景观设计学（中英文）
LANDSCAPE ARCHITECTURE FRONTIERS

中国科学引文数据库核心库来源期刊
A CSCD (Chinese Science Citation Database) Core Collection Journal

2015美国景观设计师协会交流类荣誉奖
2015 ASLA Honor Award of Communication Category

041 VOLUME 7 ISSUE 5 2019.10
CN 10-1467/TU ISSN 2096-336X
NATIONAL CIRCULATION CODE 80-985

主管	中华人民共和国教育部	SUPERVISOR Ministry of Education of the People's Republic of China
主办	高等教育出版社有限公司 北京大学	ADMINISTRATORS Higher Education Press Limited Company Peking University
承办	北京大学建筑与景观设计学院	ORGANIZER College of Architecture and Landscape, Peking University
出版	高等教育出版社有限公司	PUBLISHER Higher Education Press Limited Company

目录

主编寄语
- 4　俞孔坚 / 岐山脚下的那方神奇土地

论文
- 10　曾颖 / 场地观绘——谈景观的自然场地认知与表达
- 24　麦咏诗 / 激发现代景观创意的火花——香港大学基础景观设计课程
- 38　瓦莱里奥·莫拉比托 / 会说话的绘画：如何表达景观构想
- 58　陈峥能，蔡哲铭 / "画"画——劳瑞·欧林手绘重顾

观点与评论
- 80　吉尔·戴斯米妮 / 多元化实践：如何合理绘制地图
- 90　张东 / 景观设计的参与、解读与表达
- 98　哈尼兹·詹德 / 全球视野下的景观与地域环境

主题实践
- 108　时惠来，林中杰，陈嘉诚 / 超越场地的多维度观察：昆山杜克花园的情境生成
- 120　吴兆杰 / 遂宁锦华记忆公园
- 134　孙翀 / 城市郊野公园的观察与思考——南昌红土遗址公园设计实践

探索与过程
- 146　陆小璇 / 作为调和过程的设计表达
- 148　王芷序 / Íchni：欢乐建筑中的装置
- 156　李玉寒 / 视域策划——朝鲜半岛金刚山风景区景观规划设计

目标与范围

《景观设计学》定位于景观设计的学术研究与设计实践的交叉领域，探讨如何通过景观设计学途径，探索解决中国和世界生态与环境问题的新观念、新理论和新方法；通过介绍和推广前沿景观设计实践，倡导有助于实现美丽中国与美丽地球的新美学和新文化；架设研究与社会需求之间的桥梁、科学与艺术之间的桥梁，引领当代景观设计学科的发展。读者群为相关领域的科研人员和专业实践群体、院校师生、决策者和广大城乡环境的建设者。

Aims and Scope

Landscape Architecture Frontiers puts its focus on the intersecting spheres of academic research and design practice in landscape architecture, discussing new opinions, theories, and approaches to address environmental and ecological issues through landscape architecture; advocating new aesthetics and new culture which benefit the beauty of China and the world by introducing and promoting most recent practice of landscape architecture. It acts as a bridge connecting research and social needs, science and art, leading the development of the discipline. Our audience includes researchers and professional architects, faculties and students, policy makers in related fields, and people who work on the environmental constructions in both urban and rural areas.

本刊保留所有刊载文章及图片的文字、电子、网络版的专有出版权，未经许可，任何人不得以营利为目的复制、转载、摘编、改编、翻译、注释、整理、编辑等，本刊保留对侵权者采取法律行动的权利。

All rights reserved. The contents should not be reproduced in any form, either in whole or in part, without written permission from the editorial department. The publisher has attempted to trace and acknowledge all sources for images used in this magazine, and we apologize for any errors and omissions.

CONTENTS

EDITORIAL

4　YU Kongjian / The Wonderland at the Foot of Mount Qishan

PAPERS

10　ZENG Ying / Observation and Representation: On Recognition and Expression of Natural Sites in Landscape Architecture

24　Vincci MAK / The Spark of Contemporary Landscape Creativity — The Foundation Landscape Design Studio in the University of Hong Kong

38　Valerio MORABITO / Verbal Drawings: Mapping Landscape Ideas

58　Albert Zhengneng CHEN, Taro Zheming CAI / Draw-ing Drawing — Revisiting the Drawings by Laurie Olin

VIEWS & CRITICISMS

80　Jill DESIMINI / Plural Practices: Ideas for Drawing Responsibly

90　ZHANG Dong / Participation, Interpretation, and Representation of Landscape Design

98　Hannes ZANDER / Global Perspectives on Landscape and Territory

THEMATIC PRACTICES

108　SHI Huilai, LIN Zhongjie, CHEN Jiacheng / Observations beyond the Site: Unfolding of Landscape Process in the Design of Duke Garden in Kunshan

120　WU Zhaojie / Jinhua Memorial Park in Suining

134　SUN Chong / Observation and Reflection of the Country Park — Nanchang Red Earth Heritage Park

EXPERIMENTS & PROCESSES

146　LU Xiaoxuan / Representation as a Process of Mediation

148　Isabella Zhixu ONG / Íchni: Devices for a Joyful Architecture

156　LI Yuhan / Curated Viewsheds — Landscape Planning and Design of the Mount Kumgang International Tourist Zone on the Korean Peninsula

---

CHIEF EDITOR | YU Kongjian　**EXECUTIVE CHIEF EDITOR** | LI Dihua　**ASSOCIATE DIRECTORS** | WANG Zhifang, LI Ming-Han, XU Liyan　**HONORARY EDITORIAL BOARD** | CHENG Xuke, CUI Kai, FENG Zongwei, HE Jingtang, JIANG Youxu, JIN Jianming, LI Wenhua, LU Dadao, MA Guoxin, PENG Yigang, QI Kang, REN Nanqi, WU Liangyong, ZHANG Tinghao　**INTERNATIONAL EDITORIAL BOARD** | Jack AHERN, Henri BAVA, Catherin BULL, Gareth DOHERTY, Davor GAZVODA, Kristina HILL, Elizabeth K. MEYER, Patrick A. MILLER, Mary PADUA, Maggie ROE, Mario SCHJETNAN, Anne Whiston SPIRN, Frederick STEINER, Carl STEINITZ, Antje STOKMAN, Robert L. THAYER　**EDITORIAL ADVISORY BOARD** | BAO Jiasheng, BAO Manzhu, BAO Zhiyi, CAI Qiang, CHE Shengquan, CHE Wu, CHEN Jun, CHEN Qibing, CHEN Tongbin, CHENG Yuning, DU Chunlan, DUAN Jin, FAN Jie, GAO Chi, GU Zhaolin, GUO Zhan, HAN Linfei, HAN Xili, HONG Tiecheng, LI Jinkui, LI Shuhua, LI Weimin, LI Xiong, LIN Hui, LIU Binyi, LIU Hui, LIU Kecheng, LU Jiwei, LV Bin, LV Qinzhi, MENG Xianmin, OUYANG Zhiyun, PANG Wei, QIU Jian, SHAO Jian, SONG Wenpei, TAN Xuming, WANG Fang, WANG Hao, WANG Jianguo, WANG Shu, WANG Xiangrong, WANG Yanglin, WU Wenyuan, WU Zhiqiang, XIE Chun, XU Dawei, YANG Baojun, YANG Rui, YE Qiang, YU Baichun, YU Changjiang, ZHANG Tianxin, ZHAO Chen, ZHENG Weiyuan, ZHOU Zhihui, ZHU Yufan, ZONG Yaoguang

PUBLISHER | **EXECUTIVE EDITOR** ZHANG Xueli　**ADD** 4 Huixin Dongjie, Beijing 100029, China　**WEBSITE** journal.hep.com.cn　**TEL** 0086-10-5855 6485　**EDITORIAL OFFICE** | **GUEST EDITOR OF THIS ISSUE** ZENG Ying　**EDITORIAL DIRECTOR** SHE Yishuang　**EXECUTIVE EDITOR** Tina TIAN [Editor-in-charge of this issue]　**EDITORS** WANG Moying, WANG Ying, TIAN Xiaojie, WANG Yinyu, RAN Lingyu, Sara JACOBS, Angus ZHANG　**COLUMN HOST OF EXPERIMENTS AND PROCESSES** LU Xiaoxuan　**ART DIRECTOR** WANG Jiang　**GRAPHIC DESIGNER** Lily CHEN　**OVERSEAS EDITOR** JIANG Bin　**ADD** Rm. 303-3, Peking University Science Park, 127-1 Zhongguancun North Street, Haidian District, Beijing (100080)　**TEL** 0086-10-6274 7821　**EMAIL** lafrontiers@foxmail.com　**WEBSITE** www.lafrontiers.com　**SUPPORTING ORGANIZATIONS** | The Committee of Landscape Architecture, Chinese Society for Urban Studies (CLA)　www.landscape.cn　**OPERATION TEAM** | SHE Yishuang, WANG Xiuli　**BUSINESS INQUIRIES** | 0086-10-6274 5785　**SUBSCRIPTION INQUIRIES** | 0086-10-6274 7841　**PRINTED BY** | Beijing Artron Colour Printing Co., Ltd.　**GENERAL AGENCY IN CHINA** | Beijing Yiran Bookshop　**GENERAL AGENCY ABROAD** | China International Book Trading Corporation　**PRICE** | RMB 58.00　HKD 100.00　TWD 450.00　USD 40.00　EUR 35.00

副理事长单位
Deputy Council Directors

广州土人景观顾问有限公司
Guangzhou TUREN Landscape Planning Co., Ltd.

166-167

山水比德集团
S.P.I. Landscape Group

170-171

安博戴水道
Ramboll Studio Dreiseitl

178-179

土人设计
TURENSCAPE

180

理事单位
Council Members

深圳奥雅设计股份有限公司
Shenzhen L&A Design Holding Limited

168

罗朗园境
laurent landscape architects firm

169

北京观筑景观规划设计院
Guanzhu Landscape & Plan Design Institute

172

阿普贝思（北京）建筑景观设计咨询有限公司
U. P. Space (BJ) Architecture & Landscape Design Consulting Co., Ltd.

173

秦皇岛耀华玻璃钢股份公司
Qinhuangdao Yaohua FRP Co., Ltd.

174-175

偶木（北京）国际景观设计有限公司
O&M International Design Company

176

WADI 设计（瓦地设计）
WADI studio

177

广亩景观
GM Landscape Design

封二

EDITORIAL
主编寄语

时间 2019年8月7日　　**地点** 陕西省太白山国家森林公园　　**拍摄** 俞孔坚

　　太白山从渭河谷地拔地而起、巍峨高耸，是"中华龙脉"秦岭山脉的主峰。丰饶的"仙境"景观使这里成为了占据关中盆地的周人和秦人及其后代子孙的神圣之地。但由于缺乏对这一自然景观的深刻理解和科学规划，多年来的无序开发不免亵渎了这方净土。

Date August 7, 2019　　**Location** Mount Taibai National Forest Park in Shaanxi Province　　**Photographer** Yu Kongjian

Mount Taibai rises high from the Weihe Valley, China. It is the main peak of the Qinling Mountains. This fecund fairyland made the area a sacred place for the people and descendants of the Zhou and Qin dynasties (from around 1046 BC to 206 BC) who once occupied the Guanzhong Basin. But, due to a lack of scientific understanding and planning about this special landscape, poor development in recent years has damaged this pure land.

岐山脚下的那方
神奇土地

俞孔坚

哈佛大学设计学博士；美国艺术与科学院院士；北京大学建筑与景观设计学院教授

翻译 萨拉·雅各布斯 张健

摘要

作为中华文化定型时期各朝代的核心领地，陕西省岐山脚下的那方土地见证了周人和秦人的发展与繁荣。笔者沿着周人躲避北方强悍游牧部落的南迁之路，周人沿渭河向东攻灭大商之路，秦人一统天下的发迹之路，以及由渭河谷地攀升至秦岭主峰太白山之路共4条观察线路，探寻古人对这片土地的认知与探索过程——包括对赖以生存和发展的现实领地的观察和体验，以及对美和未来世界的向往和畅想。周人对农耕生产和生活环境的观察体验及对盆地型领地的偏好，深刻地影响了风水观念的形成，进而推动了"中国"这一理想领地意象的产生；秦朝的大一统也将为生存而抗争的崇高之意深深烙印于中国文化的艺术形态之中；对于昆仑仙境的构想更是人们对宗教理想和世俗欲望的完美表达。周人和秦人对于这方土地的景观体验深刻影响了中国的社会和文化形态的表达。

关键词

文化；观察；体验；风水；崇高；艺术表达

https://doi.org/10.15302/J-LAF-1-010004
收稿时间 RECEIVED DATE / 2019-09-18
中图分类号 / K901.9, G07
文献标识码 / C

本文引用格式 / PLEASE CITE THIS ARTICLE AS

Yu, K. (2019). The Wonderland at the Foot of Mount Qishan. Landscape Architecture Frontiers, 7(5), 4-9. https://doi.org/10.15302/J-LAF-1-010004

早在30年前，我就期望能以周人和秦人的视角，去观察和体验岐山脚下为他们带来发展与繁荣的那片神奇土地。2019年8月，我终于得以怀着无限的思古之幽情，徜徉于这片深邃无底、望不到边的文化景观的海洋之中。作为中华文化定型时期（约为秦汉时期前后）各朝代的核心领地，这里的日月星辰、大地景观，乃至生命万物的信息，都已融入以汉语为母语的人们共同的文化基因中，深刻影响着他们认知、适应、再现和改造自然及创造世界的方式，涵盖价值观、审美观和地理空间与方位的吉凶观等——简言之，这方土地在很大程度上定义了中国的社会和文化形态。

我的此次观察和体验之旅沿4条线路展开。第一条是沿着周族的迁徙之路，即从北方的旬邑南迁至豳州，再到岐山南麓的周原。这是周人作为农耕部落为躲避北方强悍游牧部落而不断寻求庇护的生存之路。我幻想跟随周先祖公刘和古公亶父，仰观天象、俯察地理，相地开垦、卜宅定都。正如《诗经》中《大雅·公刘》和《大雅·緜》所详细描绘的那样，作为部落首领，公刘和古公亶父沿着河流廊道，穿越山间盆地，环顾四周山峦，在找到安全的潜在领地之后，便登上四周高地，俯瞰河谷绿洲，欣喜于获取了丰腴的土壤；再下至平原，沿山泉溪流溯源而上，断定有丰富的水源；再丈量土地，开田地以播五谷，夯土基而筑宫室。[1][2]这种对农耕生产和生活环境的观察体验及对盆地型领地的偏好，最终通过《诗经》《易经》等古老经典著作的传播，成为后世相地术（风水）的基本模式，表达为理想的风水——如左青龙、右白虎、前朱雀、后玄武、中明堂的空间格局意象，又如"利东南、不利西北"的方位吉凶判断。

第二条观察线路是跟随日渐强大的周人，沿渭河一路向东，冲出关中，横扫中原，攻灭大商，定都洛邑（今洛阳）。所谓"余其宅兹中国"（见于西周何尊铭文），这也是"中国"二字最早的铭记[3]。正如周文王被囚禁于羑里城而演绎《周易》并将周族在岐山脚下的关中盆地对农耕生活和环境的观察与经验进行整理一样，我们有理由论断"中国"或"中央之国"的领地意象——建立于四周皆有边界的盆地中的都城——即自此形成，而后随走出关中的周族领袖传至中原大地而铭于文。

第三条观察线路是向西沿汧水（今千河）溯流而上，寻找秦人发迹的源头。途经千河与渭河交汇的"汧渭之会"，穿越关山崎岖的峡谷——这是中国地理中从第二级阶梯向第一级阶梯过渡的景观甬道，仅30km的行程之后，海拔便从900m攀升至2 200m，行至秦非子牧马之地。秦非子因精通养马之道，受周孝王之命在汧水与渭水之间肥沃的天然牧场主管牧马，深受赏识，继而获封岐山以西的狭小地带[4]。经过数百年励精图治，秦国以其强悍雄风，取周而代之，完成了一统天下的大业。同时在周朝的"中国"领地意识基础上，更深刻地实现了货币、度量衡、文字、交通工具等的统一。秦人的这条发迹之路也给农耕民族以温顺避让为主要特征的文化注入了坚韧与剽悍之风。其后的汉王朝更是将秦横扫六国的气魄发扬光大，据称此时关山一带牧养的马匹数量达30余万[5]，作战军队借此完成了由步兵为主向骑兵为主的转变，可实

THE WONDERLAND AT THE FOOT OF MOUNT QISHAN

YU Kongjian
Doctor of Design at Graduate School of Design, Harvard University; Honorary Foreign Fellow of the American Academy of Arts and Sciences; Professor of College of Architecture and Landscape, Peking University

TRANSLATED BY Sara JACOBS Angus ZHANG

ABSTRACT
As the core territory for the Zhou and Qin dynasties, the land at the foot of Mount Qishan in Shaanxi Province has significantly made the society and culture of China thrive and grow. The author retraced four routes to find out how the Zhou and Qin people explored and envisioned this landscape, both physically as settlements and spiritually as a wonderland. These routes include the migration path of the Zhou people from the north to the south of Mount Qishan to seek shelter from nomadic tribes; the path of the Zhou people moving from the west to the east along the Weihe River to conquer the Shang people and establish a new kingdom; the path of the Qin State to unify the other six states and found a great dynasty; and the route climbing from the Weihe Valley to Mount Taibai, the main peak of the Qinling Mountains. All the episodes happened on these routes had a profound influence on the ideology of Chinese society and cultural identity. For instance, the Zhou people's observation on the landscape for farming and living, as well as their preference for the basin-shaped territory, significantly contributed to forming the Chinese geomancy (Feng Shui) and developed into an ideal territorial image of being the "kingdom in the center" (literally meaning "China" in Chinese); the artistic representation of sublime reflected the Qin people's fight for survival and honor; and the described Kunlun Wonderland perfectly expresses both religious ideals and worldly desires.

KEYWORDS
Culture; Observation; Experience; Geomancy; Sublime; Artistic Representation

For nearly 30 years, I yearned to see and experience the land at the foot of Mount Qishan as though I were the Zhou and Qin people who developed and prospered because of their relationship with the mount. In August 2019, I was finally able to spend time immersed in this glamorous cultural landscape, trying to get connected with the ancient years. This land, the core territory for the Zhou, Qin, and Han dynasties, has significantly made the society and culture of China thrive and grow: the knowledge of the sun, of the moon, of the earth, and of all the beings of this place has been integrated into the culture of Chinese-speaking people, developing into their societal and aesthetic values, as well as the geomancy of a geographic space, which profoundly shaped the way how people cognize, adapt to, and transform the world they live in.

My trip followed four routes. The first was the migration path of the Zhou people (the ancient farming tribes), from the ancient Xunyi City in the north to the ancient Binzhou City in the south, and to the ancient Zhouyuan City at the south foot of Mount Qishan, to seek shelter from the nomadic tribes. On this route, I imagined myself following Duke Liu and Duke Dan (leaders and ancestors of the Zhou people), looking up the sky and down at the ground, selecting sites for farming, homes, and the capital. As described in *The Book of Poetry*, Duke Liu and Duke Dan moved along the Weihe Valley corridor, crossing basins and ranges in mountains. After finding a safe place for potential settlements, they may have climbed the surrounding highlands to overlook oases and valleys, delighting in the rich soil; they may have traveled down to the plains and to trace mountain streams to find water resource; they may have also measured the land for farms and homes.[1][2] Spread through ancient works such as *The Book of Poetry* and *The Book of Changes*, such landscape observation for farming and living and the preference for the basin-shaped territory contributed to forming an ideal Chinese geomancy (Feng Shui) that informs site and position selection and spatial pattern.

The second route I took was the path which the Zhou people took before making the ancient Luoyi City their capital. At that time, the increasingly powerful Zhou people moved along the Weihe River to the east, from the Guanzhong Basin towards the Central Plains to conquer the Shang people and establish a new dynasty, early in which period the term of "kingdom in the center" (the literal meaning of "China" in Chinese) first appeared as recorded by the inscription on He Zun[3], a ritual bronze vessel. King Wen, the founder of the Zhou Dynasty, complied *The Book of Changes* when being imprisoned by the Shang people, which became a written record of Zhou people's observation and experience of farming and living in the Guanzhong Basin. For this record, we could infer that the image of a "kingdom in the center" — a capital sitting in a basin with a clear border — was invented by Zhou leaders before inscribed on He Zun.

The third route traveled upstream along the ancient Qianhe River to feel after the prosperous history of the Qin Dynasty. The route passed through the intersection of the Qianhe River and Weihe River, through the cragged gorge of Guanshan Mountain, whose topography transitions from 900 meters to 2,200 meters over only 30 kilometers. The pastures between the Qianhe and the Weihe rivers was where Qin Feizi, the founding king of Qin State, raised horses for King Xiao of Zhou. For his proficiency in horse breeding, Qin Feizi was well-rewarded with a small piece of land to the west of Mount Qishan[4]. After hundreds of years of hard work, the Qin State ended the ruling of Zhou and conquered the other six states throughout the country. Expanding the territorial cognition of the "kingdom in the center" from the Zhou Dynasty, the Qin Emperor unified the nation in currency, metrology, written language, and vehicle size. The unexcelled prosperity of the Qin Dynasty blended a tough and courageous culture into the China's docile and modest identity as an agricultural nation. Later, the Han Dynasty carried forward Qin's domineering vigor — It is said that the number of army horses in the Guanshan area reached more than 300,000 during that period[5]. A robust cavalry then formed that made the Han army capable of completing long-distance

现长途奔袭、快速突袭和大迂回,成就了卫青、霍去病等开疆拓土、纵横漠北、却匈奴于千里之外的丰功伟绩。

这处连接关中与西域的景观也为中国文化的艺术形态注入了骨感和峻美之气。事实上,划分中国两大自然地理区域、界定农耕与游牧两种文化的关山,经过无数诗人的描绘,在中国文学中已被泛化为象征远离故土、戎马征战和战火硝烟的符号,表达为"远方"(Far)和"崇高"(Sublime)之意。这种崇高也通过五代后梁山水画家关仝的画笔表达了出来。关仝师承北方山水画派鼻祖荆浩,并青出于蓝,以其"关家山水"独领风骚。其代表作《关山行旅图》冠绝当代,为后世临摹效仿,深刻影响了中国的山水美学。画中山峰迭起、溪谷幽深、栈道险绝、驮马凄凉。这里所表达的"崇高"与陶渊明在《桃花源记》中所表达的理想农耕环境的"优美"(Beauty)完全不同。至此,象征闲适安宁的"优美"和象征为生存而抗争的"崇高"在中国文化中实现了完美平衡。

第四条观察线路是从海拔约500m的渭河谷地一直攀升至海拔约3 750m的秦岭主峰——太白山。沿太白山的主要溪谷汤峪拾阶而上,一路可感受幽谷深处的神秘莫测和生命万物之丰饶。据称峪口汤泉可治百病,所见之草皆可入药。及至山顶,大面积的冰川遗迹(通常为白雪所覆盖)和冰斗湖映入眼帘,其景观与盆地、平原景观迥异。由此俯瞰关中盆地,城廓了然、尽收眼底,大有以上帝之眼瞭望凡尘的感觉。无怪乎《尚书·禹贡》谓之"惇物山"[6]、《汉书·地理志》称之"太乙山"[7],均是对太白山的丰饶与宛若仙境的表达。据称,岐伯尝味百草即发生在太白山一带,而"药王"孙思邈则长年居隐太白山中,亲自采摘草药,研究药物性能。我个人认为,传说中的道教名山昆仑山即以太白山为原型:高峻非羽仙不可及,更有怪兽神鸟、不死之药、琼浆玉液和王母瑶池等。这无非是周人、秦人及其子孙后代将白雪冠顶的太白山表达为可满足人世间一切欲望的仙境而已。因而,太白山即昆仑仙境便成为了兼有宗教理想和世俗欲望的完美表达。

正是周人和秦人对岐山脚下这片土地的认知与探索——包括对其赖以生存和发展的现实领地的观察和体验,以及对美和未来世界的向往和畅想——才有了他们对理想景观模式的表达,进而发展为"中国"这一理想领地的意象,以及对崇高山水和昆仑仙境的艺术表达。而由于周朝和秦朝在中华文化定型时期占据着决定性的地位,对岐山脚下这方土地的景观体验也注定会在中国的社会和文化形态的表达中发挥关键作用。**LAF**

strikes, rapid assaults, and outflanking. At that time, great military generals such as Wei Qing and Huo Qubing expanded the national territory and kept the Hsiung-nu tribes thousands of miles away.

The landscape along this route that connects the Central Plain Area with the western regions is a unique charm in Chinese art and culture. Guanshan Mountain, which roughly divides China into two parts in geography, as well as in culture (farming and nomadic), has been portrayed by countless poets as a symbol for far and sublime that represents warfare. The sense of sublime has also been reflected in the landscape paintings of Guan Tong, a painter of the Later Liang Dynasty in the Five Dynasties and Ten Kingdoms period. As a student of Jing Hao who was the leading pioneer of the northern landscape painting school, Guan Tong surpassed his teacher in style and legacy. His masterpiece, the *Travelling in Mountains*, has long been intimidated and profoundly affected China's landscape aesthetic of towering peaks, steep valleys, dangerous paths, and desolate landscapes. The sublime expressed in Guan Tong's paintings contrasts the beauty depicted in Tao Yuanming's *Peach Blossom Spring* characterized for peace and tranquility, yet the both two coexist and influence the Chinese culture.

Finally, my fourth route climbs from the Weihe Valley to Mount Taibai, the main peak of the Qinling Mountains, which ranges in elevation from 500 meters to 3,750 meters. The mystery and richness of the landscape is evident walking along the Tangyu Valley, a major valley of Mount Taibai. It is said that the spring water here can heal people and all the found plants are therapeutic. The top of the mountain was covered with large areas of snowy glaciers and ice, forming a completely different landscape from the basins and plains. Cities nestled in the Central Plain Basin can be panoramically viewed from this vantage point — Mount Taibai is worthy of its name of the "Mountain of Dunwu" (mountain of richness) by *The Book of Documents*[6] or the "Mountain of Taiyi" (mountain of mystery) by *The Book of Han*[7]. It is said that famous Chinese physicians Qibo and Sun Simiao lived here for years to study the properties of herbs. In my personally opinion, Mount Taibai is the archetype of Mount Kunlun, the legendary Taoist site: it rises so high that can only be accessible by gods, and it offers the medicine of immortality. The Zhou, the Qin, and their descendants understand that the snow-covered Mount Taibai was a fairyland that contains all the desires of human world. Thus, Mount Taibai, or the Kunlun Wonderland, perfectly represents both the religious ideals and worldly desires.

It is precisely because of how the Zhou and Qin people explored and envisioned this landscape at the foot of Mount Qishan, both physically as settlements and spiritually as a wonderland, their expression of the ideal landscape model emerged and developed into an ideal territorial image of "kingdom in the center," as well as the poetic representation of the sublime landscape and the Kunlun Wonderland. Their observation and experience of this landscape in this significant period has greatly fostered and shaped China's social and cultural identity and made it thriving. **LAF**

REFERENCES

[1] Wang, X. (Ed.). (2015). Duke Liu in Greater Odes of the Kingdom. The Book of Poetry. Beijing: Zhonghua Book Company.
[2] Wang, X. (Ed.). (2015). Continuity in Greater Odes of the Kingdom. The Book of Poetry. Beijing: Zhonghua Book Company.
[3] He, Z. (2011). The Idea of "Central Country" Recorded in the Inscriptions of He Zun. Wenbo, (6), 32-34.
[4] Guo, F., Zhang, K., & Lv, J. (2000). The Dictionary of Gansu. Lanzhou: Gansu Culture Publishing House.
[5] An, Z. (2006). Horse Breeding and the Breed Improvement in Han Dynasty. Agricultural Archaeology, (4), 273-280, 296.
[6] Wang, S., & Wang, C. (2012). The Tribute of Yu. The Book of Documents. Beijing: Zhonghua Book Company.
[7] Ban, G. (n. d.). Geography (Vol. 28). The Book of Han. Beijing: Zhonghua Book Company.

场地观绘
——谈景观的自然场地认知与表达

OBSERVATION AND REPRESENTATION: ON RECOGNITION AND EXPRESSION OF NATURAL SITES IN LANDSCAPE ARCHITECTURE

本文引用格式 / PLEASE CITE THIS ARTICLE AS

Zeng, Y. (2019). Observation and Representation: On Recognition and Expression of Natural Sites in Landscape Architecture. Landscape Architecture Frontiers, 7(5), 10-23. https://doi.org/10.15302/J-LAF-1-020012

https://doi.org/10.15302/J-LAF-1-020012　　收稿时间 RECEIVED DATE / 2019-09-27　　中图分类号 / TU986.2　　文献标识码 / A

曾颖*

艺术学博士，中国美术学院建筑艺术学院景观设计系副教授、系主任；宾夕法尼亚大学景观设计学硕士

ZENG Ying

PhD in Fine Art; Associate Professor and Chair of Department of Landscape Architecture, School of Architecture, China Academy of Art; Master of Landscape Architecture, University of Pennsylvania

*通讯作者

地址：杭州市是西湖区转塘街道象山路352号，中国美术学院象山校区建筑艺术学院14号楼109室
邮编：310024
邮箱：yzeng@caa.edu.cn

摘要

在景观设计专业教育中，自然场地的观察与表达意味着在场地上"怎么看"以及"怎么画"。本文首先通过比较写实素描、设计素描、自然风景写生等传统绘画形式之间的差异来探讨景观设计学科的场地观察与表达，并提出：虽然两者都涉及对客观事物与现象的观察（观）与表达（绘），但传统绘画以"模仿"客观物象的表面形式为目的，景观设计则更强调了解并呈现客观真实场地的变化过程以及其中隐藏的复杂关联，即"再现"场地的本质。

景观设计学科对场地的观察与表达可归纳为三个要点：亲临场地、调动身体运动，以及再现事物的变化过程与事物之间的关联。本文列举了两个案例——一个通过场地尺度的设计教学阐释了基于真实场地的观察如何逐步形成抽象的设计形式，另一个则通过分析从场地到区域与全球尺度的设计实践，探讨了对场地关联的跨尺度思考如何指导具体的景观设计实践——以期为中国当前的景观设计教育与实践提供借鉴。

关键词

景观设计；场地；观察；感知；运动；表达；再现

ABSTRACT

In the education of Landscape Architecture, the way we view and depict a natural site is defined by the way we observe and express it. This paper starts with a comparison between the perspective and approach of traditional painting types (the realistic sketch, design sketch, and landscape painting) and those in Landscape Architecture. All of them involve observation (viewing) and expression (drawing) of natural beings and phenomena, where traditional paintings are in the pursuit of honest depiction of the forms or shapes. While in Landscape Architecture it emphasizes understanding and representing the evolutions and the complicated intrinsic relations of the authentic sites — in other words, to represent the nature of reality.

To be on-site, the use of body movement, and the evolutions and correlations of natural beings are the three most important principles to the observation and representation in Landscape Architecture. Combining with two cases in teaching and practice, this paper elaborates how to develop abstract forms and design concepts from the observation of authentic sites and how the trans-scaled reflection on the correlations about the sites can inspire a site-scaled design, providing references for the education and practice of Landscape Architecture in China.

KEYWORDS

Landscape Architecture; Site; Observation; Perception; Movement; Expression; Representation

基金项目
2019年中国美术学院重点高校建设科研创提升计划科研培育资助项目

RESEARCH FUND
2019 Research and Innovation Incubation Program of China Academy of Art

编辑　王胤瑜　田乐　汪默英　　翻译　肖杰　田乐　王胤瑜
EDITED BY　WANG Yinyu　Tina TIAN　WANG Moying　　**TRANSLATED BY**　XIAO Jie　Tina TIAN　WANG Yinyu

1 引言

在美术院校里，教师们有一种共识：学会观察是绘画的前提[1]。各专业中以素描为基础的造型训练的本质都是在讨论观察方法。其中，景观设计学科入门课程的教师主要面临着两个教学难点：一是探究绘画与设计之间如何建立联系，并通过一定的教学方法引导学生对此展开探讨；二是如何从观察与表达入手，引导学生对真实的场地进行认知，从而逐步生成设计概念。

本文首先比较了20世纪90年代中期中国美术院校教授的设计素描[①]与传统写实素描、自然风景写生等绘画类型在观察与表达上的共性与差异，进而对景观设计学科的场地观察与表达的要义展开探讨，并借助具体案例阐明这些原则在景观设计教学与设计实践中的应用。

2 绘画中的观察与表达

研究"观察"与"表达"的演变有助于厘清绘画与景观设计的关联。回顾自己从20世纪90年代初期绘制第一张几何石膏体素描到目前在景观设计系教学的经历，笔者认为，绘画中"观察"与"表达"的

① 尽管本文以笔者熟悉的美术院校的设计教育为例，但是类似的教学模式在中国高校的建筑和风景园林专业基础设计教育中亦有相当长的历史，许多院校至今仍在沿用这一模式。

① The design sketch mentioned in this paper mainly refers to that taught in academies of fine arts, with which the author is the most familiar. However, it has also been adopted for long in the fundamental studios of Architecture and Landscape Architecture majors in many other colleges and universities in China until now.

演变可体现在三种绘画类型中，即传统写实素描（以画石膏像明暗素描为起始）、设计素描（保留造型过程的结构素描），以及东西方自然风景写生。

传统写实素描关注物体的"可见部分"，即表面形体及其各部分比例等，如石膏头像的"三庭五眼"，强调通过整体比较和分析求得可见的"形"，并用光影加以表现（图1）。设计素描除了关注看得见的"形"外，更注重探究看不见的物体内部结构，在实际绘图中则表现为运用平行线、剖切线等辅助线来表达形体结构（图2）。这种画法源于"自然形式是由内部性质决定外部发展的，外部是内部的结果"[2]

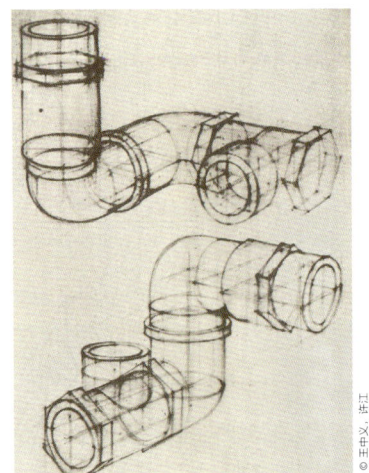

1. 传统写实素描
2. 设计素描

1. Traditional realistic sketch
2. Design sketch

1 Introduction

It is a shared knowledge among teachers in academies of fine arts that how a painter observes determines how he or she paints[1]. Related disciplines all have explored how to teach students observation approaches through pencil sketch training to learn how to depict objects in their foundation years. In the fundamental studios of Landscape Architecture, teachers especially have two primary tasks: 1) to explore the relationship between painting and design, and encourage and inspire students to think about it with proper teaching methods; and 2) to equip them with the capability to transform their understanding of an authentic site into design ideas through observation and representation.

Starting with a comparison between the approaches of observation and expression of different painting types — the design sketch taught in academies of fine arts in the mid-1990s①, the traditional realistic sketch, and the landscape painting — this paper discusses the principles of observation and expression in Landscape Architecture, and then combines them with two cases to demonstrate their application in the education and design practice of Landscape Architecture specifically.

2 Observation and Expression in Painting

Insights into the evolution of observation and expression help clarify the relationship between painting and landscape design. According to the author's own experiences from learning how to draw light and shade sketches in the early 1990s to teaching at a Landscape Architecture department today, such an evolution can be articulated from three folds, namely the traditional realistic sketch (that begins with the light and shade sketch training), design sketch (also called "structure sketch" based on the process of depicting objects), and landscape painting in both eastern and western styles.

Traditional realistic sketch focuses on depicting the visible parts of objects, i.e., the external forms and the proportion of components, which are acquired through a holistic measurement and profiling and depicted by drawing with light and shadow. For example, students are trained to study and draw the geometrical features of a head sculpture (Fig. 1). Design sketch goes further from depicting visible external shapes to invisible internal structures by using paralleling lines, section lines, and other auxiliary lines (Fig. 2). Such a method lies in the concept that natural beings' external forms are defined by their nature[2]. That is saying, one purpose of the observation of natural beings' structure is to learn and abstract forms

3. 由布鲁诺·陶特设计的德国科隆"玻璃宫"
4. 由克劳德·洛兰绘制的《风景——摩西和燃烧的灌木丛》，绘于1664年，现藏于柏林国立美术馆。

3. The "Glass Pavilion" in Cologne, Germany by Bruno Taut
4. *Landschaft mit Moses und dem brennenden Dornbusch* (1664), collected in Staatliche Museen zu Berlin.

的观点，因此，在某种程度上，观察结构正是为了从自然中提炼形式。例如，在《从素描走向设计》一书中，作者以布鲁诺·陶特设计的德国科隆"玻璃宫"形似菠萝的拱形面顶（图3）为例，说明这种以菱形为结构单位的外观体现了自然界生态成长的有机性质。其尽管已经不具备自然形态原来的功能性质，更不是自然形态本身，但无疑是从自然中提炼出来的。[2]

从传统写实素描的"重外部形式"到设计素描的"重内部结构与过程"，素描绘画始终坚持一个基本原则，即尊重客观对象，力求"模拟、模仿"，强调整体比较和分析[3]。自然风景写生的观察与表达方法则有所不同。

就观察与表达方法而言，自然风景写生主要分为两个流派：以西方风景画为代表的写实（静观）派，以及以中国山水画为代表的写意（游观）派。写实风景画忠实于对自然场地中客观对象的观察，力求尽可能还原在单一地点、单一时刻观察到的内容，这种表达与写实素描一样，可以称之为"模仿"（图4）。因此对这两类作品的评价也是以"惟妙惟肖""逼真"为佳，如古希腊画家宙克西斯和帕拉休斯分别绘制葡萄与幕帘来比试谁的画作更能以假乱真[4]。

写意风景画则倡导先在自然山水中不断游走、饱览山水特征，再闭门创作，其表达结果是物像与观察者本人主观感知的"化合"。这种方法以北宋著名画家郭熙提出的"三远法"为代表："山有三远：自山下而仰山巅，谓之高远；自山前而窥山后，谓之深远；自近山而望远山，谓之平远。"[5] "高远""深远""平远"即为三种不同的观山视角。在其代表作《早春图》中，郭熙在同一幅画面中同时呈现了这三种视角下的山景（图5）。这种基于多视点、多角度的观察是其与

from them. For example, the book *From Sketch to Design* exemplifies the arch of the "Glass Pavilion" in Cologne, Germany designed by Bruno Taut (Fig. 3), which is composed of prismatic units as a manifestation of organic natural growth. Despite of the loss of the original functions and shapes, it is still an abstraction from the nature.[2]

Be it the traditional realistic sketch that highlights the "tracing of external forms" or the design sketch that focuses on "discomposing internal structures and processes," they both follow the same principle: to honestly draw an object as much as possible through a holistic measurement and profiling[3]. Landscape painting, alternatively, accentuates different methods in observation and expression of objects.

There have long been two main genres in landscape painting in terms of approaches of observation and expression: realism (by in-position viewing and represented by western landscape paintings) and freehand (by moving viewing and represented by Chinese landscape paintings). The realism expresses what the painters observe at a particular moment and a particular site as detailed as possible, which is still an act of honest drawing, just like the traditional realistic sketch (Fig. 4), and praises verisimilitude, illustrated by the competition on painting skills between ancient Greek painters Zeuxis and Parrhasius by painting grapes and curtains in an extremely realistic way[4].

In contrast, the freehand embraces the expression of the painters' observation and perception of natural landscapes by integrating their memories and personal interpretation

5. 郭熙的画作《早春图》，现藏于台北故宫博物院。

5. *Early Spring* ppainted by Guo Xi, collected in Taipei Palace Museum.

前三种绘画的观察方法最大的不同；但其创作结果仅仅是不同场景的拼贴与并置，仍然停留在表达外在形式的层面。

3 景观设计学科的观察与表达

上述绘画类型观察与表达的内容都是纯粹的客观事物或自然现象。而"景观"是一种现象学语境下拥有丰富内涵的媒介[6]，因此，景观设计学科的观察与表达"并不是简单的摹写和复现客观事物"，还应将其背后"更多的东西"[7]——景观的内涵——呈现出来。这些信息与关联往往不是肉眼可见的，必须借助一定的方法予以探究和追溯。下文将从三个方面来探讨景观设计学科的观察与表达。

3.1 亲临场地

首先，观察者必须亲临场地。在当前的信息技术时代，尽管设计师可以在不到场的情况下便获得各种场地信息，如场地高程、卫星影像、植被分布状态等，但是对于景观设计学科来说，个人经历和文化背景的差异会导致不同设计师对相同场地形成不同的认知和解读，因此亲临场地的意义仍是不可替代的。

具体而言，这一要求源于景观的三个特征——空间性、时间性和物质性。美国宾夕法尼亚大学景观学前系主任詹姆斯·科纳在其论文《再现与景观：景观媒介中的绘画与营造》里具体讨论了这三种特征。"空间性"强调景观不是单一地点和视角下的自然风景，对景观

into drawings. A good example is the Three-Distance Theory, first employed by Guo Xi, a great painter in Song Dynasty. Guo believed that a natural scene can be viewed and depicted in three perspectives of distances, namely High Distance Perspective (viewing by looking up), Far / Deep Distance Perspective (viewing by looking beyond), and Level Distance Perspective (viewing by looking afar)."[5] In his masterpiece, *Early Spring*, Guo integrated the three perspectives in one frame (Fig. 5). The multiplicity of perspectives makes abstract landscape painting itself strikingly different from the former three, whose expression form, however, was considered still a depiction of external shapes with methods of collage and re-arrangement of different scenes.

3 The Observation and Expression in Landscape Architecture

What are depicted in the above painting types are absolutely natural objects and phenomena. However, landscapes, as a kind of medium with rich connotation in the phenomenology context[6], are considered and expressed quite differently in Landscape Architecture: Instead of simply replicating natural shapes or forms, landscape observation and expression aims at exploring and visualizing the meaning of invisible connections in the sites[7], which requires proper methods and approaches. The paper will elaborate on the observation and expression in Landscape Architecture from three perspectives.

3.1 To be On-Site

For landscape observation, to be on-site is necessitated. Nowadays, thanks to the advance of information technology, designers have access to acquiring site information, including elevation data, satellite images, and vegetation maps, without field visits. However, in Landscape Architecture, site visit is irreplaceable because designers' individual experience and cultural background result in a variety of perception and reading of a same authentic site.

The on-site observation of a landscape is determined by its spatiality, temporality, and materiality, which are articulated specifically by James Corner, the former chair of Department of Landscape Architecture, University of Pennsylvania, in his paper *Representation and Landscape: Drawing and Making in the Landscape Medium*. Spatiality refers to that the understanding of a landscape should go beyond a static scenery of a particular location from a particular perspective; the site should be perceived and experienced at different levels and from different perspectives. Temporality requires designers to

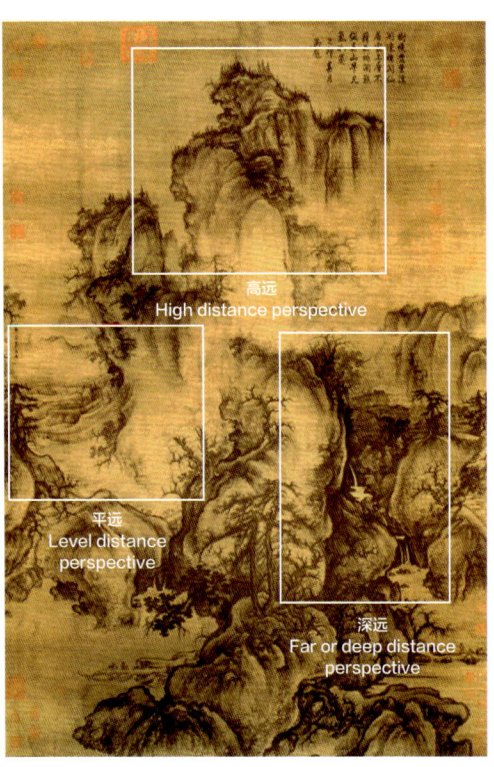

的观察即是从不同的地点和角度对场地进行感知和体验;"时间性"指景观会随着时间推移而演变,因此需要在不同时间与事件背景下对场地进行解读;"物质性"意味着人们必须通过亲身接触与感知真实的场地,才能更好地理解组成景观的物质材料的丰富性与复杂性[6]。这意味着在教室或实验室里借助科学仪器获取的数据,并不能充分反映场地上各种元素的物质材料特征。[8]

在场地中,除了观看,观察者在行走、攀爬的过程中还可以借助听觉、嗅觉、触觉等感官来感知和体验场地的物质材料特征,如感受植物的芳香、土壤的气息、阳光的"味道"等。这些感受将嵌入观察者的肢体与肌肤,留下长久的记忆,并且——正如美国著名人文地理学家段义孚所说——能够"唤起观察者强烈的情感体验"[9]。因此,亲临场地的观察不仅是视觉意义上的,还需要调动其他感官维度。

3.2 基于身体运动的观察

其次,景观的观察要求调动身体的运动进行体验与感知。在传统素描与设计素描中,观察的对象是独立于观察者之外的另一个物体,因此观察者与观察对象之间除了视觉上的"观看",并没有太多其他感知联系。而在景观设计学科中,"亲临场地的观察"意味着观察的主体(人)被观察对象(自然场地)所笼罩,这使得对景观的观察具有如下两个特征:

3.2.1 观察的连续性与序列性

对自然场地的观察需要通过身体的运动,激发观察的连续性与序列性。这种观察不是在静止状态下从单一地点观察一幅幅固定角度的静止画面,而是在运动中感知连续的动态空间片段。这种连续性、序列性的观察曾被国内外学者广泛讨论,如著名建筑历史理论家、宾夕法尼亚大学教授戴维·莱瑟巴罗在演讲"蜿蜒的法则"中指出,"多样变换"作为18~19世纪欧洲传统如画式园林的审美范畴之一,对现代建筑的空间设计影响深远,其是指多个景象的集合依次展现在观察者眼前,"就像戏剧舞台上表演的一个个片段,一幕幕剧情"[10]。对这种"多样变换"的美感的体验,实际上正是来自观察者在园林中的序列型的连续运动;著名园林史学家约翰·迪克逊·亨特提出的人在园林中的三种运动方式——"队列行进、散步及漫游"[11],也是在探讨人在运动中的观察与感知。由于园林是对自然景观进行模拟、再造的产

view the landscapes at different moments and in varied contexts. The materiality means that the abundance and complexity of the material composition of a landscape can only be comprehended with the observers' on-site perceptions and feelings.[6] Therefore, such on-site observation cannot be replaced with off-site information searching and data analyses.[8]

Besides visual perception, observers can also trace and learn the unique auditory, olfactory, and tactile features of the landscape's materiality — for instance, the fragrance of the plants and the smell of soil or even the sunshine — when they are walking around or climbing up and down on the site. Such experience would then leave the observers a memory and impression of the landscape scenes and arouse their strong emotions, as what Yi-Fu Tuan, an American anthropogeographer, stated[9]. Therefore, on-site observation is an act requiring multi-sensory approaches.

3.2 Observation through Body Movement

Second, body movements should be emphasized in on-site observation. In drawing a traditional realistic sketch or a design sketch, the only sensorial connection between the observer and the object relies on "viewing," because the observer is outside of what he / she is watching. However, the on-site observation in Landscape Architecture means that the observer is surrounded by or part of the object (the landscape). It contributes to two-fold significance as following.

3.2.1 The Continuity and Sequence of Observation

Observation through body movement should be continuous and sequential in order to generate a dynamic sequence of landscape perceptions, which has been discussed widely in the academia. In his lecture "The Law of Meander," David Leatherbarrow, an architectural history theorist and professor of University of Pennsylvania, underpinned that the "variety" of picturesque traditional gardens that has greatly influenced the spatial design in modern Architecture refers to the sequential appearance of a series of scenes in the gardens, just like "acts or events on stage in a dramatic performance"[10]. It is exactly perceived when people are moving continuously and sequentially throughout a picturesque garden; the "three kinds of movements" in gardens and other designed landscapes, namely "the procession or ritual, the stroll, and the ramble,"[11] put forward by the famous garden historian John Dixon Hunt, also elaborate how people experience the garden sceneries during continuous movements. As gardens are replications of natural landscapes, such movements also are required for the observation of natural sites. To some extent, this also finds

6. 钱贡于明万历年间绘制的《环翠堂园景图》局部。全图为一幅连续长卷，全面表现了徽州府私家园林"坐隐园"内外的109处景点。

6. A part of *Huan Cui Tang Yuan Jing Tu* painted by Qian Gong in Ming Dynasty. It is a long scroll presenting all the 109 scenic spots in Zuoyin Garden, a private garden located in the Huizhou region at that time.

物，因而对自然场地的观察也必须注重连续性与序列性。这与中国山水画创作中的"游观"法（图6）在某种程度上是相通的。

景观设计学科的观察不仅仅是发现自然场地的表象，还要探究其形成的内在逻辑，因此，观察者必须在场地上持续运动并抓住一系列连续的自然现象特征，才能分析其中隐藏的各种场地因素，及其之间的相互关联。例如，当观察到地面上有不同状态的树叶（如枯叶、新叶或被挤压进泥土中的叶片），并探究其原因时，就需要在持续的运动中对场地内与树叶有关的各种因素（如光照、树龄等）进行比较与分析，进而得出结论——或许是高处茂密的树冠影响了较矮的树木接受光照，或许是树叶在生长过程中自然凋落。显然，缺乏方向性的散点式观察无法有效帮助设计师发现这些内在关联。

3.2.2 观察的信息侦查性

景观设计学科的场地观察不仅仅是通过多种感官对场地的自然表象进行感知，还包括侦查场地信息，如坡度、坡向等自然因素，以及地方传统、社会经济发展状况等社会人文因素；除了地面上肉眼直接可见的事物与现象之外，如农作物种植模式、空气质量等需要进一步探查和搜集的信息也应包括在内。观察者不仅要如实记录上述信息，还要据此预估使用者介入场地后可能产生的反应，以形成对场地特征的评价，如什么样的坡度适宜行走，什么样的地表材质不易滑倒等。这类侦查最早来源于军事行军路线评估，观察者除了记录可见的

resonance with the "moving-viewing" approach adopted by Chinese landscape painters (Fig. 6).

In Landscape Architecture, the goal of observation and expression is to discover and present not only the forms and appearances, but also the internal relations of factors leading to natural phenomena, which often rely on tracing the clues from the continuous features on the site. For instance, to find out why there are dead, young, and mud-covered leaves on the ground, one has to move around to make a series of comparisons and analyses of all the factors that might result in such situations of leaves (e.g., light condition or tree ages). Then, the cause, either the dense canopy that blocks the sunshine for smaller trees or just a seasonal natural phenomenon, can be figured out. It is obvious that random observations can little help designers explore the internal factors and relations of natural beings.

3.2.2 Field Investigation in Observation

Landscape observation also requires field investigation to accurately and holistically profile a site by studying its environmental, societal, and cultural factors and conditions, such as slope grade and aspect, folk tradition, and the regional socio-economic context; besides, in-depth exploration is needed to collect information that cannot be acquired by "seeing" and requires a further measurement or evaluation, such as the crop farming patterns and air quality. The observers should also assess the site features by simulating users' behaviors and activities on the site — for instance, the best slope grade range for walking comfort; the best antiskid materials on the ground surface. Such

山脉、水系等自然基底，以及桥、路等人造构筑，还要对路线中的环境、交通等各方面情况进行评估。[12]因此，这种对场地的观察不再是仅仅像镜子一样折射、反映场地的客观面貌，还需要对各种细节信息与人的使用情况进行深入观察、收集、判断与评论。

这种信息的收集和侦查过程如同一个复杂的"化合"过程，使场地的客观物像与观察者的主观认知、兴趣与经历相互交织、相互作用，形成具有鲜明个体特征的印象记录，而不是机械的数据复制。这种差异和变化正是景观设计的艺术魅力的来源，为设计师的设计创作提供了无限可能。

3.3 以"再现"为目的的表达

景观设计学科的表达需要揭示景观的内涵，即客观事物与现象的"形"背后的"理"，包括自然场地在时间和空间上的变化过程，以及其间万物的关联。

3.3.1 从表达形式转向表达过程

传统写实素描表达的是准确的"造型"，要求能够尽可能还原客观对象的形态；设计素描的表达则开始追求展现对象的内部结构，并认为这种对内在结构的理解在某种意义上也是对外部造型的表达。而对景观设计学科而言，对自然场地的表达需要从还原事物的表象转变到展现事物的本质，才可能在后续设计中介入自然场地，表达的关键内容则是探究场地中的各种外部力量如何相互作用，及其影响和塑造事物形式的过程。

尽管设计素描和景观设计学科对场地的表达看似都强调"过程"，但其本质不同：设计素描表达的是观察者探究静态物体内部结构的过程，该过程不涉及外部作用力对物体的影响；而景观是由场地中许许多多彼此相关的力量共同塑造的动态对象，是具有生命力且可参与的。例如，詹姆斯·科纳景观设计事务所在加拿大多伦多当斯维尔公园设计竞赛方案中呈现了场地在未来20年间的变化过程，包括各阶段需要建造的内容和相应的管理措施，及其可能对动植物造成的影响等（图7）。其表达的重点不再是场地经过设计后的"最终状态"，

field investigations were first employed for military purposes, when the scouts investigated natural morphologies (e.g., mountains and rivers) and manmade structures (e.g., bridges and roads) to assess the environmental and traffic conditions of marching routes.[12] Such investigation help observers generate both the objective knowledge and subjective understandings of the site, covering not only the natural beings but also human activities and perceptions.

These field investigation processes realize an integration of natural objects with the observers' individual perception and personal interests and experience, giving birth to unique interpretations rather than data replication — this is the charm of the artistry that landscape architecture has and the variety of possibilities that landscape architecture brings.

3.3 Representation as Expression

In Landscape Architecture, the expression of landscapes focuses on exploring the intrinsic logics and rules that affect and generate the "shape" of natural beings, including the temporal-spatial evolution of a site and the inter-relations among all components in the system.

3.3.1 From Form Expression towards Process Representation

Therefore, a transition of the goal of expression from the traditional realistic sketch to design sketch then to Landscape Architecture can be seen from accurately depicting the image of objects, to decomposing the internal structures for interpreting the external forms better, and then to representing the essences of natural beings on the site, which is expected to reveal the interactions among all kinds of factors on the sites and the formation processes of the observed objects and phenomena. The process representation lays a foundation for the following design practices.

Notably, the "processes" expressed in both the design sketch and landscape design differ from each other in essence. The former refers to how the observers decompose the internal structures of static objects without considering the impact of external factors. In the latter, landscape is a living and participatory entity shaped by a great number of interrelated factors. One example of this kind of process representation is the proposal of Downsview Park in Toronto, Canada by James Corner Field Operations. It visualized the changes of the site in the upcoming two decades, including the specific construction in each construction phase and the corresponding management measures, as well as the possible impacts on local animals and plants (Fig. 7). Instead of showing a beautiful defined vision about the site, the proposal attempted to manifest and

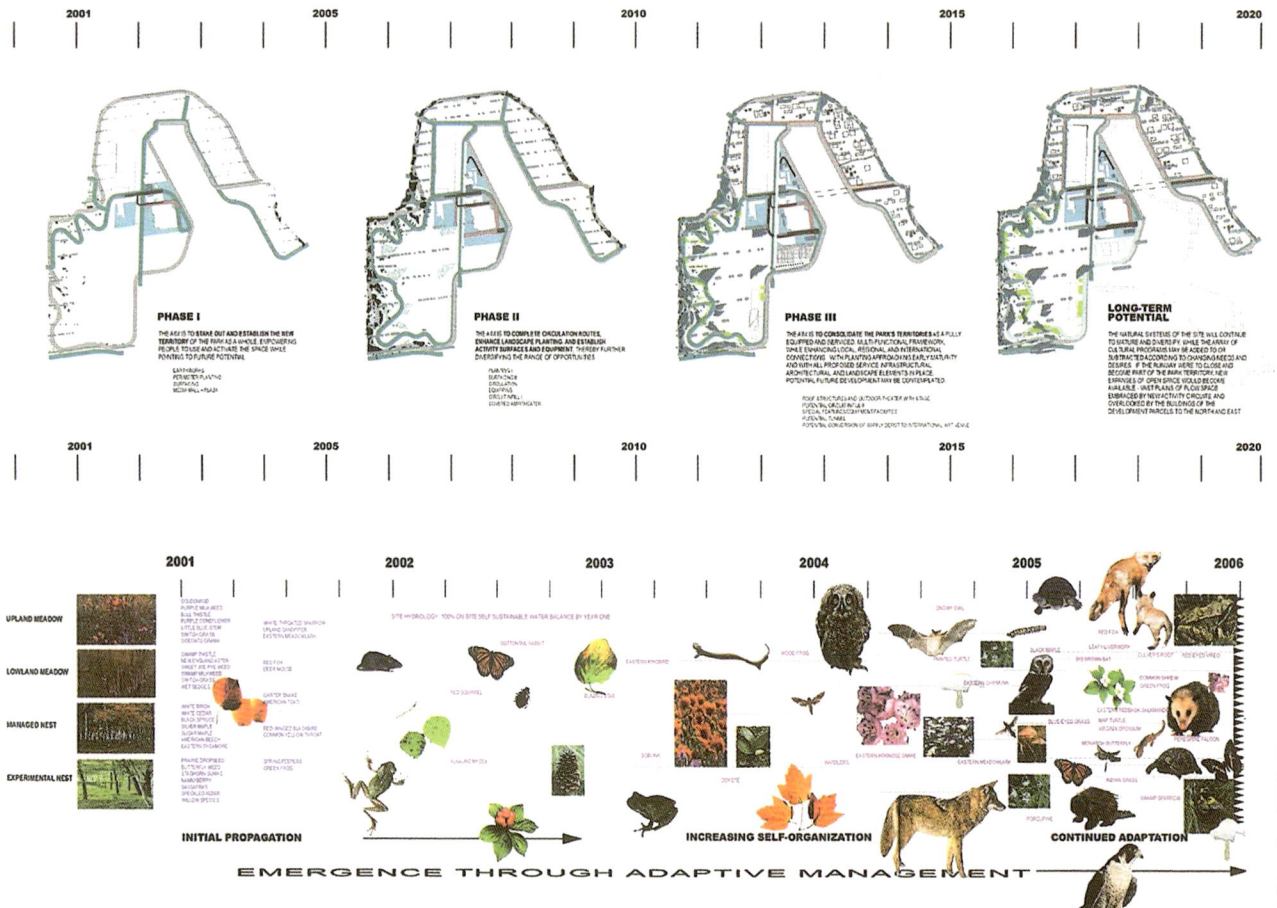

7. 詹姆斯·科纳景观设计事务所在加拿大多伦多当斯维尔公园设计竞赛中提出的"生长的生态"概念

7. The concept of "Emergent Ecology" proposed by James Corner Field Operations in the Downsview Park International Design Competition

而是其在各种外力（如砍伐、开垦等人为因素，以及阳光、风、降水、洪泛等自然因素）共同作用下逐步达到这一"最终状态"的过程。

3.3.2 表达联系与关联

另一方面，场地内各种因素的相互作用也在客观事物与现象之间建立了联系。因此，对景观的表达还必须包含这些关联。正如近代气候学、植物地理学和地球物理学创始人之一的德国自然科学家亚历山大·冯·洪堡所述，"自然是一个有机的整体"，不是"僵死的拼合之物"；在探索未知场地时，较之提出一系列彼此孤立的发现，洪堡对如何将它们联系起来更感兴趣，并认为个别现象"唯有通过与整体关联才变得重要"。[13]这种关于自然内部关联性和整体性的思考在洪堡著名的《自然之图》（图8）中得到了充分体现。

interpret how the vision and designed scenarios will evolve over time under all kinds of human and natural impacts, such as deforestation and reclamation, as well as sunshine, wind, rainfall, and floods.

3.3.2 Representation of Relations

Meanwhile, the interactions among the external factors also support the connections between all the natural beings on the site, which should be part of the representation of landscapes. According to Alexander von Humboldt, a German natural scientist and the founder of the modern Climatology, Phytogeography, and Geophysics, nature is an organic unity moved and animated by inner forces, rather than ossified combinations. He was more interested in the correlations than isolated discoveries when exploring an unknown site, holding that individual phenomenon is of no significance unless being correlated to the whole.[13] His ideas on the internal relations and the unity of nature are typically elaborated in the well-known *Naturgemälde* (Fig. 8).

8. The *Naturgemälde* (1806) painted by Alexander von Humboldt expresses a transect of the Atlantic Ocean, the South End of South America, and the Pacific Ocean.

在这张图中，洪堡建立起了位于相同海拔高度的不同事物之间的关联性。他描绘了位于南美洲厄瓜多尔的钦博拉索峰和科多帕希火山的纵剖面，并以"海拔高度"为线索，用文字描述和各种数据将有关这一地区的多种可见或不可见的信息相串联。洪堡"在画面的左右两侧排布了几列文字栏，提供一些细节信息。只要在左边栏中选择某个海拔高度，就可在图中找到这一高度下相互关联的事物，了解此处的温度、湿度和气压，以及生活在这里的动物和植物"[13]。

此外，洪堡还将人类的活动与生物圈和物理环境联系交织在一起：在1806年发表的《植物地理学随笔》中，他将植物的地理分布置

In this drawing, Humboldt tried to establish the connections among things at a same altitude: he depicted the transects of the Chimborazo Peak and the Cotopaxi in Ecuador, South America and correlated the visible and invisible information of the natural beings at the same altitude with descriptions and data: He displayed different types of detailed information in the lists on both sides of the drawing as references. One can first select an altitude from the list in left and find out the corresponding data and descriptions such as the temperature, humidity, air pressure, and flora and fauna.[13]

Moreover, Humboldt examined the distribution of plants at a broader scale to correlate plant communities with the physical world and human activities. In his work *Essay on the Geography of Plants*, published in 1806, Humboldt stated that the crop, vegetable, and fruit species travelled along with humans' migration and settlement in history, increasingly expanding the distribution of plant species and changing the

于更宏观的视野中进行观察，并指出：数千年来，庄稼谷物和蔬菜水果跟随着人类的脚步传播，人类将植物带到新的家园，也改变了地球的面貌。农业使植物与政治和经济挂钩，人类历史上的无数战争都因抢夺植物资源而爆发。[13]通过对场地关联的跨尺度思考，洪堡将对动物与植物的研究内容拓展到了它们与各种外部因素之间的关联与相互作用，如温度、湿度等物理环境因子，以及人类的迁徙、战争等经济政治因素。

值得一提的是，1905年，苏格兰城市规划大师帕特里克·格迪斯绘制了另一张"峡谷剖面"，其包含了从高山到山脚湖泊的一系列景观类型，并将它们与当地人从事的职业联系起来（图9），以强调"人、工作和场所"的关系[14]。与洪堡的发现相比，这张"峡谷剖面"表达的关联将人类活动考虑得更为细致、深入，但仍然是单一地方尺度上的；洪堡的思想则使场地尺度的景观与其所在区域乃至全球范围内的其他地方产生关联。

4 从场地观察到设计表达

正如前文所述，对景观的观察需要观察者亲临场地并基于身体运动进行多感官维度的、充分的场地感知，且其表达注重揭示自然现象背后的本质与联系。但是，景观设计专业教师需要思考如何使学生理解这种场地观察与景观表达之间的联系以及不同事物之间的关联性，并掌握通过观察与表达提炼出设计概念的方法。笔者将以两个案例具体加以说明。

global landscape. Considering that many wars on the world were about the fighting for the limited agricultural resources and products on earth, Humboldt also correlated plant species' distribution with the political episodes and economic developments in human history.[13] With such reflections on the trans-scaled relations of natural sites, Humboldt innovatively expanded his study scope to the correlations and interactions between flora and fauna with the conditions of their natural environment (e.g., temperature, humidity) and socio-economic contexts (e.g., human migration, wars).

Notably, another famous transection drawing, the "Valley Section" by the Scottish urban planner Patrick Geddes in 1905, presents various landscape types observed, from the peak to the lakes in the foothill and correlates them to different occupations of local residents (Fig. 9), highlighting the relationships among human, work, and places[14]. Human activities were examined more specifically in Geddes' work, at a local scale though. While, Humboldt's findings employed a trans-scaled perspective to map such relationships by examining the landscapes in a regional or global context.

4 From Site Observation to Design Representation

As above, the author exemplifies that on-site observation based on body movement and multi-sensory perception and the landscape representation dissecting the nature and internal relations of natural beings can help Landscape Architecture students not only learn the connection and causality between on-site observation and landscape representation, as well as the correlations between all sorts of creatures, but also master the methods and skills of how to extract and develop a design concept from such a process of observation and representation. Two cases are illustrated in the following text to elaborate how observation and representation are employed and performed in the teaching and design practice of Landscape Architecture.

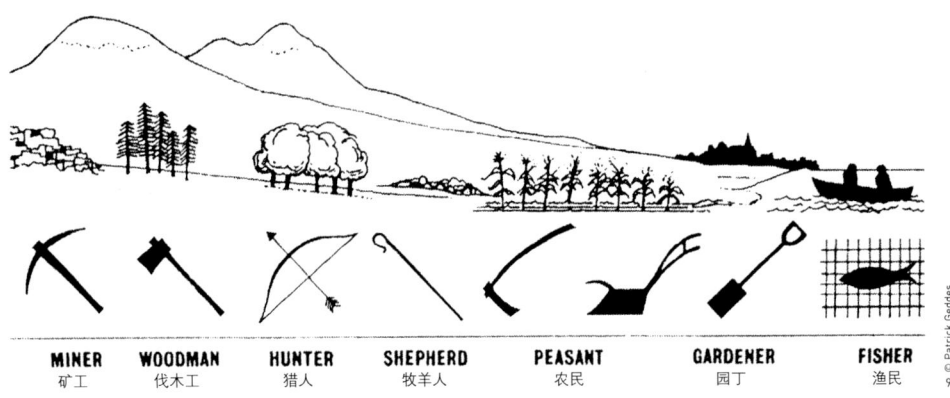

9. 帕特里克·格迪斯绘制的峡谷剖面
9. The "Valley Section" by Patrick Geddes

4.1 Developing Abstract Design Languages from Physical Sites

In the fundamental studio of the Department of Landscape Architecture of the School of Architecture, China Academy of Art, the author teaches students about how to observe and analyze natural phenomena on an authentic site and then abstract and represent them as design languages. The process consists of four phases as following, and students are asked to record each of them in a form of a stripe image / model at 1,100 mm × 150 mm (Fig. 10, 11).

First, students need to observe the sites and take one of the observed natural phenomena as his / her study topic. Then, he or she takes a series of colored photos to form the first collage strip. For instance, student Li Le noticed that there were a number of stones in different sizes scattered on the rough ground, then discovered that it was caused by water flow scouring. Therefore, she studied the interactions between stones and water flows as her interest.

However, in colored photos, the characteristics of materials on the ground is usually too rich and complicated to easily identify the elements that should be included under the study theme. Students need to transform the photos into black-white ones: through screening, clip, re-arrangement, and grayscale adjustment, the second black-white collage strip can be created. In doing so, Li eliminated the leaves and mud on the ground so as to highlight the shapes and textures of the stones and water flow traces.

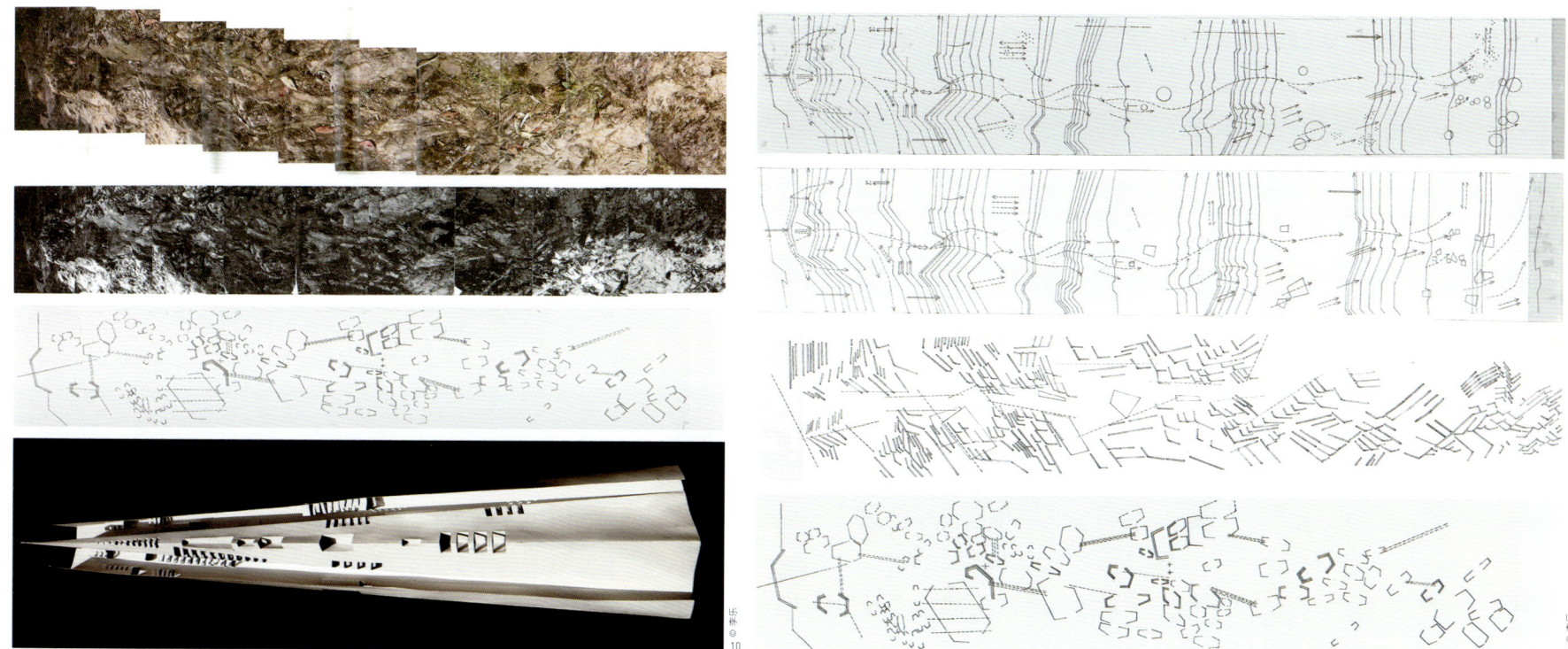

10. The colored photo collage strip, black-white photo collage strip, geometric drawing sketch strip, and 3D model strip (from top to down) made by student Li Le.
11. Student Li Le represented the varied stones, water flows, and the related factors on the site with geometric drawing sketch strips by ruler-compass drawing.

来（图11）。如李乐的尺规线描表明，石头的不同状态是由多种因素共同造成的，如石头本身的大小、位置，以及水流冲刷的强度、方向等；洼地积水对石块几乎没有冲刷作用，雨季泄洪水则有较强的冲刷力；较大的石块不易因水流冲刷或被踩踏而发生位移，较小的石子则易被踩进泥土或被水淹没；位于道路中央的石头比路旁的更容易被踩踏，等等。至此，地形地势、雨洪径流、天气状况以及人类活动等因素对场地状态的影响逐步显现出来。石头与水流这两种景观元素则是探究影响场地的各种自然力量和人为因素的透镜和媒介。

第四步是对尺规线描表达的景观元素及其与自然、人为因素的关联性进一步抽象，提取其空间特征，并以立体形式表现为3D模型。如李乐通过折叠和切割的方式来表示场地的高程变化，并着重表达场地中石头的多种状态：例如凸起处代表大块石头，凹陷处代表部分露出水面或沉没于水面以下的石头。

在上述练习中，学生首先通过亲临场地进行观察形成个性化感知，然后聚焦于自己感兴趣的现象，对其形成机制展开探究；上述4种带状图片/模型展现了这一循序渐进的探究过程，通过再现场地内"那些之前人们并未注意到的联系和共性"[15]，在真实场地的表象与抽象的概念形式之间建立起联系，而后者将成为进一步开展场地设计的重要基础。

4.2 从地方到全球的跨尺度思考

对场地关联性的观察与再现还可从更大的区域与全球尺度来推进景观设计。于1999年开放的西班牙巴塞罗那植物园便是一个很好的案例：景观设计师贝特·菲格拉斯将巴塞罗那的地中海气候作为组织花园植物展区的线索，将澳大利亚、南非、美国加利福尼亚州、智利等具有同样气候类型的国家或地区的代表性植物整合在一起，使花园景观既能展现全球不同地区的自然植被特征，又能达成某种协调统一，从而形成独特魅力（图12，13）。这种做法亦可避免外来植物无法适应当地气候的问题，大大节约了花园的养护成本。

值得一提的是，上述将植物、气候与区域相联系的思考方式并非景观设计师的首创，洪堡于1799~1804年在美洲考察期间便发现了植物、气候与区域之间的类似关联："他在安第斯山脉看到的苔藓，让他想起了千万里之外的德国北部森林中的另一种苔藓。在加拉加斯附

In the third step, students are asked to record and visualize the relations between the themed landscape elements with other factors on the site in a form of geometric drawing sketches with the vegetable parchments and fine point pens (Fig. 11). Li's sketches revealed that the varied conditions of stones resulted from a combined impact of stone sizes and locations, the magnitude and direction of water flows, etc. Her findings included that ponding water caused little erosion of the stones, while floodwater during rainy seasons eroded the stones heavily and can rush them away; the larger the stone was, the more difficult it was moved when being washed out or stepped; and the stones in the middle of path were more likely to be disturbed by passers-by. In this way, the impacts of terrain, runoff, weather, and human activities on the site was gradually visualized by analyzing the interactions between the stones and water flows.

Based on the geometric drawing sketches, students are asked to abstract the spatial features of the themed landscape elements and their relations with the natural factors and human interventions, and represent them in a 3D model strip. In her model, Li represented the elevation variation of the site with paper folding and cutting with a special focus on the diverse states of the stones: for example, the humps represent the larger stones and the depressions refer to those submerged by the water, partly or totally.

Starting with an on-site observation, students are encouraged to develop individual perceptions and study a natural phenomenon in their interests to explore the mechanisms and rules behind them. With collages, sketches, and models, the progressive discoveries during the exploration that manifests the relationships and similarities that were previously unsuspected[15] correlate the specific phenomena in reality with the abstract concepts and forms, which is fundamental to the following design process.

4.2 From Local to Global

Moreover, the observation and representation of landscape relations on a site can correlate with regional- or global-scaled landscapes. The Barcelona Botanic Garden opened in 1999 is a classic example: Taking the Mediterranean Climate of Barcelona as a clue, the landscape designer Bet Figueras introduced representative plants from other countries and regions with the same climate, such as Australia, South Africa, California in the United States, and Chile, into one garden. While displaying the diversity of plants, the garden creates the unique and harmonious charm (Fig. 12, 13). These adaptive exotic plants can also save the maintenance costs.

It is worth noting that a similar correlation has been discovered by Humboldt far earlier in his expedition to the

近的山中，他仔细观察那里类似杜鹃花的灌木丛，发现其与生长在瑞士阿尔卑斯山的一种树十分相似。后来在墨西哥，他将那里的松树、柏树与橡树和加拿大的树种进行比较……"[13]正是基于这些发现，洪堡首次提出了将植被、气候与地理环境相结合的概念——"植被带"，以及按照分布区域而非生物学特征对植物进行分类的新方法，为近代植物地理学的发展奠定了基础。而巴塞罗那植物园的案例恰好证明，这种从地方到全球的跨尺度关联思维，能够为场地尺度的景观设计提供有力支撑。

5 结语

对于景观设计学科，观察是一切知识的根本，生动的图像表达则是研究场地和设计创新的重要工具。自然场地的观察与表达的最终目的不是"模拟"，而是"再现"，即揭示事物外部形式/形态的生成逻辑，是揭示事物在不同时间、不同外力作用下的"动态的过程探究"。换言之，观察的重点是影响事物发展的各种作用力，而不是形式本身；再现的基础是对事物本质的认识和理解，而不是对事物表象的描摹。[16]因此，亲临场地的、调运多感官维度的观察是景观设计的必要前提，而对事物本质的思考及对事物之间关联的探寻更是有助于拓展设计思维。这不仅有助于设计师更好地将自然规律融入方案的推敲过程，从而为设计实践提供更坚实的科学依据，而且，面对景观设计学科入门课程的两大教学难点——一是探究绘画与设计之间如何建立联系，并通过一定的教学方法引导学生对此展开探讨；二是如何从观察与表达入手，引导学生对真实的场地进行认知，从而逐步生成设计概念——这种观察与表达亦为我们提供了一种有力的设计实验工具。**LAF**

Americas from 1799 to 1804: The moss he found in the Andes reminded him of another plant species in the forests in northern Germany. The azalea-liked bushes in the mountains near Caracas, Venezuela looked similar to a tree species found in the Alps in Switzerland. He also compared the pines, cypresses, and oaks in Mexico with those he observed in Canada.[13] Inspired by such findings in vegetation, climate, and geology, Humboldt came up with the concept of "plant communities," which leads to a new plant taxonomy method based on the global distributions of plant species, instead of biological characterlistics, laying a foundation for the modern Phytogeography. The design of the Barcelona Botanic Garden perfectly exemplifies that a trans-scaled thinking and reflection can provide strong support to site-scaled landscape design practice.

5 Conclusion

In Landscape Architecture, all knowledge about the sites comes from observation and graphic representation is significant in fostering and developing design creativity. Instead of depicting "what a natural being looks like" by seeing, such a

12. 巴塞罗那植物园的总平面图（左）与地中海气候在全球的分布范围（右）

12. The master plan of Barcelona Botanic Garden (left) and the Mediterranean climate zones all over the world (right).

1. 澳大利亚 Australia
2. 南非 South Africa
3. 智利 Chile
4. 加利福尼亚州 California
5. 东地中海地区 Eastern Mediterranean
6. 西地中海地区 Western Mediterranean
7. 北非 North Africa
8. 加纳利群岛 Canary Islands
9. 植物学研究所 Institute of botany
10. 植物园养护中心 Botanical garden maintenance building
P. 停车场 Parking

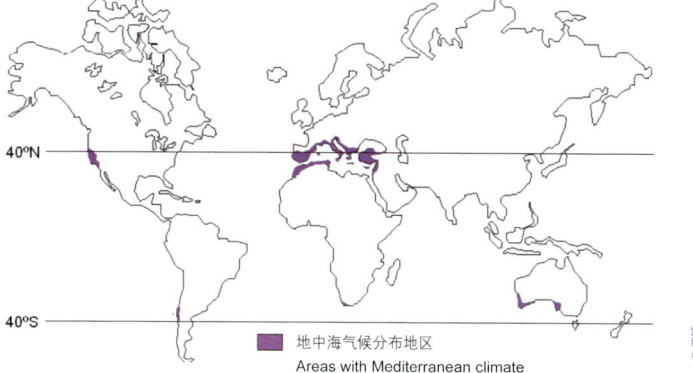

Mediterranean Climate 地中海气候

noun.
1. A Mediterranean climate is a climate that resembles those of the lands bordering the Mediterranean Sea, a climate has sunny, hot, dry summers and rainy winters. These climates generally occur on the western coasts of continental landmasses, roughly between the latitudes of 30° and 45° north and south of the equator.
2. The theme of plant collections in Barcelona Botanic Garden.

地中海气候分布地区
Areas with Mediterranean climate

13. 巴塞罗那植物园的实景图（上）与地中海气候对应的主要植物群落类型（下）

13. The built-up landscape in Barcelona Botanic Garden (upper) and the major plant communities of Mediterranean climate (below)

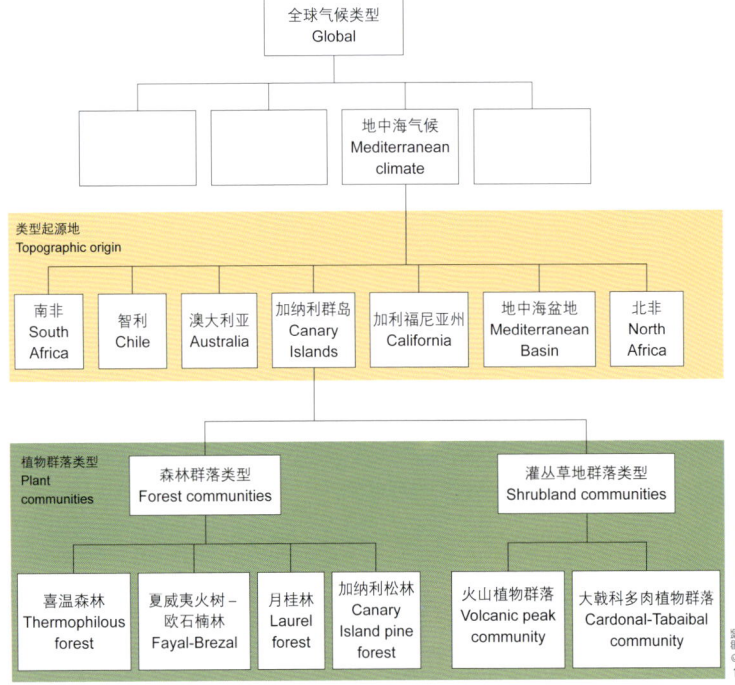

process of observation and expression is to represent "why it looks like this" by knowing, through a dynamic exploration that tries to reveal the changes of natural things in different time periods and by different external factors. In other words, what landscape architects need to observe is all impact forces impacting a natural being's evolution, rather than its form; what they need to represent is the perception and understanding of it, rather than its appearance.[16] The author thus holds that 1) the essence of landscape observation relies on on-site visits, combined with multi-sensory perception during continuous body movements, and 2) the exploration of thing's nature, as well as the correlations between things, helps landscape architects open design thinking and horizon, providing them with more scientific supports (including the rules and logics of natural processes and phenomena) that inform and improve landscape design practice. Meanwhile, to respond the two primary tasks in fundamental education of Landscape Architecture — 1) to explore the relationship between painting and design, and encourage and inspire students to think about it with proper teaching methods; and 2) to equip them with the capability to transform their understanding of an authentic site into design ideas through observation and expression — this observation and representation demonstrates itself as a powerful tool for experimental design. **LAF**

REFERENCES

[1] Wu, X. (1985). Enlighted by the Tradition — The Modern Basic Teaching for the Modeling of Chinese Figure Painting. New Arts, (3), 9-12.
[2] Wang, Z., & Xu, J. (1992). From Sketching to Designing. Hangzhou: China Academy of Arts Press.
[3] Wu, D. (Ed.). (2018). Realistic Sketching Tutorial (p. 125). Hangzhou: China Academy of Arts Press.
[4] Tanigawa, A. (2013). Art Fragments (K. Wang, & H. Wang, Trans.). Hangzhou: Zhejiang University Press.
[5] Guo, X. (2010). Lin-Quan-Gao-Zhi [The Lofty Message of Forests and Streams]. Jinan: Shandong Pictorial Publishing House.
[6] Corner, J. (1992). Representation and landscape: Drawing and making in the landscape medium. Word & Image, 8(3), 243-275. https://doi.org/10.1080/02666286.1992.10435840
[7] Zhou, X. (2015). What is Aesthetics? (p. 176). Beijing: Peking University Press.
[8] Zeng, Y. (2018). Body-Scale Perception and Experience: A terrain-Based Foundation Studio of Landscape Architecture. Landscape Architecture Frontiers, 6(5), 34-43. https://doi.org/10.15302/J-L https://doi.org/10.15302/J-LAF-20180503 AF-20180503
[9] Tuan, Y. (2018). Topophilia: A Study of Environmental Perception, Attitudes and Values (C. Zhi, & S. Liu, Trans.). Beijing: The Commercial Press.
[10] Leatherbarrow, D. (2005). The Law of Meander. In Architecture Oriented Otherwise (p. 272). New York: Princeton Architectural Press.
[11] Hunt, J. D. (2003). "Lordship of the Feet": Toward a Poetics of Movement in the Garden. In M. Conan (ed.), Landscape Design and the Experience of Motion (pp. 187-213). Washington D.C.: Dumbarton Oaks.
[12] Mathur, A., & Da Cunha, D. (2006). Deccan Traverses: The Making of Bangalore's Terrain (p. 69). New Delhi: Rupa Publications.
[13] Wulf, A. (2017). The Invention of Nature: Alexander von Humboldt's New World (H. Bian, Tran). Hangzhou: Zhejiang People's Publishing House.
[14] Geddes, P. (2012). Cities in Evolution: An Introduction to the Town Planning Movement and to the Study of Civics (H. Li, J. Wu, D. Ye, & K. Ma, Trans). Beijing: China Architecture & Building Press.
[15] Leatherbarrow, D. (2004). Topographical Stories: Studies in Landscape and Architecture. Philadelphia: University of Pennsylvania Press.
[16] Gombrich, E. H. (1987). Art & Illusion: A Study in the Psychology of Pictorial Representation (X. Lin, B. Li, & J. Fan, Trans). Hangzhou: Zhejiang Photographic Press.

PLEASE CITE THIS ARTICLE AS

Mak, V. (2019). The Spark of Contemporary Landscape Creativity — The Foundation Landscape Design Studio in the University of Hong Kong. Landscape Architecture Frontiers, 7(5), 24-37. https://doi.org/10.15302/J-LAF-1-020010

https://doi.org/10.15302/J-LAF-1-020010 RECEIVED DATE / 2019-09-05 TU986.2, J59 A

麦咏诗
香港大学建筑学院园境建筑学部高级讲师、园境学文学士课程统筹主任

Vincci MAK*
Senior Lecturer and Program Director of Bachelor of Arts in Landscape Studies, at the Division of Landscape Architecture, Faculty of Architecture, the University of Hong Kong

*Corresponding Author
Address: 6/F Knowles Building, Division of Landscape Architecture, Faculty of Architecture, the University of Hong Kong, Pokfulam, Hong Kong, China
Email: wsvmak@hku.hk

激发现代景观创意的火花
——香港大学基础景观设计课程

THE SPARK OF CONTEMPORARY LANDSCAPE CREATIVITY
— THE FOUNDATION LANDSCAPE DESIGN STUDIO IN THE UNIVERSITY OF HONG KONG

摘要

传统的景观设计课程大多以学习经典景观案例、实地考察和模仿练习作为基础教学方式。基础景观设计课的学生通常通过研习和摹拟先例来了解景观大师的设计,并通过场地调研的过程来学习空间设计。

一直以来,创意和创造性都是景观设计学所追求的学科目标。因此,景观设计教学也可以研究艺术创作的过程作为起点,引导学生欣赏艺术和设计作品,领悟设计概念的发展过程,并培养他们运用不同技法来表达设计的能力。同时,现代景观设计学不再只限于空间设计,而是需要对环境的演变进程、操作、分步机制、运动以及系统运作进行完整理解。由此可见,现代景观的表现性和动态性正受到重视。

以上对景观的理解需要一套不同的观察与表达的方式与技巧。本文旨在分享香港大学园境学文学士课程中的基础景观设计课如何基于现代景观学科语境来制定教学内容及其发展过程。

关键词

基础景观设计课;动态;过程;创意;艺术;概念;观察与表达

ABSTRACT

Traditional landscape design studio training starts with the learning of a classic or prominent landscape project, may it be through site observation or a trace-over / imitation exercise. Foundation year students in a landscape program typically take the landscape precedent project as a study ground, to learn about the landscape master's design through the mimicking process in the trace-over exercise, or to learn about the articulation of spatial design through site observation.

Landscape Architecture, afterall, is a creative endeavor. Thus, an alternative approach is to start the fundamental training with the study of artistic processes, to foster appreciation in art and design, innovative concept development, and articulation in craftsmanship. Also, the contemporary discourse of Landscape Architecture is no longer simply about spatial design, but has transformed to require understanding of process, operation, step-by-step mechanism, movement, and how a system works. The performative and dynamic aspects of landscape are being valued nowadays.

Such ways of seeing landscapes require a different set of observation and representation methods and skills. In this article, the author shares how the pedagogical content and developments of the foundation year landscape design studio in the HKU Bachelor of Arts in Landscape Studies BA(LS) Program help train students with such new interpretations to contemporary Landscape Architecture.

KEYWORDS

Foundation Landscape Design Studio; Dynamic; Process; Creativity; Art; Concept; Observation and Representation

EDITED BY Tina TIAN **TRANSLATED BY** CHANG Gengjiaqi Tina TIAN

1 背景介绍:当代景观教学和香港大学园境学文学士课程

当代景观设计在过去20年间发生了重大变化,从追求形态和装饰性的空间设计演变到重视操作性和表现性的景观设计,并主张促进这些属性的实现。景观设计学不再单纯是一门追求美学的学科,而是选取其演进过程、分步机制、运动变化和工作系统等基本逻辑,来构成景观设计课程的基础。

在基础设计教学中，另一个非常重要但却容易被忽视的组成部分是如何构思一个设计概念。有人认为设计概念的构思"只可意会，不可言传"。然而，一位景观设计师成功的关键在于他/她独特的设计概念，以及如何通过景观空间设计来凸显其概念。没有独特的概念，设计就失去了灵魂。这也是为什么设计概念的构思是景观设计教学的重点之一。

当代景观设计教学也许不能再仅仅要求基础学年的学生们复制历史上的景观杰作。现今所需要的教学方式应是培养学生发展自己的设计逻辑和敏锐性，而非"通过复制来学习"。

基于此背景，香港大学园境学文学士课程于2009年创立。该课程设置的愿景是为学生提供全面的当代景观教育，使学生在毕业后拥有可应对这个瞬息万变社会的专业技能。在这个为期4年的课程中，设计部分的教学从基础学年的"人体与物件"学习、中间学年的"环境：社群和生物物理系统"学习，拓展到毕业学年的"系统：城市和区域话题"学习。

以"人体与物件"为研究对象的基础景观设计课关注物件的构成、布局，及其与人体的尺度关系，是景观设计的入门课题，所以也是培养学生对景观设计学学科认知的最佳时机。香港大学园境建筑学部的高级讲师麦咏诗从2011年设计并开展了"景观设计概论课"（即基础景观设计课，12学分，共12周，约需300~360学时），来对基础学年的学生进行概念创新和动态过程的教学。这门课程的教学活动主要

1 Background: Contemporary Landscape Pedagogies and the HKU Bachelor of Arts in Landscape Studies BA(LS) Program

Contemporary landscape design in the past two decades has transformed a lot. From the pursuit of forms and ornamental attributes in spatial design, the discipline of Landscape Architecture now values the operative and performative aspects of design and the roadmaps to achieve such attributes. Landscape Architecture is no longer an aesthetic discipline, but emphasizes on design logics that include process, step-by-step mechanism, movement, and systematic work flow, which now lay a foundation to landscape design pedagogy.

Another essential component often being ignored (or downplayed) in the teaching of foundation design studio is how to develop a design concept. Concept development, some say, is very intuitive and cannot be taught. However, the success of a landscape architect is dependent on the creativity of his / her design concepts and how these concepts are conveyed through landscape and spatial design. Without a creative concept, a design work may lose its identity and soul. This is why developing a design concept is essential to landscape design education.

Contemporary pedagogical approaches in landscape design perhaps need to shift from simply coaching foundation year students to replicate historical landscape masterpieces. "Learning by copying" is no longer applicable to contemporary pedagogical goals to train students to develop their design logic and to improve their design sensibility.

Under such a premise, the Bachelor of Arts in Landscape Studies BA(LS) Program in HKU (the University of Hong Kong) was established in 2009. The vision of the HKU BA(LS) Program is to equip graduates with professional knowledge and skills through a comprehensive landscape education, allowing them to cope with the ever-changing world. In this four-year program, the design studio scopes and sequences start from "body and object" in the foundation years, then "context: community and biophysical system" in the intermediate year, with the final year's focus on "systems: urban and regional issues."

During the "body and object" study in the foundation year studio, students are expected to learn design fundamentals. The making and composition of an object, as well as its relationship with human scale, are explored. This offers the best time to engage students with new interpretations of landscape. Vincci Mak, senior lecturer at HKU Landscape Architecture, has developed the "Introduction to Landscape Design Studio" (the foundation landscape design studio hereafter, 12 credits, with

基于定期的师生一对一讨论、评图和公开汇报等形式，学生可从中习得如何运用绘图和模型制作等技巧来表达其设计概念。

基础景观设计课初期以研究某一物件或动作，并以其过程和步骤为题来理解景观系统；随着教学内容和方法的发展演变，后期则以分析一件艺术作品来了解创作背后的文化故事或历史景况。初期教师主要通过向学生引进景观表现性的相关内容来改变新生们对景观设计学的粗浅观念，即景观是只关于环境美化的学科。景观动态机制的教授后来在本科生课程中得到重视，并成为学生学习基础景观设计课前必修的预备课程之一。通过教学观察得知，基础学年学生遇到的一个最大的挑战是如何发展设计概念。因此，后期的基础景观设计课有针对性地侧重于设计概念发展的教学。这些课程设计上的调整有助于厘清教学目标，并为学生提供更为有效的景观设计教学。

这两种不同学习轨迹的基础景观设计课使我们可以管窥设计教育如何在观察、分析和表达方面为学生开辟新的方向和方法。指导学生们如何观察、决定表达什么，以及如何记录，有助于其形成景观设计思维，这将成为景观设计教育学中的重要里程碑。本文旨在分享这些新的教学经验，并讨论它们如何启发与加深学生对于当代景观的理解。

2 景观作为动态机制的介入

景观从来都不是静态的。"对过程的表现是景观都市主义的核心关注点；将自然看作过程的观念指导着设计师去进行设计。"[1]在当代景观设计中，我们视景观为一个动态系统，并在设计中采用"融入其中"的方法来建立与自然系统的融合。为了向基础学年的学生引进这种概念，设计课题的选取和其相关作业的布置都以培养学生对景观动态性的理解为目标。

2.1 鸟类运动的研究

运动变化是理解动态系统的重要因素之一。因此，在基础景观设计课的初期教学中，其中一个作业题目即选取鸟的身体运动作为研究对象。鸟类是景观的构成部分之一。选取鸟类做研究的部分原因是因为这有助于扩展学生对于景观设计的理解，即景观设计是为不同生物而设计的，万物其生本身就是一个动态的系统。当然，此题目选取的主要原因还是鸟能飞翔、行走，甚至游泳，它们形态各异的活动行为可为学生对多种身体运动的发生方式提供丰富的研究机会。

300 to 360 learning hours in 12 weeks) since 2011 to teach foundation year landscape students about concept creativity and dynamic processes. This course is primarily taught in the forms of regular desk crits, pin ups, and presentations. Students are trained with drawing and model-making skills to represent design ideas.

In its early years, this course engaged students to study objects or movements about their processes and mechanisms. As the course focus and pedagogical goal changed, in later years students were trained to study an art work and to understand the story and cultural / historic context of the creation. By introducing the performative aspects of Landscape Architecture, the early phases of the course reacted to the "default" notion held by foundation year students, that is the discipline is only about beautifying the environment. The importance of the study of landscape as a dynamic mechanism has then gained recognition in the BA(LS) Program. Therefore, it was then incorporated into the pre-requisite course that students need to take prior to the foundation landscape design studio. Teaching observation reveals that one of the biggest challenges for foundation year students is about how to develop a design concept. Therefore, the later phases of this course focused on design concept development to help improve students' knowledge and skills strategically. Such training would help sharpen the pedagogical objectives and provide more effective design knowledge and skills for students.

The two study tracks resulted in examples of how students were guided to expand new horizons and to explore a wider range of methods in observation, analysis, and representation, which inform their landscape design thinking. These are all important cornerstones in landscape design pedagogy. This article aims to share these new learning experiences and discuss how they make an impact on students' understanding of contemporary landscape.

2 The Teaching of Landscape as a Dynamic Mechanism

Landscape is never static. "Representation of process is the central concern of Landscape Urbanism; the movement's view of nature as process guides the designers in developing their designs."[1] In contemporary landscape architecture, we try to incorporate our understanding of landscape as a dynamic system in our design, adopting an influx approach to work with natural systems. Design studio topics and associated exercises were carefully selected, when introducing this concept to foundation year students, in order to foster their comprehension of the dynamic nature of landscape.

1. 学生王天檬以常见的乌鸦作为研究对象，并绘制当其翅膀展开至最大范围时的全身比例关系图。除了了解乌鸦身体的各个尺寸，王天檬还研究了这种鸟如何通过其翅膀的运动来实现飞行，以及其他与身体运动相关的行为，如觅食。

1. A scaled drawing of a common raven when its wings are spread to the maximum extent, by student Wang Tianmeng. Wang studied a common raven on its various body dimensions, and how this bird constitutes its movement of flying with its wings, as well as the bird's other behaviors associated with body movements, such as food hunting.

这个练习中选择的鸟类在体型和生活习性上各具特点，飞行方式及所运用的身体部分，乃至动作的速度和频率等方面都各不相同。鸟类如何运动以达到自身身体平衡，及与景观环境平衡，都是学习的一部分。

这些乍听起来好像都与景观设计无关。但是如果将景观系统的运作机制解码，就会发现二者之间拥有相似的元素。"景观的复杂性在某种意义上恰恰在于景观中的元素的固有动态和生态本质，而这取决于我们如何理解生物体与其环境之间不断发展的关系，而非孤立地理解离散的元素。"[2]景观系统是一个由各种元素构成的网络，并且所有的元素都是相互联系的，一个元素的运动（或操作）可能触发序列中另一个元素的运动变化。如果其中的某一部分无法运作，其他部分就也无法运作。这一点和身体运动发生方式十分相似：骨骼的大小与肌肉和肌腱的推拉方式相互关联。

此研究的关键在于重点学习和理解动态系统的运作机制，并将其延伸至对于景观的系统理解。因此，在基础景观设计课中，对鸟类运动的初步研究，是对其整体和身体部位的尺寸、典型运动行为和生活习性形成的概观（图1）。

鸟类的身体运动研究背后旨在向学生传达身体各部分共同合作从而产生身体运动这一观念。同时，作为设计练习的一部分，教学时亦引入了"运动变化图表"，以记录和表达随时间变化的一系列动作。这呼应了当代景观设计学的论述："……景观都市主义的表现的重要元素，就是用'图表'来表达对生物态的演进过程，从而引入时间元素……"[1]

2.1 Study of Bird Movements

Movement study is one of the most important methods to understand a dynamic system. Therefore, the anatomy and movement of birds were introduced as study topics in one of the early versions of the foundation landscape design studio. Birds are inhabitants in the landscape. The study of birds is relevant because it helps expand the understanding that landscape design is created for many different living things (and the co-existence of all creatures is a dynamic system itself), and of course the main reason is that birds can fly, walk, or swim. Its various body-moving behaviors provide rich study sources for students to explore the multiple ways of body movement.

The collection of birds selected for the course varies in size and living pattern. The ways they fly are all different. They move their body parts differently, resulting in different speeds and paces of movement. How the birds achieve a bodily balance with their movements, and create equilibrium with the landscape context, are also part of the study.

All these seem unrelated to landscape design. However, if one deciphers how a landscape system works, there may be similar elements to be found. "Landscape offers... complexities, not least of which is the inherent dynamic of its elements and the very nature of ecology, which is fundamentally about understanding the set of ongoing relationships between organisms and their environment, and less about understanding discrete elements in isolation."[2] A landscape system is a network of elements, the movement (or operation) of one element may trigger the movement of another element in the sequence, and all the parts are inter-connected. If one of them does not perform, the others will not neither. This is highly similar to how body movement occurs: the sizes of bones, and how the muscles and tendons get pushed and pulled are inter-related.

Learning how a dynamic system works is key, and such an understanding is adopted in the comprehension of landscape as a system. Therefore, the initial study of a bird's movement in the foundation landscape design studio is to form an overview of the bird's overall and body parts' sizes, typical body movements, and living patterns (Fig. 1).

While the essential message behind this study of bird movements is the inter-connectedness of various body parts, "movement diagram series" was also introduced as part of design studio exercise, to document and describe such a series of movements through time. This echoes the discourse of contemporary Landscape Architecture that "(t)he... important element of Landscape Urbanism's representation, the diagram, addresses biological and ecological processes, thereby introducing the element of time…."[1]

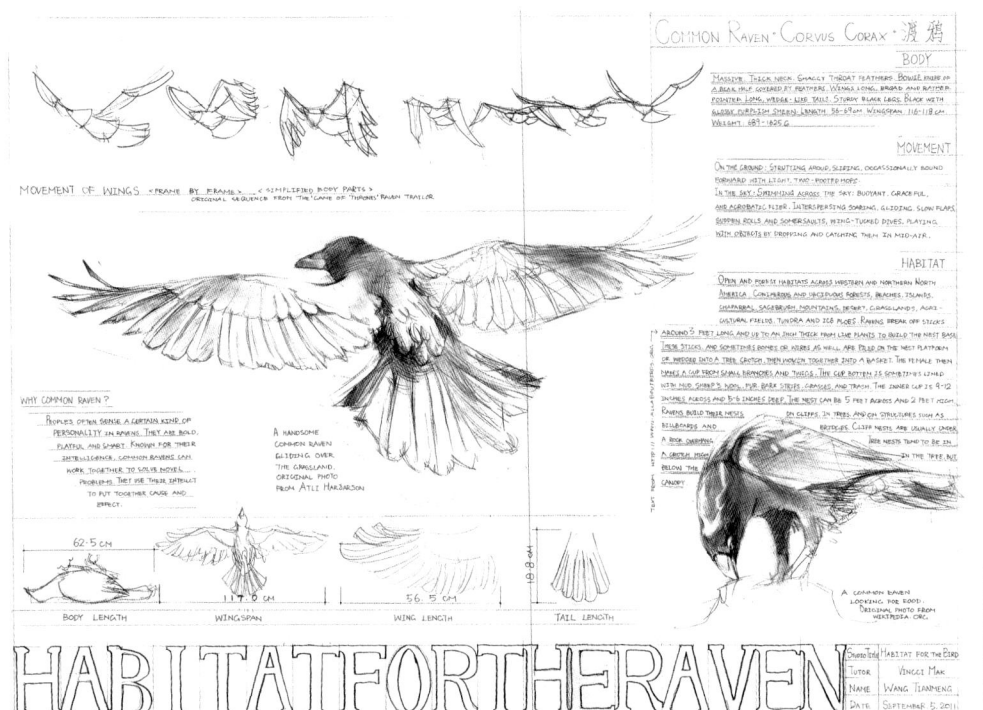

© 王天檬 / Wang Tianmeng

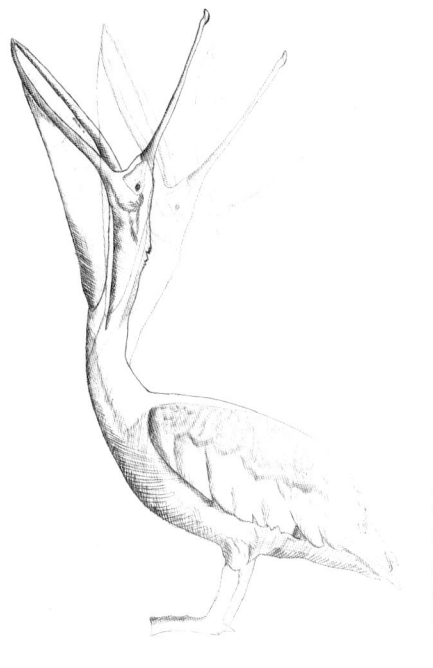

2. 学生胡承轩描述鹈鹕鸟喙动态的立面图。胡承轩以鹈鹕为研究对象，这种鸟以大口袋一样的鸟喙而闻名，因此他将研究重点放在了鸟喙的运动上。他将鸟喙（和相连的脖颈部分）与鹈鹕的立面图重叠，以此来表达这一运动。

3. 学生胡承轩记录鹈鹕鸟喙动态的运动变化图表。胡承轩对鸟喙的运动进行了进一步观察，并结合鸟喙的大小和时间的变化来描述鹈鹕如何捕鱼为食。

4. 学生李云烽记录猫头鹰准备自卫时的运动变化图表。他尝试记录猫头鹰在这一动作中各身体部位的移动和变化情况。

2. An elevation drawing of a pelican describing the bird's mouth movement, by student Woo Shing Hin Bryan. Pelican is characterized for its "big pocket" mouth, so Woo focused his study on the bird's mouth movement and represented it by overlapping his elevation drawing of the pelican with the drawing of the movement of its mouth (and neck).

3. A movement diagram series of a pelican describing the bird's mouth movement, by student Woo Shing Hin Bryan. Woo further studied the bird's mouth movement, in association with the changes of mouth size and with time, to represent how a pelican hunts fish as food.

4. A movement diagram series of an owl when it prepares for a self-defense, by student Lee Wan Fung. Lee tried to document how the body parts of an owl changes during the movement.

© 胡承轩 / Woo Shing Hin Bryan

2

© 胡承轩 / Woo Shing Hin Bryan

3

© 李云烽 / Lee Wan Fung

4-1

© 李云烽 / Lee Wan Fung

4-2

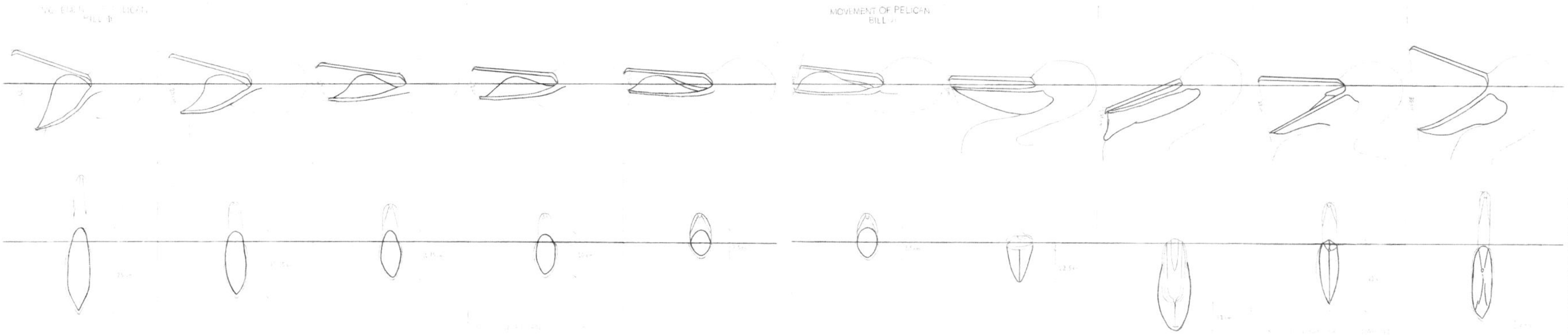

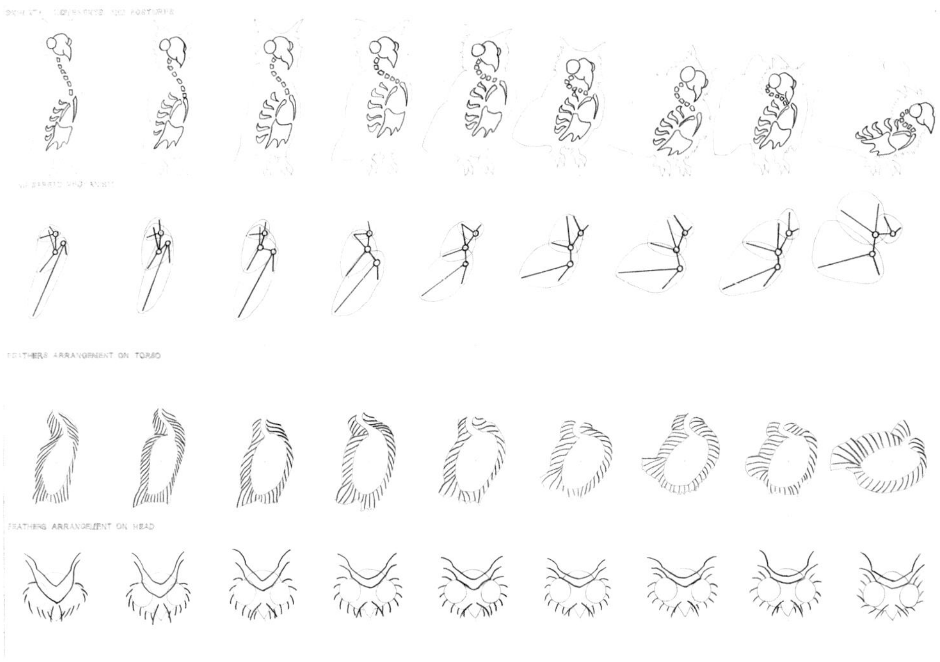

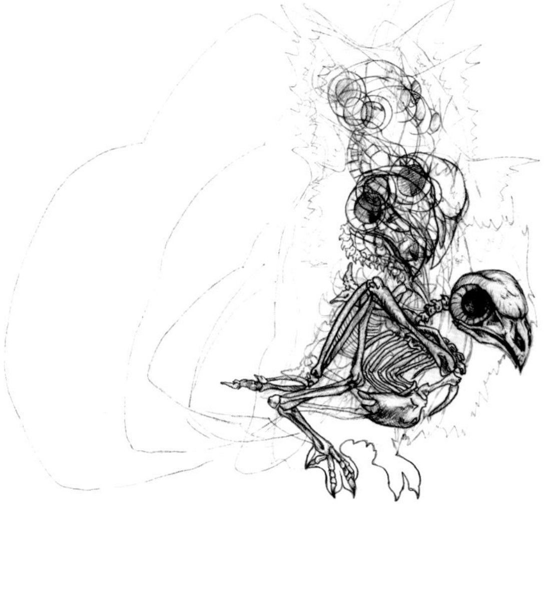

所以，除了以平面图和立面图这些典型的表现手法来绘制鸟类外，学生还要绘制一份"运动变化图表"。这种表现方法帮助学生观察和分析鸟类身体特定部位的运动细节，并将这种运动的步骤与时间联系起来。"这种系列图是描述时间与空间之间复杂关系的有效工具。"[3]这种表达方式也参考了早期电影发展时的连续摄影法，例如艾提安–朱尔斯·马雷和埃德沃德·迈布里奇的作品。"（在连续摄影中）一个身体关节的动作被记录为一连串点象，连接起来就成了图形。"[4]

学生可以分别画出每一步的运动图，也可以把每一步的运动在画面上进行叠加。两者均可帮助学生对生成运动的每一步骤形成清晰而深刻的理解（图2~4）。

作为一项观察分析练习，这种对运动行为的观察为学生奠定了理解景观机制的基础，亦为学生下一步的设计概念学习做了准备。该课程最终要求学生设计一处虚构的"鸟类栖息地"，学生要从他们对鸟类动作的理解中发展出一个设计概念，并通过绘制概念图展开学习。由于运动变化与身体部位的形状、大小和比例有关，学生们可利用之前研究所得的形状比例，以及各身体部位的移动机制来绘制概念图。这样的概念图为学生鸟类栖息地三维空间设计提供了二维基础（图5~9）。

2.2 对体育运动的研究

之后的基础景观设计课沿用了相似的教学手段，目的仍然是使学生了解运动变化是如何进行的，但研究课题变为了体育运动，并以研究体育运动步骤为概念，设计一个体验场馆。借由此，学生的研究重点可以集中在人体尺度的运动变化上，有助于训练他们空间设计的能力（图10）。

以体育运动作为研究对象的优点在于其对学生而言相对容易理解，毕竟人最熟悉的还是自己的身体。但由于参考照片或图像选取的拍摄角度，会使学生容易混淆尺度和运动幅度，从而影响研究效果。

Therefore, besides the typical representation of drawing plan and elevation views of the birds, students were also asked to make a "movement diagram series." This representation method helps students observe and analyze a bird's movement of a particular body part in details, and to relate the steps of such a movement with time. "Serial drawings are effective tools for illustrating the complex relationship between time and space."[3] This way of representation also adopts the chronophotography in early history of motion picture, for example, the works by Etienne-Jules Marey and Eadweard Muybridge. "The points (on the chronophotograph) traced by the movement of a joint on a body can be readily connected to form a graph."[4]

Students diagramed the drawings of each step of movement, or overlaid all the steps onto one drawing. Both comprise very strong and clear understanding of how the steps come together to make one movement happen (Fig. 2 ~ 4).

As an exercise of observation and analysis, the movement study laid a foundation for understanding landscape mechanism, which prepared students for the next step exercise: to develop a design concept. The final project of the course was to design a hypothetical habitat for the bird. Students were asked to develop a concept inspired from their understanding of the bird's movement and to represent it through concept drawing. Having learned that a movement relates to the shape, size, and proportion of body parts, students started using forms and proportions, and how the pieces collide and detach, to compose their concept drawings. Such drawings then served as the two-dimensional basis that supported students in developing three-dimensional design for the bird's habitat (Fig. 5 ~ 9).

2.2 Study of Sports

The next iteration of the exercise in the foundation landscape design studio adopted a similar pedagogical approach, aiming to continue engaging students to learn how movement works. The difference was the subject: it became a study of sports, and by studying the motion steps of the sports, students were to design a sports pavilion. This exercise facilitated students' understanding of human-scale movements and improved their learning of spatial design (Fig. 10).

The advantage of studying movement in sports is that it is easy to understand as people are familiar with the human body. However, the reference photographs or images are often taken from angles confusing to students in terms of scales and the range of motions, causing impacts on study results.

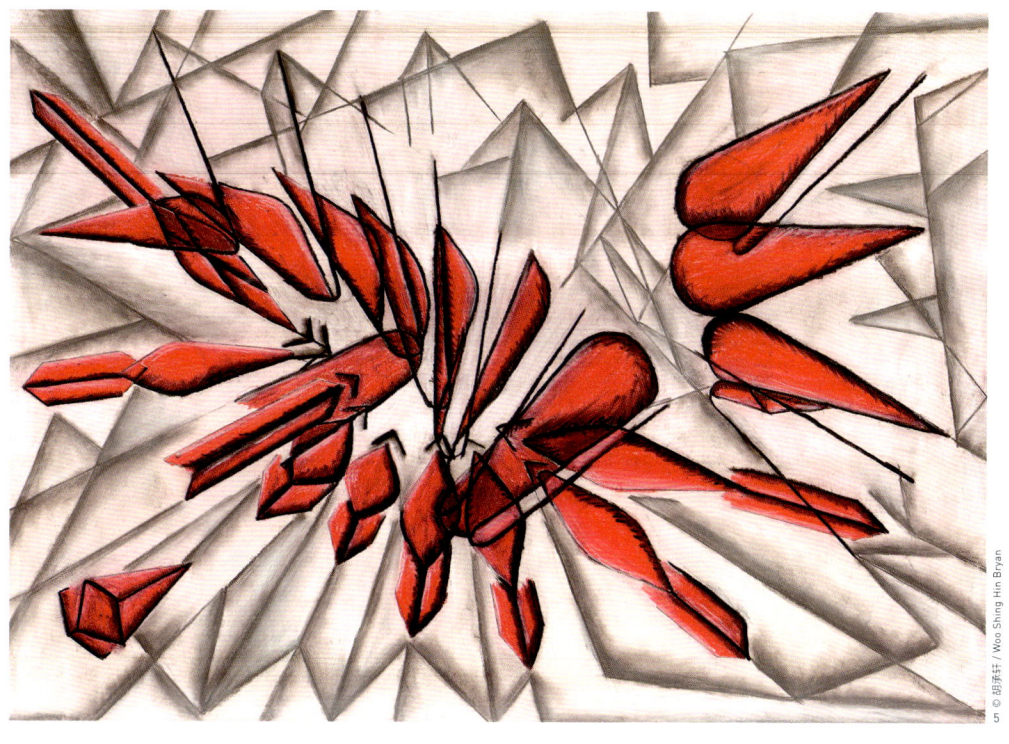
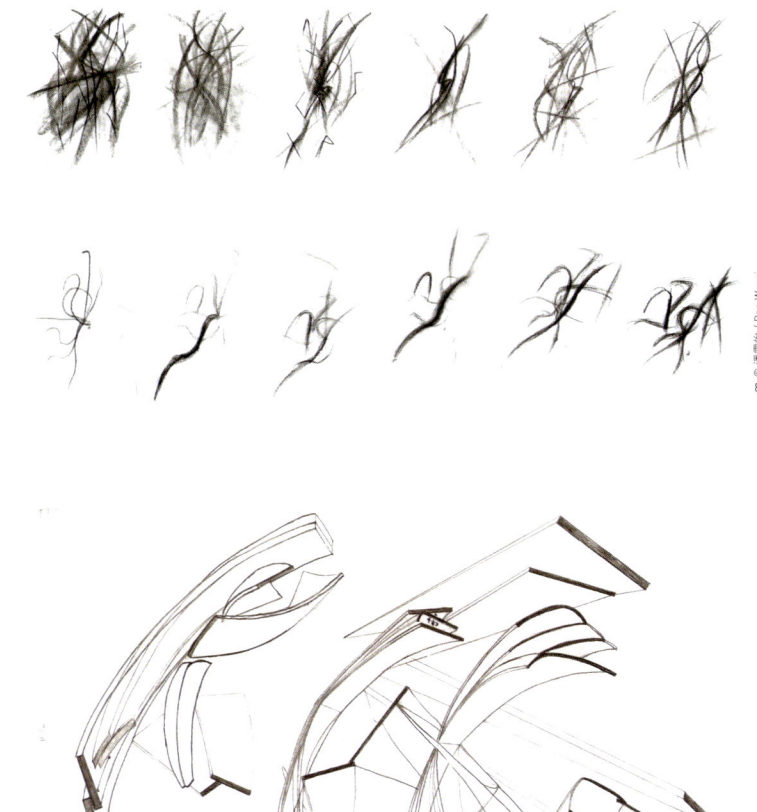
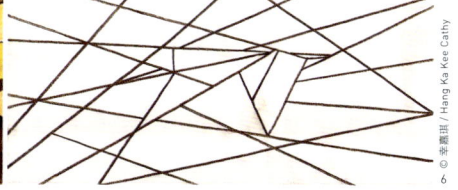

5. 学生胡承轩基于鹈鹕行为研究进行的概念图绘制。该概念图上所呈现的形状、大小和角度，都来自于他早期对鸟喙运动变化的观察。
6. 学生幸嘉琪把蓝脚鲣鸟行为抽象化的概念图系列。蓝脚鲣鸟以其流畅而快速地从空中潜入水中捕鱼的行为而闻名。在此系列概念图中，她一步步地重点描绘了蓝脚鲣鸟的这一特点。
7. 学生幸嘉琪基于对蓝脚鲣鸟所绘的概念图发展而来的概念模型。她从概念习作中提取外形轮廓，从而进一步形成鸟类栖息地的空间设计；她将长三角形引伸为鸟类栖息地的设计概念，创建线性空间，以呼应此鸟快速和精确的动作。

5. Concept drawing abstracting a pelican's movement, by student Woo Shing Hin Bryan. In his concept drawing, the shapes, sizes, and angles of the forms were informed by his earlier study of the bird's mouth movement.
6. Concept drawing series abstracting blue-footed booby's movement, by student Hang Ka Kee Cathy. The bird blue-footed booby is famous for its smoothness and speediness to dive in to water from air for fish hunting. In Hang's series of concept drawings, she accentuated the bird's characteristic step by step.
7. Concept model derived from the concept drawings of the bird blue-footed booby, by student Hang Ka Kee Cathy. She extracted the forms developed in her concept work to form the spatial design of the bird's habitat. Hang derived to use a long triangulated form to create linear spaces for the habitat to echo the speedy and precise movement of the bird.

8. 学生潘雯怡将火烈鸟行为抽象化的概念图系列。学生潘雯怡以火烈鸟为研究对象，在其概念图中表现了火烈鸟腿部的细长形状和它们的动作。
9. 学生潘雯怡鸟类栖息地设计剖面图。从图中可以看出，她从早期概念阶段学到的关于鸟的腿部形状、组成、比例和运动模式的知识，应用到最终的设计中。
10. 学生张爱惠研究并记录掷铅球这项运动的运动变化图表。

8. Concept drawing series abstracting a flamingo's movement, by student Pan Wenyi. Pan studied the bird flamingo, and the concept drawing manifested her interests in the elongated shape of bird legs and their movements.
9. Section drawing of the bird's habitat design, by student Pan Wenyi. She applied the knowledge learned from the earlier concept phases about the bird's leg form, composition, proportion, and movement pattern into the development of her final design.
10. Movement diagram series studying and recording the sport "shot-putting," by student Cheung Oi Wai Charity.

2.3 对达·芬奇发明的研究

受以体育运动为研究课题的教学经验的启发，基础景观设计课后期对达·芬奇的发明进行了研究。记录达·芬奇装置器械发明的文献丰富，可供学生挖掘的参考资料众多，而且达·芬奇令人惊叹的素描也会对学生的制图学习有所启发，他对细节、尺度和比例的专注也激励着学生们对于普适设计的探索。达·芬奇所发明的仪器往往需要由人来操作，因而也就需要考虑到人体的尺度和运动。最重要的是，达·芬奇精心设计的装置中详细而复杂的操作和运动机制完美地契合了培养学生理解动态系统的教学目标（图11~14）。这种理解与当代景观论述中理解基础设施的作用及其相关的表现、机制和过程密切相关。"虽然基础设施本身是静态的，但是它们组织和管理的是复杂的过程、运动和交换系统……在基于基础设施的都市主义中，形态的确很重要，但更重要的是它能做什么，而不是它看起来像什么。"[5]

事实上，通过研究一个机械来理解景观系统并非首创，来自美国加利福尼亚大学伯克利分校的奇普·苏利文教授曾在其《空间观察和分析表达》一文中借用美国的著名风景画家埃里克·撒隆绘制的机械图纸表达了此观点："埃里克·撒隆……使用分析图来理解过去的

2.3 Study of Da Vinci Inventions

Lesson learned from the study of sports exercise led to the evolution of the project topic of the course. It was later developed into the study of Da Vinci inventions. Da Vinci left abundant documentations of his inventions for students to reference. His amazing sketches inform students in drawing techniques. His dedication to details, scales, and proportions inspires students in the understanding of universal design. A Da Vinci apparatus often requires a manual operation, from there the movements at human scale also come in to consideration. And most importantly, a Da Vinci invention is often a well-designed apparatus with a sophisticated mechanism in operation and movement, making it a perfect topic to meet the pedagogical objective of nurturing students to understand dynamic systems (Fig. 11 ~ 14). Such understanding closely relates to infrastructure's role in contemporary landscape discourse and its performances, mechanisms, and processes. "Although static in and of themselves, infrastructures organize and manage complex systems of flow, movement, and exchange…. In infrastructural urbanism, form matters, but more for what it can do than for what it looks like."[5]

In fact, the study of a machine as a means to understand landscape system is not new. Professor Chip Sullivan from the University of California, Berkeley illustrated this point with the machine drawings made by Eric Sloane, a renowned American landscape painter, in his article Observation and the Analytical

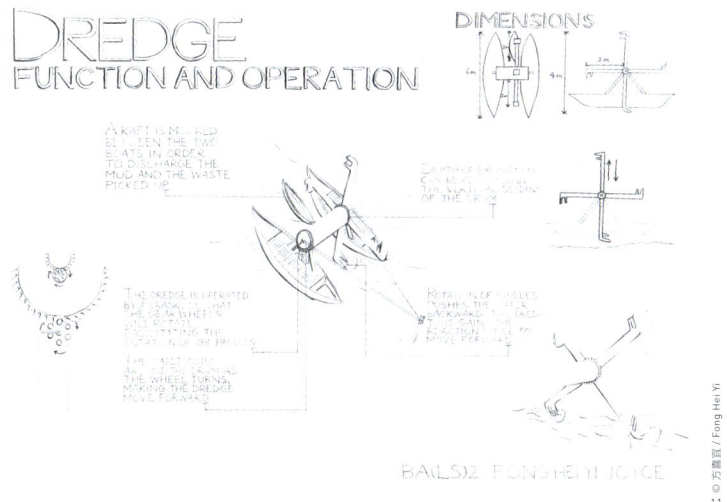

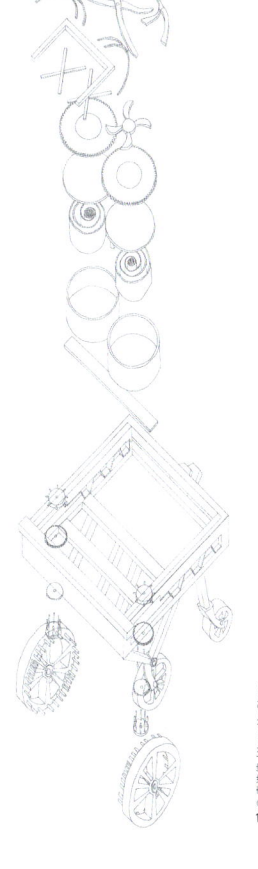

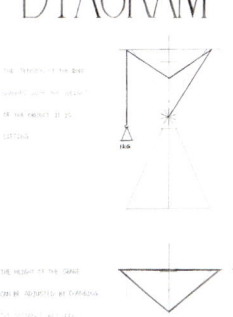
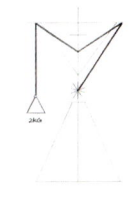
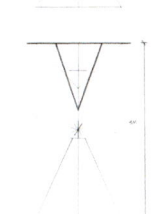
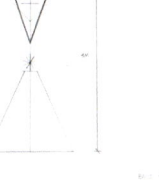

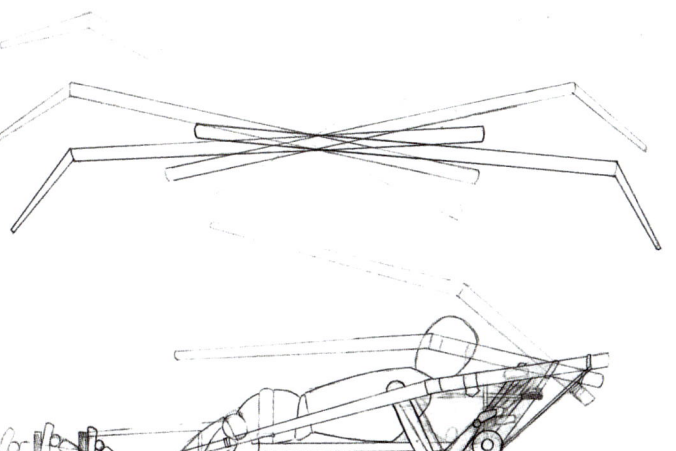

11. 学生方喜宜解析挖掘机工作原理的绘图。
12. 学生袁浩信解析计程器不同部件的轴测图。
13. 学生林之琪探究带有中心绞车滑轮系统的起重机如何随着设备张力及高度的变化而运作的图表。

11. Drawing analyzing the operation of a dredge, by student Fong Hei Yi.
12. Axonometric drawing deciphering the parts of an odometer, by student Yuen Ho Shun.
13. Diagrams exploring a crane with central winch, by student Lin Zhiqi. Lin studied how the crane's pulley system operates as the tension and height of the apparatus changes.

14. 学生蔡景欣对于飞行器的绘图。学生蔡景欣探究了达·芬奇的飞行器发明，并将重点放在人的运动如何操作飞行器上。
15, 16. 学生吴丽晶通过对带中心绞车滑轮系统的起重机的运动进行研究，推导出动词"拉扭"，来建立概念模型并绘制概念图。其概念模型中，纸板间材料力度的大小以及概念图中笔触的样式都帮助吴丽晶发展出空间中与"拉扭"的相关概念。
17. 学生王俊文对灯笼状骨架的旋转起重机进行了研究，并推导出了"围绕"这一动词。他以概念图探讨当有多于一个围绕动作同时发生时并置的空间质量。
18, 19. 学生邹丹叶以水力锯为研究对象，并选择了动词"流动"来进行概念学习。她基于其对"流动性"的理解制作概念模型，并将这一概念转化为空间设计的模型。

14. Drawings exploring a flying machine, by student Tsoi King Yan Ingrid. Tsoi studied Da Vinci's flying machine with a focus on how human's movement engages in the operation of the flying machine.
15, 16. Through her movement study with a crane with central winch, student Ng Lai Ching derived the verb "strain" to develop concept model and drawing. The magnitude of strain between the cardboards in the concept model, as well as the pattern of strokes in the concept drawing, helped Ng develop her idea of "strain" in space.
17. Student Wang Junwen studied a revolving crane with lantern framework and selected the action verb "revolve" for further study. His concept drawing explored the spatial quality of the juxtaposition of multiple revolving actions.
18, 19. Student Zou Joy Liu studied the hydraulic saw and selected the verb "flow" to further her concept study. She made concept model to explore the attribute of fluidity in "flow," and translated such a concept into a spatial form.

机械和工具是如何制造和使用的……其对每一个单独的部件进行了图解，并通过一系列细节和流程的绘图对机械进行了重现。"[3]

在学习了达·芬奇的发明之后，学生们要推导出一个动词来描述他们所研究的仪器的运动。然后，他们基于该动词绘制概念图并制作模型，这一中间步骤有助于他们介入相应的空间设计练习。这种练习构建方式旨在使学生意识到景观是动态的，且常常处于不断的运动之中。动词不仅有助于学生们描述和表达在本领域应该掌握的景观操作机制，动态随着时间对空间环境的演变影响亦对学生在空间设计品质及体验方面有所启发。这些都能指导学生在理解景观动态性的前提下去发展自己设计的基本原理。在此启发下，学生们可以进一步深化他们的设计概念，而该练习正旨在指导这一创作过程的发生（图15~19）。

此练习的另一重教育价值是，达·芬奇在设计装置时是有其独到的设计决策的，通过潜移默化地学习达·芬奇的设计逻辑和解读仪器的操作，学生们可以间接地学习设计决策的产生过程。这样的学习过程某种意义上借鉴了经典景观先例的研究方法，不同的是，学生还需要将他们所理解的设计逻辑，分析和转换为可应用到景观设计的知识。相对于以经典景观先例研究来直接学习空间设计，达·芬奇发明的研究更侧重于针对学生基础、概念和逻辑的训练。

Representation of Space: "Eric Sloane… used analytical pen and ink drawings to understand how the machines and tools of the past were fabricated and used…. Sloane diagramed each individual part and reconstructed the machine through a progression of details and processes."[3]

After learning about the Da Vinci inventions, students were asked to derive an action verb to describe the movement of the apparatus they studied. Then, they developed concept drawings and models based on the verb — this intermediate step helped them ease into the spatial design phase. The framework of the exercise aimed to deduce the understanding that landscape is always influx and in constant motions. The derivation of action verbs helps describe and articulate the landscape operations that students should learn about in this discipline; moreover, how a motion occurs over a given timeframe affects the characteristics of a space also inspires students to consider the experience and quality of the space they design. This step guided students to develop their design rationales based on the understanding of the dynamic nature of landscape, and to articulate their design concepts — coaching students through this creative process to happen is the exact goal of the exercise (Fig. 15 ~ 19).

Additionally, this exercise allowed students to indirectly study the logic of design decisions of Da Vinci when he developed a piece of apparatus. By deciphering the operation of the apparatus, students learned how design decisions of these masterpieces were made. Such a learning process weaves back to the typical landscape precedent study approach, yet here the design logic students understand still need to be analyzed and transformed into knowledge to apply into their future landscape design. The study of Da Vinci inventions focuses more on training students in design fundamentals, concepts, and logics, rather than a typical landscape precedent study which one learns directly about an existing space.

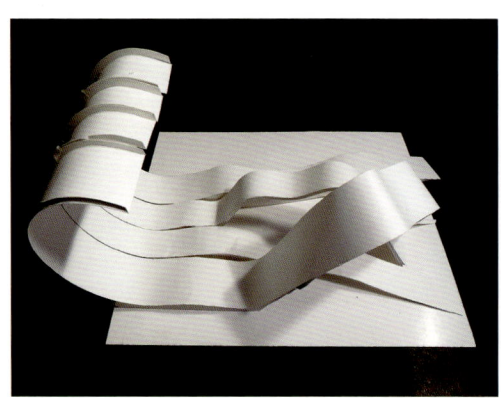

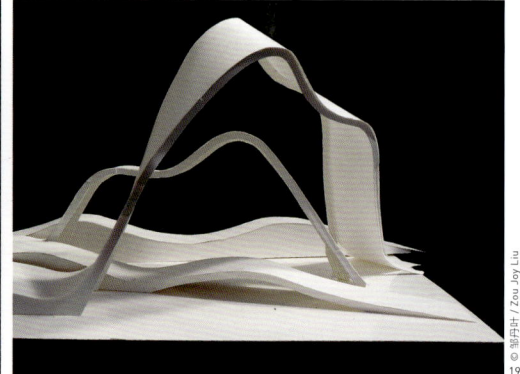

3 景观设计的创作过程

自2011年起,香港大学园境学文学士课程进行了以动态系统为教学目标展开基础景观设计课的教学工作。教学经验显示,大多数加入该学位课程的学生都已适应这样的教育方向。所以,后来在课程更新时,在基础景观设计课之前为学生安排了一门与视觉表达相关的手绘课,并在教学内容上引入了将运动、操作和景观视作动态系统的学习。因而,这门基础景观设计课也需要开发新的教学课题。经由教学观察到的是,许多基础学年的学生在发展设计概念时常常容易没有头绪,无从下手,所以引导学生如何适应设计这一专业领域的思维和工作模式便成为一个重要的新任务。

因此,基础景观设计课将教学重点转向发展创意概念的过程,通过引导学生一步步建立自己的设计理念,使其有独立设计的能力。基础景观设计课的课题从2015年开始致力于培养学生对艺术和设计的欣赏和概念构思的能力。

景观设计学是一门内涵广泛的学科,与其他学科之间存在着许多共同点与交叉点。创意艺术是和景观设计学有许多共通之处的学科之一。许多优秀的景观设计大师也受到了艺术的影响。"在他(劳伦斯·哈普林)办公室里展示的图纸中可以看出,他早期(哈普林)借鉴了胡安·米罗等现代画家的作品,其(哈普林)后期的概念速写作品也深受立体主义的影响。"[1]艺术作品中包含的艺术史知识,以及每位艺术家的创作过程,都有助于年轻的景观设计学生理解创意概念是如何构思的。学生在接到设计作业时,通常会先考虑空间设计是否实用。虽然这是衡量一个设计是否成功的标准之一,但设计也寻求由创作概念所创造的附加价值。设计的力量在于能够看到和构思出超越常规的想法,从而启发新的思维和生活方式。所以基础景观设计课的新教学内容也致力于培养学生对设计的理解和概念构思的能力。

以创意艺术为切入点让基础景观设计课学生参与设计创作过程亦有先例可循。苏利文教授分享:"我一直认为景观应被视作为一种艺术形式。我教授的所有景观课程都以艺术视角出发,并鼓励每个学生都能在直观理解、灵感和想象力等方面拥有自己独特的认知。每个课程作业大纲都会建立一个支持并推动学生发展其个人创作过程的框架。"[6]

3.1 对艺术作品的研究

与之前的基础景观设计课相似,新的基础景观设计课在进入实际的项目设计之前亦需要进行分析研究,只是研究对象变成了一件艺术作品。课堂选用的艺术作品的筛选标准包括其在艺术史上的重要意义、对当时文化发展的反思、创造性的突破,以及在形式、材料、空

3 Creative Processes of Landscape Design

Since 2011, the BA(LS) Program at HKU has run this foundation year design studio with pedagogical goal to strengthen students' understanding of dynamic systems. Since then, most students coming in to the program are well-tuned to this educational direction. When the program went through a curriculum development later, a hand drawing representation course was introduced prior to this foundation year design studio, and the learning about movement, operation, and landscape as dynamic systems was incorporated there. The foundation landscape design studio could then gear towards another agenda. One observation made through teaching was, many foundation year students had struggles to start a design process and to come up with a design concept. How to ease their mind and mode of working into design became an important task.

Therefore, the foundation year landscape design studio has shifted its emphasis towards the process of developing creative concepts, empowering students with design creativity by guiding them through the steps of building up their own design concepts. Since 2015, the selection of studio topics has developed to foster students' appreciation in art and design and to nurture their capacity in concept development.

Landscape Architecture is such a broad and inclusive discipline, and there are many overlaps with other disciplines, in particular the creative arts. Many outstanding landscape architects are influenced and inspired by arts. "In his (Lawrence Halprin's) early office presentation drawings, he referenced (Joan) Miró and other modern painters. In his mature work, the notebook drawings seem closer to Cubism." [1] Knowledge of art history and the creative process that each artist pursues benefit young landscape students to understand how creative concepts are conceived. The common approach a student may first resort to when being given a design task is to develop a pragmatic spatial solution. While this is one of the criteria to evaluate if a design is successful, design also looks for the added-value created with artistic concepts. The power of design is to see and conceive ideas beyond norms which lead to new ways of thinking and living. It is the level of design understanding and concept creation that the new version of the foundation landscape design studio aims to train students with.

Drawing inspiration from the creative arts to engage foundation landscape design studio students in creative process is not new. Sullivan once shared, "I have always believed that landscape architecture is an art form and should be accepted as such. I teach all of my classes through an artistic lens, with each

20. 学生樊立雪以野口勇的《从火星上看到的雕塑》这一作品为研究对象。虽然这是一件虚构的作品，但樊立雪基于人可以走近该作品这一假设，巧妙地绘制出该艺术品的立面图。这件作品通常是从鸟瞰的角度来进行解读的，而她决定使用立面这一表达角度，展现出对这一作品的一种少见的诠释。

20. Student Fan Lixue studied the work *Sculpture to be seen from Mars* by artist Isamu Noguchi. It is an imaginary piece of work. Fan smartly derived its elevation view, assuming someone is approaching the sculpture. This masterpiece is often understood from a plan view, so Fan's decision to make an elevation drawing brought alternative interpretation of the piece which is rarely seen.

间等方面的创新运用。选用的艺术作品可视为一个系列，学生们可以接触到各种各样的艺术创作过程，并了解它们在创意世界中产生了何种影响。

学生们对艺术作品的学习从绘制该艺术作品的平面图和立面图开始。他们通常基于艺术作品的透视角度照片，对其真实尺寸进行研究推断，以便按比例绘图（图20）。

接下来的则是最重要的练习，即对概念构思的探究。通过初步的学习和研究，学生需要了解当时的文化历史背景，以及这种背景如何影响艺术家的创作过程。和景观设计一样，艺术创作也会经历反复迭代。许多艺术家可能有一件广为人知的代表作品，但学生通过研究，会发现艺术家往往会以相同的艺术创作轨迹创造出许多类似的作品。我们可以把它们理解为一系列艺术作品，学生们需要学习的正是这背后的艺术创作过程或创意发展过程。尽管学生们的研究对象只是一件艺术品，但此练习会让他们意识到，为了理解一件艺术作品，他们需要对艺术家的整个系列作品进行研究。这样有助于他们了解如何对一个想法进行初步构思，然后经过多次调整，最终成为一个概念。这种迭代和自我反思的过程实际上在艺术学和设计学中是非常独特的，对于很多景观基础课程学生来说，这也是一种非常新颖的实践方式。这样的练习对于他们理解设计实践的基本原理是非常有建设性的。

在推导出一个概念是如何形成的之后，学生需要通过抽象的绘画

student encouraged to develop his or her own sources of intuition, inspiration, and imagination. Each project brief establishes a framework that allows exploration and pushes students to develop their individual creative processes." [6]

3.1 Study of Art Works

Similar to the previous version, the new foundation landscape design studio started with an analytical study before getting into an actual design project. Each student was asked to study a piece of art work. The collection of art works was selected based on their significance in art history, reflection of cultural development at the time, creative breakthroughs, and innovative ways in the use of forms, materials, and spaces. Such selected collection of art works was seen as a series, for students to expose to a variety of artistic processes and to understand what impacts these art works made in the creative world.

The way students engaged with the study of an art work started with the documentation drawings of the art work in its plan and elevation views. After finding photographs of the art piece in perspective views, students needed to research and figure out the art work's dimensions in reality, in order to develop the scaled drawings of it (Fig. 20).

Students' next task — the most important one — was the research of concept creation. Through an initial study and research, students were aware of the cultural / historic context at the time, and how such a background influenced the artist's creative process. Like landscape design, an artistic process also goes through iterations. Many artists may have a very famous piece of work, but through research students realized the artists often create a number of similar pieces with the same creative trajectory. We may understand the similar works as a series, from which students were to explore and learn the artistic process or creative journey. Even though the ultimate study was only focused on one specific piece of art work, students' findings led them to understand the need to study the whole series in order to comprehend one of the pieces. Such a learning process helped them understand how an idea may be first conceived, then tuned and edited, in multiple times, then finally became a concept. Such iterative and self-reflective processes are in fact very unique in art and design. However, they are very new to many foundation year landscape students as a way of practice, so the concept creation training is very critical to shape students' understanding of the fundamentals of design practice.

After deducing the process of concept creation, students needed to represent their conceptual understanding of the art work by making abstract drawing and model. In their work, students applied what they learned from the concept creation

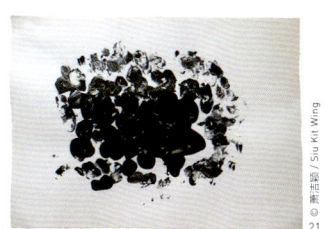
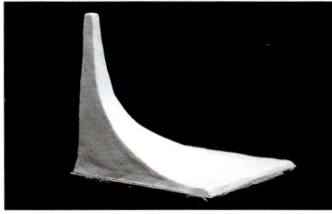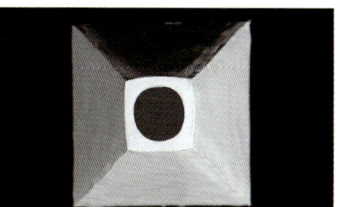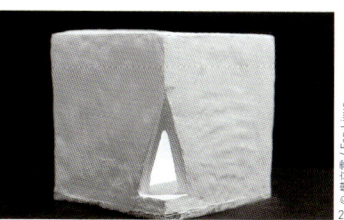

和模型来表达他们对艺术作品的概念理解。他们需要运用从概念创作研究中学到的知识，以及从艺术家工作流程中学到的迭代和自我反思过程来完成这项练习（图21~24）。

3.2 露天博物馆设计

这些诠释艺术作品概念的抽象画为学生下一步的学习打下了基础：他们需要设计一个露天博物馆来陈列他们学习的艺术作品。通过抽象绘画的过程，学生对艺术作品进行自我诠释，从而启发他们在景观设计一段旅程/经历，来引导参观者体验和理解艺术作品。

要把这个概念贯穿到露天博物馆的空间设计中并不容易，但学生们都进行了积极的探索。例如，有学生在为野口勇的作品《从火星上

research, as well as the iterative and self-reflective processes learned from the artist's work flow (Fig. 21 ~ 24).

3.2 Open-Air Museum Design

The abstract drawing exercise laid foundation for students' next step: the design of an open-air museum to display the art work they studied. The making of the abstract drawing became a process for students to develop their own interpretation of the artist's work, helping them introduce a journey or narrative in the landscape to guide visitors to experience and understand the art work.

To realize such a concept in the spatial design for the open-air museum was not straightforward. Here are some good examples. The student who designed an open-air museum for Isamu Noguchi's *Sculpture to be seen from Mars* used landscape design to create an opportunity for visitors to go up front to the art work displayed in the middle of the proposed site, and used the landscape technique of creating elevation difference to allow visitors to view the work from above. Following the Noguchi's creative approach, the student also applied the minimalistic style in the design of the manmade landscape parts (Fig. 25). In another project where the student designed an open-air museum for Olafur Eliasson's *The New York City Waterfall*, the landscape design was intended to illustrate the student's thinking about how waterfalls are viewed, experienced, and interpreted. This student also used the project's spatial design to guide visitors to experience the intellectual pursuit she had when studying the art work (Fig. 26).

4 Impacts and Reflections

The two tracks of the foundation landscape design studio created a significant impact on students' subsequent comprehension

21, 22. 学生萧洁颖研究的是威廉·德·库宁的作品《侧躺的人》。她从最初的研究中得出关键词"触"，并将她对触觉的研究概念反映于图纸和模型之中。

23. 学生樊立雪从野口勇的作品《从火星上看到的雕塑》中学习了极简主义的表现手法。因此，她在概念研究中专注于借助概念模型制作过程来探索什么是极简主义。

21, 22. Student Siu Kit Wing studied Willem de Kooning's *Reclining Figure*. She derived a concept keyword "tactile" from her initial study and dedicated her concept study with drawings and models to represent a sense of touch.

23. Student Fan Lixue learned about the minimalistic approach from Isamu Noguchi's *Sculpture to be seen from Mars*. Hence, in the concept study, she dedicated her focus through the concept model making process to explore what minimalism is.

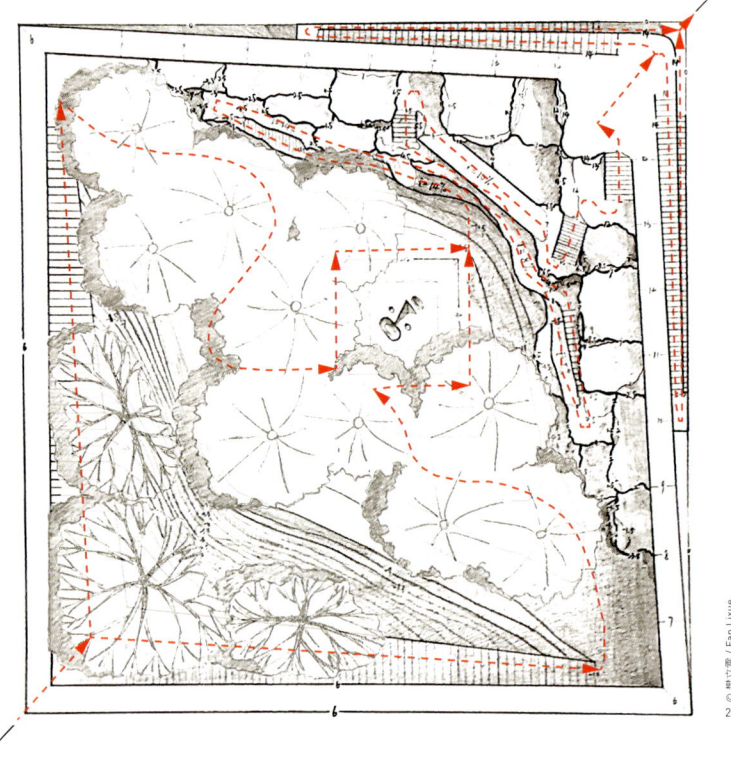

of landscape. Compared with landscape programs that start the foundation year studio with studying landscape masterpieces via tracing-over exercises, the foundation landscape design studio of the HKU BA(LS) Program aims at teaching more about the systematic characters of landscape and the creative concept logic universal to many design disciplines. Students are not given a definite answer of what Landscape Architecture is, instead, they are introduced to the logics of thinking and means of seeing, through studio exercises, to explore what landscape is by themselves. It is quite reflective in how BA(LS) graduates develop their thesis topics when they get into the Master of Landscape Architecture (MLA) Program: when preparing their thesis projects, they tend to select topics or scopes that are challenging the conventional territory of Landscape Architecture, integrating knowledge and expertise from allied disciplines into their own landscape projects. The intellectual capacities they present as thinkers and innovators are exactly the qualities that the next generation of Landscape Architecture leaders should have. **LAF**

REFERENCES

[1] Balmori, D. (2014). Chapter 4: Contemporary Landscape Architects and Landscape Artists. In Author (Ed.), Drawing and Reinventing Landscape (pp.81-111). Chichester: John Wiley & Sons Inc.
[2] Rovira, R. (2012). Exactness and Abstraction in Landscape Architectural Reproduction. In N. Amoroso (Ed.), Representing Landscapes: A Visual Collection of Landscape Architectural Drawings (p. 81). Oxon; New York: Routledge.
[3] Sullivan, C. (2008). Observation and the Analytical Representation of Space. In M. Treib (Ed.), Representing Landscape Architecture (pp.64-65). New York: Taylor & Francis.
[4] Doane, M. A. (2002). Chapter 2: Temporality, Storage, Legibility: Freud, Marey, and the Cinema. In Author (Ed.), The Emergence of Cinematic Time: Modernity, Contingency, the Archive (p. 60). Cambridge (Mass.): Harvard University Press.
[5] Allen, S. (1999). Infrastructural Urbanism. In Author (Ed.), Points + Lines: Diagrams and Projects for the City (pp. 55-57). New York: Princeton Architectural Press.
[6] Sullivan, C. (2012). The Art of Representing Landscapes. In N. Amoroso (Ed.), Representing Landscapes: A Visual Collection of Landscape Architectural Drawings (p. 175). Oxon; New York: Routledge.

24. 学生常耿家祺以奥拉富尔·埃利亚松的作品《纽约市瀑布》为研究对象，在概念图中使用了不同的色彩、笔触和纹理来诠释瀑布。
25. 学生樊立雪设计的露天博物馆平面图
26. 学生常耿家祺设计的露天博物馆剖面图

24. Student Chang Gengjiaqi studied Olafur Eliasson's *The New York City Waterfall*. She developed ways to use colors, strokes, and textures to describe the waterfall in her concept drawing.
25. Plan drawing of an open-air museum design, by student Fan Lixue.
26. Section drawing of an open-air museum design, by student Chang Gengjiaqi.

看到的雕塑》设计露天博物馆时，以景观设计引导参观者走到场地中央的艺术作品面前，还使用了创造高程差异的技巧，使参观者可以从鸟瞰角度观察作品；除此之外，其人造景观部分也延续了艺术家极简主义的这一创作手法（图25）。另外，亦有学生在为奥拉富尔·埃利亚松的作品《纽约市瀑布》设计露天博物馆时，把自己对瀑布是如何被观看、体验和诠释的关注延续到设计之中，希望借由空间设计使参观者体验到其在研究这一艺术作品时的思维过程（图26）。

4 影响和反思

景观设计概论课的两种学习轨迹对学生之后对于景观的理解产生了巨大的影响。相比于以模仿和研究经典案例为基础景观设计课的传统景观专业课程，香港大学园境学文学士课程的景观设计概论课旨在将教导景观的系统性和普适于设计领域的创意思维逻辑用作启蒙教学。学生们学习的并不是景观设计的既有定义；相反，他们可以运用习得的逻辑思维和方法，通过设计课的练习自己去探索景观的定义。在该课程的毕业生步入园境学硕士课程后开展硕士论文课题时，这种教学模式带来的效果十分明显：他们往往会选择一些挑战传统景观设计学科边界的课题或研究范围，并将其他相关学科的知识融入到自己的景观项目之中。他们展示了自己作为思考者和创新者的知识能力，这正是下一代景观设计学科领头人应当具备的素质。**LAF**

本文引用格式 / PLEASE CITE THIS ARTICLE AS

Morabito, V. (2019). Verbal Drawings: Mapping Landscape Ideas. Landscape Architecture Frontiers, 7(5), 38-57. https://doi.org/10.15302/J-LAF-1-020011

会说话的绘画：
如何表达景观构想

VERBAL DRAWINGS: MAPPING LANDSCAPE IDEAS

https://doi.org/10.15302/J-LAF-1-020011　　收稿时间 RECEIVED DATE / 2019-08-19　　中图分类号 TU986.2, J2　　文献标识码 / A

瓦莱里奥·莫拉比托
宾夕法尼亚大学斯图尔特-韦茨曼设计学院客座教授，意大利地中海雷焦卡拉布里亚大学副教授

Valerio MORABITO*
Adjunct Professor, University of Pennsylvania Stuart Weitzman School of Design; Assistant Professor, Mediterranea University of Reggio Calabria

*Corresponding Author
Address: M3-89122, Reggio Calabria, Italy
Email: morabito@design.upenn.edu

摘要

本文探讨了绘画中的一个特殊类别——语言绘图——的历史、特征及其在当代景观设计领域的设计交流中所扮演的角色。语言绘图的定义来自于对岩绘艺术本身的观察和解读，以及对其绘制过程的了解。作为先于语言文字的人类最早的通过书写进行交流的方式，岩绘艺术不仅是可供观赏的绘画，也是可供阅读的信息。这些由象形语言、表意语言和抽象表意语言构成的，经由特定语法和句法逻辑组合而成的图像具备三大特质：直观感、美感和轻盈感。岩绘艺术描绘了人类在特定环境中的特定活动，它们不仅是人类最早的景观表达方式，也是地图绘制艺术的雏形，由此制图艺术和语言绘图之间建立起了紧密关联。本文通过实例试图说明古代和现代地图绘制艺术对当代景观设计的重要性；相较于现今单调，追求视觉刺激、快速制作、快速消费的数字图像，当代语言绘图必须体现出如岩绘艺术般的三个特质：直观感、美感和轻盈感。最后，本文提出了介于安伯托·艾柯的"开放式作品"和语言绘图之间的概念：语言绘图更像是一种"开放式框架"，其有助于设计想法的拓展和延伸，并激发出更多的创新性。

关键词

语言绘图；地图绘制艺术；解读；设计表达

ABSTRACT

Verbal drawings, as a particular drawing category of drawings, are discussed in this paper about its history, qualities, and what kind of role they could play in the design communication of contemporary landscape architecture. The definition of verbal drawings arises from the observation and reading of Rupestrian art and its process in making drawings and paintings. Rupestrian art was the first human written communication prior to the emergence of words and spoken communication. For this reason, Rupestrian art drawings and paintings are not just images to be seen; above all, they are texts to be read. They are written drawings using pictograms, ideograms, and psycho-ideograms to compose images with a specific grammar and syntax. These written images have three qualities: a sense of immediacy, a sense of beauty, and a sense of lightness. Representing human activities in particular environments, Rupestrian art drawings are not only the first landscape representations but also the early representations of the act of mapping, opening a connection between the art of cartography and the art of verbal drawings. Using examples, this paper explains the importance of ancient and modern mapping arts in connection with the discourse of contemporary landscape architecture by demonstrating how the senses of immediacy, beauty, and lightness help contemporary verbal drawings compete with the neutral, beautiful, quickly produced and consumed digital representations nowadays. In the end, the text proposes a confrontation between Umberto Eco's concept of "open work" and verbal drawings — Verbal drawings might be intended more like "open frameworks" than "open works." It is a concept that considers verbal drawings able to accept new ideas for extending their meanings and significance throughout the design process.

KEYWORDS

Verbal Drawings; Art of Mapping; Reading; Representation

翻译　沈欣欣　田乐
TRANSLATED BY　SHEN Xinxin　Tina TIAN

1 岩绘艺术

岩绘艺术被认为是人类最早通过书写进行交流的方式。这些艺术作品体现出了一套由精确语法和句法构成的通用语言[1]。我将这些岩绘称为"会说话的绘画"（语言绘图），并认为它们具有三个基本特征：直观感、美感和轻盈感。最重要的是，这些画作不仅可以记录场地，并使人们通过记忆和想象再现场景；而且这些画作对场地和事件的描绘和诠释，有时甚至会改变场地或事件本身的意义。正因如此，在当代制图语境下，语言绘图所具备的特质可为景观设计提供不同的表现方法参考，从而激发景观设计师的灵感和创意。

埃马努埃尔·阿纳蒂[1]曾分析了上百万张岩绘艺术作品，并将其中的语言绘画划分为三类：1）象形语言（描绘动物或领土的画作）；2）表意语言（出现在象形图案内外部的符号/记号）；3）抽象表意语言（与写实表现手法完全不同的、高度抽象的符号/记号）。阿纳蒂认为，借助这些语言绘画，人们日常现实生活的未知维度得以呈现。此外，这些语言绘图也是人类对自然景观的首次再现[2]。创作这些画作的艺术家们必须亲眼见过或亲身参与过画中所描绘的场景，记住所见所闻，并将之抽象概括为图形或文字信息[3]。这项艺术活动的另一个重要贡献是激发了人们对色彩进行更广泛的探索，从在绘画创作中使用单一的赭石色，到运用多种从自然中获得的颜色。

由于岩绘艺术被认为是先于文字语言的人类第一语言，其所运用的语法和句法是成为快速情感表达的最佳示例：它主要以象形语言来描绘场景，以表意语言来解释含义，以抽象表意语言来表达时空的神秘性。通过这三种语言元素的不同组合，即能够在一张作品中同时传达出包含思想、行为、运动，以及人类对想象力的渴求的完整过程。就将个人与整个世界联系起来这一点来说，岩绘也称得上是人类最早的制图艺术。

此文以岩绘艺术为出发点，探讨语言绘图之于当代景观设计的意义——其可以成为景观设计师表达方式的借鉴和创造力的源泉——以及相较于当今流行的制作精美的数码图像，语言绘图所具有的竞争力。为此，作者将结合历史上著名的制图艺术代表作，以及其个人的艺术实践和在宾夕法尼亚大学的教学案例进行论述。

1 The Paintings of Rupestrian Art

The paintings of Rupestrian art are considered the first examples of human written communication. It was a universal language organized with precise syntax and grammar made by signs and symbols[1]. I describe these paintings as "verbal drawings" with three fundamental characteristics: a sense of immediacy, a sense of beauty, and a sense of lightness. Most importantly, such verbal drawings could read places and represent them through the imagination and memory; they depicted and interpreted places and events, sometimes changing their meaning. For these reasons, in the contemporary production of images, the qualities of these verbal drawings can play a fundamental role to be sources for different methodologies of representations that might generate new ideas and creativity in the contemporary landscape architecture.

Analyzing over one million examples of Rupestrian art, Emmanuel Anati[1] defines three main types: 1) pictograms (bodies of animals or territories), 2) ideograms (signs and marks inside or outside the pictograms), and 3) psycho-ideograms (abstract transcendental signs and iconic elements far from any realistic representation). Anati considers them as instruments to connect the reality of daily life to unknown dimensions. Further, these verbal drawings are the first manifestation of man's spontaneous landscape representation[2]. Artists had to see or take part in the scenes being described; they had to memorize what they saw and abstract it into drawn or written information[3]. Another important activity of this art was that it inspired a wide-ranging exploring of landscapes for ochre and other colors with which to create art.

Since Rupestrian art is recognized as the first language before the invention of alphabets, the grammar and syntax of Rupestrian art is a perfect example of quick emotional communication: pictograms dominate scenes; ideograms surround them to explain the meaning and psycho-ideograms represent mystical ideas of space and time. In just one view, composed of these three different groups of elements, it is possible to convey thoughts, actions, movements, and the aspirations of the human imagination as a whole process. Insofar as it linked individuals to their world, Rupestrian art can also be understood as the earliest form of cartography.

With Rupestrian art as the point of departure, this paper discusses the role of verbal drawings in the contemporary landscape architecture both in representation and as sources of creativity, and how they can compete with the pervasive beautiful digital contemporary production of images. For doing it, the paper uses some prominent historical examples of cartographic representations and briefly describe the author's art practice and that of his students at the University of Pennsylvania.

2 Verbal Drawings in the Art of Mapping

Speculating about the meaning and metaphor related to the famous Queen shape European map[①], Trevor J. Barnes affirms that "No matter which metaphor we choose, the presumption is that the map is a text that is to be read."[4] And he adds, "The art of mapping related with the word 'geography' is literally 'earth writing' (from the Greek geo, meaning 'earth,' and graphien, meaning 'to write'). It is also ironic in another sense because the one thing that links all geographers of whatever stripe is that they write."

Mappa Mundi, marking a crucial moment in the art of mapping, were instruments to control the known and unknown world. Mappa Mundi wrote beautiful landscape texts representing the continents in the form of pictograms made by "visual rhythm, regularity, and symmetry,"[5] using codified signs in types of ideograms to inform about microcosms, and imaging psycho-ideograms to envision unknown territories and morphologies.

An example of verbal drawings is the Mappa Mundi, contained in the *Commentary on the Apocalypse of Saint John* by Beatus of Liebana, dating from around the middle of the eleventh century. The continental masses occupy almost the entire scene of the surface, making it the pictogram of the stage as the whole. The Ocean was marginalized to the borders of the drawn surface, with the Mediterranean Sea skirting the shapes of the continents. The marginal sea space is populated by ideograms of explored and unexplored islands, fish, and sea vessels, all different in shape, scale, and size. Together with the intricate mosaic of symbolic ideograms and psycho-ideograms incorporated in the continents, they gave shape to the grammar and syntax of verbal medieval landscape drawings.

The Map of the World made by Fra Mauro around 1459, is another example of the art of mapping that can be related to the category of verbal drawings. The map, having political navigational purposes[5], followed the same descriptive representation of the Mappa Mundi made by Beatus of Liebana. Continents, representing the main pictograms, occupied almost the entire scene. The sea represented all around the border of the map creates relationships and adds information, even distances. With more than three thousand texts, the language of this beautiful map expresses real data, including legends and tales, to be codified and read like a book.

After "discovering" the American continent and new sea routes to India and China, there was a flowering of different types of maps. Ocean was no longer marginalized along map borders but acquired primary importance at the center of

① Europa regina (Latin for Queen Europe), made in the European Middle Ages, is the map-like depiction of the European continent as a queen.

② 更多信息请访问大卫拉姆斯地图收集网站。

② For more information, please visit the website of David Rumsey Map Collection.

1. 由瓦莱里奥·莫拉比托绘制的《移动岛》，手绘稿扫描件，绘制于2017年。

1. *Movable Islands* by Valerio Morabito, hand digital drawing, 2017.

上述提及的这些地图及其他制图艺术作品都是语言绘图的范例，它们向人们传递已知和未知的场地信息。同时，像岩绘艺术一样，这些地图必须激发冒险家、君主、航海家和普罗大众们的想象力。为此，地图中也对神话般的秘境、未知的文化与外来动植物进行了描绘（图1）。[6]

地图绘制者必须学习如何讲述故事，选择哪些信息应着重表达，哪些应隐去[5]。他们需要从现实生活中收集经验，亲自到访某处，或是记录下从朋友、商人、旅人口中听说的遥远故事。这些地图绘制者要把这些非书面的信息转化为图形符号、色彩、形状和线条，再通过他们的技艺在有限的图纸上表现船只、航线、城堡、建筑、城市、地貌、动植物等内容。亚历山大·冯·洪堡绘制的地图可被视为语言绘图的例子，它们展现出了"错综交织的生态网络图景"。[7]

3 语言绘图与现代地图绘制艺术

关于现代地图绘制艺术，20世纪中一个著名的说明性地图案例是《世界地图集：人类环境综述》。[8]这部地图集体现了语言绘图在实现科学、想象和美学之间的微妙平衡方面的重大进步。在应对难以处理的科学数据时，赫伯特·拜耳曾说："科学家不会以我这样的工作方式思考。"为了追求他理想中的美感，拜耳与马丁·罗森茨威格、

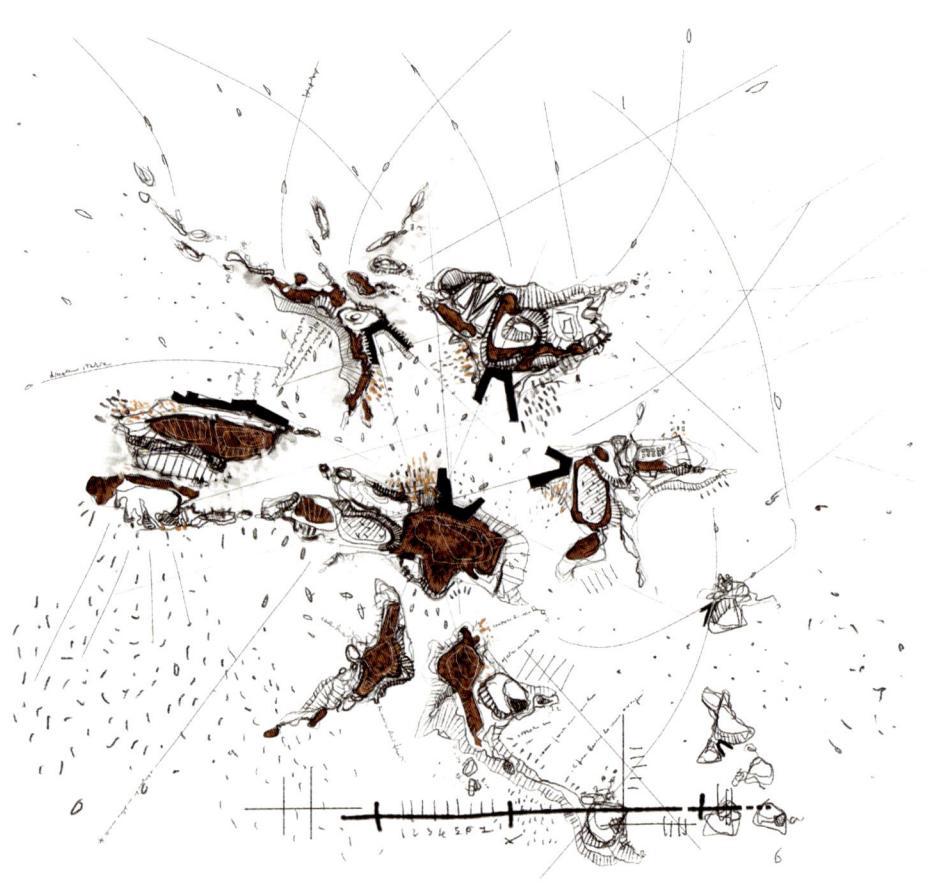

cartographies. This strategic change opened up unexpected scenarios, and Europeans began to explore and imagine new landscapes. The Planisphere created by Urbano Monte in 1587, realized in many little pieces drawn on the pages of a book — recently restored② — is an example of this new perception of the world. Newly, these pieces were recomposed in a circular version and a linear extension of the entire Planisphere. These contemporary versions of the Planisphere reveal the new role of the ocean, which became the central pictogram of the whole scene, while a multitude of ideograms and a series of psycho-ideograms were settled in strategic places along with the sea coasts and in the ocean.

These mentioned maps and cartographies, together with many others, are verbal drawing examples used to give information about places discovered and to be explored. At the same time, like Rupestrian art, they had to enhance the imagination of explorers, kings, navigators, and ordinary people. To do so, they described, among other things, fabulous places, unknown cultures, exotic animals, and plants that came from mythological stories and mysterious legends (Fig. 1).[6]

Cartographers had to learn the process to write stories, selecting what they had to represent and what they wanted to reveal,[5] collecting real-life experiences, and visiting sites or having descriptions of faraway places from travelers, friends, and merchants. They had to transform verbal messages and information into graphic signs, colors, shapes, and lines, developing their artistic skills to display ships, lines, castles, buildings, cities, morphologies, animals, and plants on a limited surface. Also, Alexander von Humboldt's maps could be used as examples of verbal drawings; they speak about "views with images of richly intertwined ecological networks."[7]

3 Verbal Drawings in the Modern Art of Mapping

A famous example of writing maps from the last century is the famous *World Geo-Graphical Atlas: A Composite of Man's Environment*[8], which enhanced the comprehension of verbal drawings' significance that maintains a precarious balance between science, imagination, and the necessity of beauty. Herbert Bayer, having difficulty in evaluating scientific data, said that "a scientist would not think in terms in which I worked." To reach his ideal of beauty, he had a lot of collaborations with many designers such as Martin Rosenzweig, Henry Gardiner, and Masato Nakagawa to develop a modernist graphical language never applied to cartography before. Bayer "used the color theories of Egbert Jacobsen, the statistical representations of Otto Neurath, and the dynamic design of

László Moholy-Nagy."[9] From the preface of the Atlas, it is possible to read that "this book is called 'World Geo-Graphic Atlas' because it includes, in addition to GEO-graphic maps, many GRAPHIC illustrations of subjects closely related to modern geography."[8]

Among many examples of the contemporary art of mapping that avoid taking into consideration only scientific collections of data and information, but poetic intuitions and inventions, there are James Corner's maps[10][11]. The syntax and grammar of his maps are based on the use of significant central territorial representations, which are pictograms of their narrations. Small traces, little details, morphological exceptions, and imperfections are emphasized by transforming them into ideograms. Corner's narrative achieves a high level of prose with the use of particular psycho-ideograms: they are elements that reveal trajectories of creativity, to imagine unexpected geographical relationships, even if they seem arbitrarily introduced. Corner invented a new process of writing landscape representations, opening a different approach to the Landscape Architecture discipline.

4 Thinking and Imaging Hand Verbal Drawings

Ludwig Wittgenstein, in one of his famous aphorism, wrote: "I really do think with my pen, because my head often knows nothing about what my hand is writing."[12] This process of thinking by pen implies the importance of hand writing in the process of imagining and creating ideas. Sketches and hand drawings select, meticulously, what elements would be remembered, kept, and erased from landscapes, territories, and cities[3].

Hand verbal drawings have a critical dynamic perception of time and space in representing both emptiness of deserts and space of rooms, drawing both centers of cities and deep inner space of forests, and visualizing both novels and data from territories.

There are many artists, landscape architects, and architects (especially in the past) who take seriously the use of sketches and hand drawings to represent their creativity. Among others, artists like John Cage, landscape architects like Lawrence Halprin, and architects like Louis I. Kahn took this inclination to sketch extreme consequences and results, from which it is possible to recognize particular kinds of verbal drawings.

Cage was a musician who used his hands both to play music and to sketch maps of ideas. For example, his sketch entitled *Rocks and Cleaning My Pen* is an exercise of using hand and pen to imagine an atlas of abstract music space. A lot of marks are placed on the left side of the paper, forming the pictogram of the entire composition. A stain, together with a few signs, drawn on the right side of the sheet of paper, complete the whole narrative. His verbal / sound drawing is an act of mapping that, through

③ For more information, please see the Laurie Olin's interview video titled "Laurie Olin on Design: Drawing as a Powerful Tool."

2. 由瓦莱里奥·莫拉比托绘制的《想象中的城市》，手绘稿扫描件，绘制于2018年。

2. *An Imaginary City Map* by Valerio Morabito, hand digital drawing, 2018.

康在草图中运用象形语言、表意语言和抽象表意语言来表达他对于空间的设计想法。在他的众多手稿中，象形文字（建筑主体）周围都会出现大量信息。精确的技术符号和标记是其当代表意语言，而抽象表意语言就是他那些创新性的形式、形态和线条。

但是，在当代设计交流语境下，手绘和草图似乎都已经消失了。设计师们渐渐放弃了这种蕴含着艺术的微妙表达形式，可能是因为这类带有个人绘画技巧特色的图纸已与当代复杂的、不带感情色彩的数字绘图格格不入。但是，语言绘画这一概念却可以帮助手绘和草图在当代设计交流语境中重新找到其新的角色定位和意义。

在当代文化背景下，对于环境认知的抽象描绘（个性化绘图）与岩绘艺术有着共通之处。作者的艺术实践旨在创造一种具有岩绘艺术效果的心理认知绘图。例如，在《想象中的城市》（图2）这一画作中，沿海岸线随机分布着一些与现实或想象中（来源于故事传说）的地理空间相互关联的元素。

另外，作者在宾夕法尼亚大学景观设计系教授设计课和表达课④，在那里，有很多学生通过语言绘图的形式对设计表达进行了探索，思维也得以开阔。他们通过将自己的手绘、印象速写或是涂鸦与数字技术结合，尝试在这两种表达方式中寻求平衡。许多非常擅长手绘的学生已经探索出了一套不再依赖于技术的表达方法。另一方面，有些不太擅长捕捉场地特质的学生则通过发现绘图中的错误和不准确的地方，来优化他们的手绘表达。

例如，画作《水之城》（图3）是对某一非真实地点展开的地理想象，但其描绘的等高线、棕榈树以及坐落于岩石上的城市，都与真实世界别无二致。出发与到达地点的选择、航船的方向，连同其他细节

the use of ideograms and psycho-ideograms, envisions a creative process of rhythms and exceptions.

Halprin spent a considerable amount of time making sketches of the natural landscape forms of the Grand Canyon. This experience was crucial in his landscape architecture practice, and there was an evident poetic connection between the nature that he sketched and the forms he designed.

Kahn's sketches are maps in which pictograms, ideograms, and psycho-ideograms created the space of ideas. In many of his sketches, pictograms, which are the bodies of his architecture, are, sometimes, surrounded by long sentences. Precise technical signs and marks resemble contemporary ideograms, while psycho-ideograms are inventions of new forms, shapes, and lines.

However, in contemporary design communication, hand drawings and sketches seem to have disappeared. Their nuanced artistic expression is often rejected, probably because it resembles specific personal skills that are alien to any contemporary, sophisticated, and neutral digital presentations. Hand drawings and sketches have to find its new role and meaning in contemporary design communication, and the idea of verbal drawings can help achieve this aim.

In contemporary culture, representations of psycho-geography (personalized maps) work in a similar way to Rupestrian art. The author's art practice aims to create the effects of Rupestrian art and psycho-geographical mapping. For example, in *The Imaginary City Map* (Fig. 2), a series of objects and elements randomly displayed

共同构成了一副引人探索的动态景观地图。

而在《褐城：摩洛哥的沙漠》（图4）一图中，沙漠广袤无垠的形象在传统村庄的反衬下愈发凸显：正是这些村庄中的留白空间衬托出沙漠的辽阔与空旷。

通过大量的对于真实与虚构的城市的想象练习，学生们得以掌握如何通过对线条、形态和形式的和谐构图，发展出属于他们自己的语言绘画。

5 语言绘图的设计表达

在20世纪末，尤其是在紧随其后的21世纪初，数字绘图掀起了一场设计过程的革命。无论是概念性的设计想法，还是分析图、剖面图和透视图，都得益于这种新型的表现方式。总平面及分区平面图变得越来越真实，以突显色彩、人物、植物和很多其他现实元素为目的的效果图进一步加强了这种真实感。这种超现实的表达方式强烈影响了景观的设计和交流。可以说，在设计师纷纷聚焦于理念创造的当下，这些数字绘图在辨识度和影响力方面取得了巨大成功。此外，数字视频也为人们提供了一种动态的空间感知体验，在不久的将来，虚拟现实技术将更加普及，让我们有机会直接"走进"我们所设计的空间中。

这些当代的数字表达方式倾向于如实地描绘现实世界。数字图像被广泛应用于设计教育和设计实践的各种形式的交流中——除去个别不重要的情况——这与数字技术的发展密不可分，更是大势所趋。这往往会导致设计师针对同一项目制作大量的数字图像。然而，这些场地分析图、总平面图、分区平面图、立面图、透视图等都在"自说自话"，彼此之间缺乏明显的关联。

这些图像主要借助从视觉上迅速吸引观者的方式来传达设计信息——我无意批判此类绘图，我认为它们的确非常漂亮而且是一种强有力的交流方式；但这些绘图的语法和句法过于单一，仅仅追求对"美丽的"景致的描绘以及对未来的乐观畅想：井井有条、光鲜靓丽的城市，拥有良好的生态景观，蝴蝶和鸟儿在其中翩翩起舞。

相较那些略显复杂、需要花些时间才能"读懂"的绘画而言，制作"美丽的"数字图片可以让人一眼就明白图面中的信息。但是，数字图像的泛滥引发了关于是否需要重新定义并发明新的当代设计交流形式的激烈讨论：学生（和设计师）的"想象和创作就像小说家写小说一样"[7]，需要在整个设计过程中发挥创造力，将从场地特质感知到对设计的表达视为一个整体的"故事"来讲述，最终想象并创造出自己的语言绘画。当我们用"语言"这个词来形容"绘图"一词时，已经定义了一种语法/句法特点鲜明、强调特殊表达技巧的绘图方式。例如，在语言绘图中，通过巧妙地运用象形语言、表意语言和抽象表意语言来构建或拆分图像，观者可以清晰地了解绘者的思考过程及设计目的。

在意大利尤佳宁山区景观设计策略细节图（图5）和意大利珊瑚港滨水区景观设计细节图（图6）中所展示的具有清晰语法/句法结构的表

along the coastline are linked with imaginary geographical connections of existing places and unreal sites from novels.

At the Department of Landscape Architecture at the University of Pennsylvania④, where the author teaches design and representation, a lot of students have developed their thinking by exploring representations made by verbal drawings. Combining personal hand drawings, intuitive sketches, and doodles with the neutrality of digital techniques, they have been trying to create a balance between these two different tools of representation. Many students who are particularly good at hand drawings have developed a methodology with which their skills do not dominate the entire narrative. Conversely, a few students without unique qualities in their hand drawings have explored their mistakes and inaccuracies to enhance the presence of hand drawings in their description.

The City of Water (Fig. 3) is an exercise of imagining geographical connections of a non-real place built on the reality

④ MLA course in "Topic in landscape representation," instructor Valerio Morabito, at the Department of Landscape Architecture, University of Pennsylvania Stuart Weitzman School of Design.

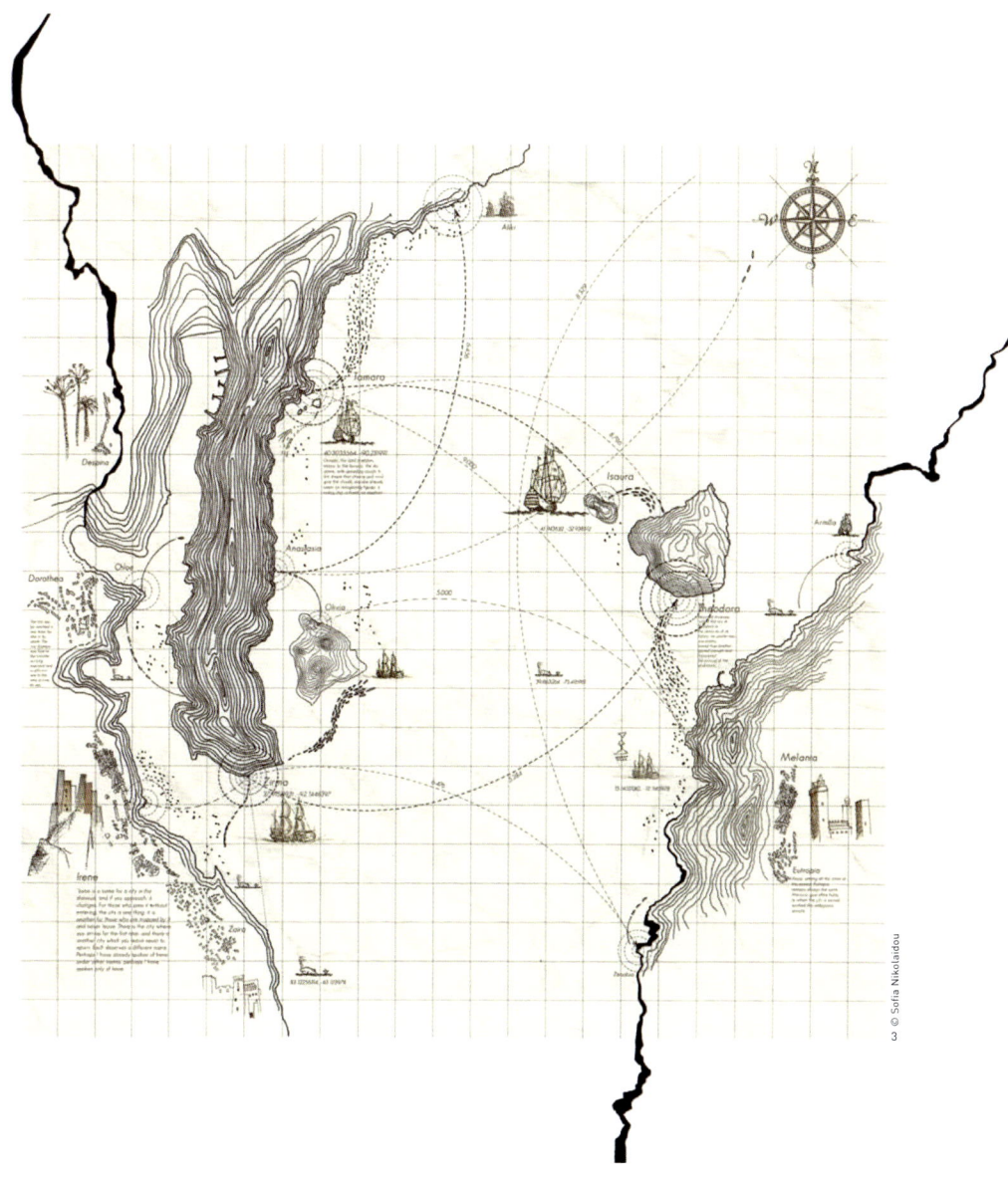

of contour lines, precise images of palms, and a city that seems perched on a rock. The positioning of many points to reach or to depart, the directions of the vessels, and other details contained in the map complete the idea of representing a dynamic landscape to discovery.

In the representation *The City of Brown: Desert of Marocco* (Fig. 4), the idea of the infinite space of the desert is designed according to a sequence of traditional villages. The white area among the villages shows the openness and vastness of the desert.

Through many exercises in imaging both real and unreal cities, students develop their verbal drawings that are written ideas made through harmonious compositions of lines, shapes, and forms.

5 Verbal Drawings for Mapping Design

At the end of the last century, and especially at the beginning of this one, digital illustrations generated a revolution in the design process; conceptual ideas, diagrams, sections, and perspectives have benefited from an extraordinary new quality of representation. Masterplans and site plans have become more and more realistic; views, populated by colors, people, plants, and many other elements, compete with reality. Sometimes, the hyper-realistic representation of landscape produces symbolic images that have strongly influenced our design and its communication. Nowadays, by feeding our capacity to create ideas, these images are very successful because they are easily recognizable and influential. Besides, digital videos provide a real dynamic perception of spaces, and soon virtual reality will be a standard tool giving us the chance to walk into our newly designed spaces.

These contemporary digital representations tend to mirror reality. Strongly linked to the pervasive evolution of digital technologies — from which it seems impossible and not entirely necessary to escape — digital images pervade any form of design communication, both in schools and in the workplace, with a few exemptions that are too rare to be significant. As a consequence, self-sufficient images are being produced, though they belong to the same project; site analysis, masterplans, site plans, sections, elevations, and perspectives are autonomous narration, without sharing any apparent relationship with each other.

These drawings share a primary role of satisfying and impressing their messages immediately on eyes that respond instantly to the design quality. Having no intention to criticize these typologies of drawings, which are attractive and sturdy forms of communication, it is evident that their languages use simple grammar and syntax to reproduce images like "beautiful"

3. 由宾夕法尼亚大学斯图尔特－韦茨曼设计学院景观设计系研究生索菲亚·尼克莱多绘制的《水之城》。此为景观表达作业练习，绘制于2017年，指导教师：瓦莱里奥·莫拉比托。
4. 由宾夕法尼亚大学斯图尔特－韦茨曼设计学院景观设计系研究生索菲亚·尼克莱多绘制的《褐城：摩洛哥的沙漠》。此为景观表达作业练习，绘制于2017年，指导教师：瓦莱里奥·莫拉比托。

3. *The City of Water* by Sofia Nikolaidou, MLA student of the Department of Landscape Architecture, University of Pennsylvania Stuart Weitzman School of Design. An exercise for Landscape Representation, 2017. Instructor: Valerio Morabito.
4. *The City of Brown: Desert of Morocco* by Sofia Nikolaidou, MLA student of the Department of Landscape Architecture, University of Pennsylvania Stuart Weitzman School of Design. An exercise for Landscape Representation, 2017. Instructor: Valerio Morabito.

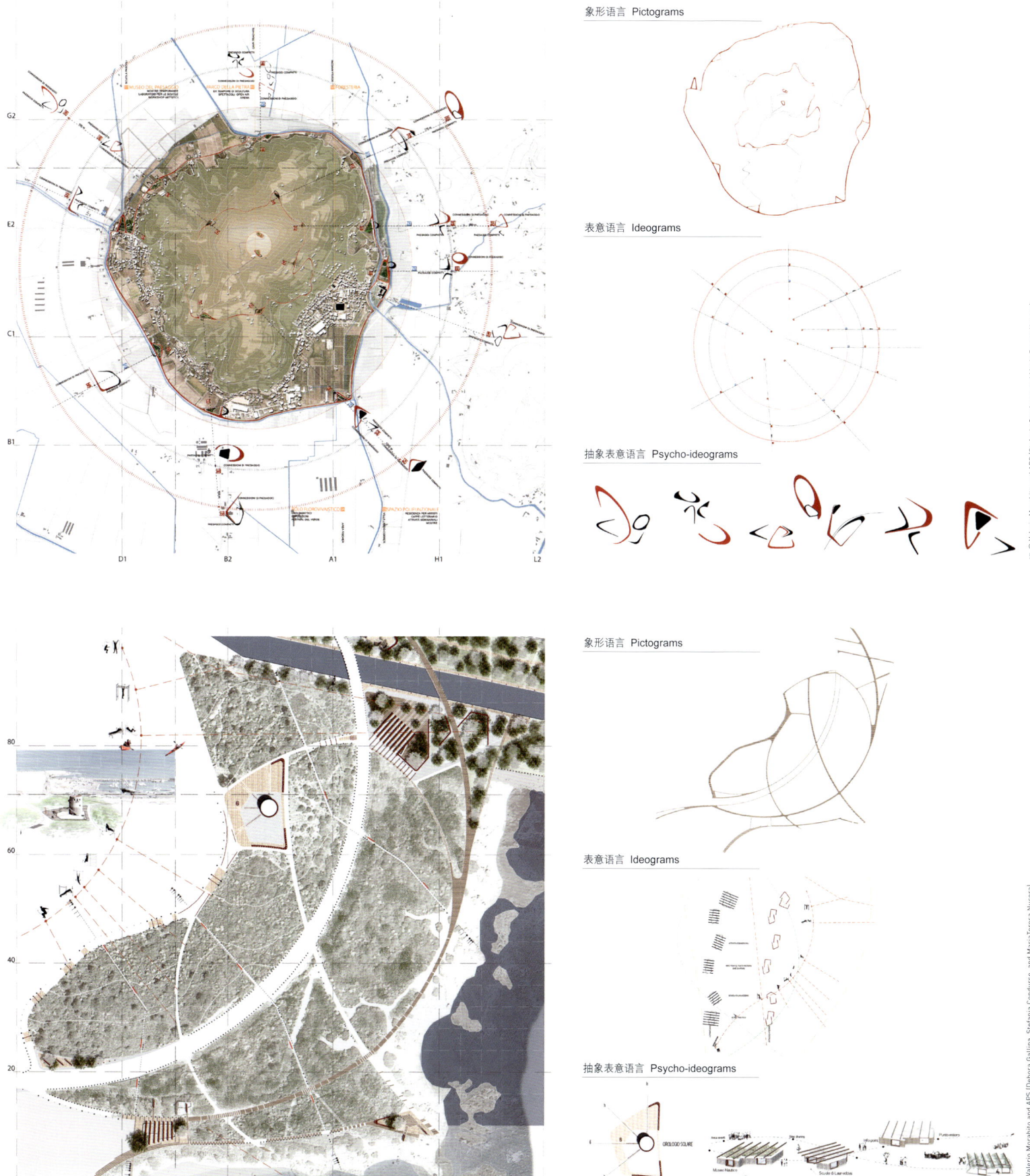

5. Mapping design details of the landscape strategy for Colli Euganei, Italy, by Valerio Morabito and APS (Stefania Condurso and Maria Teresa Nucera), 2017.
6. Mapping design details of the waterfront of Porto Corallo, Italy, by Valerio Morabito and APS (Debora Gallina, Stefania Condurso, and MariaTeresa Nucera), 2018.
7. Sketch of the Cityscape of the Shanghai City, China by Valerio Morabito, hand digital drawing, 2019.

意语言和抽象表意语言的组合形式，直观地表达了主体设计思想。相较于现今快速制作、快速消费的数字图像，当代语言绘图必须体现出如岩绘艺术般的三个特质：直观感、美感和轻盈感（图7）。

6 语言绘图的直观感

正如本文伊始所述，直观的情感表达是岩绘艺术最重要的一大特质。岩绘艺术使用简单的语法进行快速描述，除了讲述真实的故事，也对切身体验之外的来世进行了探索。类似地，当代景观设计的语言绘图也需要具备这种直观感，以吸引观者仔细阅读，从而获得更为深入的解读。

在上千张岩绘艺术作品中，有两幅画作尤其能够体现语言绘图直观感的特点：一幅是法国拉斯科洞窟壁画中所描绘的马（图8-1）；一幅是西班牙阿尔塔米拉洞窟壁画中描绘的狩猎场景（图8-2）。第一幅画中，象形语言是动物的身体，表意语言是图中的箭头（解释场景

realities. These images envision a not critical optimistic perspective of the future, well organized in shining cities, set in ecological landscapes, and populated by butterflies and birds.

Producing "beautiful" images to gaze upon is a common language that everybody can understand at a time when it seems complicated and need to spend time on "reading" drawings. However, the proliferation and the pervasive presence of these images open a critical debate as to whether one should rewrite and invent a different contemporary form of communication. Students (and designers) that "imagine things in the same way a novelist constructs a piece of fiction"[7] need to show the entire process of their creativity, from the perception of the site to the representation of the design, as a whole specific narration, imaging and creating their pictures in forms of verbal drawings. The term "verbal," in conjunction with the word "drawing," is a way to describe drawings in which grammar and syntax are evident and developed through particular techniques of representation. For example, there are drawings that use pictograms, ideograms, and psycho-ideograms to decompose and recompose images from which it is possible to elicit the sequence of ideas together with the purposes of design.

The map for a new landscape strategy for Colli Euganei (Fig. 5) and the one for a new waterfront of Porto Corallo (Fig. 6), both in Italy, have been divided into layers to better explain how the combination between ideograms and psycho-ideograms organize and explain the main landscape idea, which is based on an explicit grammar and syntax. In the intense competition with contemporary images that are quickly produced and consumed, contemporary verbal drawings have to embody the three specific qualities recognized in Rupestrian art: a sense of immediacy, a sense of beauty, and a sense of lightness (Fig. 7).

6 Immediacy in Verbal Drawings

At the beginning of this paper, the quick emotional narrative of Rupestrian art was mentioned as one of the most important qualities they have. Using a rapid description made by simple syntax and grammar, they wrote about real stories and also represented the afterlife that exists beyond our actual physical experience. Such as the Rupestrian art drawings, contemporary verbal drawings in landscape architecture have to reflect this characteristic of immediacy, guiding deep into their meanings when they are read carefully.

Two common examples of Rupestrian art, among thousands, better explain this process of immediacy: one is the painting of a horse painted inside the Cave of Lascaux, France (Fig. 8-1); the other one is the representation of a territory used for hunting

中的活动的运动方向），而抽象表意语言则是一个包含了一些线条的矩形——这一符号与画中的象形语言或表意语言没有明显的关联，但其也是描绘场景时所运用的语汇的一部分[1]。这幅画以象形语言开始叙述，用表意语言解释场中的活动，并用抽象表意语言延伸了画面含义。第二幅画的象形语言是一个由线条围合成的具有边界的场地（描绘的可能是一个狩猎场景），画面中的表意语言映衬出了场地的尺度，而抽象表意语言则丰富了画面内容，引发人们进行更深远的联想。

意大利托雷德尔格雷科滨水区的景观设计方案基于场地本身与意大利索伦托海湾一带的美丽岛屿之间的地理关系而展开（图9）。这片滨水空间本身缺乏特色，而其周边的普罗奇达岛、伊斯基亚岛、卡碧岛以及索伦托却拥有悠久的历史、迷人的景观和诗意的城市空间，于是设计以对这些特色的描绘作为切入点。画面以维苏威火山⑤为中心绘制了一些线条，来表达那些岛屿与滨水区之间的地理联系。设计在滨水岸线上选取了5个重要的景观节点，并依照与每个节点有着地缘关联的岛屿和村镇的特色设计了一系列开敞的花园。当地传统的色彩、

that was painted in the Cave of Altamira, Spain (Fig. 8-2). The first example visualizes the pictogram represented by the body of an animal. Ideograms, resembling arrows, explain techniques used for the activity, while a psycho-ideogram completes the entire scene: it is a kind of rectangle cut by lines. Without having any apparent relationship with the pictogram and ideograms, this symbol, is part of the syntax of the scene[1]. The painting starts its narration with the pictogram, explains the activity with ideograms, and opens the interpretation with a psycho-ideogram. The pictogram of the second painting is a territory traced by different lines enclosed by a boundary; it is probably a hunting landscape. The territory representation is emphasized by an ideogram that seems to measure it. The psycho-ideogram completes the entire scene, opening it to different meanings and interpretations.

For the design of the Torre del Greco waterfront, the landscape strategy was based on geographical relationships related to the incredible context in front of it made by beautiful islands and traditional villages of the Gulf of Sorrento in Italy (Fig. 9). The waterfront itself was without any particular feature, but the islands of Procida, Ischia, and Capri, together with the city of Sorrento, are plenty of history, amazing landscapes, and urban poetic spaces. All these qualities generated the beginning of the design process. Taken into consideration the center of Vesuvio⑤, some lines were traced to visualize the geographical connection with the waterfront and its contexts. Five main points along the waterfront became the main points of the entire waterfront landscape strategy, where a series of open gardens were designed according to the features of the islands

⑤ 维苏威火山是罗马庞贝古城附近的一座著名的火山。

⑤ Vesuvio is a famous volcano near the ancient Roman Pompei city.

8-1. 由瓦莱里奥·莫拉比托临摹的法国拉斯科洞窟壁画中所描绘的马，绘制于2019年。
8-2. 由瓦莱里奥·莫拉比托临摹的西班牙阿尔塔米拉洞窟壁画中描绘的狩猎场景，绘制于2019年。
9. 由瓦莱里奥·莫拉比托与来自APS景观设计事务所的黛博拉·贾琳娜、斯蒂菲尼亚·康多索和玛利亚·特瑞莎·纽萨拉合作绘制的意大利托雷德尔格雷科滨水区景观策略图，绘制于2018年。

8-1. Hand digital drawing copy of the horse painted inside the Cave of Lascaux, France by Valerio Morabito, 2019.
8-2. Hand digital drawing copy of the representation of a territory used for hunting painted in the Cave of Altamira, Spain by Valerio Morabito, 2019.
9. Mapping for the landscape strategy for the waterfront of ToPorto Corallo, Italy by Valerio Morabito and APS (Debora Gallina, Stefania Condurso and MariaTeresa Nucera), 2018.

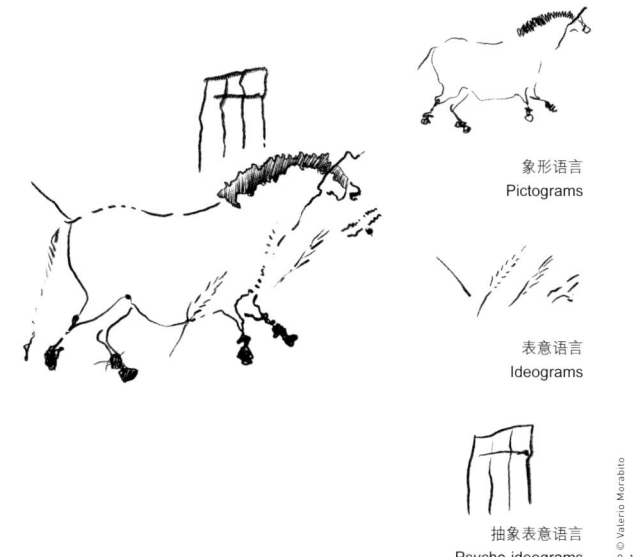

象形语言 Pictograms
表意语言 Ideograms
抽象表意语言 Psycho-ideograms 8-1

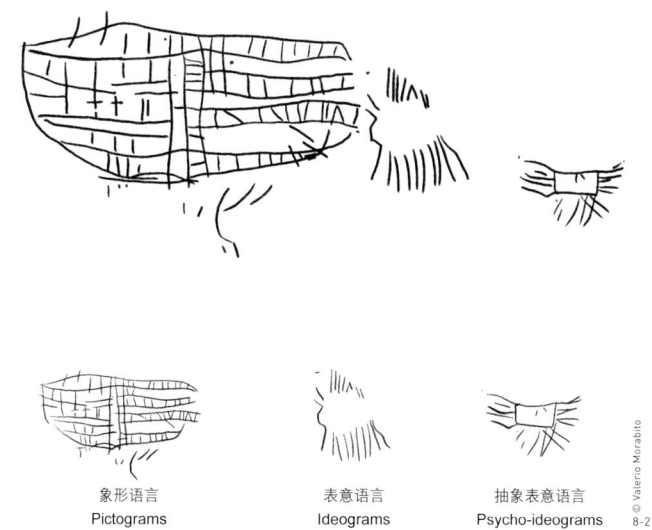

象形语言 Pictograms
表意语言 Ideograms
抽象表意语言 Psycho-ideograms 8-2

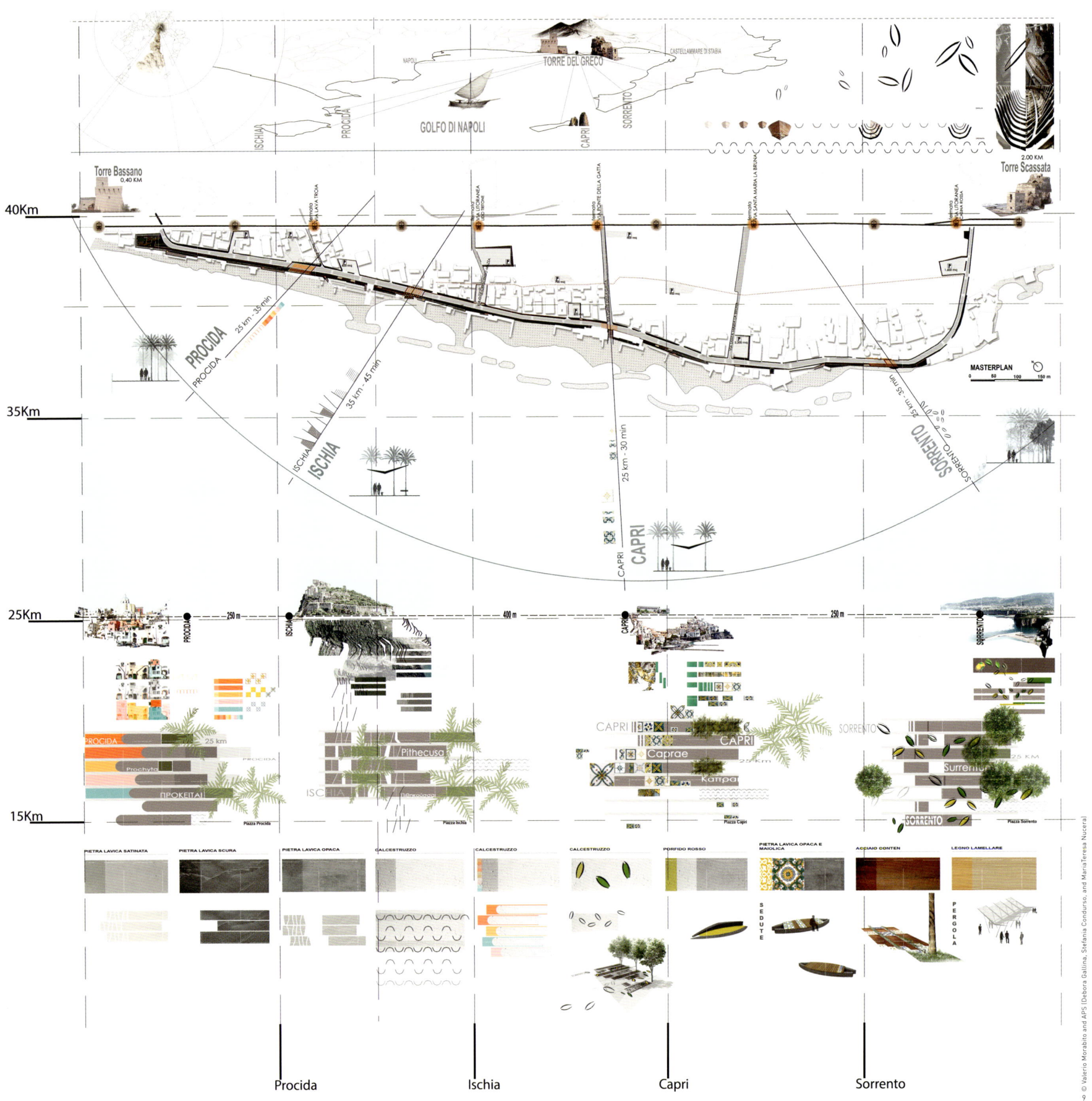

10. Mapping for the waterfront of Alicante, Spain by Valerio Morabito and APS (Debora Gallina, Stefania Condurso, and MariaTeresa Nucera), 2018.
11. *Along the Shanghai River* by Valerio Morabito, hand digital drawing, 2018.

形状、形式及元素（如陶瓷装饰）均体现在花园的设计中。仅在这一张景观设计图中就体现了设计者思考创作的过程，场地与其所处的地理环境之间通过长长的线条建立起了空间上的动态关联。当沿着滨水空间漫步的游人进入这些开放的花园中时，他们便能立刻感受到空间中的色彩、材料、形式和形态都来源于他们所熟悉的当地环境；与此同时，花园还能激发游人对远方的无限想象。

and villages that were geographically connected. Traditional colors, shapes, forms, and elements like ceramic decorations were transformed and used for the design of gardens. The map for the landscape design strategy represents, in one drawing, the process used to create new physical and ephemeral relationships between the long line of the waterfront and its geographical context. People walking along the waterfront and engaging the design of these open gardens can have the immediate physical perception of colors, materials, forms, and shapes coming from the well-known context, and at the same time, they might be transported by imagination to other places.

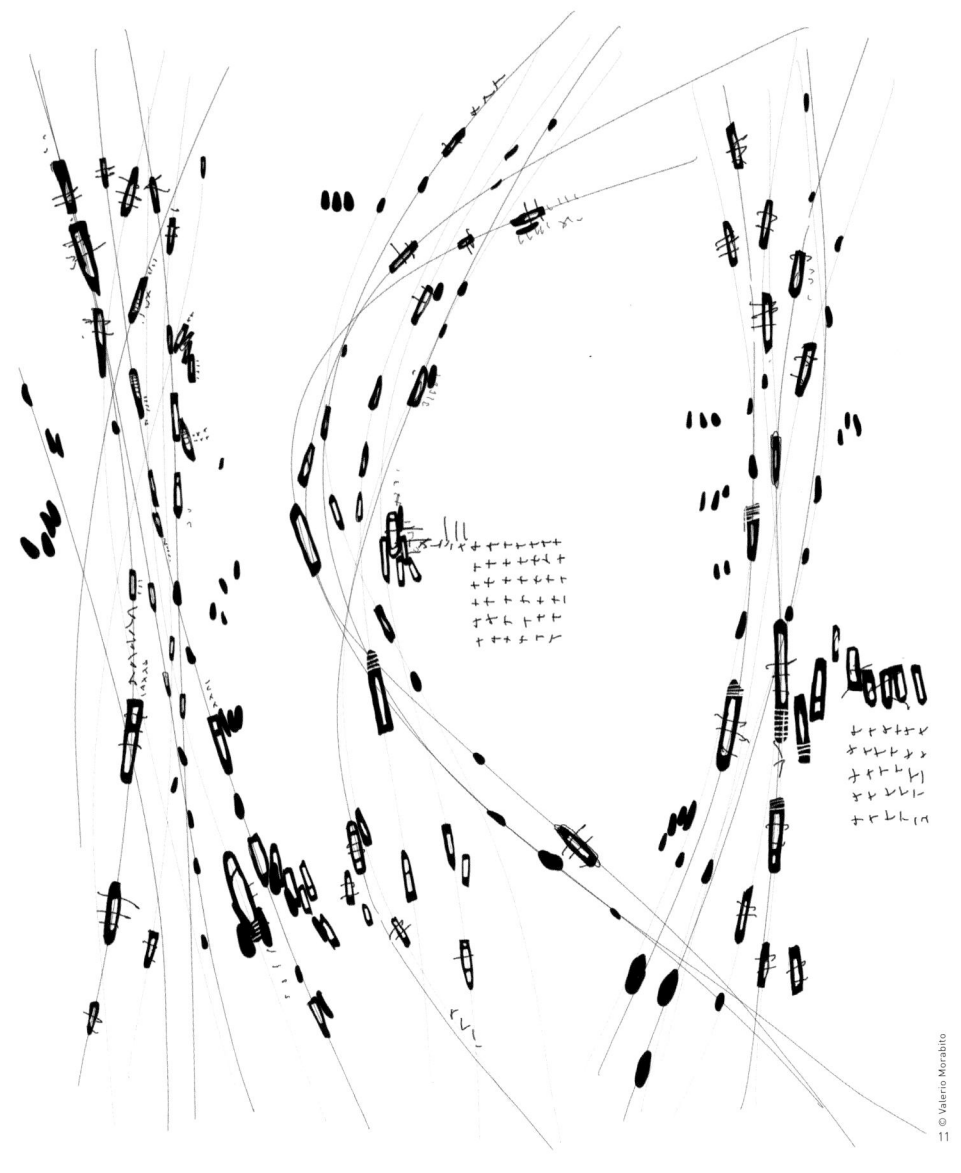

7 Beauty in Verbal Drawings

Old maps, having lost "the gaze, or the intellectual operations established by their users," are now, "abstract objects hovering between graphic curiosity and decorative devices."[5] Being abstract objects, old maps are artistic representations from which it is possible to learn how beauty was created in displaying graphics curiosity and decorative devices.

Old maps are archives containing a multitude of signs, iconic marks, objects — both abstract and tangible — diagrams, and multitudes of lines to be interpreted and used. Cartographies are surfaces of complex and interrelated compositions of different scales that create geographical connections and relationships both with real and imaginary places.

Miller Atlas (1519, probably by Lopo Homem) is one of the most beautiful examples of map archives. The quantity and quality of ideograms and psycho-ideograms collected in the sheets of the Atlas testify the incredible cartographer's representation skills. It is a storage device of endless variation of graphic signs, shapes, measurement, words, lines, and complex shores information assembled by creative combinations. Packed with lions, elephants, warriors, ships, trees, cities, castles, and many other symbolic items, this archive is a written narration of events.

Using the alphabets of ideograms and psycho-ideograms contained in old maps and cartographies, contemporary verbal drawings have many opportunities for writing about places, design strategies, and geographical inventions in a different way. In the map for the waterfront of Alicante, Spain (Fig. 10), the elements of the design strategy are carefully chosen and arranged in a dynamic combination of plans, views, and diagrams.

8 Lightness in Verbal Drawings

Many recent drawings tend to occupy the entire surface where they are represented. These drawings are compact and closed that do not concede any space and margin. John Dixon Hunt[13] spoke about the necessity of having margins in contemporary landscape design, affirming that, in these spaces, it might be possible to add personal notes, the same which can be found on the pages of books as they are read. In contemporary verbal drawings, margins are places where imagination might find a place to operate. They are not only intended like frames surrounding pictures, but margins, being integral parts of the entire scene, are white spaces that measure,

7 语言绘图的美感

今天，即便人们已不再"去关注或解读古老地图中的内容"，但它们仍然是"能够激发人们兴趣的、抽象的、颇具装饰意味的图形"。[5]作为抽象图像，古老地图中的艺术表现形式依旧值得我们去探索，如何通过吸引人的构图和装饰性的表现技法在图纸上创造美感。

古老地图中蕴含着丰富多样的标识、标志性符号、抽象及具象的元素、分析图，以及大量的线条，有待人们来了解和使用。地图绘制通过对不同尺度上的要素进行复杂又相互关联的整合，来表现真实或想象的地缘联系。

其中,绘制于1519年的《米勒地图集》(可能为罗伯·欧蒙所绘)是最能体现古老地图美感的经典之作。地图集中所包含的表意语言和抽象表意语言数量繁多且精美至极,体现出绘制者超凡的表达能力。这部地图集犹如一个庞大的资源库,其中运用的图形符号、形状、量度、词汇、线条和集合极为丰富,以一种创造性的方式向观者传达着信息;地图集中还随处可见诸如狮子、大象、士兵、舰船、树木、城市、城堡等象征性符号,仿若一本精妙的故事书一般。

参考古老地图及其他绘图中的表意语言和抽象表意语言,当代制图者可以借助语言绘图创新性地描绘场地、阐释设计策略,或表达地理关系。比如,在西班牙阿里坎特滨水区地图(图10)中,设计元素即以巧妙而多样的组合方式出现在平面图、透视图和分析图中。

8 语言绘图的轻盈感

近年来,许多绘图的画面往往都被填得很满,图面局促且封闭,没有任何留白或间隙。约翰·迪克逊·亨特[13]在谈到当代景观设计中留白的重要性时强调,绘图者可以利用这些留白空间添加个人标注,就像他们看书时在页面留白处写下笔记一样。在当代语言绘图中,留白给人以想象的空间,它们可以如画框般起到界定画面的作用,图中的间隙也是整体构图中的必要组成部分,可以凸显、塑造及平衡(设计理念及表达上的)轻盈感。

一个最能体现轻盈感的例子就是中国传统山水画。中国传统山水画不再仅仅是对可见世界的描摹,绘者将对外部世界的理解转化为理想化的图像,更是其内心深处精神寄托的映射。郭熙的名作《树色平远图》[14]有助于我们理解语言绘图中轻盈感的概念。在这幅画中,轻盈感是通过精心设计的留白实现的。留白使得整幅画面更加灵动,自然元素和人物活动流畅排布。这些留白也为不同尺度和不同视角的场景转换留下了想象空间。与岩绘艺术类似,我们也可以从这幅画中辨析出象形语言(古树)、表意语言(桥、灌丛、亭、船舶),乃至抽象表意语言(印章)。

另一个例子是彩绘版画《京都及其周边地区盛景图》[6]:城市中的标志性建筑物从云层间的留白处升起,营造了一种独特的轻盈感,同时也将其他不必要的元素隐藏了起来。另外,在米开朗基罗创作的西斯廷教堂壁画中,上帝和亚当的手指之间的留白还隐喻了天神与人类之间的距离,使得整幅壁画散发出引人入胜的宗教轻盈感。并且对于这处人神之间的留白,每个人还可以发挥自己的想象,从而激发出多样性的解读。

20世纪初期的达达主义运动探索了不同寻常的思维导图的表现形式。他们通过将大小不同、形状各异的随机词汇随意地分布在空白的纸张上,完成对形状的切割与组合,在形成美感和直观感的同时,也营造了一种美妙的轻盈感。

control, and balance the sense of lightness both about ideas and their representations.

One of the most significant examples concerning the lightness in representing ideas comes from traditional Chinese landscape painting, which became no longer a description of the visible world but by conveying the artist's inner heart and mental perceptions, transformed the mere representations of the external world into idealized images. The famous painting *Old Trees, Level Distance* by Guo Xi[14] helps visualize the idea of lightness related to verbal drawings. In this representative example, lightness is achieved through the use of precisely designed white spaces. Leaving them in the painting, the artist enhances the entire dynamic perception of the scene, allowing the natural elements to move freely concerning human activities. The understanding of a multitude of scales and perspectives are supported by these blank absences that are places where imagination can be fed. As well as Rupestrian art, this painting might be decomposed into pictograms (main trees), ideograms (bridges, bushes, pavilions, and boats), and even psycho-ideograms (stamps).

Another example is the painted panel representing the panoramic views of Kyoto and its suburbs, known as *Scenes in and around the Capital of Kyoto*.[6] The city monuments, rising from the white space of clouds, generate a particular lightness of power, where all unnecessary elements are covered. In the fresco of the Sistine Chapel, by Michelangelo, the white space between the finger of God and Adam measures the distance between divine genius and human genius, giving to the entire fresco an incredible religious lightness. Everybody can add ideas into the open space between God and human nature, creating multitudes of personal significances.

At the beginning of the last century, the Dada artistic movement explored the path to compose uncommon geographical mind maps. Using random words different in scale, shapes, and characters, artists displayed them casually on the empty paper space, achieving an incredible sense of lightness that, combined with a sense of beauty and immediacy, divided the meaning by its shape.

The Maps of Japan, a triptych of drawings made by the artist Waltercio Caldas, cited by James Corner in the famous essay *The Agency of Mapping*,[11] are perfect examples of lightness in the art of mapping. The composition of the drawing is made up of a regular square frame surrounding the square surface of the paper; in this white square, the artist placed imaginary geographical points and numbers. The white space is the psycho-ideogram of the entire representation, the fundamental absence of nonessential information.

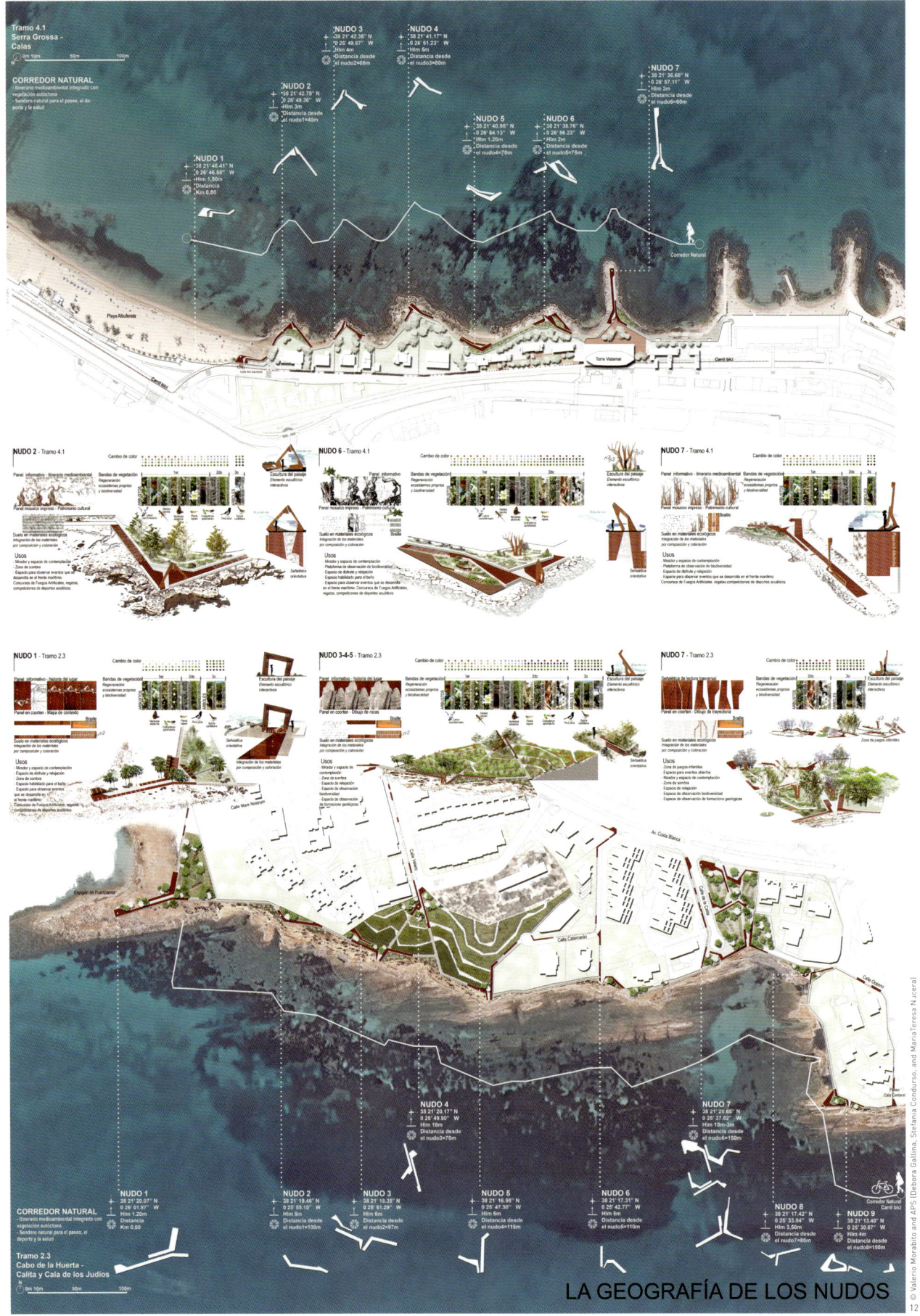

12. 由瓦莱里奥·莫拉比托与来自APS景观设计事务所的黛博拉·贾琳娜、斯蒂菲尼亚·康多索和玛利亚·特瑞莎·纽萨拉合作绘制的西班牙阿利坎特滨水区景观设计图，绘制于2018年。

12. Mapping design details for the waterfront of Alicante, Spain by Valerio Morabito and APS (Debora Gallina, Stefania Condurso, and MariaTeresa Nucera), 2018.

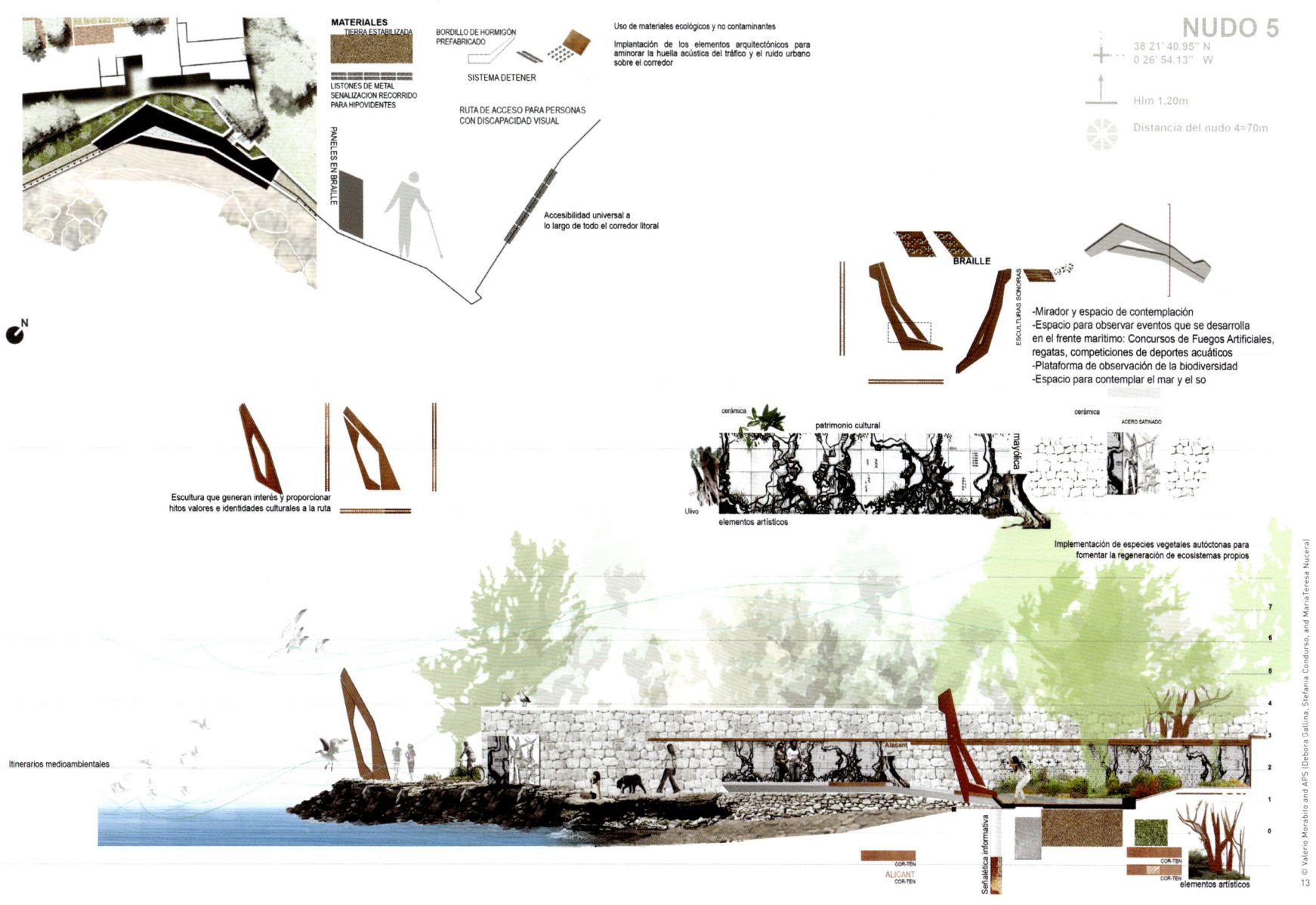

另一个能够体现绘图轻盈感的经典案例是沃尔特西欧·卡尔达斯的三联画《日本地图集》，该画作曾被詹姆斯·科纳在著作《地图术的力量》一书中予以引用。画作的纸张和边框都采用了正方形，在这个正方形的画面中，艺术家绘制了一系列虚构的地理位置和数字。整个画面的留白部分就是其抽象表意语言，绘者刻意利用留白隐去了一些不必要的信息。

《黄浦江上》这一画作（图11）所体现出的轻盈感，亦能使观者从画中感受到上海黄浦江上的航运不分昼夜的繁忙。虽然画面中的黄浦江不再被具象的形状所限定，城市的边界也随之消失。

The drawing *Along the Shanghai River* (Fig. 11) represents the lightness with which it is possible to perceive the infinite flow of boats and black ships that pass during the night and day in Shanghai. The river no longer has its shape, and the city disappears.

9 Verbal Drawing as Open Frameworks

The concept of "Open Work" was conceived by Umberto Eco to defines a work of art not as a concluded experience. Speaking

13. 由瓦莱里奥·莫拉比托与来自APS景观设计事务所的黛博拉·贾琳娜、斯蒂菲尼亚·康多索和玛利亚·特瑞莎·纽萨拉合作绘制的西班牙阿利坎特滨水区景观设计剖面图，绘制于2018年。

13. Landscape section for the waterfront of Alicante, Spain by Valerio Morabito and APS (Debora Gallina, Stefania Condurso, and MariaTeresa Nucera), 2018.

14. 由瓦莱里奥·莫拉比托与APS景观设计事务所的斯蒂菲尼亚·康多索和阿莉西亚·雷特拉合作绘制的意大利伊格莱西亚斯旅游区景观设计图，绘制于2018年。

14. Perspective for the landscape strategy for a touristic development of Iglesiente, Italy by Valerio Morabito and APS (Stefania Condurso and Alessia Latella), 2018.

about the new art of music, and using specific examples, he writes that "these new musical works instead consist not in a closed and defined message, not in a uniquely organized form, but the possibility of various organizations entrusted from the initiative of the interpreter. And therefore, they present themselves not as finite works that ask to be relived and understood in a given structural direction, but, as 'open works,' which are carried out by interpreters at the same time as they are aesthetically used."[15] Adding that the aesthetics has been repeatedly addressed in philosophy, a work of art has an aesthetic value when it leaves possibilities and opportunities to many subjects to formulate different interpretations of it, even if the author concluded and "closed" it in meaning and intentions.[15] To better explain his concept, he added the example of a road sign: it has a specific purpose and function that does not allow any other interpretation of it.

But musical performances and verbal drawings have two different aims to reach and different aesthetics significance. The musical aesthetic is related to the quality of music, to the performance, and to the capacity of listeners to be involved. When music and its performance are tremendous, and the listeners are well educated, interested, or intuitively inspired, the aesthetics produces a new significance and perception of the original artistic intention. But this new status does not create any change of the work that instead remains in its original physical aspect: a painting remains a painting, a musical score is written in the same way, a sculpture does not change from its original form.

Conversely, it might be said that contemporary verbal drawings are between artworks and road signs. A verbal drawing can be transformed after academic discussions, clients' desires' and citizens' critics, without invalidating its original significance; it is possible to assert its aesthetics extends[16] and adds rather than to change their meanings.

Verbal drawings can be maps that visualize design strategies coming directly from poetic and narrative site analysis. The cartography for a design proposal of Alicante waterfront (Fig. 12) shows the coastline features, the urban structure, the existing topography together with the idea of the new landscape strategy based on the creations of several nodes. Sections in the shape of verbal drawings (Fig. 13) can simultaneously represent the design of elements and their materials, ecological processes, activities, and programs. Also, perspectives can be conceived according to the idea of verbal drawings. These are drawings that do not attempt to photograph a precise moment in time, but the elements that are part of the scene are selected and arranged according to

9 语言绘图：开放式框架

"开放式作品"（Open Work）的概念由安伯托·艾柯提出，是指那些能够引起观者多样性解读和体验的艺术作品。在谈及具体的新的音乐艺术作品时，他说"这些新的音乐作品表达的不是封闭的限定性的信息，也摒弃了单一的组合方式，而是通过多样化的组合形式来激发人们多样化解读的可能。因此，这些作品并不需要通过既定结构来呈现。不过人们对于这些'开放作品'的欣赏和解读水平也取决于他们当时的审美能力。"[15]其实，美学问题已在哲学领域反复讨论，当一件艺术作品本身能为观者留下许多探讨的可能性并能激发出差异性的解读时，其本身就具有了美学价值，即便有时候作者试图赋予作品某种确切意义。[15]为了更好地理解"开放式作品"的理念，艾柯还举了一个交通指示标识的反例：交通指示标识具有非常明确的功用，不容有其他形式的解读。

然而，音乐演奏和语言绘图有着不同的目标和美学意义。对于音乐的美学欣赏与音乐的品质、演奏效果，以及听众的欣赏水平有关。当音乐本身及其演奏效果非常精彩、听众又拥有良好知识背景并且受到情绪感染时，音乐的美学欣赏便赋予了音乐新的意义和解读。但这种新的意义和解读并没有改变作品本身：画还是那幅画，乐曲还是那首乐曲，雕塑也还是那尊雕塑。

相反，语言绘图或许介乎于艺术作品和交通指示标识之间。基于学术讨论、客户需求和市民的意见反馈，语言绘图可以改变形式，但仍保留其原本含义——换言之，语言绘图可以在不改变其原本意图的基础上，实现美学意义上的扩展[16]和丰富。

语言绘图可对那些缘于场地分析与诗意解读的设计策略进行可视化表达。如西班牙阿里坎特滨水区设计方案图（图12）展示了包含海岸线特征、城市结构、现有地形以及多个新建节点的景观构想。当我们以语言绘图的形式来绘制剖面时，可以同时表现设计元素以及它们

a moveable and active narrative. In the view of landscape strategy for a touristic development of Iglesiente[17], elements, such as the cliff, the wind sculpture, and the agave, are composed together in accordance with white spaces (Fig. 14), in which, over time, it is possible to add notes, thoughts, and new ideas that might be generated during the process of landscape.

After visiting the city of Chengdu, the author made this sketch to imagine a new waterfront (Fig. 15). It tries to embody the energy of the space, extending its lines to envision which kinds of relationships it is possible to establish with the river, with people, and their way to use the space. The image of the hand drawings *City Objects* (Fig. 16) showing the process of transformation and reshaping of verbal drawings generates a map for an urban park.

Therefore, contemporary verbal drawings might be described as open frameworks rather than "open works." Like frames of buildings, they extend their meanings, adding further technical and poetic requirements and, at the same time, they are also tools to imagine and create innovative ideas of contemporary landscape architecture. **LAF**

15. 由瓦莱里奥·莫拉比托绘制的中国成都滨水区设计概念图，数字手绘稿，绘制于2019年。

15. An idea for the Chengdu Waterfront, China by Valerio Morabito, hand digital drawing, 2019.

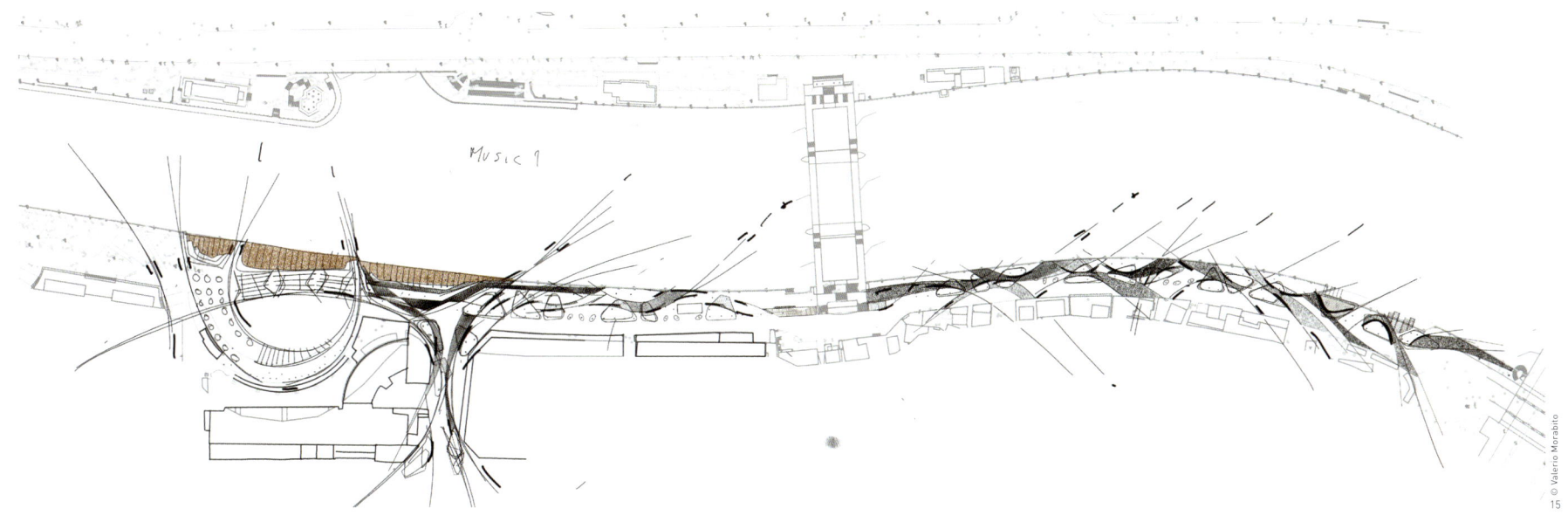

16. 由瓦莱里奥·莫拉比托绘制的《城市事物》，手绘稿扫描件，绘制于2018年。

16. *City Objects*, hand digital drawing, by Valerio Morabito, 2018.

的材料、生态过程和场地中的活动安排（图13）。同样，透视图也可以运用语言绘图的思路来构想：透视图不再是像照片一样尝试精准捕捉场地的某个瞬间，而是基于一种动态的叙述方式来选择和排布场景中的元素。在意大利伊格莱西亚斯旅游区景观设计图[17]中，场地元素（如峭壁、关于风的雕塑、龙舌兰等）与画面中的留白相互组合（图14）；随着时间推移，人们可以为场地添加更多注解，而随着景观不断变化，设计师也可能产生新的想法。

另外，在游历成都之后，笔者还绘制了一张草图来描绘其构想的一个新的滨水空间（图15），试图通过线条的延展来表达河流、人和空间之间的联系，从而展现空间的力量。手绘图《城市事物》（图16）则通过描绘一座城市公园，来展示语言绘图的转换和重塑过程。

综上所述，当代的语言绘图可被理解为一种开放式框架，而非"开放式作品"。就像建筑物的架构，绘图的意义借由这种开放式框架得到扩展与延伸，技术和美学内涵也能得到深化与丰富。与此同时，对于当代景观设计来说，它也是激发想象和创新思考的工具。**LAF**

REFERENCES

[1] Anati, E. (2002). La struttura elementare dell'Arte. Italy: Centro Camuno di Studi Preistorici.
[2] Geoffry, J., & Susan, J. (1987). The landscape of man: Shaping the environment from prehistory to the present day. New York: Thames and Hudson.
[3] Lommel, A. (1967). The world of the early hunters. London: Evelyn, Adams & Mackay.
[4] Barnes, T. J., & Duncan, J. S. (1992). Writing Worlds. Discourse, text and metaphors in the representation of landscape. London: Routledge.
[5] Jacobs, C. (2006). The Sovereign Map: Theoretical Approaches in Cartography throughout History. Chicago: The University of Chicago Press.
[6] Vigra, V. (2008). Cartographia: Mapping Civilization. New York: Little, Brown and Company.
[7] Desimini, J., & Waldheim, C. (2016). Cartographic Ground: Projecting the Landscape Imaginary. New York: Princeton Architectural Press.
[8] Bayer, H. (1953). World Geo-Graphic Atlas: A Composite of Man's Environment. Chicago: Container Corporation of America.
[9] CODEX99 Website. (2013, September 10). The World Geo-Graphical Atlas [Web log message]. Retrieved from http://www.codex99.com/design/the-world-geographical-atlas.html
[10] Corner, J., & MacLean, A. S. (2000).Taking measures across the American landscape. New Haven: Yale University Press.
[11] Corner, J., & Hirsch, A. B. (2014). The Landscape Imagination: Collected Essays of James Corner 1990-2010. New York: Princeton Architectural Press.
[12] Wittgenstein, L. (1984). Culture and Value. Chicago: University of Chicago Press.
[13] Hunt, J. D., & Morabito, V. (2012). Sette lezioni sul paesaggio. Melfi: Libria.
[14] Foong, P. (2000). Guo Xi's Intimate Landscxape and the Case of Old Trees, Level Distance. Metropolitan Musum Journal, (35), 87-115.
[15] Eco, U. (1989). Open Work. Cambridge: Harvard University Press.
[16] Morabito, V. (2004). The extended representation of landscape. Paisea, (14), 18-24. Retrieved from http://www.paisea.com/wp-content/uploads/paisea-014-ART-2.pdf
[17] Morabito, V. & Morabito, V. A. (2013). Processi di paesaggio. Roma: Aracne.

本文引用格式 / PLEASE CITE THIS ARTICLE AS

Chen, A., & Cai, T. (2019). Draw-ing Drawing — Revisiting the Drawings by Laurie Olin. Landscape Architecture Frontiers, 7(5), 58-79. https://doi.org/10.15302/J-LAF-1-020009

"画"画
——劳瑞·欧林手绘重顾

DRAW-ING DRAWING
— REVISITING THE DRAWINGS BY LAURIE OLIN

https://doi.org/10.15302/J-LAF-1-020009 收稿时间 RECEIVED DATE / 2019-08-16 中图分类号 / J2 文献标识码 / A

陈峥能
Stoss景观都市主义工作室景观设计师

蔡哲铭
OLIN景观设计事务所景观设计师

Albert Zhengneng CHEN*
Landscape Designer of Stoss Landscape Urbanism

Taro Zheming CAI
Landscape Designer of the OLIN Studio

*Corresponding Author
Address: 54 Old Colony Ave 3rd Floor, Boston, MA 02127, USA
Email: albertchen@alumni.upenn.edu

摘要

　　景观的概念在某种意义上与人们对眼前世界的不断解读息息相关，是人类与自然及文化之间关系的体现。因此，我们不能将景观视作一种先验知识，而应通过观察与表现对其加以理解。在如今众多的媒介之中，无论是描绘现状还是构思方案，手绘或许都是最为古老而简易的表现手段，但这一富于创造之功又常在所见之外的绘画过程却不及成作更为观者所瞩目。本文旨在探究这一有赖于绘者手（娴熟表现）眼（深刻观察）协调的看似复杂的观察与思考过程。文章首先解读了美国景观设计大师劳瑞·欧林在近期一次展览中的部分画作，并着眼于三处重点：景观表现的留白与省略、景观构图（透视构图与修辞构图），以及笔墨技艺背后的潜在意图。其次，试图梳理欧林几十年来在景观手绘与实践之间耕耘的脉络，并借此阐明观察和表现能力的培养在当今景观设计教育中的意义。

关键词

手绘；观察；表现；劳瑞·欧林

ABSTRACT

The idea of landscape is, to some extent, a cumulative interpretation of the way we see the world, reflecting our relationship with nature and culture. Landscape is thereby impossible to be assumed a priori but only to be understood through observation and representation. Between a broad spectrum of media, hand drawing presents presumably an oldest and simplest means for landscape representation, whether it is existing or imaginary. However, the creative yet oftentimes invisible process of draw-ing receives less attention from the spectators than its result. The paper takes an inquiry into this seemingly complicated process of looking and thinking based on the coordination of the draughtsman's critical eye and skilful hand. First, the paper gives a careful reading upon some selected drawings from a recent exhibition of the renowned American landscape architect Laurie Olin, with three particular focuses — the reduction in representation, the composition of the observed landscape (perspectival composition and figurative composition), and the conjecturable intention behind drawing skills. Second, the paper attempts to unveil the evolution of Olin's decades of training and practising of drawing and observation, and further argues the significance in the training of hand and the cultivation of the critical eye in Landscape Architecture pedagogy.

KEYWORDS

Drawing; Observation; Representation; Laurie Olin

编辑　田晓劼
EDITED BY　TIAN Xiaojie

1 引言

　　景观是一个复合概念，它为人们从多角度审视自身与自然及文化之间的关系提供了共同基础。因此，景观的概念在某种意义上与人们对眼前世界的不断解读息息相关，这种解读并非先验的，而是基于对事物的观察与表现。对于合格的景观设计师而言，观察与表现是两项最基本的能力。一边用敏锐的眼睛来观察，一边用娴熟的手来作画，几乎是设计师的一种本能。这一过程不但需要眼、手、心的协调，而且要将"批判性观察"视为景观表现的核心。景观的手绘表现从来不只是简单地描摹视觉投影，而是要在脑海中重新诠释所见之景，并表达所见之外的新意。这种"新意的表达"因此蕴含了绘者颇具洞见的观察和思考过程，进而启发观者通过仔细观摩眼前的画作，了解这一不可言传的过程。

此文落笔的初衷缘于劳瑞·欧林近期的一次手绘展览。欧林是美国颇负盛名的景观设计大师，他于2018年将自己的大部分画作、手稿，以及速写本赠予宾夕法尼亚大学（以下简称宾大）建筑档案馆。由此，宾大建筑档案馆策划了一场名为"手绘"（Drawing）的展览，从记录了欧林近70年来对景观的观察、思考和学习的手绘作品中精选出一部分呈现给公众，包括20世纪60年代末的写实铅笔素描、旅居英国乡村时的钢笔白描、在美国南部自驾游时作于自制牛皮纸画簿上的钢笔画、经年累月留在速写本上的钢笔与淡墨画、行走地中海与中国时所画的水彩画、关于意大利和法国园林的大画幅炭笔素描，以及数量可观的景观设计实践草图。一方面，欧林的铅笔素描呈现出逼真而适意的细节刻画；另一方面，其速写作品则反映了他对设计的深刻理解以及在众多实践中的不断探索。对欧林而言，手绘是领悟世界的有效途径[1]；对于观者而言，品析画作亦是一种通过探索绘者的好奇心和求知欲而引发批判性思考的方法。正如《园冶》中的"拟入画中行"[2]所述，这是一种有别于欣赏既成意象的画作体验方式——以批判性视角重游绘者的"景观"构建过程。

1 Introduction

Landscape is a complex idea, which confers a common ground for viewing and reflecting our relationship with nature and culture through different lenses. Therefore, the idea of landscape is to some extent linked to a cumulative interpretation of how we see the world, which is almost impossible to be assumed a priori but only to be understood through observation and representation. For a reliable landscape architect, observation and representation of landscape are two most fundamental capabilities. For designers, it is almost instinctive to see with a keen eye and to draw by the skilful hand. This process requires not only the coordination of the eye, the hand, and the mind, but also the placing of "critical observation" in the center of landscape representation. To represent the landscape through drawing, however, is never simply to delineate the object projected on the retina, but to construe in mind the existing and to express the new. This "new expression," therefore, embeds the process of seeing and thinking from the draughtsman's "critical eye," suggesting the spectator could revisit this unutterable process through a careful reading of a drawing.

The initiative in writing this paper was struck by a recent exhibition of drawings from Laurie Olin, a renowned and much-awarded American landscape architect. In 2018, the Architectural Archives of the University of Pennsylvania was gifted a vast collection of his drawings, writings, and particularly the sketchbooks from Olin. The exhibition named "Drawing" was then curated by the Architectural Archives, selectively displaying Olin's almost seven decades of observing, thinking, and studying landscape through his continuous hand drawing. The selected drawings include his naturalistic graphite drawings in the late 1960s, ink delineation from his stay in English countryside, ink drawings on self-bonded craft paper sheets during his road trips towards the South, ink wash in stacks of sketchbooks over years, watercolor from the Mediterranean and China, charcoal on large format about Italian and French gardens, and a considerable amount of drawings from his design practice. While his graphite drawings bring the eidetic and agreeable details, Olin's sketchbooks reflect more of his design insights and experimentations in his productive practices. For Olin, drawing is an efficient approach to learn the world[1], while for spectators, reading the drawings also provides a critical pathway to learn through the draughtsman's curiosity and wonder. This is similar to the idea "to walk in the painting"[2] from the classic Chinese landscape literature *Art of Garden-Building*, which suggests a critical revisit upon the draughtsman's constructing of his / her conception in lieu of imagining the constructed imagery as it is.

此次手绘作品展在为观者带来观赏体验的同时，更启发大家进一步思考：手绘呈现了什么？绘者想要表达什么？观者从画作中领会了什么？观者如何通达画外之意及画作背后的创作过程？带着这些耐人寻味的问题和对手绘的基本理解，本文的两位作者——分别为欧林的学生和同事——对"手绘"展览中的几幅画作进行了评析，并试图探讨观察与表现之于当代景观设计师的意义。本文选取的这部分画作分属不同类别，表现媒介与内容也各有差异，这些均取决于欧林对周遭景观的观察与感知，以及在纸面上进行探索与实验的迫切渴望。

2 作为观察媒介的手绘

2.1 什么是手绘？

在展开讨论之前，我们需要明确"手绘"一词是指什么。在文艺复兴时期的画家眼中，"素描"（disegno）是一种写生与表达想法的技艺，用以在成作前确定画作的主题与表现内容。通常，画家需要绘制相当数量的草稿，以为最终的油画定稿做准备。但需要强调的是，手绘的定义不应取决于作画的工具、媒介，或着色与否，而主要在于绘者的作画意图与目的——这远比画作的媒介与表现技巧更为重要。意大利语"disegno"一词的拉丁词源意味丰富，蕴含着标记、描摹、描绘、图示等动作含义，并可由此引申为规划与设计行为，表明手绘这一实践来源于对世界的观察与理解，并最终落于笔头。

尽管绘画领域中涉及线条和色彩的争论从未间断，手绘作为沟通外部与内在世界桥梁的初衷却从未改变。手绘与个人感知的这种联系正是瓦西里·康定斯基所谓的为了实现"确切的观察和确切的呈现"而进行的手眼训练过程，最终通过绘者"清晰的观察与描绘来呈现环境与文脉的本质"[①]。对于欧林而言，手绘既是一种身体行为，也是一种思维反应。手绘过程需要依靠手的移动、眼的捕捉，以及两者之间的相互协调来实现，从不局限于事先拟定的主题和内容。就观察与表现的即时协调而言，手绘过程要求绘者分析其所见，同时将捕捉到的

Besides the appreciation of the accomplishment of these drawings, the exhibition has also brought with recognition of some more inspiring inquiries. What does the drawing say? What does the draughtsman try to tell? What do we apprehend, and moreover, how can we access to the invisible message and the creative process behind the drawing? Developed from these interests and preliminary understandings of drawing, the co-authors of this paper, a student of Olin and a colleague of the OLIN Studio, reviewed a selection of Olin's drawings from this exhibition and attempt to discuss the significance of observation and representation to landscape architects today. These drawings from the exhibition demonstrate a creative spectrum in kinds, media, and contents, yet all determined by Olin's observation and perception from the surrounding landscape and his immediate desire to explore and experiment on the paper.

2 Drawing as Observation

2.1 What Is Drawing?

What does the term refer to when we discuss drawing? The term "disegno" was then considered by Renaissance painters as certain techniques to learn from nature and to visualize the thoughts and affirm the ideas for their final oeuvres. In many cases, a considerable amount of preliminary drawings have to be tested and prepared for their ultimate paintings (pittura). However, it is essential to know that drawing cannot be defined by the tools or media or whether it is colored or not. The definition of the practice of drawing depends mainly on the draughtsman's intention and purpose that matters more than its media and representation techniques. The Latin root of "disegno" implies the action to mark, to trace out, to depict, to denote, from which the term has extended its meaning to plan and design, suggesting the practice of drawing in the vein from observation and comprehension to eventually "figuring-out."

Despite the continuous discourse upon drawing and painting (the mastery of coloring) among the painters from later generations, the purpose of drawing to bridge the internal and the external world has never altered. This connection between drawing and perception is what Wassily Kandinsky called a process of training towards "the exact observation and exact presentation" to seek to present the essence through one's "clear observation and clear rendering of the contexts."[①] For Olin, the action of drawing is physical as well as responsive. The process of drawing, relying upon a continuous correspondence between the moving hand and the searching eye, is never limited by a clear goal regards to the content or the theme of a work. In terms of this instant coordination between observation and

---

① 源自康定斯基被广泛引用的一段话："绘画指导是指对绘画对象的构成要素和内在张力（而非外观）进行感知、准确观察，以及确切呈现的训练，并可以从给定对象的逻辑结构或通过对其所处环境进行观察与表现方面的训练去发现，进而从表面现象迈向三维认知。"

① From Kandinsky's famous quote "Drawing instruction is a training towards perception, exact observation and exact presentation not of the outward appearances of an object, but of its constructive elements, its lawful forces-tensions, which can be discovered in given objects and of the logical structures of same-education toward clear observation and clear rendering of the contexts, whereby surface phenomena are an introductory step towards the three-dimensional."

个人体会和感触呈现在画面上。因此，手绘是一个探索的过程而非制式的流程，无法彻底做到事先规划。绘者在手绘中所追求的——无论是具体的存在还是隐喻的内涵，抑或是如伊波利特·丹纳所言代表事物本质的"特征"[3]——从来不是对结果的呈现，而是想法的酝酿与发酵。手绘即是忠实于自己的好奇心与求知欲，不断地去追问、去疑惑，在未知中不断求索。

2.2 手绘背后的创作过程

如上所述，手绘实践与观察一脉相承，观察是贯穿整个绘画过程的基础。观者审视画作的不同视角也产生了迥异的感受与解读。但对画作的批判性解读往往需要观者着眼于成作的图像之外，从绘者的视角聚焦其创作过程。保罗·塞尚曾如此盛赞克劳德·莫奈的艺术创造力："莫奈只是眼力好而已，但这是何等的眼力啊！"[4]塞尚对莫奈观察力的赞叹表明，艺术家画作背后独特的洞察力与富于创造性的表现力，虽然通常不直接显露出来，但仍可能被有心的观者捕捉。如果说画作本身在对所观之景进行二次回应时将观者与绘者相联结，那么画作背后的创作过程则展现了绘者首次与周遭世界相联结的情形。这一所见之外的创作过程恰恰是笔者的兴趣所在。

通过有意识地观看、分析、追问、推敲以及表现，绘画创作过程为个体创造了与周遭景观对话的条件。从认识论来讲，这一过程主要是个体对所处世界的解构与重构，因而可以被视作一种个人的、内在的对话。从这一角度而言，通过感知与反应，手绘过程成为了构建个体与外部世界身心联系的桥梁和入口。随着手绘一笔一划地成形，个体与世界的交流也在不断推进。在最后一笔从纸面上提起之前，整个绘画过程都记录了绘者对景观的原初体验，即亲历。

然而，观者只能通过画作的最终呈现来领会绘画的经过。如果绘画的过程被视为绘者对景观的最初领受与反馈，那么观者对画作的解读则是一种"二次"应答。当欧林的精选画作呈现在眼前，作为观者的我们会有怎样的期待？约翰·伯格曾断言，每一次观看行为的背后

representation, drawing requires the draughtsman to analyze what he or she sees and to decide what to capture and how to present simultaneously with his or her perception. That said, drawing is not a consolidated orchestration but an explorative process and therefore cannot be fully planned. What the draughtsman seeks in the drawing, whether they are the physical occurrence, allegorical connotations, or what Hippolyte Taine called the essential "character"[3], is never presented as a given result, but pregnancy of an idea. To draw is to stay honest to one's curiosity, to question, to wonder, and to seek the answer without having it beforehand.

2.2 Draw-ing behind Drawing

As previously discussed, the practice of drawing is in the vein of observation. Observation endures as fundamental in both the end result and the process of drawing. People approach the drawing from different perspectives, and produce various perceptions and readings. However, rather than the recognition of the outcome image, the critical reading of a drawing requires more focuses on the process of drawing from the artist's perspective. As Paul Cezanne remarked in a letter on Claude Monet's artistic ability, "Monet is nothing but an eye. But what an eye!"[4] Cezanne's exclamation of Monet's keen eye suggests the artist's unique observation and creative process of representing that are often not explicitly visible but possibly accessible to us. From this perspective, if drawing connects the spectator and the artist in a secondary reception of the landscape observed, draw-ing connects the artist to the world with a first immersion. This process of draw-ing behind the presenting outcome is what we are interested in.

Draw-ing offers the capacity to initiate the dialogue between the individual and the surrounded landscape through carefully looking, analyzing, questioning, reconciling, and representing. Epistemically, this process is mostly the individual's deconstruction and reconstruction of the world surrounded, which is therefore considered as a personal and internal dialogue. From this standpoint, draw-ing becomes the bridge and portal that connect the individual and the world physically and mentally, through perception and reception. As draw-ing moves on, the communication between the draughtsman and the world continues. Before the final stroke ends on the medium, this whole movement of draw-ing records the draughtsman's primary experience of landscape.

However, for the spectator, one could only apprehend the process of draw-ing through drawing, an end presence of interpretation. If draw-ing is considered as an initial reception of landscape, then our reading through drawing is a secondary

都是对意义的追寻[5]。如果将"观察"置于欧林手绘的核心，那么我们所期待的意义应当显露于两者目光的交叠处——绘者彼时的探求与观者此刻的追寻。笔者期望探寻是什么捕获了欧林的目光，而他又聚焦于何处，进而理解欧林如何感悟周遭的景观，及其通过手绘对景观进行的思考。带着这些期待，笔者试图再现欧林画作中不可见的创作过程，并通过三个方面切入这一隐含的创作过程：事实之景与呈现之景、透视构图与修辞构图的景观叙事，以及笔触背后的意图。

2.3 事实之景与呈现之景

在此次展览上与威廉·惠特克的对谈中，欧林称手绘对其而言是一种观察的媒介，"手绘就是去观察、去认知、去吸收"。欧林的大多数手绘作品，尤其是那些速写本里的画作，都绘于现场，这表明手绘不只是视觉记录，更是一种感知周遭声音、气味、光线、温度和湿度的沉浸体验。在欧林的速写本中，景观弥漫交织的丰富性以一种取舍与凝练的方式呈现出来。不同于相机胶卷通过镜头与快门对光线的忠实记录，手绘的过程并不照搬描摹现实，而是呈现经过思考和选择的结果。笔者认为，欧林在他的手绘作品中有意进行了简化和省略，以更明确地呈现其所思之景。

one. Now we are in front of this selection of drawings by Olin. What do we expect for? John Berger asserts that the search for meaning is behind every act of looking[5]. If our assumption places observation in the center of Olin's drawings, then our expectation of the meanings is revealed in the overlapped eyes — the search by the draughtsman and the search by the spectator. We are interested in what captures the eye and where he puts the spotlight and hence to understand how he receives the surrounding landscape and his reflection of the landscape through drawing. With these expectations, we attempt to revisit this almost invisible process of draw-ing behind Olin's drawings. Our approach to this underlying message relies on three particular concentrations: the factual versus the presented circumstance, the narrative of drawings through the perspective and figurative compositions, and the intention behind strokes.

2.3 The Factual versus the Presented Circumstance

In a conversation with William Whitaker at the exhibition, Olin stated that drawing (to him) is a medium of observation, "drawing is to observe, acknowledge, and absorb." Most of Olin's drawings, particularly the ones from his sketchbook, are drawn in situ, which suggests that drawing is more than visual

1. 画作《普罗旺斯里巴斯》
2. 画作《翁布里亚托迪》

1. Ribas, Provence
2. Todi, Umbria

3. 画作《多利亚·潘菲利庄园》，2008年绘于罗马

3. *Villa Doria Pamphili*, Rome, 2008

documentation but as an immersive experience of perceiving the surrounding sounds, the scents, the lights, and the feeling of temperature and humidity. This richness of contextual information from the permeating landscape is presented in Olin's sketchbooks in a selective and distilled manner. Unlike the camera film that honestly captures light passing through lens and shutter, movements of the drawing hand do not trace the reality in the same way. Instead, they often follow the selection from the mind. We assume an intentional reduction of the circumstance is adopted in Olin's drawings in order to present something more explicitly.

Some distinct reductions are noticeable — ample space reserved from the lush woods and shrubs, or vast Italian plaza and lawn exposed in the warm glare with a few stubbles or hints of pavers (Fig. 1, 2). Nonetheless, one should recognize these withholds are made on purpose to present the distilled facts without being distracted with overwhelming details. In effect, the blank space always invites the spectator to fill with their own search and imagination. With some sporadic strokes and lines provided as clues in adjacency, the spectator is encouraged to search the contextual interrelationships drawn out from the circumstance.

However, not all reductions in the drawings are explicit. Here a relatively large format of ochres chalk sketch depicts an overlook from the terrace of campo downward to the pond and parterre in Giardino Segreto (secret garden) of Villa Doria Pamphili (Fig. 3). This is not an easy perspective to capture, as the prospect is manifold. In the center of the reflective pond, an erect swamp cypress (*Taxodium distichum*) punches the ceiling of the tableau. Through the graceful branches and twigs, it unfolds an airy depiction of the sixteenth-century fashion maze garden flanking the façade of Casino. The springy lines scribble through the Palladian motifs of the pedimented windows and the volume of low-clipped hedges, and never languish nor omit any components, such as the haut-reliefs above the cornice and the alignment of citrus pots. From the parterre, one has a glimpse of the clouding stone pines (*Pinus pinea*) rising over the exuberant bushes and palm trees (*Trachycarpus fortunei*) in the far end of the secret garden. Now if we withdraw our look from the distant background to the tall swamp cypress, we could fathom why the withered-appearing tree looks so out of season. The draughtsman chose to present the naked and drooping branches to compose a deeper pictorial space whereas depict the delicate rustling leaves on the tip to indicate its factual vitality and species. Here we could possibly conclude that the implicit arrangement sacrifices the actual appearance

其中一些省略较为明显——例如，在一片茂密葱翠的树林与灌木丛中大块留白，抑或在艳阳下宽阔的意大利广场与草坪中仅点缀以零星的草株和铺装（图1，2）。但观者应当意识到，这些在表达上的保留乃绘者有意为之，对事实之景进行概括和提炼，从而避免对次要细节着墨过多。实际上，留白总能引导观者填补其个人期待与想象。绘者以零星的笔触和线条在留白间埋下伏笔，鼓励观者大胆追寻此情此景间的文脉。

然而，并非所有省略都如此直白。在这幅较大画幅的赭石色粉笔速写中，欧林描绘了一个从多利亚·潘菲利庄园的露台俯瞰秘密花园中水池与花圃的视野（图3）。这一多层次叠合的视角透视复杂，不易拿捏。一棵落羽杉（*Taxodium distichum*）挺立在明镜般的水池中央，树梢都快刺破画面顶端。笔触在婀娜的枝桠间穿过，轻快地呈现出府邸一侧风行于16世纪的迷宫花园。柔韧紧凑的线条扫过建筑立面上帕拉迪奥母题的窗饰和花园里修剪整齐的矮树篱，笔触既不滞留一处，也不忽略任何（建筑与花园的）要素——如檐口上方的高浮雕和花圃里排放整齐的柑橘盆栽。从花圃望去，观者得以瞥见远处秘密花园另一端冠盖如云的意大利五针松（*Pinus pinea*）从郁郁葱葱的灌木丛和棕榈（*Trachycarpus fortunei*）间升起。现在，若将视线从背景落回到近处

4. 画作《罗马纳沃那广场"四河喷泉"》
5. 画作《卢森堡公园》

4. *Four Rivers, Piazza Navona, Rome*
5. *Jardin du Luxembourg*

高大的落羽杉上,我们便能明白绘者将此树刻画得如此凋萎及不合时宜的缘由。欧林在此处选择性地呈现了裸秃而低垂的枝条以实现一个具有深邃视野的绘图空间,同时通过刻画树顶部婆娑的羽叶来表明其在事实之景中的活力与物种特征。这里笔者可以初步得出结论:绘者在此画中含蓄地省略了落羽杉的真实形态,以呈现一个更为重要的洞察——在视野中,远处富于自然面貌的英国园林与中景秘密花园内精美的矫饰主义花圃之间形成了完美对比。

有趣的是,省略手法在景观手绘中的运用还能让设计师发现和思考所观对象的形式生成。笔者在欧林的速写本中发现了一个耐人寻味的例子——一幅关于吉安·洛伦索·贝尔尼尼雕塑作品"四河喷泉"的钢笔速写(图4),这一雕塑以对自然的拟人化刻画著称。绘者的目光专注于石灰华基座和四位河神巨大的大理石雕像,而将置于雕塑顶部的方尖碑弃于画面之外。紧邻位于画面中央的河神,欧林快速勾画了一系列微缩的(也可能是从更远视点观察的)雕塑速写,一个比一个舍弃更多细节,直至最终以简洁的草图呈现出扭转的石块体量。绘者在创作的过程中探求了这一动人的巴洛克喷泉的最初概念,这一逐步提炼的过程多么富有感染力和启发性!从一开始对四位河神的阳刚之气以及基石上明暗关系的仔细刻画,到最终草图中四个人体在整个喷泉的动态"旋涡"中被略去,这幅速写呈现了对雕塑动态构成本质的有序有法的探究过程。

2.4 叙事性的景观构图

生生不息的景观自然地呈现在绘者眼前,而绘者则沉浸于对此情此景的感受之中——这一感知和表达的过程需要通过时间去将多维的感知表现在绘图板上。从笔尖接触画面的一瞬间开始,表现过程便紧

of the swamp cypress to reveal a more important discovery: the perfect contrast between the more natural-appearing English Garden in the background and the delicate Mannerist parterre in the secret garden.

Interestingly, this act of reduction allows the designer to discover and reflect on the form of an object in the landscape. Here is a fascinating example we find in Olin's sketchbook — an ink sketch of the famous personification of nature, Gian Lorenzo Bernini's stunning fountain *Quattro Fiumi* (*Four Rivers*) (Fig. 4). The draughtsman's eyes are fixed on the travertine base and culls the marble bodies of four gigantic river deities from the obelisk perched atop the sculpture. Next to the central deity of the drawing, Olin included another three sequential sketches with each a smaller scale or perhaps from a farther distanced vantage point, removing more details one after another, until eventually a brief scribble of the twisting volumes of the rock. How inspiring it is to see this sequential process of distillation, through which the draughtsman sought to grasp the original concept of this spectacular baroque fountain. From an initial careful depiction of the masculinity of the four gods and light and shade of the rock base to the last sketch with the four figures omitted in the holistic vortex of the fountain, the sketch presents a sequential and methodical search that approaches the essential dynamism of the sculptural components.

2.4 The Composition as Storytelling

The living landscape presents itself in front of the draughtsman's eyes, and the latter is immersed in the reception of such scenes, which requires time to seize the perception and expression within the specified dimensions of a drawing pad. From the very moment when the tip of the tool touches the surface of the paper, the process of representation pivots on the visual narrative of the story. As the eye rolling from here to

② 本文将修辞构图运用于手绘实践是受到德·塞尔托的启发。德·塞尔托在介绍将行走作为一种创造性的空间行为（"脚印的构成艺术"）时，借用了诗歌文学中"文体修辞"的概念。提喻与连词缺省是德·塞尔托着重强调的修辞，他将二者分别与行走体验相比较，用以解释语言与文学结构如何在象征层面展现出"（语言与空间实践的）存在与作用方式"（来源：参考文献[7]）。

② The idea of figurative composition in drawing practice is inspired from de Certeau's borrowing of the "stylistic figures" in poetry to introduce his idea of walking as a creative spatial practice, "an art of composing a path." The two particular figures, synecdoche and asyndeton, are highlighted and compared with the walking experience by de Certeau to indicate how the linguistic and literary structure manifests "the way of being and operating" (of the verbal and spatial practice) at a symbolic level (Source: Ref. [7]).

随视觉叙事而动。目光流转之处，俯仰天地之间，我们通过丰沛的周身知觉来与身边的情景相交融。"我们并非先看到世界，而后再听到、嗅到或触碰到它"[6]——对景观的联觉感知在同一时间共同涌现，而非框定于一块凝固的背景帷幕上。因此，对于绘者而言，最大的挑战莫过于将感知到的在时空中持续流动的景观重新呈现在有限的画纸内。

故而，构图乃是一种关于绘者所观之景的叙事过程，并为观者探寻绘者目光流转的观察过程提供了线索。这里我们看到一幅宁静祥和的巴黎卢森堡公园水彩速写（图5）。修剪后树冠低矮的七叶树（Aesculus hippocastanum）占据了将近一半合页画面。苍翠欲滴的肥枝大叶以整簇的笔触铺陈开来，有如成群的银鱼在炫目的日光中闪烁着不同明暗的绿色，在细石子铺地上洒下慵懒而迷人的树荫。此画的构图可以从两个维度进行解读。垂直维度上，绘者略去了高大七叶树阵的树梢以及苍白大理石雕像的上部，让透光而弥漫的绿色树冠营造出一个宜人的公共集会场所——树冠的底部正与雕塑基座的饰带平齐。富于生机的生活场景被浓缩在这一由树冠和铺地清晰勾勒出的尺度怡人的空间中，将观者的目光导向躺坐着的人们；水平维度上，从左至右，绘者观察并捕捉到了处在不同景深中的休憩和交谈的人们。从前景中铜绿色椅子上躺着的一对男女，到背景中在固定长凳和可移动座椅上聊天的人们，画面记录了人的身体和城市座椅贴合的多种可能，描绘出一段城市花园中悠闲宁静的时光。这一构图方式着重表现了园艺设计如何塑造城市公园景观，反过来也表明了城市空间如何被公众自主使用。

欧林手绘作品中运用的多种构图思路蕴含了绘画过程中多样的可能性——从对叙事的掌控到持续不断的观察与分析。包括卢森堡公园水彩速写在内的多数手绘以一种传统的透视构图来表现所观之景，而另外一部分画作则代表了一种富于艺术创造性的探究，以一种摒弃传统透视的修辞构图②来探索景观。

对比诗歌中的修辞手法，我们可以更好地理解此处笔者所谓的"修辞构图"及其背后的叙事意图。米歇尔·德·塞尔托将行走看作

there, from the touch of the firm ground to a gust of head-on soft wind, we engage with the encompassing landscape in a flux of embodied senses. "We do not see the world and then hear it or smell it or touch it"[6] — this synesthetic perception of the permeating landscape comes all together at a time, never being something framed in a frozen backdrop. Therefore, not least of the great challenges for the draughtsman is to compose the perceived duration and the movement of a landscape within a defined sheet of paper.

A composition is, therefore, the storytelling of what the draughtsman sees, providing clues for the trajectory of the moving eye and the process of observation. Here presents a placid watercolor of Jardin du Luxembourg (Luxembourg Garden) (Fig. 5). Less than half of the facing tableaux are filled with the chunky, low-clipped canopies of horse chestnut trees (*Aesculus hippocastanum*). The thick and verdant leaves are spreading in multiple clusters of palpable strokes like an enormous herd of glitter fish, shining in the faint sunlight through different shades of green while casting mesmerising shades on the crushed gravel. The composition can be read from two dimensions. Vertically, the draughtsman clips the tops of the towering horse chestnut trees and the pale marble statuary. A light-penetrable and permeating green canopy defines a comfortable gathering space, with its bottom aligned to the pedestal's frieze. The living landscape is compressed into a tightly framed, intimate space between the treetops and ground plain, directing the viewer's gaze to the seated figures. Horizontally, from left to right, the draughtsman observes then captures people resting and socializing at varying depths. From the couple in the foreground reposing in the verdigris lounge chair, to the people in the background chatting on the fixed benches and flexible metal chairs, the image depicts many ways of body engagement with the seating and describes a peaceful moment in the garden. This compositional decision emphasizes particularly how the landscape is shaped by strategic horticultural design, which in turn informs how space is used spontaneously by the public.

Olin's drawing encompasses a multitude of compositional decisions that reflect abundant possibilities within the act of drawing, from the mastering of storytelling, to unrelenting dedication to observation and analysis. Most of the drawings, like the watercolor sketch from Luxembourg Garden, represent the observed landscape with a conventional perspectival approach, while other drawings are representative of the artistic searching and exploring place through figurative composition② and disregard for the perspectival tradition.

A comparison with the rhetoric in poetry will shed some

5 © Laurie Olin

一种空间艺术性表达，为了诠释这一概念，他引入了演说与诗歌中的语言学概念——文体修辞，并认为，正如演说中区别于事实陈述的具有象征意义的修辞手法一样，对步行的修辞表达体现了行走体验中空间风格的变化，这种变化由行人自身的行走风格产生，且和实际空间有别。[7]

德·塞尔托的这一有关行走与文字之间修辞运用的横向比较很有启发意义。如果富有感染力的修辞能让讲述者超越平铺直叙进行更加生动的表达，那么将这一修辞运用到绘画构图中也是适宜的——由此，笔者所谓的"修辞构图"便可充分运用于表现独到的景观视野以及个人对所观之景的洞见与体悟上。

与前述手绘表现中具象的省略和留白类似，修辞构图通过个人对景观的领会对事实之景进行转译和诠释，使绘者得以传递传统学院派透视构图所无法捕捉和表达的内容。因此，面对这一非传统透视构图，我们需要对画作进行诗意的解读，通过这种解读，观者或许能领会那些所见之外的情景与持续凝结在画面中的时空——由此，观者可以从二维的景观表现中再现绘者彼时将观察进行概括和提炼的过程。然而，这并不意味着运用了修辞构图的手绘作品就一定是象征性的、远离现实的，恰恰相反，源于文学修辞的修辞构图填补了观者与绘者之间的时空鸿沟。修辞构图可使观者身处真实可感的沉浸式环境中。

德·塞尔托强调了两种诗歌中基本的文体修辞：提喻法（指用一个部分或一个特殊的描述物来代表整体或用整体代表部分）和连词缺省（指不同的部分在连词缺失的情况下并列呈现在一起）。当我们将这两种文学性建构置于绘画的语境中，第一种修辞即将视野中的景观隐喻地构成在画面上，例如近距离细致描绘一朵标志着无垠野草甸和乡间景象的罂粟花（*Papaver somniferum*）；第二种修辞则是对景观中情境转换与必要过渡信息的刻意省略，从而呈现所见之外的内容，例如将"此间"与"彼处"、"当下"与"过往"的景观并置于同一张画作中。有趣的是，这两种修辞构图频繁出现于欧林游历英国时的手绘中。

一个可供观者寻味的例子是一幅乡间小径的速写。画作竖向构图，一只丰满的雏燕和切过小径穿过栅栏的木阶梯清晰地上下并列呈现（图6）。这两个不同尺度的对象未经场景变换或任何过渡性背景提示即被直接并置于一幅画作之中。二者都可见于英国巴克兰乡间田野，它们共同讲述了当地农业景观和乡村发展的历史。正如欧林在画作的补充文字中所言，燕子（*Hirundo rustica*）"在英国民谣和文学作品中常被视为自由的象征"，也代表了其他在乡村私有农田间飞来飞去的本土鸟类，如知更鸟（*Erithacus rubecula*）和云雀（*Alauda arvensis*）[8]。这些大自然中生性自由、无忧无虑的鸟类与小径、栅栏、

more light on this second category of composition and the draughtsman's intention behind this narrative of drawing. To construe his idea of walking as a creative spatial expression, Michel de Certeau introduced the linguistic concept of "stylistic figures" from speech and poem, arguing that the figures of pedestrian rhetoric provides a stylistic metamorphosis of space in walking experience — like the use of figures in processing of the symbolic other than the actual fact in speech.[7]

This comparison between the stylistic operating of steps and words is inspirational. If the affective use of stylistic figures allows the storyteller to express the meaning in a broader context beyond the normal structure of words, it is also possible to appropriate this rhetoric to drawing composition — thence what we call "figurative composition" can be comprehensibly adopted to represent a unique sight and personal insights from the landscape observed.

Similar to the representational reductions, these figurative compositions distort the actual prospect according to the personal apprehension of the landscape, which allows the draughtsman to deliver what cannot be captured from academic perspectival composition. Therefore, it requires a poetic reading of drawing, through which the spectator could possibly apprehend the almost invisible contextual message and the crystallized duration in the field — one can, therefore, seek to revisit the encapsulated process of observation from a two-dimensional representation. However, this is not to say these drawings with figurative composition are symbolic and hence distanced from reality. On the contrary, the figurative composition inspired from literary figures closes the gap between the spectator's gaze and the draughtsman's reception. The latter is presumably palpable and immersive.

De Certeau highlighted two fundamental stylistic figures in poetry: synecdoche (where a part or a special is used for representing the general and vice versa) and asyndeton (where the parts are juxtaposed in the absence of conjunctions). To situate these two literary constructs in the discourse of drawing, the first figure can be understood as an analogical composing of the landscape in sight, for instance — a detail depiction of an emblematic poppy flower (*Papaver somniferum*) to represent the vast wild meadow in the country; the second figure is elliptical in providing contextual transition or necessary visual conjunction within the landscape observed, which allows the invisible to speak, for example — a juxtaposition of "here" and "there," "now" and "then," in the same drawing. Interestingly, these two manners of figurative composition can be frequently found in Olin's drawings from his trips in England.

One appreciable example here is a sketch of footpaths

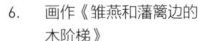

6. 画作《雏燕和藩篱边的木阶梯》

6. *A Young Swallow and a Stile*

篱墙和灌木树篱等用于划分物权、界定田地、阻断非法侵入的人工构筑物形成了对比。在画面的下半部分，一小段连续的木栅栏横在一条通往牧场或麦地的田间小路上，划出了一条清晰的产权边界。栅栏代表曾经的争议达成了共识——这条边界很可能曾在数十年间不断变迁，代表一种由当地农民维系的自然之熵不断叠加的秩序。但这架乡间简易自制的木阶梯如同"一个公共通道的象征"[8]，为人类（并非为牲畜）提供了某种游离于边界之间的灵活性。

修辞构图手法的使用为观者解读画作的文脉信息，甚至重现绘者的观察过程创造了更多可能。观者就这幅手绘的欣赏可以始于一系列追问：为何选择田间的燕子与阶梯作为描绘对象？又为何略去二者之间的环境信息？从中我们也许可以理解绘者的注意力是如何从固定的人工设施转移到动态的自然造化，进而感知英国乡间的社会习俗、严格的私产界定和保护，以及当地人经年累月含辛茹苦的耕种畜牧。在欧林于英国旅行途中创作的其他手绘中，修辞构图手法的运用不胜枚举——绿篱与编条篱墙的比较解读、移动的牧群与白云苍狗之间的联想，以及对麦地里野花的形态细节与麦田全景的并置描绘——所有这些构图都体现了绘画过程中绘者对于当地及地域景观情境的呼应性解读。

2.5 笔触和质感背后的意图

在绘画的过程中，要想在图面上实时呈现对景观的观察，既要求绘者要有敏锐的洞察力，又要求绘者有娴熟的手上功夫。手的移动和

crossing the land. The drawing is in a portrait format, with two parts composed together plainly — a chubby young swallow and a wood stile at a fence cutting the footpath (Fig. 6). The two objects are depicted at different scales yet juxtaposed together without a change of scene or any hints of a transitional background. Both two objects are found in the fields in Buckland, sharing the same agricultural landscape and history of the rural development. As Olin states in his complemental texts to the drawing, the swallow (*Hirundo rustica*) is "often used as a symbol of individual freedom in English folk songs and literature," representing other native birds, like red robin (*Erithacus rubecula*) and lark (*Alauda arvensis*), flying here and there over the private farmlands and properties.[8] The wayward behavior of these unfettered creatures from nature contrasts with the footpaths, fences, palisades, and hedgerows which delineate legal ownership of lands and properties and prevent the wrongful trespass. Here, at the lower part of the drawing, a small portion of the continuous post-and-rail wooden fence cuts across a small footpath entering the pastureland or barley field, drawing a clear line between the two sides of the ownership. A fence represents an agreement of contestation, presumably changing and shifting for years and decades, a superimposing order from farmer's maintenance on natural entropy. However, a bricolage of stile, "a symbol of public access,"[8] offers some flexibilities for humans — not for livestock.

The draughtsman uses the figurative composition to infer greater possibilities for the spectator to read the contextual information, and to review the process of observation as well. We can start with questioning ourselves the selective presenting of the swallow and the stile from the landscape and the ellipsis of the rest of the circumstance, from which we might seek to understand the draughtsman's changing focus from the steady human device to the movement of natural creation, to further acknowledge the social protocols and strict sense of ownership and protection in the English countryside, along with their struggles and efforts of cultivation and animal husbandry. There are various other similar adoptions of the figurative composition, including the comparative reading of living fence and wattle fence, the association between the moving herds and the caprice of clouds, the careful observation on the wildflower morphologies abut to the panorama of the same barley field — all encourage the critical intertextual and contextual analysis of the local and regional landscape through drawing.

2.5 The Intention behind Strokes and Textures

As we have discussed in the process of draw-ing, the coordination between the observation of landscape and its

手腕的弯曲度掌控着画笔与媒介间的接触，线条由此自然流出。在这一过程中，绘者对景观的感知融于恰当的笔触与质感中。而观者所接收到的则是景观的"二次体验"。在有关艺术与知识创造的古典语境中，这一体验不仅经由纯熟的绘画技巧塑造和演绎，更通过绘者个人的技艺[3]去吸收和解读"一次体验"中的深层含义。从这个角度来看，手绘是一项智力活动，其所要求的具体能力不可简化为一种技能训练。这里对笔触背后可能意图的推敲并行于对绘画应用技巧的理解。

能够欣赏一幅画作如何通过生动的笔触和富于表现力的手法来表现所描绘的对象始终是一种乐趣。在一些难得的瞬间，观者几乎能感受到画笔的脉动与节奏。但是，要想明确绘者缘何以某种方式作画，通常比弄清其所使用的技巧类型更加困难。在此问题下，我们应开展更为深入细致的研究，以对欧林不断发展的手绘技艺及其习得与运用进行更为连贯和整体性的理解。碍于篇幅，本文仅给出一些例证来阐述笔者对于笔法技巧背后绘者心理的揣测。

在欧林众多的手绘笔法中——疾行、逆锋、停顿、游丝、湿抹（用手指）、枯笔（用旧笔）——这些多样的墨迹构成了欧林在西北太平洋沿岸的一系列手绘作品，涵盖山海湖谷、近海岛屿，以及迷雾

almost simultaneous representation on paper demands for both the keen eye and practised hand. Driven by movements of the hand and twists of the wrist, lines flow out through the controlled touch between the tool and the medium. In this process, the draughtsman's reception is resolved in the right strokes and textures. Received by the spectator is only a secondary experience of landscape, which, however, in a context of art and knowledge, has been formed and performed with skills and techniques as well as by the draughtsman's personal techne[3] to absorb and disclose the latent information and meanings in what he or she sees primarily. At this point, the intellectual activity of draw-ing requires specific skills that cannot be simplified into technical training. A consideration of intention behind the frozen strokes hereby goes in parallel to understand how the skills of drawing are applied.

It is always an enjoyment to see how the object is expressively represented with animated strokes and vivid portrayal. In such lucky encounters, the spectator could almost feel the impulse and tempo of the pen. However, to determine why the draughtsman draws in a certain way is often more difficult than figuring out what type of skills he or she has used. Further close studies under this task are necessary to present a more coherent and holistic understanding of Olin's acquiring, adopting, and operating of an evolving palette of drawing skills. Hereby, we give some exemplifications that we have drawn our conjectures to enter the draughtsman's possible psyche behind the operation of skills.

Among Olin's expansive breadth of skills — running, dragging, lingering, fine tress, wet smear, moistureless scribble — these monochrome patterns of ink movements constitute a series of drawings from the Pacific Northwest with unique geography of mountains and sea, lakes and canyons, offshore islands and

[3] 笔者在此处引用希腊语"techne"（通常在英文中被简化翻译为"艺术"或"手艺"，但事实上，其涉及人类创作与求知的更广泛含义，特别是可以通过它来揭示自然的本质）是为了区别于"技术"（technique，源于希腊语"teckhnikos"）一词，以此强调对景观手绘的认识不能只停留在手上功夫，认为它只是一种工具化的技巧和手段，而必须理解其具有洞察和探究的意图。关于对这两个术语的深刻区别，另见马丁·海德格尔撰写的《对技术的追问》一文（来源：参考文献[9]）。

[3] By using the Greek word "techne" (often translated simply in English as "art" or "craft", however, referring to a broad sense of human capacity of making and knowing, particularly in a relation to unveil nature, or physis), we intend to distinguish from the word "technique," which is derived from the Greek word "teckhnikos," in order to argue that drawing skills should not be considered merely the techniques or instrumentalities to acquire, but with intent to see and to know. The differentiation between the two words draws upon Martin Heidegger's essay The Question Concerning Technology (Source: Ref. [9]).

7. 华盛顿海岸线折本速写《清晨的新月湖》，绘于2009年
8. 华盛顿海岸线折本速写景象：从位于奥林匹克国家公园红宝石海滩的艾比岛上方的山顶向北望，绘于2009年。

7. Washington coast folding sketch — *Lake Crescent, Early Morning*, 2009
8. Washington coast folding sketch — Looking North up the Crest past the Abby Island (at Ruby Beach in the Olympic National Park), 2009.

雨林等独特地理类型。这卷折本水墨速写从一幅夏季清晨新月湖的景色展开（图7）。这不是一幅精致细腻的手绘。从轻快的笔触中，可以看出绘者下笔迅速。没有过多的细节，绘者勾勒出层叠山脉的起伏轮廓，更多着墨于漫山针叶林的明暗层次，凸显了湖面的清澈与宁静。

通过少量的着墨，线条与质感间的刻意对比有效拉开了景深。西海岸成年花旗松（*Pseudotsuga menziesii*）的浓粗枝叶以浓墨点甩的手法呈现，为画面提供了一个框架。为了表现近山针叶林的质感，绘者简洁地描绘了高耸的树干与层叠的水平枝叶，在单棵树形的抓取与丛生植物群落的表现之间取得了很好的平衡。视线延伸之处，温带雨林的质感从粗重的笔触显著变化为有层次的锯齿状线条，以强调林冠层的垂直机理。同时，观者亦可注意到绘者运用笔触提速和笔尖轻提的手法（很可能是通过旋转笔尖的角度或者换用一根快干了的针管笔）来表现空间的远近和山坡的朝向。从前景的黑到中景的灰，不断变化的笔触终于远山的留白。这些表现手法呈现出一幅引人入胜的画面，在某种程度上可以说，这是欧林在湖岸获得的"一次体验"。

欧林在此折本第一幅速写中惯用的笔触在随后西北海岸线景观的序列手绘中得到了延续——舒展而低沉的云、苍白而斜倚的峭壁和离岛、堆叠的树家、散落的嶙峋怪石和砂砾（图8）。先前用于描绘轻薄云彩的技法再次应用于表现潮涨潮落。这些微妙的笔触变化生发于一套连贯而流畅的笔法，将当地的气象、地质和生态捕捉联结于纸面的方寸之间，使西海岸的原始景观变得触手可及。依笔者所见，通过这一系列笔法不仅可以推断自然栖息地间的相互关系，还可以揭示绘者从自然形态中观察到的内在冲动与生命力。绘者可能忽略了沙滩上的阴影和机理，因此并未在图面上有所体现。与此同时，绘者可能将注意力集中于掌握岩石与乱木的形态与特质上。通过娴熟掌控画笔的徐疾，绘者以笔触的移动精练地记录下了他与景观在那一时刻的对话。

foggy rainforest. Here a folding scroll of ink sketches starts with a horizontal vista of Lake Crescent early in the summer morning (Fig. 7). It is not a delicate illustration. From the brisk strokes, one can tell that the tempo is quite fleeting. Without many depictions of detail, the draughtsman outlines the undulating profiles of layered mountains, placing more ink in varying shades of the predominant conifers, accentuating the serene reflection in the lucid lake.

The intentional contrast between the lines and textures effectively distorts the depth of the view without a massive flow of ink. Characterized with dashing of thick ink, the shaggy branches of the mature coast Douglas-firs (*Pseudotsuga menziesii*) provide a frame for the foreground. The texture of the conifer forest on the near mountain is expressively represented with brief denotations of the towering trunks and stacks of lateral brunches — a well-handled balance between the discernible morphology of individual Pinus and the dense clustering of plant life. Where the sight extends, the texture of the temperate rain forest changes dramatically from thick strokes into a layering of toothy lines to emphasize the verticality of the forest canopies. At the same time, the spectator can notice the intentional acceleration of tempo, the pen tiptoes (very likely by twisting the angle or using another moistureless pigment liner) to depict the distance and aspect of the slope. The changing technique — from the foreground depicted in black to the mid-ground scribbles in grey — ends in the background where the mountains are outlined with reserve. The representational techniques offer an inviting prospect, which we might say, in a certain likelihood, is the primary experience Olin received at the lakeshore.

This proclivity of strokes and scribbles continues in the sequential sketches of the North-western shoreline landscape — stretched, condensed clouds, tumbling pale cliffs and offshore islands, piles of thickly fallen trees, stacks of grotesque rocks and eroded detritus (Fig. 8). The same sweeps of gossamer for the elongated clouds are extrapolated again to describe the swing of the wave and foam. These subtle inflexions born from a consistent, fluent stroke language draw together meteorology, geology, and biology, contributing to the palpable presence of a primordial landscape. Not only inferring the interrelationships within the natural habitat, this stroke pattern, as we read, also reveals the inherent momentum and impulse of what the draughtsman sees in the forms shaped by natural forces. The shadow and texture on the sand are presumably neglected by the eye, hence reserved by the hand. Very likely that the draughtsman's attention was fixed on grasping the morphology and personality of the rocks and logs. Through the fine skills of pause and run, the draughtsman uses the movement of strokes to concisely record his conversation with the landscape at a precise moment in time.

3 The Practice of Drawing and Observation

Draw-ing is interactive, and the analytical reading of drawing, as previously discussed in this paper, seeks to communicate to this invisible process. How can we enter the psyche of the designer through analyzing drawing and drawing? One possible access is through text, the annotation in the drawing.

Olin draws during travel, and often he writes and composes text directly within the drawing as a whole. Some of the text are notes with factual, intended to record Olin's observations. These notes include descriptions of temporal sensations, such as the note here from his Luxembourg Garden sketch: "A beautiful day, temperature seventy, blue sky with clouds moving all day." The notes on temperature and atmosphere can quickly place the spectator into this visual and sensorial imagination so that they may share the feeling virtually. Other factual notes provide clues into Olin's observation of the landscape and present the findings in sequence as small vignettes in the composition. In the Pompidou sketch (Fig. 9), one may presume that Olin began the drawing with a sketch primarily of the fountain at the Pompidou Center. The central sketch illustrates factual information of the fountain, the sculpture inside the fountain, the people near the fountain, and the crowds and buildings in the background. He continued to analyze the plaza via annotated plan, section and fountain details (ideal drainage of sorts). These complimentary

9. 画作《蓬皮杜速写》，绘于1997年
10. 画作《农场、废墟、荒野》

9. *Pompidou Sketch*, 1997
10. *A Farm, a Ruin, a Rampant Nature*

3 手绘与观察的实践

手绘是一个交流的过程，如前文所述，对于画作的分析解读即是对绘者背后创作过程的探寻。我们应当如何通过分析手绘及手绘过程进入绘者的精神世界？一种可行的方式是通过文字，即手绘上的标注。

欧林在旅途中的手绘经常会辅以文字注释。其中一些文字是事实类注释，旨在记录自身观察。这类注释也包括即时感受的描写，比如他在卢森堡公园手绘中记录的文字："美好的一天，气温21℃，云朵终日在蓝天上漂浮"。关于温度与氛围的文字注释可以快速将观者置入充满画面感的想象之中，观者几乎可以与绘者分享感官体验。其他事实类注释包括欧林观察记录的小插图，插图的顺序揭示了欧林观察方式的线索。在关于蓬皮杜的速写中（图9），可以认为欧林的手绘主要从蓬皮杜中心喷泉的速写开始。画面中央描绘了喷泉、喷泉中的雕塑、聚集在喷泉周围的人，以及背景中人群和建筑的事实信息。紧接着，欧林继续通过绘制带有标注的平面图、剖面图以及喷泉的细节（理想的排水等）对蓬皮杜中心广场进行分析。这些辅助的小图既是透视速写构图的组成部分，亦以图解形式清晰地展现了欧林的分析过程。通过观察、思考、手绘和分析，欧林将喷泉置入城市街区、地形环境、空间活动、社交活动，以及设计构造的情境之中。这一页的手绘（或许可以看作一幅绘画）展现了对于空间的一种自发式观察方式，即审视"那里有什么"，并询问"它好在哪里"以及"为什么好"。

通过记录不可见的元素（例如氛围）或构图中被省略的元素，（绘画中的）文字为观者提供了一种更为直接的途径去解读手绘，同时记录并揭示了艺术家的精神世界。手绘中的注释实质上是邀请观者进入绘者的内心世界。那些具有描述性、即时性、情感性和背景阐述作用的文字可在观者和绘者/设计师之间建立共同的体验基础。

欧林关于将手绘作为观察媒介的观点还暗示了一种将手绘与专业实践相联系的途径。为了达成对欧林景观设计师身份的某种推测性理解，笔者尝试通过比较阅读来研究其手绘作品。相应地，笔者力求使欧林的手绘实践与其设计哲学的发展保持一致，并将这一不断演进的过程置于文化语境之中，同时将对其产生重要影响的时刻与人物关系一并考虑。由此，手绘成为连接欧林的批判性观察与专业实践的主体。在通过手绘探寻这一不断发展的过程时，相关研究本质上是检视内外部的观察与表达（景观的感知、内部的构造，以及外部的呈现）之间的协调性。此外，对欧林所受手绘训练及其发展过程的探索可为回顾景观设计学教学法有所启发——将对眼、手和思维进行训练的重要性与专业实践联系起来。

欧林的英国风景手绘已在前文中提及，人们可能会从这些画的绘画技法中看出其具有建筑学的教育背景。除建筑表现手法之外，欧林的作品还呈现出了更多外来的影响（图10）。在《穿过旷野》一书中可以看到很多具有倾斜视角的手绘作品。这些画作的背景被向前推，所描绘的事物在画面中被挤压。由于画面中的前景和中景的景深被压缩，致使画面变得更加扁平。这种倾斜透视手法使得画面中描绘的对象缺乏明确的主次，观者的目光因此得以在画面中漫游。在《穿过旷野》一书中，许多画作都通过不同比例的并置和大量留白的使用来进行构图和叙事。具体而言，在这幅野花手绘中，罂粟花和雏菊（*Bellis perennis*）占据了大部分画面，只留下页面底部窄窄一条用于描绘周边的草甸和形单影只

drawings are both compositional to the perspective sketch, as well as diagrammatic in which they clearly illustrate Olin's analytical process. Through observing, thinking, drawing, and analyzing, Olin contextualized the fountain in the city block, the topography, the program suggested by the space, the social activities, and design tectonics. The page, as one may refer as one drawing, demonstrates a spontaneous way of observing the place, reviewing "what is there," and asking "what is good about it" and "why it is good."

Text can be utilized to describe the act of drawing in an accessible manner, by including the invisible elements such as atmosphere or elements omitted from the composition. It records and reveals the artist's psychological state. Annotation in drawings essentially is an invitation for spectators to enter the draughtsman' / designer's inner world, by providing a descriptive, temporal, emotional, and contextual situation to form between speculator and draughtsman / designer an experiential common ground.

Olin's remark on drawing as a medium of observation also suggests a purposeful approach connecting drawing to professional practice. In an attempt to provide some speculative understanding of Olin's becoming of a landscape architect, we try to examine his drawing through comparative readings. Correspondingly, we seek to align Olin's drawing practice with the development of his design philosophy and to situate the evolving process in its cultural context with benchmarks on influential moments and figures. Draw-ing, therefore, becomes the subject connecting Olin's critical observation and professional practice. In searching for this evolving process through drawing, the research essentially looks at the coordination between observation and representation both internally and externally — how landscape is perceived, internally constructed, and externally represented. Moreover, the exploration for Olin's training and development can shed lights on reviewing the landscape architecture pedagogy, associating the significance of the cultivated eye, hand, and mind in professional practice.

Olin's drawings of the English landscape have been previously noted in this paper, and one may see these drawing techniques suggest background in architecture. In addition to the architectural rendering influence, Olin's work reveals further foreign influence (Fig. 10). Many drawings from *Across the Open Field* can be found with tilted perspective, in which the background is pushed forward until everything is compressed in the picture plane. The visual depth between the foreground and the middle ground is significantly reduced, which results in a flattened image. In such a way, there is no clear hierarchy

in the objects depicted, rather, it allows the eyes to wander in the drawing. Amongst the drawings from *Across the Open Field*, a juxtaposition of different scales and ample intentionally unfilled space are used frequently to create wise composition and narrative. Particularly, Olin's wildflower drawing depicts poppies and daisies (*Bellis perennis*) that dominate the plate with only a sliver of the surrounding meadow and solitary oaks (*Quercus palustris*) at the bottom of the composition (Fig. 11). The composition plays with the scale of the very large and the very small, creating a rather dynamic visual experience. Such techniques are commonly used in Chinese landscape scrolls and the wood prints from the Floating World of Edo. However, we argue that Olin did not intend to borrow these techniques from classical Chinese and Japanese representation to recreate the similar visual effect. Olin studied many ways of representation, but it is his skilful hand developed through drawing from life, that defines his approach to composition and narrative. It is not the image (from the eye) that one needs to learn, but the critical representation (the hand) that one should understand and absorb in order to create one's vision (the mind) (Fig. 12 ~ 14).

In the drawing of *Two Views to the Northwest from Buscot House*, the above portion depicts the vista looking over the ha-ha from a distant point, and the bottom portion is viewed from an elevated perspective, looking down and revealing the ha-ha (Fig. 12). Depending on how one views the drawing, whether from top-down or bottom-up, the image creates ascending or descending perception. The juxtaposition of the two compositions suggests movement, recreating the draughtsman's

11. 画作《麦田上永恒而宁静的野花——罂粟花和雏菊》
12. 画作《从巴斯考特大宅向西北望的两个视图》
13. 画作《奶牛山丘》所描绘的丘陵之景与在大片浅水池塘下的山坡上吃草的奶牛。
14. 画中为在宅子北部公园草坪上吃草的雄鹿,以及草坪上方的护栏栏杆。

11. *Timeless and Tranquil Wildflowers — Poppies and Daisies — in a Wheat Field*
12. *Two Views to the Northwest from Buscot House*
13. Up on the downs and cows grazing the hillside below the large dew pond on *Cow Down*.
14. A drawing of bucks grazing in the park north of the house in the meadow and parapet rail of the terrace above this meadow.

15. 墨水画《费尔班克斯的回忆》，1967年绘于纽约。该手绘收录于本次展览图录中。
16. 画作《小木屋》，1968年绘于阿默甘西特。该手绘收录于本次展览图录中。

15. *Fairbanks Memory* (an ink drawing), New York, 1967, from the "Drawing" exhibition catalogue.
16. *The Cabin*, Amagansett, 1968, from the "Drawing" exhibition catalogue.

的橡树（*Quercus palustris*）（图11）。这一构图在极大与极小的尺度间游走，创造出颇具动态的观画体验。这种技法常见于中国山水卷轴画和江户浮世绘木版画中。然而，笔者认为欧林并未打算从中国和日本的古典绘画中借鉴这些技法来重现类似的视觉效果。虽然欧林研习了诸多绘画表现手法，但其通过绘画生活训练出的艺术之手，定义了属于他个人的构图和叙事方式。艺术家要学习的并非图像画面（眼之所见），而是需要通过理解和吸收绘画中的关键性表达（手上功夫）来创造出可以展现艺术家构思（思想）的作品（图12~14）。

在《从巴斯考特大宅向西北望的两个视图》一画中，画面的上半部分描绘了从远处的视点略过隐垣所见的景致；画面下半部分则是从高处俯视所见的风景，从上向下的视角显露了隐垣（图12）。根据人们对画作自上而下或自下而上的浏览方式，图像会产生上升或下降的感觉。两种构图的并置呈现了一种动态，重现了绘者的空间体验。

对于欧林绘画所受影响的探索揭示了关键性的学习过程。艺术家需要通过持续的手绘练习不断训练手、眼、心在观察、分析和表达方面的协调性，以磨练出能够准确呈现艺术家理念的绘画技巧。

从此次建筑档案馆的画展中可以清楚地看出欧林手绘的变化。展览中展示了欧林一系列从20世纪60年代末到70年代初的墨水画，笔触松散，近乎抽象，与同期的英国风景手绘有很大不同（图15）。艺术家必须放弃对于精确的控制，才能用极少的笔画描绘出对象的形态特征。2018年10月8日，在画展的开幕活动上，欧林解释称这一系列的手绘是由树枝代笔蘸墨水绘制而成。虽然表达的目的不同，亨利·马蒂斯于20世纪50年代创作的《杂技演员》和布莱斯·马登受日本书法影响的"冷山"系列都采用了相似的绘画手法。对于欧林而言，他把这种绘画方式当作通过其他绘画媒介以打破自身"常态"的尝试。

在另一幅绘于20世纪60年代末的《小木屋》素描中，欧林选择性地描绘了阴影中的建筑和景观，在画面上留下了很大的留白空间（图16）。

spatial experience of place.

Discovering Olin's influences in drawing reveals the critical process of learning. Artists need to coordinate eye and mind into viewing, analyzing and infusing representation skills through the unceasingly practice of the hand, in order to develop the skill needed to accurately render the artist's vision.

The transformation of Olin's drawing is apparent in exhibition at the Architectural Archive. The show presented a series of very loose and mostly abstract ink drawings from the late 1960s to the early 1970s, greatly different from the English landscape drawings of the same period (Fig. 15). One must relinquish control and forfeit the ability to be precise in order to depict character of form with fewer strokes. During the exhibition reception in 8th October, 2018, Olin explained that the series of work was done using a stick with its tip dipped in ink. Both Henry Matisse's large drawing of *Acrobats* in the 1950s and Brice Marden's Cold Mountain series, which is influenced by Japanese calligraphy, have adapted similar drawing methods but for different purposes. For Olin, he called it as a way to break from his "norms" and to try out other mediums.

Looking at *The Cabin*, another drawing from the late 1960s, Olin drew the architecture and the landscape selectively only in the shade, creating substantial empty spaces on the plate (Fig. 16). However, the areas represented are described with great focus and

不过，他所刻画的部分笔触精细入微，可以看出花费了很多精力。安德鲁·怀斯同样也选择特定区域进行细致描画，而不会占满整个画面进行构图，画面的留白部分为观者提供了个人想象的空间，怀斯的许多关于农田和谷仓的速写也都运用了这一表现方式。在另一张木炭画《多利亚·潘菲利庄园》中，欧林以类似的方法，仅以描绘树干上的阴影的方式绘制了画面中心的树，故意忽略了树叶和大部分背景（图17）。与《小木屋》相比，这张木炭画的绘画表现方式明显不同，其笔触更加随意，但仍呈现出精细的描绘。本次展览呈现了欧林丰富的绘画媒介和表达技法，其在绘画上的实验性尝试和对于手的训练似乎从未停止。

然而，笔者认为展览中最具才气，或许也是最具多样性的作品是欧林在20世纪60年代至80年代初期间创作的一系列手绘。这些画作创作于欧林接受建筑教育以及他早期从事建筑及景观设计工作期间。在这一时期，欧林完成了大量用于捕捉和记录其所见所感的手绘，以为他的设计工作和设计理念提供助力。

手绘是景观设计师重要的训练实践，为了加深这一理解，我们必须思考欧林作为绘者和设计师的想法及其设计理念的形成。欧林在美国阿拉斯加州长大，之后举家搬迁并在多个城市居住过，对于不同的城市景观，他一直饶有兴趣。他不仅观察身边的生活环境并随手记录，还积极融入到当地人之中。1958年，即在西雅图华盛顿大学建筑学院学习的第二年，欧林才开始学习景观设计，当时他的一门设计课由著名景观设计师理查德·哈格执教。欧林在华盛顿大学接受了布扎体系建筑教育，并接受了哈格的一些景观设计教育。不要忘记，那时

exquisitely precise stroke. Andrew Wyeth, too, had drawn in selected focus areas instead of a fully composed plate (Wyeth has many field sketches of barns and farms which can see this techinique), in which the empty space provides room for the spectator to fill with personal imagination. In another charcoal drawing *Villa Doria Pamphilli*, the central tree is drawn in the similar technique by including only the shadow on the truck, where Olin intentionally neglects the foliage and most of the background (Fig. 17). Compared to *The Cabin* drawing, the charcoal depiction is notably different, in which the strokes are much more loose yet still show great attention and precise depiction. The exhibition has presented a great diversity in the medium and technique acquired by Olin. Olin's experiment and training of the hand never seem to have stopped.

However, we argue that the most intellectual and perhaps the most diverse selection of drawings from the exhibition were created between the 1960s to the early 1980s, and it was during Olin's architectural education and early practice in architecture and landscape architecture, wherein he produced a great amount of drawings, which were used to capture and record his observations and to aid in his considerable design work and philosophy.

In order to deepen the understanding of draw-ing as critical training and practice for a landscape architect, we must consider the development of Olin's design philosophy, the mind of the draughtsman and designer. Growing up in Alaska and having moved and lived in multiple cities, Olin had always been interested in the landscape — through being in and observing the landscape, drawing the landscape, and always engaging with the people who live there. Olin did not study landscape architecture until his second year of architecture school at the University of Washington in Seattle in 1958 when he had a studio taught by the famous landscape architect Richard Haag. He received a Beaux-Arts training at the University of Washington, and some landscape architecture training with Richard Haag. Although not to forget that it was the 1960s' golden period of Modern gardens on the West Coast, with designers such as Thomas Church, Garrett Eckbo, and Bob Royston having strong presence in design schools. Given Haag's Mid-western background, we can certainly guess that Haag must had recommended Olin to read John B. Jackson's works on vernacular American landscape and cultural landscape on which Olin already had lots of curiosities. Later Olin also worked for Haag for several years. It was the time when both Beaux-Arts and Bauhaus training coexisted in the architecture school at the University of Washington. Olin has received the traditional fine art training in drawing and architectural design in addition to studies in modern arts, music and poetry.

After graduated with degree in Architecture, Olin practiced

17. 画作《多利亚·潘菲利庄园》，2008年绘于罗马。该手绘是本次展览图录的封底。

17. *Villa Doria Pamphili*, Rome, 2008 — backcover of the "Drawing" exhibition catalogue.

是西海岸现代主义景观的黄金时期，托马斯·丘奇、盖瑞特·埃克博，以及鲍勃·罗伊斯顿等设计师的理念在设计院校中占有重要地位。考虑到哈格的美国中西部背景，我们当然可以猜测，哈格一定向欧林推荐了约翰·B·杰克逊关于美国乡土景观和文化景观的作品，而欧林对此亦有不少好奇心。此后欧林还为哈格工作过几年。那时的华盛顿大学建筑学院兼施布扎学院风格和包豪斯学院风格的教学。除了绘画和建筑设计方面的传统美术训练之外，欧林还进行了现代艺术、音乐和诗歌方面的研习。

在获得建筑学学位后，欧林于20世纪60年代开展了几年建筑实践。在这一时期，美国景观设计领域还同时发生了若干重要运动，这些运动必然对欧林产生了影响，继而也影响了他的职业路径。这些影响首先源自城市理论家关于人与城市环境方面的著作。凯文·林奇于1960年出版的《城市意象》介绍了人们如何构建自己所居住城市的心理地图这一概念；作家和社会活动家简·雅各布斯于1961年出版的《美国大城市的死与生》，批评了理性主义的规划，并赞美了多样化的社区和城市社交生活。民族志学和行为学也在这一时期兴起并相互促进。我们可以从欧林众多相关主题的手绘作品看出他一直对人（社会）充满兴趣，这种兴趣甚至从很早就开始了。可以猜想，这些运动对欧林颇有影响，特别是在他已经对人及其所居住的环境产生兴趣之后。他之后在英格兰和罗马申请了学者奖学金，完成了可以被视作文化人类学的研究成果。在回到西雅图工作之后，欧林参与了多个社区项目，特别是贫民窟社区的公共菜市场保护工作——这也从一个侧面佐证了上述猜想。1972年，欧林整理并记录了自己的观察和发现，出版了一本名为《镜子上的哈气》的小册子，介绍了个体、团体与地方之间复杂而无形的关系。欧林可能是第一位以民族志学方法研究无家可归者的景观设计师。

20世纪70年代末，公园和城市广场已成为社会学家研究的主题。其中，威廉·H·怀特通过直接观察法来研究和描述城市中行人的行为，这些研究后来呈现于《小城市空间的社会生活》一书中。同一时期，受奥尔多·利奥波德于20世纪50年代提出的"土地伦理"的影响，蕾切尔·卡森撰写了《寂静的春天》。随后，环境运动逐渐兴起。1966年末，包括伊恩·麦克哈格在内的一小群景观设计师在费城发表了"景观宣言"，他们关注环境危机，并呼吁景观设计师采取行动。后来，麦克哈格于1969年出版了著名的《设计结合自然》一书。这本著作对于景观设计学教育的巨大影响一直延续至今。欧林之后还加入宾夕法尼亚大学任教，并与麦克哈格共事。生态思想在欧林主持的诸多公司总部设计中均有明显体现。

欧林曾多次提及他对平凡事物的喜爱。笔者认为，能够欣赏普通事物代表一个人可以通过批判性的观察和思考，具备对设计的感受力和敏感度。欧林曾提起过他与普利策奖得主西奥多·罗特克一起学习现代诗歌的经历。在最近的一次谈话中，他表达了对埃兹拉·庞德诗歌作品的赞赏。尽管庞德和托马斯·S·艾略特都被认为是现代诗人且他们的

professionally for several years in the 1960s. The period also aligned with several important movements in American Landscape Architecture that must have influenced Olin and impacted his development. This influence firstly was through the urban theorist's works in studying people and the urban environment. Kevin Lynch in his 1960 book *The Image of the City* introduced the concept of how people can construct a mental map of city they live in. Writer and activist Jane Jacobs published *The Death and Life of Great American Cities* in 1961, criticizing the rationalist planning and proposing the appreciation for diverse neighbourhood and urban social lives. There was also the rise of ethnology and behavioral studies, all contributed into one another. Olin has always been interested in people and it is much apparent as shown in Olin's numerous drawings on this topic even from an early stage. We can conjecture that these works had been influential for Olin, especially since he was already interested in people and the environment they occupy. He later perused fellowship works in England and Rome, producing works that can be considered as cultural anthropology. After moving back to Seattle for work, Olin participated in community projects, notably working to preserve a public market in the Skid Road community — partly supports such a speculation. He put together a pamphlet titled *Breath on the Mirror* in 1972 of his observation and finding, unveiling the complicated and invisible relationship between individuals, groups and the place. Olin may have been the first landscape architect who has studied homeless in an ethnographic approach.

By the late 1970s, parks and urban squares had become subjects for social scientists. Among them, William H. Whyte used direct observation to study and describe pedestrian behavior in cities which went on to develop into the book of *The Social Life of Small Urban Spaces*. Simultaneously, there was a rise of environmental movement after the publication of Rachel Carson's *Silent Spring* which followed Aldo Leopold's "land ethics" from the 1950s. Later in 1966, a small group of landscape architects including Ian McHarg announced the Declaration of Concern in Philadelphia, sharing concerns on environmental crisis and calling for landscape architects' action. McHarg later published the famous *Design with Nature* in 1969 which became instrumental in shaping the pedagogy of Landscape Architecture education as of today. Olin also joined as a faculty member at the University of Pennsylvania working with McHarg later in his career, where environmental thinking had become quite evident in many of his corporate headquarter designs.

Olin has repeatedly mentioned his fondness of ordinary things in several occasions. We argue the appreciation of the ordinary entails design sensibility and sensitivity through the critical eye and mind. Olin has mentioned his experience of learning modern

作品都与历史有关，但欧林显然更偏爱庞德，因为庞德的作品强调的是即时和直接的感受。这一特质在欧林本人的写作中也很明显——几乎没有严格的学术措辞，相反，文字语气随和、平易近人，仿佛在与读者同处一室面对面聊天。欧林希望他的文字也能引起即刻的感受。非学术的写作方式不仅不会影响文章质量，还可以实现更加流畅的阅读体验。更重要的是，这一写作方式可以带来更广泛的受众。

如果将欧林置于他所处的文化背景中进行研究，那么他对土地、美学以及人的极大热忱就显而易见了。他的设计理念并非"随波逐流"的结果，而是根据其最初的个人兴趣，并伴随相关思考和研究的不断积累而逐渐产生的。因此，20世纪60年代到80年代初期的经历对于他的职业生涯异常重要：他接触了丰富的理论思想，并经历了社会、经济和政治状况的巨大变革。笔者认为70年代是欧林职业生涯的重要节点，在此期间他游历美国并在海外游学，同时获得了学者奖学金，并进行了文化景观方面的研究。他观察、思考，并用手绘记录；大量的手绘作品向我们展示了他内心世界（思想）的形成。笔者也将70年代视为欧林从建筑领域过渡到景观设计领域的转折点。自1974年在宾夕法尼亚大学任教以来，他对人与景观的兴趣不断加深，并最终在费城创立了自己的景观设计和城市设计事务所。通过各种尺度和地域的设计项目，欧林展示了其设计对于人的敏感和温情。他最新出版的书籍《就座》集中体现了其设计理念与实践。通过将重心集中于座椅设计，《就座》展现了欧林对公共座椅历史的研究与观察概述，以及关于公共座椅从设计理念到实物构造的见解和具体设计案例。在书中，他呼吁设计师关注人的"处境"和"坐的状态"，并表明"当一个人选择了自己的座位并将自己置身于景观之中时，他也成为了景观的一部分，同时也处于一个更广阔的文脉之中"[10]。这一陈述回溯了沉浸式体验在批判性观察中的重要性。"绘者作画时必须保持安静，一动不动地坐着并非常仔细地观察。如果你做到这些，事物的本质将会自然呈现出来，世界将由此打开。"[11]

在"911"恐怖袭击之后，欧林参加了加强华盛顿特区国家广场安

poetry with the Pulitzer Prize winner Theodore Roethke. In a recent conversation, he has expressed his appreciation of poetry and works by Ezra Pound. Although both are considered modern poets and both have works related to history, Olin clearly prefers Pound over Thomas S. Eliot because Pound writes for immediate impose and direct reception. This quality is also evident in Olin's own writing. Almost all Olin's writings are not in strict academic rhetoric. Instead, the tone of the writing is casual and approachable, as if he is chatting to you in an intimate and more direct setting. Olin's writing, too, hopes to bring immediate reaction. The non-academic format does not discount the intellect of the content but provides a more fluid and organic experience in accessing the information via reading, and most importantly, it can be accessible to a wider range of readers.

By situating Olin in his cultural context, his great passion for the land, for beauty, and for people is quite evident. His design philosophy developed slowly by accumulating associated thinking and studies based on his original personal interest. It was not merely a result of drifting along with the "trend." The period between the 1960s and early 1980s thus becomes remarkable in his career in which he has been exposed to a richness of thoughts and has experienced great shifts in social, economic and political conditions. We would argue the 1970s as the benchmark in Olin's career, wherein he has travelled across the country and abroad, and has conducted fellowship research in cultural landscape. He observed, thought and drew, and he drew a lot which revealed to us his internal construct. We also see the 1970s as the turning point where Olin has transitioned into the field of landscape architecture. His interests in people and landscape continued to develop as he began teaching at the University of Pennsylvania in 1974 and eventually founded his own practice of landscape architecture and urban design firm in Philadelphia. Through his design works in various scales and locals, Olin has shown sensitivity and tenderness for people. His latest book *Be Seated* exemplifies his philosophy and practice. By focusing on designing seating, the book shows an overview of Olin's study and observation with the history of public seating, his insights and design cases in both philosophical and physical construct. In the book, he called for attention to "situate" and "sitting," and suggests that "as one takes one's fixed spot in the landscape, one also becomes of it, situated within a larger context."[10] This statement circles back to the significance of the immersive experience in critical observation. "To draw, one has to be quiet and sit still and look very carefully. If you do, things will reveal themselves. The world will open and unfold."[11]

Olin participated in a design competition to enhance

18. 瓦格纳公园内的无靠背长椅

18. Backless bench in Wagner Park

全性的场地设计竞赛。其中，广场的公共座椅设计概念进行了多种考量，例如防止车辆（炸弹）袭击的安全措施，考虑最需要安排休憩座椅的位置，可满足大量游客使用需求的座椅尺寸和形式，呼应国家广场物质性文化的座椅材质，如何在各个方向上保持最佳视野，以及如何通过尺度和比例的设置，以优雅的形式去呼应纪念碑而不喧宾夺主。在瓦格纳公园固定长椅这一设计案例中，欧林解释道，设计的目的是希望座凳宽度可以使人们能"在面朝不同方向背对背坐着时不会互相干扰"[10]（图18）。在这里，长椅设计的重点不再是外观、材质或样式风格。此外，无靠背长椅的设计也源于这种对人的使用方式的关注。无论是站立还是坐着，无靠背长椅都有助于保持人们望向海港和自由女神像时视野的通透性。这样设计的长椅还为人们坐着、躺着、"瘫坐着"[10]提供了极大的灵活度，也为人们彼此之间无障碍的互动提供了便利。

尽管固定长椅通常仅被视为空间营造的元素，但欧林旨在通过使用诸如长椅之类的单一对象来强调围绕设计产生的社会行为和表现，并在更大的文脉里拓展其含义与影响。现实中的设计实践不仅需要建造技术知识，还需要观察和决策方面的敏感性和批判性。在设计哥伦布环岛广场时，无靠背长椅成为激活空间的关键元素。长椅的材质、形状、构造和照明皆为满足公众需求而设计（图19）。当市政官员要求增加扶手以防止流浪汉在长椅上睡觉时，欧林从美学和社会学的角度予以反驳。在《就座》一书中，他甚至称这些官员为"愚蠢无知的官僚主义破坏分子"[10]。作为在美国推广可移动座椅的设计师之一，欧林在公共场所中采用可移动的桌椅体现了其人文素养。设计绩效中的社会层面需要事实性和感知性两方面的观察。因此，对批判性观察的训练在景观设计领域尤为重要。

4 结语

本文无法概括或总结景观手绘的定义，这也并非笔者的意图。笔者通过对欧林的绘画作品及其手绘和设计实践发展历程的简短回顾，

the security at National Mall in Washington, D.C. after the terrorist attack of September 11, 2001. The thoughts behind the bench proposal includes security measure to prevent vehicular assault, consideration of location where seating is most needed, dimension and forms that can accommodate large quantity of visitors, materials that resemble the material culture of the National Mall, consideration to maintain maximum vision in all direction, and how the scale and proportion can result in a refined manner to the memorial yet with minimal disturbance to the context. In the case of designing the fixed bench at Wagner Park, Olin explained that the intention is to provide the width that allows people to "be able to sit back to back while facing different directions without disturbing each other"[10] (Fig. 18). The emphasis on bench design was not the look, the material or the style. This also applies to the decision of proposing backless bench. The backless helps to maintain the visibility to the harbor and the Statue of Liberty whether one is standing or sitting. It also offers great flexibility regarding how people sit, lay or "drape"[10] themselves and how people may interact by providing no obstacle in between.

Although the fixed bench often implies spatial construction, Olin means to underline the social behavior and performance that can occupy the design, using the singular object, such as the bench, and extends its implications and impacts within a larger context. The actual design practice requires not only the technical knowledge in making but also the sensitivity and criticality in observation and decision making. At Columbus Circle, the backless bench is designed as a key element to activate the space. The bench's material, shape, tectonics, and lighting are designed with the singular intent in serving the needs of the public (Fig. 19). When city officials requested the addition of armrests to prevent homeless people sleeping on the benches, Olin displayed opposition both aesthetically and socially. In *Be Seated*, he even calls out the officials as "knuckleheaded bureaucratic vandalism"[10]. Being one of the designers who proliferated the use of movable seating in American, Olin's contribution of the movable tables and chairs in public spaces demonstrates humanistic qualities. The social aspect of design performance demands both factual and perceptual observation. Therefore, the training of critical observation becomes especially crucial in the profession of landscape architecture.

4 Conclusions

The paper is not able to generalize or conclude here the definition of drawing in relation to landscape, which has never been our intention. Instead, through a short revisit of Olin's

19. 哥伦布环岛广场内的无靠背长椅
19. Backless bench in Columbus Circle

探究了画作创作过程与景观批判性观察之间的密切关系。对于绘者而言，绘画过程是一种持续的沉浸，是领会所观之景的途径，而这一过程最终将通过画作呈现出来。对于观者而言，通过研究绘者的创作过程，可以理解手绘背后的内容和含义。除了坚持主张将手绘作为观察的媒介之外，笔者还探索了解读绘画过程及其潜在信息的可行途径。本文通过举例，简要介绍了三种可能的方法：解读事实之景与呈现之景，通过透视构图和修辞构图进行手绘叙事，以及理解绘画技巧背后的意图和心理。

这种对绘画过程的理解进一步将手绘视作培养景观设计师的一项重要训练内容，特别是在手眼协调方面。对于我们这代人而言，技术进步促进了借由外部替代物（例如摄影、胶片、GIS、无人机，以及其他相关计算设备）增强"看到"和"渲染"景观的能力。一方面，这些替代工具带来了前所未有的"眼"（视野）"手"（工具）体验，可以对景观进行极为逼真的"二次"观察和景观表现。但另一方面，它们也使我们对景观的"一次"体验失去了沉浸感和敏感性。由于实证主义模型在空间和时间上的局限性，清晰精确的图像或模拟既不等于对景观更为透彻的理解，也不代表对于景观的精确解释。相反，如果在视觉上过度依赖这种二次景观体验，可能会使我们更加难以通过敏锐观察与好奇心来探求真实的景观。

这种对景观"二次"体验的普遍假设与消费已经对我们与景观之间的关系产生了影响。正如克里斯托夫·吉鲁特所言，"景观设计学科正在经历意象性的巨大损失"，他将这一危机归因于泛滥的图片中"视觉参考物的错置和丧失"[12]。有趣的是，吉鲁特对大众传媒和传统景观标志性视觉系统的批判促使他开始另寻景观设计领域中用于表现和观察的新型主导媒介——这将产生并传播更多的景观"二次"认知。但笔者认为问题并不在于景观媒介，无论它们是新是旧、是静态抑或是动态，问题出在我们自身：我们已经失去了对于景观"一次"体验的信仰，并停止了对观察过程和"参考图像"的质疑。因此，由

drawings and his personal development on drawing and design practice, we have examined the idea of "draw-ing" in its affinity with the critical observation of landscape. For the draughtsman, draw-ing is an immersive duration and a portal to apprehend the landscape observed, which will be eventually achieved in the drawing as an end result. While for the spectator, by focusing on draw-ing, it becomes possible to revisit the invisible meaning and message behind the drawing beheld. Besides this maintained argument asserting drawing as the medium for observation, we have also explored the accessible approaches to read draw-ing as a process and latent message. Three possible approaches are briefly introduced through exemplifications: first, reading between the factual and presented circumstance; second, the narrative of a drawing through the realistic and figurative composition; third, the intention and psyche behind the drawing techniques.

This understanding of draw-ing further considers drawing as a critical practice for training a landscape designer, with a particular concentration on the coordination of the critical eye and the skilful hand. For our generations, the technological advancement facilitates a growing capacity to "see" and to "render" landscape through external surrogates, such as photographic media, films, GIS, drones, and other relevant computational devices. On the one hand, these surrogates have brought with the unprecedented "eye" and "hand" for an eidetic, secondary observation and representation of landscape. While on the other hand, they also take away our immersions and sensitivities in the primary experience of landscape. Due to the spatial and temporal limitations in positivist models, an eidetic image or simulation of landscape does not necessarily equalize a more thorough apprehension, neither a precise interpretation, of landscape. On the contrary, the proclivity of our visual overreliance on this secondary experience of landscape could further distance ourselves from sensitive observation and curiosity through the haptic immersion in a landscape.

The prevailing presumptions and consumptions of this secondary experience of landscape already have had the impacts on our relationship with landscape. As Christophe Girot has argued, "the landscape architecture is experiencing an extraordinary loss of imageability" — the crisis that he attributed to "the misplaced and lost visual references" in flux and overabundance of images[12]. Interestingly, Girot's criticism on the mass media and the traditional iconic visual system of landscape led him to seek for new dominating media of representation and observation in landscape architecture, which eventually would produce and circulate even more secondary perceptions of landscape. However, we argue that the problem

于蓬勃发展的媒体载体带来的影响，景观的"二次"或"三次"体验已叠加到景观的社会和文化感知之上。

笔者对欧林的手绘及其在景观设计领域数十载的求索进行了回顾，尽管简短，却激发了我们对在学习和领悟景观中起关键作用的"一次"体验的见解。作为一种理解景观的有效方法，手绘没有捷径，只能通过循序渐进的训练习得。欧林认为艺术"不像科学那样可以在前人的基础上继续攀登"，而是要求每一代艺术家都"从头开始……朝着既定目标不断前进"[13]。景观设计作为一门从实用艺术走向复杂科学的学科，永远不能否认"每个艺术家都必须在洞察与判断、感知与表现方面"不断努力[13]。

鉴于此，笔者主张重新审视景观设计实践及教学中手绘的创作过程，以重新思考艺术与工具的关系，以及观察与表现的方式。通过回溯绘画的过程，我们可以摆脱对科学全知性的虚幻信念，认识到我们在观察身边景观时的局限性和想象力，从中领悟自身问题并不断反思。**LAF**

is not in the media of landscape, whether they are old or new, static or dynamic. The problem lies with us, who have lost faith in the primary experience of landscape and stopped questioning the process of observing and the creation of the "referential image." The production of the secondary or tertiary experience of landscape has therefore superimposed on the social and cultural perception of landscape via the vehicle of thriving media.

Our revisit of Olin's drawings and his decade-long pursuit in landscape architecture, even though very brief in this paper, has still struck us with provoking insights into the primary experience that plays a critical role in learning and understanding landscape. Drawing as an effective method in this process offers no shortcut but incremental practices. Olin asserts his reflection upon art as "not really additive like science," which instead requires each generation of artists to "start from scratch… to climb toward such achievement"[13]. Landscape Architecture as a discipline marching from a practical art towards a complex science can never deny the indispensability of continuous pursuit "in the realm of insight and values, feelings and skills in each individual in the course of one life"[13].

Having these concerns, hereby, we argue for a revisit to draw-ing in landscape design profession and education in order to rethink the relationship between art and instrumentality in the discipline and the way we observe and represent landscape. By returning to draw-ing, we are able to retreat from our illusory faith in the scientific omniscience, to recognize both our limitation and imagination in observing the permeating landscape around us, and to start figuring out our questions and reflexions from landscape. **LAF**

REFERENCES

[1] Whitaker, W. (2018, October 8 – December 21). What is good about the good [Introduction in the "Drawing" exhibition catalog]. Kroiz Gallery, the Architectural Archives, University of Pennsylvania School of Design, Philadelphia.

[2] Ji, C., & Chen, Z. (Annotation). The Craft of Gardens. (2015). Chapter 10. Beijing: China Building Industry Publishing House.

[3] Taine, H. (1980). Philosophie de l'art [Philosophy of art] (Vol. 102). Genève: Éditions Slatkine.

[4] Vollard, A. (1914). In M. Doran (Ed.), Conversations with Cézanne (p. 122). Oakland: University of California Press.

[5] Berger, J. (2013). Understanding a photograph. London: Penguin Books.

[6] Tilley, C., & Cameron-Daum, K. (2017). Anthropology of Landscape: The Extraordinary in the Ordinary (p. 9). London: UCL Press.

[7] De Certeau, M., & Rendall, S. (Tran.). (1984). The practice of everyday life (pp. 100-101). Berkeley: University of California Press.

[8] Olin, L. (2000). Across the Open Field: Essays Drawn from English Landscapes (p. 168). Philadelphia: University of Pennsylvania Press.

[9] Heidegger, M. (1954). The question concerning technology. Technology and values: Essential readings. New York: Garland Publishing.

[10] Olin, L. (2017). Be Seated. San Rafael: Applied Research and Design.

[11] Olin, L. (2012). Oyster Light: Pacific Northwest Reflections. SiteLINES: A Journal of Place, 7(2), 3-5. Retrieved from https://www.jstor.org/stable/24889402

[12] Girot, C. (2004). Movism: Prologue to a New Visual Theory in Landscape Architecture. In M. Koll-Schretzenmayr, M. Keiner, & G. Nussbaumer (Eds.), The Real and Virtual Worlds of Spatial Planning (pp. 199-206), Heidelberg: Springer.

[13] Olin, L. (2012). Across the Open Field: Essays Drawn from English Landscapes (pp. 20-21). Philadelphia: University of Pennsylvania Press.

PLEASE CITE THIS ARTICLE AS

Desimini, J. (2019). Plural Practices: Ideas for Drawing Responsibly. Landscape Architecture Frontiers, 7(5), 80-89. https://doi.org/10.15302/J-LAF-1-030007

https://doi.org/10.15302/J-LAF-1-030007　　RECEIVED DATE / 2019-08-12　　P28, TU318+.5　　B

多元化实践：
如何合理绘制地图
PLURAL PRACTICES: IDEAS FOR DRAWING RESPONSIBLY

吉尔·戴斯米妮
哈佛大学设计研究生院景观设计系副教授，"制图场地：表达想象中的景观"展览策展人

Jill DESIMINI*

Associate Professor of Landscape Architecture, Harvard Graduate School of Design; Curator of the exhibition "Cartographic Grounds: Projecting the Landscape Imaginary"

*Corresponding Author
Address: 48 Quincy Street, Cambridge, MA 02138, USA
Email: desimini@gsd.harvard.edu

1 "制图场地"项目：景观设计学与地图制图学的思想交融

2012年，"制图场地"项目启动，并通过在哈佛大学设计研究生院举办的名为"制图场地：表达想象中的景观"的展览（展期为2012年10月29日至2013年1月1日）和2016年由普林斯顿建筑出版社出版的同名书籍予以呈现和发表。

在设计文化中，"构图"和数据可视化概念正日渐兴起，抽象派艺术作品的地位与传播也开始占据更重要的地位。鉴于此，"制图场地"项目期望重新畅想制图实践在更加接近场地表达效果与掌控场地本身特征上的主观潜能。项目所提出的各项举措使景观设计学科迎来了期待已久的调和状态——对设计场地的刻画实现了地质学与地理学、区域尺度和国土尺度的融合。

项目选取了设计历史悠久的瑞士、东京、巴塞罗那和洛杉矶等特定区域作为研究对象，同时这些场地需尽可能毗邻不同的大洋、分属不同的大洲、归于不同的地理环境，以在尺度、地形和类型方面进行对比。所有的地图和规划都必须保证图面完整（例如，需标明不同线型和通用制图符号的含义）和尺度准确，且多以大尺度绘制来激发想象。项目选取1:25 000的图纸作为最大范围，其他图纸的比例多为1:10 000或更大（图1、2）。所有的制图方案均与设计方案成对呈现，以展现二者的相似性，加强它们的联系。

"制图场地"项目不仅聚焦于当代设计实践，更畅想了现实材料与数字技术、数据信息与经验知识相互交织的未来图景。项目展示了借鉴自其他不同学科的一系列地图表达基础技术，以及用以描绘地下、瞬时、水域及陆地等不同情境的工具包。这些表达工具既可用于

摘要

本文基于绘图技术、尺度以及对图像的观察、解读与想象等，对地图制图和景观设计话题进行了探讨。通过细致观察和严谨思考，可以开发更为合理的绘图工具包，使地图解读和空间营造更丰富。这就要求设计师对其所获取到的信息保持质疑，并进一步提升其准确性、扩展其涵盖范围。制图工作正面临更为复杂的挑战，与之相适应的表达媒介和方法也需要更加多元与稳健。文章探讨了以展览和书籍形式呈现的"制图场地"项目，项目期望重新畅想制图实践在更加接近场地表达效果与掌控场地本身特征上的主观潜能，在推动景观设计学与地图制图学两大学科交融的同时，试图将二者应用于更为基础的实践中，并呈现和畅想更加多元化的设计领域。此外，通过介绍哈佛大学设计研究生院的观察与表达训练课程，文章指出，观察是所有工作的根本，而对于设计而言，最终的表达必须超越对现实世界的记录与理解，畅想更加公平、更具适应性的未来。

关键词

景观设计学；地图制图学；表达；可视化；多元

ABSTRACT

The article discusses the topics of cartography and landscape architecture, with a few ideas about technique, scale, observation, translation, and imagination. The charge is to look closely, think critically, and develop sensibly a drawing toolkit that allows for an expansion of possible readings and spatial outcomes. It asks designers to question the information before them, and to respond with precision and range. The challenges are increasingly complex, and thus, media and methods must be plural and robust. The replies herein build on the Cartographic Grounds project, an exhibit and book that again reimagines the projective potential of cartographic practices that afford greater proximity to the manifestation and manipulation of the ground itself, and promotes the intersection between the disciplines of Landscape Architecture and Cartography towards a grounded practice of representing and imagining multiple terrains for design. The introduction of the observation and representation training in Harvard Graduate School of Design further suggests that observation is fundamental, and for design, representation must extend beyond documenting and understanding the world that exists, towards imagining a more equitable and adaptive future.

KEYWORDS

Landscape Architecture; Cartography; Representation; Visualization; Plurality

EDITED BY　Tina TIAN　　TRANSLATED BY　WANG Ying

1. 2012年，莫斯巴赫景观设计事务所的获胜作品——台中相移公园平面图（原图以1∶25 000比例绘制）。层叠的地形突出了其"岩石圈"设计中所应用的地层学知识。在与菲利普·拉姆建筑事务所和刘培森建筑师事务所的合作下，项目以微气候营造引领设计，将台中市中心原有的军事用地改造为一处公共空间。

2. 2012年，由LCLA建筑事务所设计师路易斯·卡列哈斯和梅丽莎·纳兰霍设计的基辅战术群岛平面图。设计师将不同的建筑方案应用于动态的水陆交界处，使其变得更加错综复杂。剖面线与图样填充之间的鲜明对比体现了陆地与水域、植被郁闭区与开阔地带之间的差异。不同海拔处的植被经过渲染，呈现出植被的密度。在这一景观中，设计师在临近海域运用了一系列程序化单元来构建微型岛屿。

1. In the Phase Shifts Park 1:25,000 scale competition drawing from 2012, Mosbach Paysagistes represent their winning design as a series of layers, highlighting the Stratigraphy present in their designed lithosphere. The project converted a former military site in downtown Taichung to a public amenity — done with Phillippe Rahm Architectes and Ricky Liu & Associates Architects + Planners, focuses on microclimate as the way to organize design.

2. In Tactical Archipelago, Kiev from 2012, designers Luis Callejas and Melissa Naranjo of LCLA Office use the aggregation of architectural interventions to populate the land-water interface, adding intricacy to a dynamic edge. The hatching versus solid fill offers contrast between land and water, between vegetated and open ground. Plantings are rendered in elevation, as a field of implied density. Within this landscape, a system of programmatic units is deployed to form micro-islands within a relational sea.

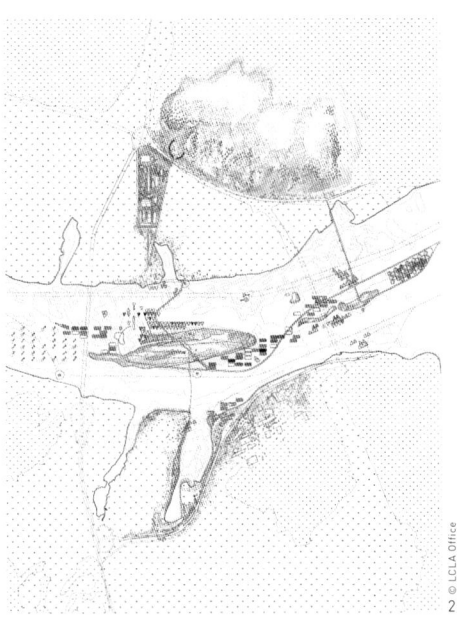

1 The Cartographic Grounds Project: Cross-pollination of Ideas between Landscape Architecture and Cartography

The Cartographic Grounds project was initiated in 2012, and included the exhibition "Cartographic Grounds: Projecting the Landscape Imaginary," at the Harvard Graduate School of Design which ran from October 29, 2012 to January 1, 2013, and a book with the same title, published in 2016 by Princeton Architectural Press.

In light of the ascendance of "mapping" and data visualization in design culture, and the privileging of abstract forces and flows, the project reimagined the projective potential of cartographic practices that afford greater proximity to the manifestation and manipulation of the ground itself. The approaches presented offered Landscape Architecture a long-overdue reconciliation of the depiction of the ground as a site of design with the geological and geographic, the regional and the territorial.

The project focused on particular geographies — Switzerland, Tokyo, Barcelona, and Los Angeles — with rich design histories but included as many seas, continents, and planets as possible, for a comparison across scale, geography, and type. All the maps and plans had graphic integrity as exemplified by their line types and conventional signs; they had scalar precision and were drawn at a large scale to engage imagination. The selected drawings used the scale of 1:25,000 as an outside parameter, with more examples closer to 1:10,000 and beyond (Fig. 1, 2). Cartographic examples were paired with design examples to show parallels and force greater connections.

The project provided contemporary design practice with clues to the imaginative intersection of the material and the digital, the data-driven and the experiential. It demonstrated a series of foundational techniques used in the representation taken from various disciplinary sources, offering an instrumental array for describing various conditions: subsurface, aqueous, and terrestrial. These representational tools were analytical and projective, precise yet speculative. Taken together, they formed a rich symbolic language capable of describing existing and imagined landscapes, promoting a fruitful cross-pollination of ideas between Landscape Architecture and Cartography.

2 Coding and Decoding

Developing codes and language have long been an interest of the discipline of Landscape Architecture, especially as it relates to mapping. For the Cartographic Grounds project, we were looking to cartographer and theorist Jacques Bertin and others to enhance our understanding of signs. As the project progressed, the focus,

场地分析，辅助获取精准结果；也可用于场地设计，辅助进行推测想象。当这些特性融于一体，便生成了一种丰富的象征性语言，来描绘现有的或构想的景观，显著实现了景观设计学与地图制图学思想的交融。

2 编码与解码

代码和语汇开发一直以来都是景观设计学关注的焦点之一，尤其在涉及制图领域的时候。"制图场地"项目的初衷是通过制图学家、理论家雅克·贝尔坦等学者的研究来加深人们对符号的理解。但随着项目的进行，大家关注的重点却转向了地图上的通用制图符号或图例。这一焦点不仅贯穿了整个项目,更帮助设计师扩展了他们的绘图工具箱。

在项目的同期展览和书籍中,我们均试图呈现更多的通用制图符号——不仅仅将它们置于图的一角,而是作为绘图过程中的基本组成部分来予以强调。除贝尔坦的研究外,法国国家地理研究所收藏的一本精美的法国地图集(1949年)也给了我们极大启发。在这本手册中,图例占据了左侧全页,右侧全页则为地图节选(图3)。通过这一呈现方式,我们发现,地图组件本身与其地理空间分布同等重要。据此,笔者认为,可以从图例中窥见对于绘图过程至关重要的各项要素。

正如每个传奇(legend)都是一个故事,每张地图上的图例(legend)也都讲述着这张地图背后的故事。图例帮助我们从视觉和文字角度解读地图上的信息。于制图者而言,图例记载了选择所需呈现元素及转译并记录主题的过程。于读者而言,图例罗列着不同符号、色彩和纹理背后所传达的丰富含义。究其本质,图例记录了地图上的所有要素(即告诉人们图纸上包含什么)——正如食谱的配料清单会透露食物的大致类型和味道,图例也能展现出地图独特的内涵与倾向。有关图例的思索也促发了人们对更多潜在绘图方式和干预措施的探索。

in fact, turned to the conventional signs — or legend — found on maps. This has become an ongoing interest in the project, and a means for designers, to expand their drawing toolkit.

In both the exhibit and the book, we tried to include as many conventional signs as possible, not relegating them to the corner but featuring them as a fundamental part of the drawing process. In addition to Bertin, we were inspired by a beautiful 1949 French catalog from the Institut Géographique National. Therein, the maps were displayed with the legend full page on the left and an excerpt of the map full scale on the right (Fig. 3). It gave equal weight to the components of the map and their deployment in geographic space. It made me think about the legend, as a synthesis of everything essential about the drawing.

The legend is a story; the legend on a drawing tells the story of the drawing. It is the visual and written explanation needed to decode the information being represented. For the maker, it is a listing of the choices made about what to include on the map and how to translate and document this subject matter. For the user, it is a listing of the meaning behind the symbols, colors, and textures. In essence, the legend tallies the ingredients — it tells what is included in the drawing — and in the same way that scanning the ingredient list of a recipe divulges the general type and taste of the food, scanning the legend of a map reveals its content and bias. To explore the potential of this idea is to explore the range of possible drawings and interventions.

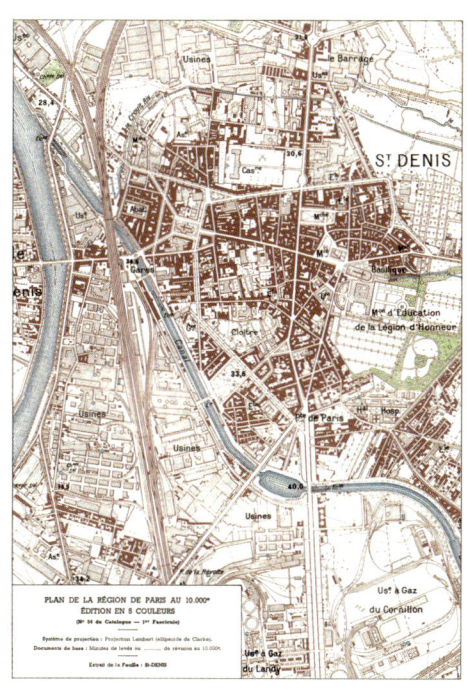

3. 由法国国家地理研究所出版的地图集节选

3. Excerpts from a catalogue of published maps by the Institut Géographique National

4. 在2014年的"图底技术"项目中,笔者通过对琼·布斯克茨的《巴塞罗那老城区规划(2000)》、大都会建筑事务所的《哈伊马角市布局规划(2007)》和《柏林市总体规划(1903)》进行调整和比较,探索了巴塞罗那图底关系的不同组织方法。绘图首先以鲜明的黑白二色呈现,而后增加了图面的层次性和复杂性,以通过运用传统绘图手法来改变对城市的解读。

5. 在2014年的"土地分类技术"项目中,笔者对代表不同土地用途的各个系统进行了对比:首先以字母命名这些系统,其次运用不同颜色进行表达,最终以Google地球或Google地图卫星常用的摄影测量视图来予以呈现。我们通常不会对航拍图提出任何异议,但实际上,航拍图是由分类后的多个时间段和多个视角的视图拼接而成的。

4. In Figure-Ground Techniques from 2014, we explore different means of codifying the figure-ground of Barcelona, adapting and comparing methods from: Joan Busquets, Old Town Barcelona from 2000; OMA's Ras Al Khaimah Structure Plans from 2007; and the Ubersichtsplan von Berlin from 1903. The drawings starts with a black and white binary distinction and adds layers and complexity, thereby changing the reading of the city through the drawing conventions employed.

5. In Land Classification Techniques from 2014, we compare systems for representing land use, beginning with an alphanumeric designation, followed by color assignments, and ending with a photogrammetric view typical of Google Earth or Google Maps satellite. We often take aerial images for granted as an unbiased representation. But in fact, aerials are classified and stitched, representing multiple time periods and points of view.

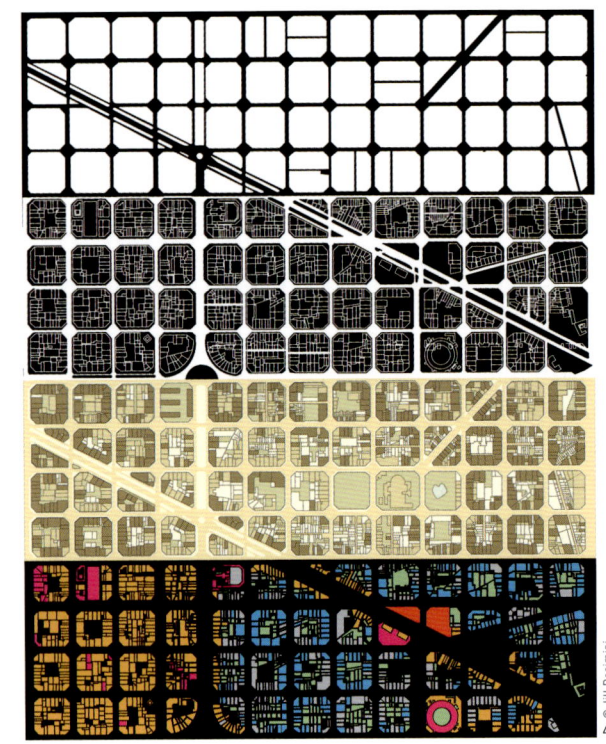

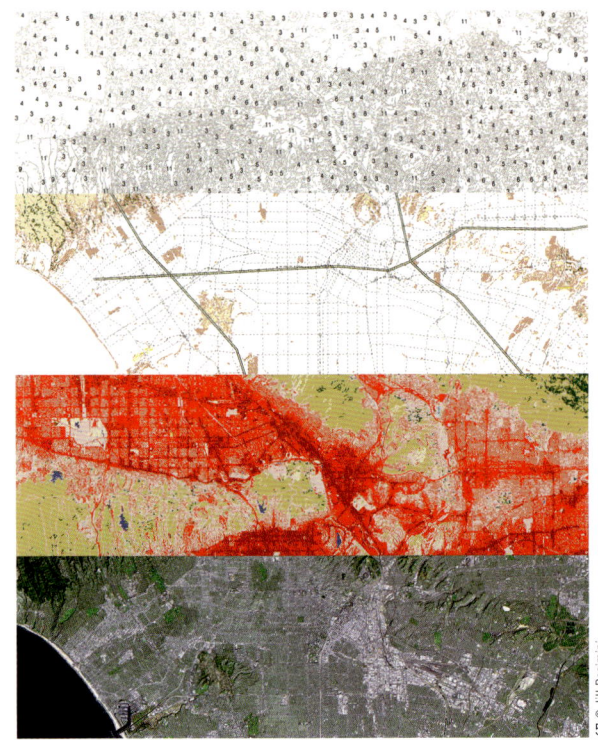

3 多元的叙事手法

随着景观设计学涉猎范围的不断扩大,如何既通俗又精准地解读愈发宏大和复杂的问题,成为了学科的一大挑战。与此同时,地图制图学也面临着同样的挑战——随着景观设计实践逐步脱离比例图与平面图,地图这一最基本的表达模式也拥有了更为广阔的舞台。已有的绘图技术考虑到了建造性设计与创造性设计的双重需求。"制图场地"项目期望突破绘图最基本的示意功能,解锁更加多元的图解方式。但在这一过程中,我们又重新注意到单色线条的重要性——线条的长短、指向和粗细可以描绘变换的地形。这无疑是对我们的适时提醒——当身处数据与资源的洪流之中,我们极易将问题看得过于简单或过于复杂,然而如何通过最简单的方式来实现最恰当的表达才是重点。由此,确定表现元素及其组合方式也成为了实现项目目标的一种途径。

多元的叙述手法和针对技术的实验研究都至关重要。每一种表达形式都像是一种论证,既包含论点,也包含一系列用以支撑论点的材料(图4,5)。表达形式的好坏取决于背后的思想与拟定的空间。

3 Plurality of Narratives

As Landscape Architecture increases its purview to address greater and more complex territories, maintaining legibility and precision becomes a challenge. This is a challenge shared with mapmaking — and as landscape practice seemed to be moving away from scaled and planar drawings, there was an opportunity to expand the potential agency of this fundamental type of representation. The techniques explored allow both for constructive and imaginative projections. The goal was to expand the literal techniques of drawing to allow for more plural interpretations. Oddly, in so doing, we were also reminded of the power of the monochromatic line — with changing lengths, orientations, and thicknesses — to describe varied terrain. As we face more data and resource, we tend to under-edit and over-complicate, so it was a timely reminder to aim for maximum impact with minimal means. Defining the representational palette becomes a means of setting the ambition for a project.

I would emphasize the plurality of narratives and the experimentation of technique. A representation is like any argument: it has a thesis and a set of materials to support the assertion (Fig. 4, 5). The representation is only as good as the idea behind it, and the space ahead of it. Rather than rules,

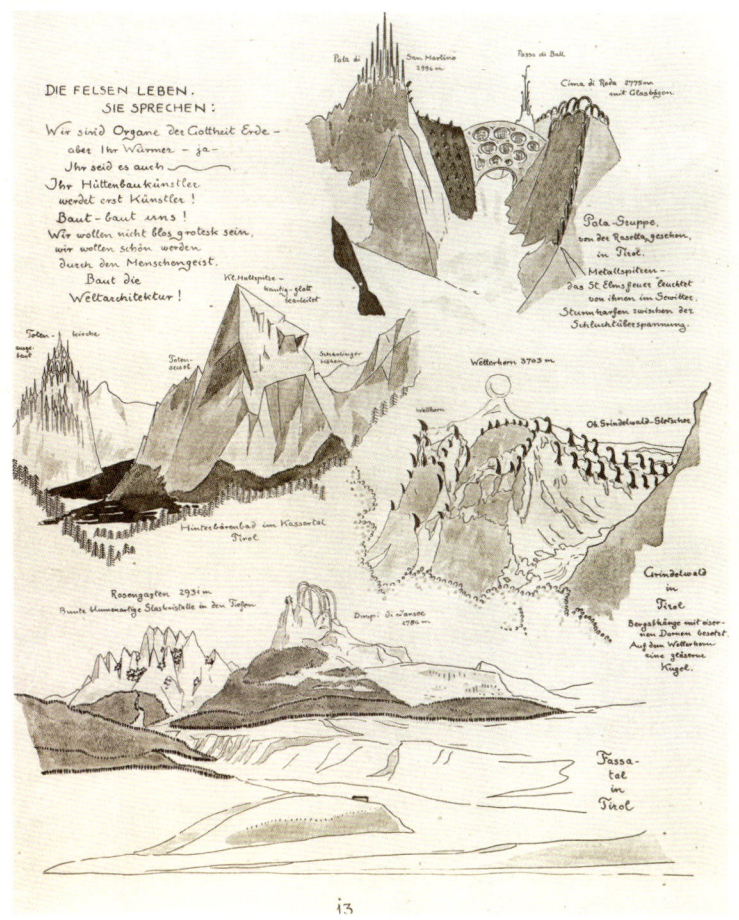

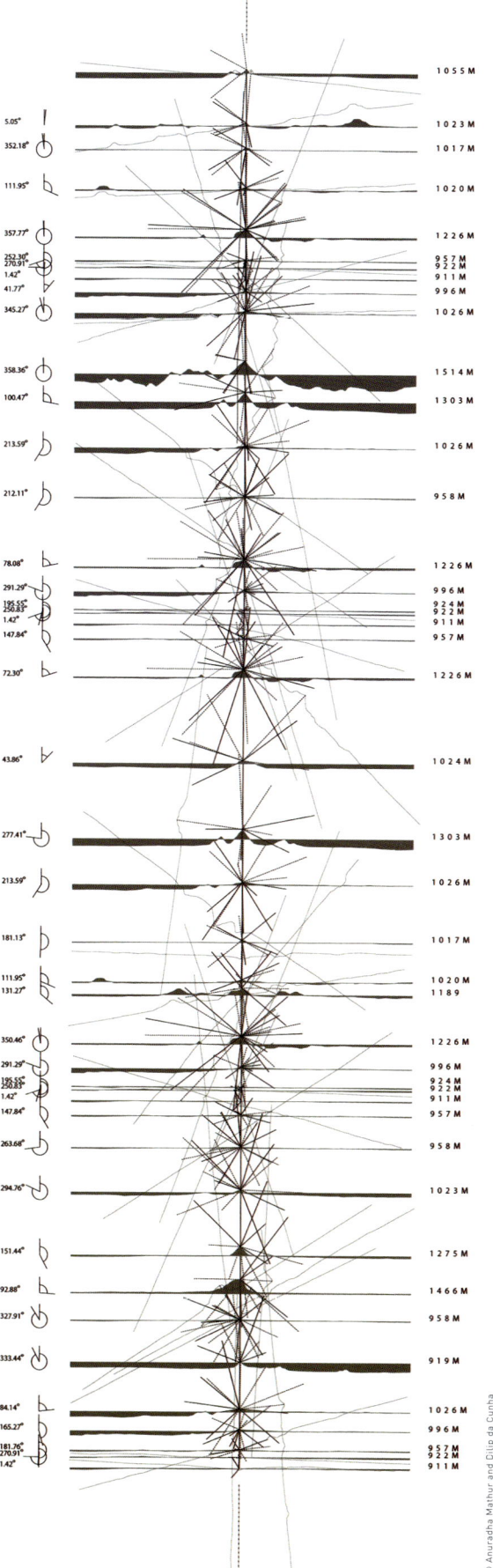

6. 在第一次世界大战的背景下,布鲁诺·陶特设想了一种乌托邦式建筑,这一愿景主要呈现于由5部分宣言组成的《高山建筑》一书中(来源:参考文献[1])。书中包含一系列带注解的插图,主张用晶体结构增强高山建筑的稳固性。插图色彩丰富、阴影清晰,能够让人回想起过去的高山全景,但经过人类干预后的景观又更显丰富。

7. 比克·卡图尔和布鲁诺·德·缪德尔于2011年所著《基础设施:公路和铁路图集》中的"切分为线条片段的N43国道"项目,呈现了随着时间的流逝,道路是如何被切分的(来源:参考文献[2])。通过对道路图形进行提取、隔离和编码,作者分析了不同时刻下应当如何定义道路和景观之间的相互作用。该图集提出了一种象形文字般的基础架构语言,由串连为直线的路段图形构成了复合的道路结构。

6. In response to World War I, Bruno Taut envisioned a utopia, largely articulated through his five-part manifesto *Alpine Architektur* (Source: Ref. [1]). The vision unfolds in a series of annotated illustrations, arguing for the enhancement of alpine architecture with crystalline structures. The illustrations are rich, shaded articulations reminiscent of past alpine panoramas but augmented by human invention.

7. Bieke Cattoor and Bruno De Meulder's N43 National Road Breaks into Segments of a Line, from their 2011 volume *Figures Infrastructures: An Atlas of Roads and Railways*, illustrates how the road has been fragmented over time (Source: Ref. [2]). Roadway figures are extracted, isolated, and coded to analyze how different moments define the interactions between the road and the landscape. The series presents a hieroglyphic-like language of infrastructure. The figures, connected by straight road segments, form the composite roadway structure.

8. 阿奴拉德哈·马图尔和迪利普·达·库尼亚在其《德干高原：班加罗尔市地形的营造》一书中绘制的基线图参考了威廉·兰布顿在班加罗尔基线周边应用的三角测量法（来源：参考文献[3]）。作为关键引导的矢量基线确定了图面的中心。图中将三角形转化为直线线形，描述了线条的运行路线、测量过程，以及在地标与地标间移动的轨迹。

9. 2007~2008年间，沃格特景观设计事务所从步行者视角绘制的"哈德斯本住宅区：步道形态"截面图。中央的红线指代路径，截面长度代表视域范围。线条的长短表示视线可及的远近。因此，从较低视角处绘制的截面较短，较高视角处绘制的截面较长。截面的高低变化体现了地势的起伏。

8. Anuradha Mathur and Dilip da Cunha's Baseline Plottings from their book *Deccan Traverses: The Making of Bangalore's Terrain* traces William Lambton's triangulation around the Bangalore Baseline [Source: Ref. [3]]. The baseline — a critical navigational vector — defines the center of the drawing. The drawing straightens the triangles, describing the lines of journey, the process of measurement, and the trajectory of bouncing from landmark to landmark.

9. Vogt Landscape Architect's Hadspen House Estate: Shape of a Walk sections from 2007 to 2008 focus on the walkers perspective. The central red line represents the route while the section length is determined by viewshed. Distance seen is distance drawn. Thus, the section from a low point is short while the section taken from a high point is long. Topography is reflected, as the sections wax and wane along the undulating route.

每一种表达都并非基于固有规范而产生，相反，尺度和设计手法的差异、经验和可应用度差异，以及理解和体验的偏差都会影响表达。在研究制图的过程中，我们试图找到更多约定俗成的规则，但最终却发现自由表达才能最有效地促进地图制图学实现更广泛的应用。

另外，有趣的是，设计师经常忽略这样一个事实：地图的阅读者同时也是可以主观描述和展开畅想的观察者。例如，英国作家阿尔佛莱德·温赖特曾花费大量时间徜徉于莱克兰瀑布的美景中，或远足，或写生，将这片他深深迷恋的景色绘制成册。如今这一系列的旅游指南已经深受全球读者的喜爱。德国建筑师布鲁诺·陶特的乌托邦式高山建筑设计图则表达了战争语境下对美好人居环境的向往（图6）。所有在"制图场地"项目中呈现的案例都鼓励人们去观察、去想象、去记录、去畅想。我们要怀抱雄心，探寻更多观察世界的方式，并通过设计改善居住环境。可以说，绘图体系产生于绘图者对事物的观察。例如，通过学者比克·卡图尔和布鲁诺·德·缪德尔的道路研究可以发现，对景观的解码和效果图的生成与解构过程，均清晰地展现了交通基础设施与土地之间的关系（图7）。在这些地图中，道路不再只是存在于数据库中的简单线条，而是一系列时而相互关联、时而相互干扰、时而又彼此孤立的空间信息。很多案例——包括阿奴拉德哈·马图尔和迪利普·达·库尼亚的印度德干高原研究（图8）和沃格特景观设计事务所为哈德斯本住宅区设计的步道（图9）等——都表明，能够观察到的空间特征本身即可被抽象为符号和标志。在后一个案例中，地形条件和视域范围决定了剖面的长度，因而步道被抽象为一种基本

there is accountability for scale and projection, for experience and accessibility, for understanding and exposing bias. In looking to cartography, we expected to find more conventions but, in the end, what we found was a freedom of expression ready to be critically tapped for wider uses.

Interestingly, there is a fact that is often ignored by designers: that audience of cartographic drawings are observers as well, who narrate and imagine too. For example, with the guides to the Lakeland Fells, Alfred Wainwright spent countless hours immersed in the Fells, hiking, drawing, and translating a landscape he loved for himself and others. They have become loved guidebooks worldwide. At the same time, these guides reminded me of the drawings of the German architect Bruno Taut for a utopian alpine architecture, a provocation for a beautiful form of living to counter the wartime condition (Fig. 6). The examples found in the Cartographic Grounds project are observation and imagination, documentation and vision. Again, there is an ambition to expand the way we see the world, and in turn, how we design and live within it. The systems of drawing — for example in Bieke Cattoor and Bruno De Meulder's work on roadways where the coding of the landscape and the construction and deconstruction of the drawing renders evident a thesis about the relationship of transportation infrastructure to land (Fig. 7) — come from observation. The road is not a single line, as found in a dataset, but a set of spatial conditions that connect at times but fragment and disrupt at others. The observed spatial characteristics themselves form the signs and symbols — and this is true of many of the examples — like Anuradha Mathur and Dilip da Cunha's work in the Deccan Plateau (Fig. 8), and Vogt Landscape Architects' walk through the Hadspen Estate (Fig. 9). In this last example, topographic

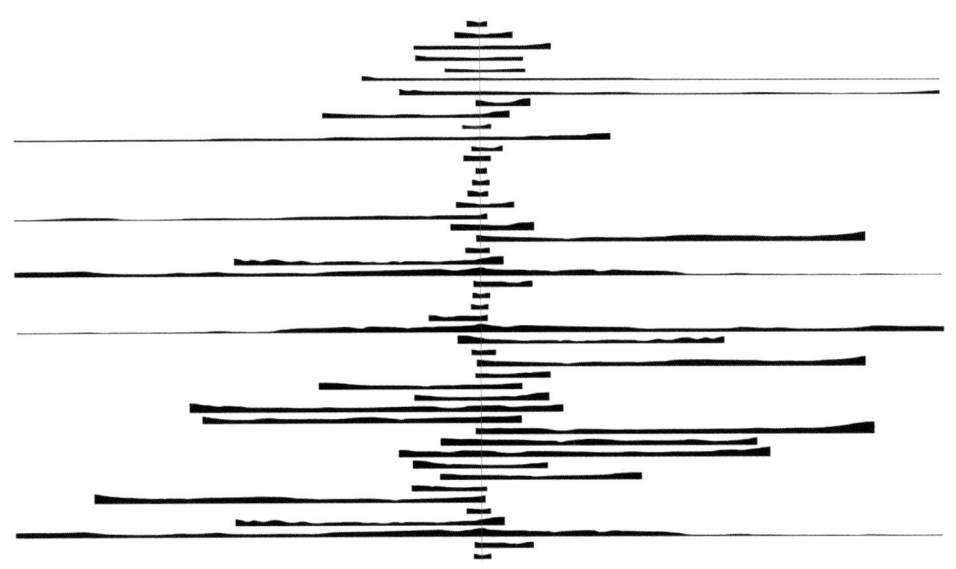

condition and viewshed inform the length of the section. The walk is abstracted to an essential relationship. These are the kinds of observations and translations that can form the basis for drawing and design. The way you draw is the way you think, and is the way you act. We wanted to make a simple point — there are many ways to think about a landscape — and thus, many ways to imagine and design alternative futures for it. I think I keep repeating myself but still, plurality cannot be lost — and perhaps, it is through close observation and careful translation that we can best find multiple meanings and ways forward.

4 Observation and Representation Training in Harvard Graduate School of Design

Observation is fundamental. At Harvard Graduate School of Design (GSD), a number of faculty are doing great work on both observation and fieldwork as it relates to design, including Design Critic Emily Wettstein, Associate Professor Gareth Doherty, and Associate Professor Rosetta S. Elkin. In seminars on fieldwork, in design studios, and in representation courses, they teach students to observe, collect, engage, and represent, as a means of developing a personal toolkit for design. It is difficult but invaluable.

Each course tackles the question of observation differently. In Wettstein's courses on representation (Fig. 10), first-year master students of Landscape Architecture are developing tools to express their own voices, and using in situ experiences to frame their

10. 在埃米莉·维特斯坦副教授的表达课上，由学生们的场地测绘方案拼接而成的图像。学生们探索了查尔斯河周边废弃区域植物和人为垃圾之间的关系。场地中杂草与废弃物的混合物经由现场观察、收集与记录，场外重新整理与再记录，最终以视频、图像和实物的形式得以再现。

11. 一位学生在爱尔兰奶牛场实地考察时基于观察绘制的图解。这项考察是加雷斯·多尔蒂副教授和尼尔·科克伍德教授开设的名为"田野调查：脱欧、边界与爱尔兰西北部的新城区"的设计课的一部分。

10. This image, compiled from a series of site mappings done in Associate Professor Emily Wettstein's representation course, explores the entanglement of plant life and human debris in an under-maintained area of the Charles River. An eclectic mix of ruderal plants and discarded objects were observed, collected, and documented on-site, arranged and re-documented off-site, and re-presented as a hybrid installation of video, image, and object arrangement.

11. A diagram translating observations made on an Irish dairy farm during the fieldwork component of Associate Professor Gareth Doherty and Professor Niall Kirkwood's studio — Field Work: Brexit, Borders, and a New-City Region for the Irish Northwest.

的空间关系。以上案例所呈现的观察和转译过程构成了制图和设计工作的基础。绘图的方式反映了制图者思考和行动的方式，我们希望借此表达一个简单的观点——观察景观的方法多种多样，基于景观的想象和设计方案也便千差万别。尽管已是老生常谈，但笔者还是希望强调，多元化切莫丢失。或许唯有经过细致的观察和谨慎的转译，我们才能发现场地所蕴含的多重价值与设计方向。

4 哈佛大学设计研究生院的观察与表达训练

观察是所有工作的根本。在哈佛大学设计研究生院，设计评论家埃米莉·维特斯坦、加雷斯·多尔蒂副教授和罗塞塔·S·埃尔金副教授等教师都在与设计相关的观察和田野调查方面有所造诣。他们通过实地考察过程中的研讨课、设计课和表达课，教导学生如何观察场地、收集资料、参与设计和展示成果，由此来拓展每个学生自己的设计工具箱。这一过程艰难却珍贵。

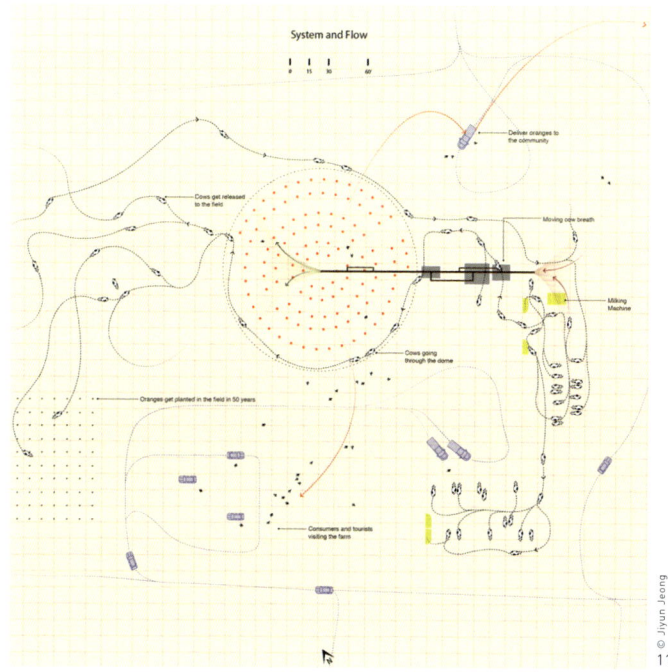

面对"观察"这一问题,不同课程的处理方式各有差异。在维特斯坦开设的表达课程中(图10),景观设计专业的硕士研究生会在第一学年中尝试开发不同的工具来表达他们的设计理念,实地考察的经验一方面塑造了他们的设计视角,另一方面也为绘图、建模和动画制作提供了素材。在多尔蒂副教授的研讨课和设计课中,实地调研主要聚焦民族志研究、本土发展现状与未来机遇(图11)。设计专业与人类学专业的学生一同参与课程,思想的火花在学科交叉过程中碰撞而生。而埃尔金副教授的课程则设置在哈佛大学的阿诺德树木园中,学生们向这里的科学家和工作人员学习知识,探索园中植物的奥秘(图12)。

在某种意义上,观察的过程也是收集资料、建立资料库的过程。以埃尔金副教授的研讨课为例,这门课程的开设缘于"植物盲"这一术语,即我们常常忽视身边的植物。在多数人眼中,植物只是绿化的工具,它们应当并且永远都会在那里。这种对植物的依赖和对环境的漠视是相当危险的。哈佛大学设计研究生院的学生均可参与这门课程,但主要授课对象还是来自景观设计系的学生和专攻风险和韧性研究的设计学硕士生,且课程非常强调与真实世界的接触。学生们在此观察植物的变化,并将实时观察结果与设计意图联系起来,再以动画、摄影、绘图、装置和讲座的形式表述各自的发现。这一能够启发灵感的过程十分必要。

以上课程的核心内容其实也是"制图场地"项目的关键理念之一。由于项目地图和航拍图大多来自谷歌、门户网站上的GIS图层,以及常用数据库,因此生成的地图、图纸和动画等结果都呈现出一定的同质性。我们应当批判性地看待这件事,并以准确性和适宜的尺度为前提,通过综合有形和无形的观察来重新定义这套机制。我们应当致力于实现多元化,尊重、理解和敬畏场地,并且创造更多可能性。

perspectives as well as provide material for their drawings, models, and films. In Doherty's seminars and studios, the fieldwork focuses on ethnography and local encounters and chance (Fig. 11). Design students work with anthropology students, and ideas cross-pollinate between the disciplines. Finally, in Elkin's courses, students work at Harvard's Arnold Arboretum, learning from the scientists and staff, while exploring live matter in situ (Fig. 12).

In a way, observation is a means of collection and library building. For Elkin's seminar course in particular, the genesis is the idea of "plant blindness" or put otherwise the notion that we fail to see the plants around us. We reduce them to a green wash, taking them for granted and assuming that they will always be there. Given our dependence on plant life and general disregard for the environment, this seems dangerous. Again, the course, taken by students across the GSD but especially those in Landscape Architecture and in the Master of Design Studies Risk and Resilience concentration, forces close encounters with the real. Students look at the variability and connect live observation with meaning and then abstract these findings into many types of media — animation, photography, drawing, installation, and presentation. It is inspiring and necessary.

Something core to this experience is also fundamental to one of the ideas behind the Cartographic Grounds project. As we acquire maps and aerials from Google, GIS layers through online portals, and common datasets, there tends to be a homogenization of the output — the map, the drawing, and the animation. We need to be critical of this — and to regain agency — through observation both tangible and intangible — without losing precision and measure. We aim for diversity, respect, understanding, awe, and creativity.

12. 在罗塞塔·S·埃尔金副教授的课堂上,一位学生正在阿诺德树木园中向同学们介绍其所在小组制作的红杉装置。

12. A student in Associate Professor Rosetta S. Elkin's course was showing her group's redwood installation at the Arnold Arboretum to her fellow students.

这就意味着设计中所应用的方法和设计结果均不同于科学领域及其他学科的观察和实验结果。对于设计而言，最终的表达必须超越对现实世界的记录与理解，畅想更加公平、更具适应性的未来。这就要求设计领域的观察工具具备比科学观测仪器更为丰富的功能。当然，科学研究所具备的试验性、循序渐进和多方协作等优势还是值得借鉴的，若能将这些特性引入更具思辨性的设计工作中，将发挥锦上添花的功效。

最后，谈及对观察结果和设计意图的转译，笔者认为，我们不应提倡"签名式设计"。首先，设计师的本职工作就是要学会倾听，而后将自己和他人的理念转译到空间设计中。设计是一个反复迭代的过程，需要不断收集来自外部的反馈以持续优化最终方案，这同样也是设计表达的重点。设计中不存在放之四海而皆准的模型，设计之美在于空间的清晰组织和营建，而不在于堆砌令人眼花缭乱的设计手法。其次，设计领域正从强调单一创作者向注重团队协作的方向发展。例如，设于伦敦的Assemble集合体的成员拒绝将个人标榜为某一项目的设计师，因为他们是作为集体而工作的。这是一种令人振奋又颇具意义的实践方式，标志着设计师已从"签名式设计"（由个人或单个企业独立承担设计）向注重团队协作和更广泛的公共利益迈进了重要一步。

5 新的挑战

景观设计学及其他同类学科正在应对更为宏大的领域，涵盖气候变化、社会不平等、政治经济危机等复杂而严峻的问题。若发挥得当，设计表达可以实现多元化、可靠性和高品质等政治抱负；若发挥不当，设计表达则可能沦入机械、刻板的固化形象中，甚至具有误导性。当前，场地转译正在变得更为直接，设计亦跳脱对等比例仿真模型的固执坚持，转而探讨建造形式和材料选择。在这一背景下，设计表达更需要呈现其批判姿态。虚拟现实等先进智能仿真工具和更加便捷的数据获取途径成为了设计师的宝贵财富，可以帮助他们畅想并检验空间设计方案。但与此同时，设计师也要认识到这些技术和信息可能带来的偏差与限制。当面对更为庞大的数据时，我们需要意识到细节数据的获取其实是有门槛的。进行精准测量和获取高分辨率的数据往往耗资巨大。例如，只有具备经济实力的国家才能够实现对国土（甚至是他们认为具有殖民意义的土地）进行1:25 000比例的测绘。地理空间数据的获取始终与国家实力紧密相联。可以说，地球上的每一寸土地都已经经过测绘，但测绘结果的分辨率却大相径庭，这种差异同样也表现在地图的特征性表达之中。

此外，视觉表达日渐呈现动态特征，为了保障它们在不同尺度和时间背景下都清晰可读，我们需要把握工作中所运用到的表达媒介的特性。景观设计师应当探寻能够协调单纯地理信息和其他抽象信息的途径，同时找到整合自然地形、社会、政治、环境和经济状况等各

That said, the methods and outcomes in design are distinct from those of the sciences and other disciplines that observe and experiment. For design, representation must extend beyond documenting and understanding the world that exists, towards imagining a more equitable and adaptive future. This requires tools of observation that go beyond scientific representation. What I admire about the scientific process is the ability to test, to be slow and incremental, and to collaborate. It would be great to find a way to bring these qualities more into speculative design work.

Finally, in thinking about the translation of observation and intent, the practice of "signature drawing" is not one to encourage. First, as designers, it is our job to listen to, transform, and make spatial our own ideas and those of others. The design process is iterative and requires feedback, indicating an evolving outcome. This should be reflected in the representation. There is not a one-style-fits-all model. The beauty of design is found in the clear organization and creation of space, not in the visibility of the hand of the designer. Secondly, the design fields are rightly moving away from an emphasis of single authorship towards recognition of the collaborative nature of the work. In fact, there are practices — like Assemble in London — whose members refuse to identify individually as the designer behind any given project. They work as a collective, demonstrating an exciting and vital way of practicing. It is a move away from the signature of any one person, or even one firm, towards a communal effort and a greater public good.

5 New Challenges

Landscape Architecture and their cognate disciplines are tackling broad territories and addressing multiple complex and sobering issues, ranging from climate change, social inequality to political and economic instability. At its best, representation shares the political ambition of diversity, authenticity, and quality. At its worst, it is machinic, formulaic, and misleading. In a world, where translation is becoming more direct, where designs are moving from 1:1 model and simulation into a built, material form, representation must adopt a critical stance. Advanced tools, such like virtual reality and other intelligent simulations, and greater access to data, are extremely valuable assets for designers to envision and test their spatial proposals. But, in doing so, designers must be aware of the biases and limitations behind the technologies and information. As we encounter more data, we should acknowledge that detail is a privilege. Accurate

13-1. "汹涌海洋"项目采用交互式动态制图过程来呈现美国纽约市的海平面上升问题。不同于常见的通过未被淹没的陆地来展现水位上升的视角，该项目将重点放在了已经或即将被淹没的土地上。

13-2. 这张来自"汹涌海洋"项目的截图显示了人口与经济等因素影响下的海平面上升问题。复杂的气候变化危机将给较为弱势的地区带来巨大风险。

13-1. This capture from the Surging Seas interactive and dynamic mapping project shows the sea level rise in New York City. Unlike most maps of rising waters that focus on the land left over, it places the visual emphasis on the land that will be lost as the ocean rises.

13-2. This capture of the Surging Seas project indicates a combination of the sea level rise with the population and economic indicators, underlining that the climate crisis is a complex concern that places great risk on vulnerable constituencies.

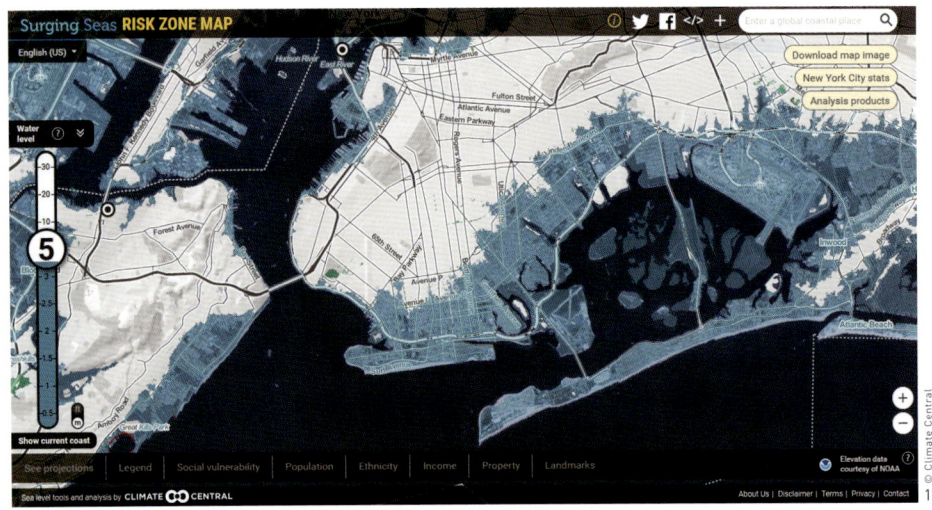

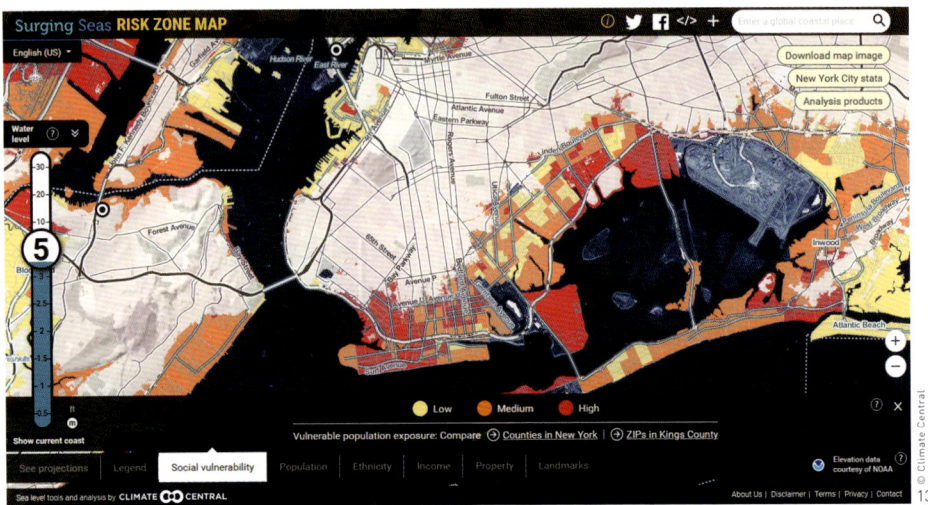

surveying and high-resolution data is expensive. For example, the 1:25,000 topographical map is a product of wealthy nations, either mapping their own territories or those of colonial interest. There is, and always has been, a correlation between power and the availability of geospatial data. Now, we tend to think that everywhere is mapped, but the resolution varies tremendously and this is reflected in the character of the representation.

In addition, as visual representations become more dynamic, requiring legibility across scale and time, it is important not to lose track of the characteristics of the medium with which we work. Landscape architects must develop means to reconcile the purely geographic with the highly abstract, as well as find ways to combine different forms of information to relate the social, political, environmental, and economic conditions to the physical terrain. Further, in the face of daunting predictions about the state of our world, we must open narratives that are both critical of harmful practices and optimistic about future potential. It is one of our tasks to change dominant perceptions that limit the palette and extent of practice. Our visualizations form the context and argument for our work. The stronger case we can make the more impactful the outcome will be. For example, we often look at sea level rise from the perspective of the land that remains dry and the result is visually underwhelming, indicating, perhaps, that there is a lot of land available and less pressure to act. However, the San Francisco based cartographers Stamen Maps, with the introduction of an interactive Surging Seas project lead by Climate Central, focus instead on the watery lands submerged (Fig. 13). It is a simple inversion but has dramatic effect. They combine economic and environmental data to make a strong case for action. The visualizations are clear and edited, yet complex and subversive. We need more of these types of projects — both cartographic and not — that relate multiple factors, dynamically, to create a context for change. **LAF**

类信息的方法。尽管人们对于世界发展的预期并不乐观，我们还是应当对各种言论保持开放的态度，既接受针对无益实践的批评，也对未来的发展潜力保持乐观。我们的职责之一便是改变限制了实践方法与范围的主流观念。可视化过程既是我们工作的基础，也为设计提供重要的论据：论据越充分，得到的结果也就越有说服力。例如，我们总是立足于未被淹没的陆地来探讨海平面上升问题，视觉冲击力往往不足，甚至可能传达出可用土地充足而不必急于采取行动的误导性信息。但与此同时，由美国气候中心组织主导、旧金山Stamen制图公司参与的"汹涌海洋"交互式项目却将重点放在了已被淹没的土地上（图13）。尽管这一反向操作非常简单，效果却十分显著。他们结合了相关的经济和环境数据，为采取行动应对海平面上升提供了有力依据。这样的可视化过程看似清晰简单，实质上却复杂且颇具颠覆性。我们需要持续关注更多类似的、涉及多种因素的项目（无论是否涉及制图），为未来设计的转型创建语境。**LAF**

REFERENCES

[1] Taut, B. (1919). Alpine Architektur. New York: Prestel Publishing.
[2] Cattoor, B. & De Meulder, B. (2011). Figures Infrastructures: An Atlas of Roads and Railways. Amsterdam: SUN Architecture.
[3] Mathur, A., & Da Cunha, D. (2006). Deccan Traverses: The Making of Bangalore's Terrain. Kolkata: Rupa & Co.

景观设计的参与、解读与表达
PARTICIPATION, INTERPRETATION, AND REPRESENTATION OF LANDSCAPE DESIGN

张东*
张唐景观合伙人

ZHANG Dong
Partner of Z+T Studio

*通讯作者
地址：上海市新华路543号1号楼
邮编：200052
邮箱：info@ztsla.com

摘要

在本次访谈中，作为张唐景观合伙人，受访人张东首先指出每个民族的景观都应与当地的文化密切相关，认为设计具有中国文化识别性的景观应当是中国景观设计师价值体系的一部分，并强调景观设计在考虑可持续性和韧性提升策略的同时，也应注重与环境教育的结合。随后，基于将景观设计过程视为"两个客观、一个主观"的总结，张东认为设计师对场地的解读，以及个人的知识储备、价值判断和审美倾向都会影响其从场地中获取信息、做出判断和进行设计。在承认生态效益、公众参与是景观设计的重要议题的同时，他格外强调设计的核心价值是创造性地解决问题，景观设计师不可忽视空间营造和对美学的追求。最后，他介绍了张唐景观目前采用的"全过程参与"工作模式，以及这种模式对设计师观察与表达能力的重要意义。

关键词

景观设计；观察；表达；文化景观；美学；"全过程参与"工作模式

ABSTRACT

At the beginning of this interview, Zhang Dong, partner of Z+T Studio, believes that landscapes of each nation should be closely rooted in its own culture and designing landscapes which praise China's cultural identity should be a part of Chinese designers' values and beliefs. Beside of integrating with strategies of sustainability and resilience, landscape design should also combine with environmental education. Zhang summarizes a landscape design process into "two objective aspects and one subjective aspect," and points out that a designer's professional knowledge, social values, and aesthetic preferences together influence his / her acquisition of information from sites and the design what and how he / she will make. While recognizing the importance of ecology and public participation to landscape design, he stresses that design essentially is to solve problems in a creative way and landscape designers should not neglect the fundamentality of spatial creation and aesthetics to the profession and the discipline. Finally, he explains the Whole-Process Participation design mode adopted by Z+T Studio, and how it helps improve designers' capacity in observation and representation.

KEYWORDS

Landscape Design; Observation; Representation; Cultural Landscapes; Aesthetics; Whole-Process Participation Design Mode

采访 田乐　编辑 冉玲于　田乐　翻译 田乐　李慧彦
INTERVIEWED　Tina TIAN　EDITED BY　RAN Lingyu　Tina TIAN　TRANSLATED BY　Tina TIAN　LI Huiyan

---

您曾说，"一个人……只生存在某个时代，接受这个时代的价值观，面对这个时代的问题。"[1]对于设计师而言，这个时代的价值观是什么？

张东（以下简称张）：首先，身为中国人，我们都希望随着中国经济的增长，中国的文化影响力也能够不断提升扩大。我经常思考的一个问题是：中国究竟能向世界文明贡献什么样的景观？正如那句话，"最民族的就是最世界的"，每个民族的景观都应该与当地的文化密切相关，即形成独特的文化景观。我认为设计具有中国文化识别性的景观应当是中国景观设计师价值体系的一部分，而这种带有中国文化印迹的设计并不只是简单的对景或置石。

此外，我们还应看向未来。未来，我们将面临诸多环境问题，因此张唐景观在每个项目中都在尝试引入可持续性和韧性提升策略，同时——最为重要的是——注重与环境教育的结合。当前的生态环境之所以如此糟糕，就是因为大多数人并未真正意识到环境健康的价值，以及洁净的水和空气对我们每个人的日常生活是多么珍贵。我们希望通过设计途径将人引入自然，唤醒人对自然的敬畏之心。例如，我们在项目中营造的洁净的水体，人们可以在里面奔跑、触摸，帮助人们意识到自然与我们的生活息息相关，健康的环境对我们至关重要（图1）。

您将景观设计过程总结为"两个客观、一个主观"，"两个客观"即设计过程应当尽量客观地进行场地观察和分析，客观地聆听客户和使用者的需求，"一个主观"是设计师对场地的个性化解读和表达。您如何理解这种观察与表达之间的相互关系？

张：首先，我认为设计的目的并不是为了展示设计师自己的个性，而是要通过解读场地进行创作。面对同样的场地、同样的使用群体，不同设计师的解决方案会千差万别，是因为每个人的关注点不同。他们对场地的理解和解读不一样，设计成果也就千差万别。

1. 长沙中航城国际社区山水间公园。景观设计尝试与环境教育相结合。

1. Hillside Eco-Park of Zhonghang Caticity Community, Changsha. The landscape design integrates with environmental education.

You once said that "A man... live only in his age, so he must follow the values of the time and face the problems of it." As a designer, what do you mean by the values of this age?

ZHANG Dong (ZHANG hereafter): First, as Chinese, we all hope China's cultural influence can continuously increase along with its economic growth. I often ponder that what kind of landscapes can China actually contribute to the world civilization? As a saying goes, "what best represents a nation can be most cognized by the world," each nation should create its unique cultural landscapes that are closely rooted in its own culture. I think that designing landscapes which praise China's cultural identity should be a part of Chinese designers' values and beliefs. But such imprints of Chinese culture are not simply about creating echoing landscapes or stone arrangements that is referred from traditional Chinese gardens.

Besides, we need to think forward. In the future, humans will face more serious environmental challenges, and Z+T Studio attempts integrating strategies of sustainability and resilience, and — most importantly — environmental education with landscape design of each project. Today, the world's ecosystems are deteriorated so badly, and most people are actually unaware of the impact of ecosystems on human's well-being — they do not realize how precious clean water and air is to everyone's daily life. We hope to reconnect people with the nature through design approaches and with our respects in awe. For example, we create waterscapes with crystal-clear water where people can run in and touch, helping them realize the association between nature and our life, as well as the value that a healthy environment means to us (Fig. 1).

You have summarized a landscape design process into "two objective aspects and one subjective aspect." The former refers that designers need to systematically observe and analyze site conditions, and to be clear with clients' demands and users' needs. The latter refers that designers are expected to represent the sites with individual's interpretations and thoughts. What do you think of the relationship between observation and representation in a landscape design process?

ZHANG: First, I believe that design is not to show how novelty a project can be, but to originally create based on what designers read and interpret about the sites. Facing a same site and the same users, the proposals by different designers may greatly vary. The different ways they each observe, read, and represent the site make the individuals' design so diversified.

场地是景观设计的限制，也是它的魅力所在。张唐景观注重符合场地的独特性设计，这不仅有赖于对场地的分析和研究，更多的是如何从场地出发寻找设计灵感，最终形成只能发生在该场地上的景观。

对设计师而言，明确的使用者信息是保证设计能够满足需求的一大前提。然而，中国很多设计项目缺少公共参与环节，项目的使用者是不明确的。尽管委托方往往会对项目的未来使用人群进行预估，但与项目建成后的实际使用群体之间会存在偏差，因而这种根据虚构使用者来推进设计的方式本身即存在问题。

在使用者需求不明确的情况下，设计师至少要尽可能地去了解不同使用者的需求是什么。设计师的个人职业经验和生活经验，以及对场地的感知非常重要，只有经历过才会明白什么样的空间才是使用者所期望的。以居住区设计为例，设计师需要换位思考：城市社区中的居民到底希望居住在什么样的景观中？

和我自己一样，现在很多城市居民都是从小城镇迁到大城市定居下来的，人们对于新社区的景观往往抱有想象，会希望它是"高档""大气"或者"尊贵"的，能够彰显他们生活水平的提升。很多时候，设计师追求所谓的"欧式生活""法式景观"意象，或者从一些传统中国园林经典中寻找灵感，将居住小区设计成度假酒店的模样。但这种意象的描绘并不等同于美好的生活，它们往往过于注重视觉感受而忽略了景观的社会价值。过去，中国人大多生活在村庄或者大院里，彼此非常熟悉，形成了和谐的"熟人社会"。但在城镇化进程中出现了越来越多的封闭社区，社区居民也都被防盗门窗隔离，大家的关系变得疏离陌生。基于生活体验，我们发现居民们普遍向往亲切、平等的社区氛围，认为能够促进大家交流的空间才是好的社区景观——这与从想象出发、追求意象的设计有着本质区别。因而我们希望能够打造一种类似社区公共客厅的景观空间，鼓励居民交流互动，形成一种和谐的社区氛围。我们的社区景观设计项目正在努力传达这种价值观。

The limits of a site also offer the charm to the design. Z+T Studio focuses on developing design works that are specifically suitable to the sites. It depends not only on thorough site analysis and investigation, but also on the ideas how to create a landscape that is utterly rooted in the site and can only occur right there.

For designers, being aware of the users of a project is a prerequisite to guarantee that their design plans work. In China, however, public participation is absent in most cases and designers often have no idea about the users of their projects. Besides, the predicted user profiles by project clients usually mismatch with actual scenarios, verifying that it is problematic to develop a design based on unreliable information.

But, in the cases where users' needs are unclear, designers should at least learn about the needs of different users as far as possible. It requires designers perceiving the site with their professional knowledge and life experience, only after which will they know what kind of space is expected by users. For example, to a residential project, designers need to put themselves in the shoes of residents: what kinds of landscapes in urban communities do we want?

Now, people who migrate from small towns to big cities, just like me, tend to live in new communities with "high-end," "grand," or "noble" landscapes that could manifest the high living standard they have. In many cases, designers seek to create the so-called landscape images of "European lifestyle," "French villas," or traditional Chinese gardens, making residential communities look like resorts. However, creating such a visually depicted landscape is not equal to creating a wonderful life for the residents, because designers neglect what social benefits a landscape can make. In the past decades, most Chinese lived in villages, communes, or compounds, enjoying a harmonious "community of acquaintances." However, today more and more enclosed communities are built during the aggressive urbanization, where the residents are isolated by burglar-proof doors and windows and becoming alienated from each other. Life experience tells us that people generally long for living in friendly communities where they feel a sense of belonging and feel free to communicate with others. This is landscape designers' job to create such places — it is completely different from those design works based on fictions or seeking for images. Z+T Studio makes efforts in making landscapes that serve as a public living room in communities, encouraging interactions between residents. Our landscape design for residential projects is conceived under and tries to spread such concepts.

2, 3. 北京万科时代中心。水景采用玻璃材料结合LED互动灯光设计，将"光"引入城市，使这里成为了一个颇具吸引力的城市场所。

2, 3. Vanke Times Center Plaza, Beijing. The waterscape is constructed with glass and interactive LED lighting design. The project that takes light as the design theme has turned the site into an inviting urban space.

"一个主观"是我们更感兴趣的话题。如果将建筑设计和景观设计进行对比，我认为建筑设计的本质是割裂——或部分割裂——人与自然的联系，而景观设计的本质是连接人和自然。我最近在罗德岛设计学院教授一门设计课，进行了一些实验性练习。例如，每个学生选择一个自己感兴趣的自然现象（海浪、闪电、暴风雨等），然后研究如何将这种自然现象引入到设计中并应用于城市环境中。传统园林设计将自然的山川象征性地"再造"于城市中，这一个过程本身就是一个客观-主观-客观的过程。而在这项训练中，学生先对自然现象进行主观解读，然后再将其"翻译"成现代景观设计语汇，并恰当地应用在城市环境中。这个过程非常有趣，在其中，"主观"包括对场地的解读，也包括对场地相关的自然（如阳光、风、雨等）本身的解读，设计师的知识储备、价值判断和审美倾向都会影响设计师从场地中获取信息、做出判断和进行设计。在某种程度上来说，设计师对场地的"主观"解读与创作比"客观"地重视自然事物更有意思。

例如，在北京万科时代广场项目中，建筑北侧的广场由于是消防通道，除了铺装外不能进行绿化，也不能建造任何凸起或下凹的结构。巨大的铺装广场需要被激活，成为周边居民愿意前往和停留的场所。我们在现场踏勘的时候发现"光"是这个场地最大的问题：场地上总是有周边建筑投射的阴影，对于北方地区来说，这是一个负面因素，但同时我们也认为在这种场地中人们会对"光"更加敏感。建筑的投影会随着季节变化在场地上产生丰富的变化。除了利用不锈钢反光材料映射出光线在不同季节和时间的变化之外，我们也将"光"引入到互动性水景中。场地得以被成功激活，成为了受周围社区居民欢迎的城市公共空间。甲方很喜欢我们提出的用光线变化记录时间季节变化这一概念，并将项目称作"光之广场"（图2，3）。

张唐景观的设计项目中大量运用了精雕细琢的人工性设计元素、艺术装置、游乐设施等，而比较少见对于自然生态系统的营造。这些

Here I would like to address about designers' individual interpretation and representation. Personally, I hold that architectural design is to contrast, at least partly, human with nature, and landscape design is to tie the two together. Recently, I am teaching a design course in Rhode Island School of Design with experimental training programs. For example, each student is asked to choose a natural phenomenon (tide, lightning, storm, etc.) he or she is interested in, and then to combine the natural phenomenon with landscape design and introduce it into urban environments. Traditional garden design tends to make natural landscapes symbolically "reappeared" in cities — it is an objective-subjective-objective process of design. In this exercise, instead, students are expected to interpret natural phenomena in their individual way, "translate" them into modern design language, and apply into the creation of urban landscapes. This is a quite interesting process, which reflects a diversity of designers' reading and interpretations of sites, as well as the natural elements associated (e.g., light, wind, rain, etc.). A designer's professional knowledge, social values, and aesthetic preferences will together influence his / her acquisition of information from sites and the design what and how he / she will make. In a certain sense, compared with honestly creating natural environments, this is an ability that exactly manifests the charm of landscape design.

For example, in the Vanke Times Center Plaza in Beijing, the existing big-size square in the north of buildings is nothing but an area of pavement since it serves as a fire control space where no landscaping, structure or elevation changes is allowed. The landscape design needs to transform the square into a dynamic recreational place for residents of surrounding neighborhoods. During field survey, we found that the biggest challenge on the site was that there is always the shade of the surrounding buildings in daytime, which is a negative fact to places in northern China. However, our design was also inspired by this challenge of light — the shadow of the buildings varies between seasons. The design not only used stainless steel reflectors to manifest the changes of light and shadow in daytime and over seasons, but also created an interactive waterscape that combines with lighting design. The site now becomes a popular urban public space serving the residents of surrounding communities. The client loved the design idea of highlighting light changes in different time around a year and named the project "Plaza of Light" (Fig. 2, 3).

In Z+T Studio's landscape design works, delicate constructed features, artistic installations, and recreational facilities are commonly found, instead of natural elements or ecological

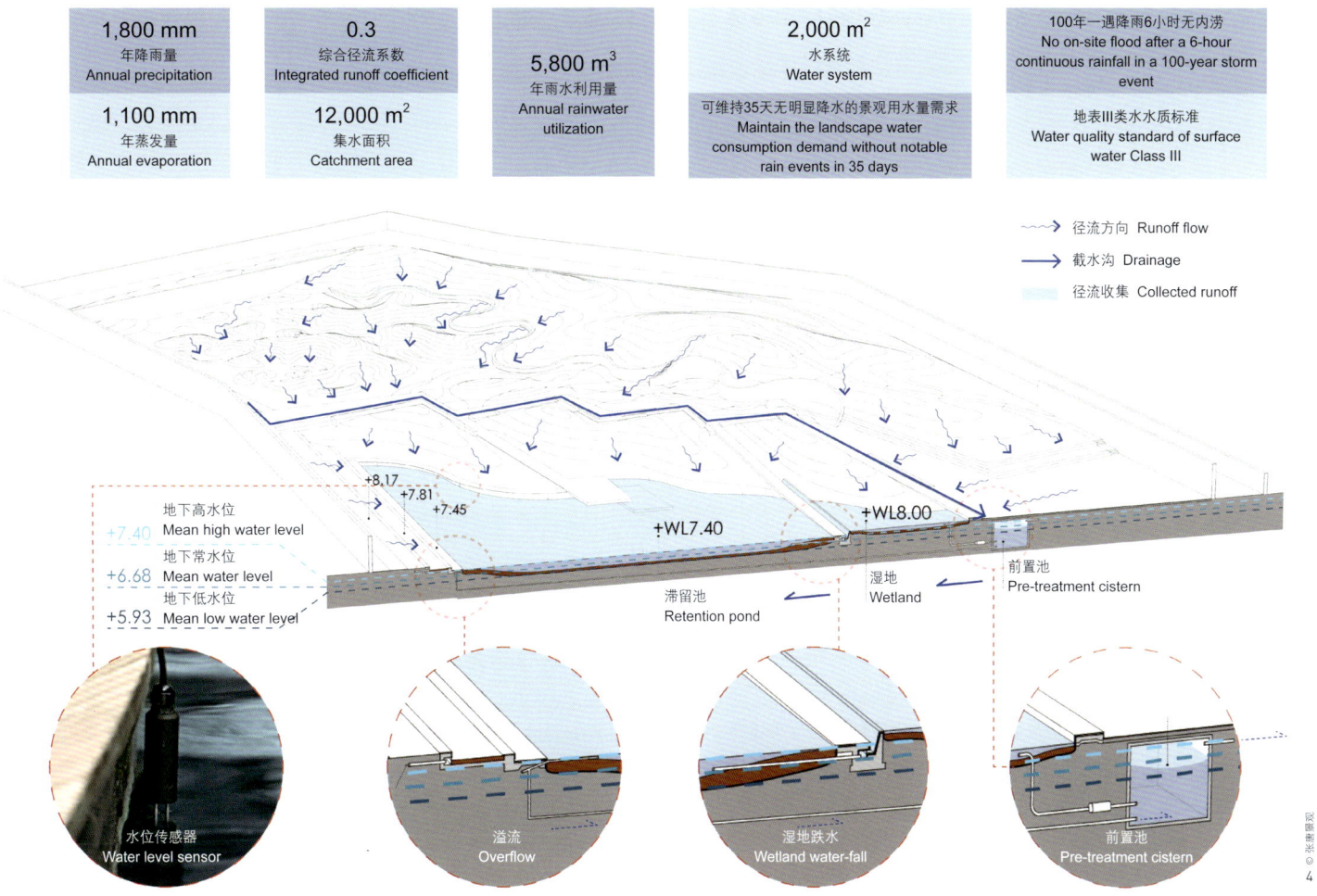

4, 5. 广州大鱼公园。通过收集场地的降雨,并借由沉水植物湿地系统净化水体,形成公园中重要的湖区景观。

4, 5. Dory Park, Guangzhou. The important lakescape was created through rainwater harvest and with a submerged-plant wetland system that is used for water purification.

设计决定是出于哪些考虑?您如何考虑这些装置、设施的地域独特性?

张:由于事务所的性质和规模,我们的项目尺度大都比较小,也多为地产商委托项目。这类项目有其特殊性,有优势,也有限制。我们的项目会给人以上的感觉,或许是因为这些元素会更加吸引大家的关注。其实,我们每个项目基本上都会对场地的自然条件进行一定的梳理;在条件允许的情况下,我们都尝试在满足周边人群日常使用需求的前提下,为场地设计一套自维持的水文循环系统。可以说,自然生态系统的营造是我们设计中很重要的一方面,不过这部分工作往往不太容易引起关注(图4,5)。

景观设计中真正独特的东西是有一定限度的,并不是所有的东西都需要是独特的,也应该考虑这些元素与场地的适配性。任何"表达"都不会是没有限制条件的,设计师需要根据场地条件通盘考虑设计元素的运用,尤其需要考虑项目后期的管理及维护问题。可持续性不仅仅是生态环境上的,还包括社会和经济层面。我们项目中的许多精雕细琢的元素都是在充分考虑其独特性的同时,反复权衡项目的附

creations. Why do you make such design decisions? How do you consider regional identity and site uniqueness when introducing artistic installations, facilities, and other man-made landscape features?

ZHANG: Due to the type and size of the studio, our commissions are mostly small-scaled and often by real estate

6. 苏州樾园。曲溪采用整石雕刻，在工厂分段制作之后运至现场拼装。
7. 南京汤山矿坑公园采矿乐园。经过和甲方的多次沟通，设计团队将原来的采石场废料堆积场改造成了一个儿童探索乐园。各种活动设施的设计基于原有地形，并充分考虑到管理和维护因素。

6. Yue-Yuan Courtyard, Suzhou. The sinuous "creek" was created with the whole-piece crafting techniques; all the pieces were crafted in factory and assembled on site.
7. Mining Garden of Tangshan Quarry Park, Nanjing. After long-time negotiations with the client, the design team conceived of transforming the dumping place of quarry waste into a children playfield. All the programs were designed based on the existing terrain and with considerations in built-up operation and maintenance.

developers. These projects have both obvious advantages and restrictions. A reason why people have such an impression about our projects may be that those artist features are more eye-catching. Actually, in each case, we analyze and improve the natural setting and the ecosystems of sites under a certain scope; if possible, we always try to design a self-sustained hydrologic system for the sites while meeting users' everyday needs. Improving a site's natural landscape and ecosystem is a very important part of our job, though it less attracts people's attention (Fig. 4, 5).

In landscape design, truly unique things are limited in number. Not everything needs to be unique, and we should care about the suitability of such artist elements with a site. A representation of design is stemmed from yet limited by the site. Design decisions have to be made site-specifically, carefully, and holistically, especially in management and maintenance after the project's completion. The sustainability of a landscape design is defined by the negotiation between ecological, social, and economic considerations. In Z+T Studio's cases, our design decisions of introducing installations or constructed elements were made after a holistic understanding of cultural and social importance, costs, construction conditions, and time limits, and built-up maintenance, in addition to site peculiarities. For example, in the Yueyuan Project, Suzhou, we create an exquisite sinuous "creek" that cost about RMB 200,000 in the courtyard of an area of nearly 900 square meters. This unique piece of art not only pays homage to the culture of Suzhou traditional garden, but also is allowed by the site conditions for installation and the budget of built-up maintenance — The design is appropriate for the site, but not for others (Fig. 6). Another fact in China is that now many parks have no specific funds for operation. To such cases, we would make quite different design plans if they had long-term and sufficient funds or public support (Fig. 7).

Last but not least, I do not understand since when making efforts in creating beauty seems to become something negative or

加值、造价、施工条件、工期以及后期养护之后做出的决定。以苏州樾园项目为例，在总面积约900m²的内庭院里塑造了一条"曲溪"，造价大约20万元。在场地安装条件允许和后期维护经费支持的情况下，这一精致的艺术化景观元素表达了设计师对苏州当地园林文化的致敬。这个设计可能不适合其他项目，但在这个项目中，它是适合的（图6）。再比如，当前中国的很多公园都没有设置专门的运营资金，如果我们能明确知道某个项目在未来是否会有稳定和足够的资金投入或社会支持，我们在设计上的决定可能会大不相同（图7）。

另外，非常重要的一点是，不知道从什么时候开始，好像追求美变成了一件负面的、肤浅的事。当前，国内外的景观设计行业愈发强调生态效益、公众参与等议题，而忽视了对于审美的思考。我认为这种趋势有些矫枉过正，甚至是道德绑架。我承认生态效益、公众参与很重要，但空间的营造、美学的追求亦是景观设计的核心。设计的核

心价值即创造性地解决问题，可我认为当前景观设计的价值在倒退，或者说在异化；如果景观设计师过度地迷失于管理者的身份中，那么其创造性势必会被弱化。社会变得更加美好是需要全社会共同推进的，我们不能要求每个景观设计项目都去解决社会问题。而且，不同的设计师关注不同的维度，创造出不同的价值，才造就了多样化的社会。

请您介绍一下张唐景观的"全过程参与"工作模式，以及这种模式是如何训练设计师观察与表达的能力的。

张：这是一个很有意思的话题。在传统中国造园中，设计师根据自己对场地条件的观察和对自然的理解，指挥匠人表达、营造一个新的"自然"；而现代景观采用的方式已经将这个由"观察"到"表达"的过程拆分成了许多小的步骤。这样的拆分符合分工需要，但也大大地压缩了设计师"观察"的时间和参与"表达"的机会。当前很多设计公司甚至会将设计阶段进一步细分为概念、方案、扩初、施工等阶段，每个阶段都由不同的设计师负责。张唐景观采用设计师全过程参与的工作流程，不仅仅是参与设计阶段，也深度参与到施工阶段。这种做法某种程度上能将"观察"和"表达"更紧密地联系起来。许多信息是在项目推进中逐渐明晰的，设计师需要根据实际情况与需求进行及时调整和优化。相较于分块设计模式，这样的全过程参与模式的经济回报相对较低，但是却有利于设计师个人的全面成长。

我们项目的最后建成效果往往要优于设计平面图或施工图，正是因为方案会随着设计过程不断调整、改善——这也是我们不太愿意参加设计竞赛的原因，设计竞赛通常比拼的是平面方案设计、效果图或是动画水平，这些并不能突显我们的优势。

此外，与现代景观行业相配合的工种和各种咨询方也越来越多样和复杂，出现了结构设计、水景设计、植物设计、土壤设计、灯光照

shallow in landscape design. Currently, landscape profession at home and abroad increasingly emphasize ecological considerations and public participation in design practice while neglect explorations in aesthetics. I think this is somewhat overcorrect, or even like a morality hijacking. Ecology and public participation are of course important, but spatial creation and aesthetics are also fundamental to the profession and the discipline. Essentially, design is to solve problems in a creative way, but today I see a regression or an alienation of it. If a landscape designer is too obsessed with acting as a manager, he or she will less care about the leverage of design creativity. A wonderful society can only be built and promoted by the whole society itself, rather than a number of landscape design projects; it is unrealistic to ask designers to address big social problems in each of their cases. The variety of design focuses leads to a rich diversity in values, thus contributing to building a wonderful society.

Could you introduce Z+T Studio's Whole-Process Participation design mode, and how does it help improve designers' capacity in observation and representation?

ZHANG: This is a very interesting topic. In traditional Chinese garden making, through site observation and with their knowledge and understanding of nature, designers used to direct craftsmen to create landscapes that represents the nature. While, the working mode adopted by modern landscape architects divides the observation-representation process into a series of steps. This meets needs of nowadays labor division, but largely decreases designers' opportunities in site observation and design representation. In some cases, the design process is subdivided into stages of conceptual design, master plan, detailed design, and construction plan, each of which is in the charge of different designers. Z+T Studio adopts the Whole-Process Participation design mode, which encourages designers participating in the entire design and construction process, making the observation and representation of a project a holism. It also helps designers have a comprehensive understanding of a site as the project gocs and make adjustment and recalibration of design plans to respond to site changes and actual needs. Although the Whole-Process Participation mode sees a relatively low economic return, it greatly contributes to the professional capacity of landscape designers.

Such constant adjustment and recalibrations made Z+T Studio's projects have a better built-up appearance and performance than what we expected — This is also why we tend to decline invitations of design competitions, our

8. 西安创意谷风之亭。在位于4层楼高的屋顶花园之上，设计团队希望利用场地多风的特征，设计一个与风相关的装置，并在设计过程全程中对材料、尺度、模型、空间感受等进行了大量尝试。最终建成效果或许并不完美，但很难想象这类设计构想可以通过常规的设计工作模式产生。

8. Pavilion of Wind, Innovation Valley, Xi'an. As a roof garden of the four-storied building, the design team conceived to manifest the windy rooftop with an artist installation and made a considerable effort in improving its appearance and performance with experiments in material selection, size, modeling, spatial experience, etc. The built-up result may not be perfect, but it still is a good example that realize innovative design ideas through an unconventional working mode.

明、艺术装置、户外家具等专项机构及产品供应商。设计行业越来越像是一种统筹协调行业，而且似乎多学科、多工种合作已成必然。而我常常思考：这是唯一正确的发展趋势吗？

我们在许多项目中也的确体会到多行业合作的必要性。术业有专攻，不同专业合作的结果往往会更好。但是，我相信行业的细分应该有一定的限度。行业细分随现代工业的发展而发展，而且往往和商业化相关。但对于景观行业而言，我们不应过分迷信工业化以及行业细分，因为景观设计师面对的项目千差万别，每个项目都应进行个性化设计。过多的分工可能会对景观设计行业带来两个负面后果。其一是流水线工业化的设计和建造会让景观变得单一，缺乏独特性和识别性——你会在不同城市、不同项目中看到同样的家具和设施。其二是可能会导致景观造价过高，如果市场总量固定，行业细分会导致单个项目造价过高，进而导致景观的简化处理，这样反过来会影响市场规模与行业风气。

在全过程参与模式中，虽然也会有跨专业合作，但我们可以进行统一调配和把控，在总体上节约建造成本，并确保设计师的设计理念能够恰当地表达出来。当然，分工不是目的，全程参与也不是目的。这一模式是我们在实践中摸索出来的，可能适合张唐景观这种规模的设计事务所，并不适于大型综合设计公司；适合我们做的项目类型，并非适用于所有项目（图8）。各个景观设计公司应当探索适合自己的方式，甚至针对不同的项目采用相应的恰当方式，以求更好地"观察"和"表达"，更好地为客户、为使用者服务。**LAF**

strengths can be hardly reflected by design plans, renderings, or animation.

In addition, landscape architecture now is collaborating with more and more other disciplines and professions — these collaborations get increasingly thorough too. New design institutes have emerged which provide customized design services in structure, waterscape, planting, soil, lighting, artistic installations, outdoor furniture, etc. In my opinion, landscape design now becomes an industry that relies on, coordinate, and lead transdisciplinary collaborations, and it seems that this trend is inevitable. However, I often ponder: Is this the only future of landscape design?

Indeed, we have learned the necessity of transdisciplinary collaborations to landscape design. Professionals with different expertise working together often leads to a greater outcome. However, landscape architects need to carefully consider the suitability of such a collaboration-and-segmentation mode in our profession. Industrial segmentation is a product of modern industrialization and somehow influenced by commercialization. To landscape industry, however, we should not exaggerate the advantages of industrial segmentation, because landscape designers face a huge variety of cases, each of which requires a specific scheme. Excessive segmentation of landscape design may lead to two reluctant consequences. First, either design or construction may lose diversity or identity — the same furniture, amenities, and facilities will be indiscriminately used in different cities and projects. Second, it may cause a higher cost of single projects if there is too much labor division, which would result in a compromise to the design, eventually in turn having an impact on the market size and the ethos in the profession.

The Whole-Process Participation mode not only encourages transdisciplinary cooperation, but also emphasizes landscape architects' leading role in the coordination. It helps ensure budget management and the quality of design. Of course, introducing a new working mode is not our goal; it comes out from our experience in practice, and may be suitable for design studios of a similar type and size like Z+T Studio and applicable to the projects like what we do (Fig. 8). Each landscape design firm needs to explore their own working mode, or adopts different modes in different cases, which supports designers for a better observation and representation of sites while meeting the needs of clients and users. **LAF**

REFERENCE

[1] Zhang, D., & Tang, Z. (2019). Participatory Landscape (p.4). Shanghai: Tongji University Press.

本文引用格式 / PLEASE CITE THIS ARTICLE AS

Zander, H. (2019). Global Perspectives on Landscape and Territory. Landscape Architecture Frontiers, 7(5), 98-107. https://doi.org/10.15302/J-LAF-1-030005

全球视野下的景观与地域环境
GLOBAL PERSPECTIVES ON LANDSCAPE AND TERRITORY

哈尼兹·詹德

哈佛大学设计研究生院景观设计学硕士，奥斯陆建筑与设计学院博士生

Hannes ZANDER*

Master in Landscape Architecture, Harvard Graduate School of Design; PhD Fellow at the Oslo School of Architecture and Design

*Corresponding Author
Address: Maridalsveien 29, 0175 Oslo, Norway
Email: hannes.zander@aho.no

摘要

《南半球的观察：全球视野下的景观与地域环境》是国际景观合作组织（ILC）出版的首本书籍。该书倡导透过"景观"这一媒介来解读当下的环境挑战和社会政治变革，讨论不同尺度的场地及其环境背景。随着全球城市化进程的日益推进，城市中的自然特征不断被人类社会改变，每一处场地、每一个人都变得与整个区域乃至整个地球息息相关。因此，提升对这种多维度依赖关系的敏感度和理解至关重要。在这种跨学科、多尺度的讨论中，通过共同努力，景观途径能够有效地解决当下自然和建成环境中的问题。作为独立智库，ILC试图创建一个平台，促进来自不同地区的景观规划、管理与设计等专业领域的学者与从业者进行对话。在该书出版发行之际，本文将介绍ILC基于人类世背景所提出的景观与地域环境营造途径。

关键词

景观途径；人类世；国土规划；关键格局制图；跨学科合作；南半球

ABSTRACT

From the South: Global Perspectives on Landscape and Territory is the first book publication by the ILC (International Landscape Collaborative). The book promotes a landscape approach that aims to understand today's environmental challenges and socio-political transformations through the medium of landscape and to discuss sites of different scales in connection to their territorial context. While the world is increasingly being urbanized and its natural characteristics are being transformed by human societies, the individual site or person is connected to regional and even planetary systems and interrelationships. It is therefore important to create a sensitivity and understanding for such multi-dimensional dependencies. In this interdisciplinary and multi-scalar discourse, the landscape serves as a common ground to productively address contemporary issues of natural and built environments as a collective effort. The ILC as an independent think-tank wants to provide a platform and facilitate a dialogue among scholars and practitioners from different geographies and disciplines, including landscape planning, management, and design. The ILC's approach to landscape and territory, the group's mission in the context of the Anthropocene, as well as the content of the book publication is discussed in this article.

KEYWORDS

Landscape Approach; Anthropocene; Territorial Planning; Critical Mapping; Interdisciplinary Collaboration; Global South

EDITED BY　Tina TIAN　RAN Lingyu　TRANSLATED BY　RAN Lingyu　Tina TIAN

1 人类世背景下的景观

由于城市化、工业化进程和农业活动，人类文明的足迹已从根本上改变了地球的大气、生物化学和地质特征，并从生态学意义上进入了一个全新纪元——人类世[1]。人类社会以一种不可逆的方式塑造着地球上的水陆系统——在未来，人类也将生存在这种人工化的自然系统之中[2]。社会和生态系统的耦合是基于资源开发模式发展起来的，而千万年来的景观塑造过程开始受到即时物质需求驱动型发展模式的影响，或转变、或被替代。今天人类所面临的环境挑战——如气候变化和日益频发、程度不断加剧的自然灾害——是我们改造自然环境的后果。这些灾害提醒着我们，从长远来看，这种模式是不可行且不可持续的。因此，人类迫切需要反思当前的开发模式与过程，探索与强大的自然循环系统协同发挥作用，并在高度人工化的景观环境中预留出供其他物种生存的空间，借此减轻人类聚落和基础设施对生态的影响，同时提升环境韧性。国际景观合作组织（ILC）即期望在此种地球环境剧变的语境下讨论景观的媒介角色。

在人类世的时代背景下，景观设计学迎来了学科机遇：景观设计师在环境系统修复以及创造基于人类开发目的的各种尺度的宜居空间（包括花园尺度、城市尺度、城乡尺度等）方面拥有丰富的积淀[3]。景观设计师不仅擅长进行系统性思考，还在根据不同维度观察复杂环境方面训练有素。另外，他们还掌握了在不同地域背景下表现和模拟空间过程与关系的技能。通过利用多维度的敏感度来批判性地观察与分析不同地理空间，为可预期的未来提出设计方案并将之可视化，景观设计师在地域景观系统的规划与开发中发挥着关键作用。因此，景观设计师应当带头探索一种协调人类影响与生态可持续性的新型开发模式。[4]-[6]然而，比起其他学科，景观设计学长期以来并没有得到足够重视，且尚未参与到面向气候韧性和地域环境保护的大尺度规划进程之中。

当今世界所面临的环境和社会问题要求基于各个地区特有的生态挑战和机遇，审慎审视资源的开采及产品的生产与消费。为了确保与场地的联系，设计师、规划师和景观设计师必须获得影响环境政策、土地管理制度、工程系统和社会生态过程的媒介与途径，并创造较之以往范围更广的影响力。《南半球的观察：全球视野下的景观与地域环境》（以下简称《南半球的观察》）一书提出了一种途径，即景观

1. 《南半球的观察》封面

1. The cover of the book *From the South: Global Perspectives on Landscape and Territory*

1 Landscape in the Age of the Anthropocene

Through urbanization, industrialization, and agriculture activities, the imprint of human civilization has fundamentally transformed atmospheric, biochemical, and geological characteristics to such an extent that an entirely new epoch of the Anthropocene has been coined to describe the planet's ecological reality[1]. Societies have shaped land-water systems in ways that have irreversibly linked humanity's future to modified natural systems[2]. This coupling of social and ecological systems evolved within an exploitative paradigm where processes that have shaped landscapes for eons started to be transformed and suspended by development patterns driven by immediate material needs. Today's environmental challenges, such as changing climates and occasional shocks from increasingly frequent and intensive natural disasters, are consequences of human's impact on the natural environment. They remind us that such a paradigm is no longer viable and sustainable in the long run. Regenerative models and processes that work with powerful natural flows and make room for ecology to enrich non-human life within highly modified landscapes are urgently needed to mitigate the impact of settlements and infrastructures while making them more resilient. The ILC (International Landscape Collaborative) positions the medium of landscape in this context of planetary environmental transformations.

The discipline of Landscape Architecture finds itself in an opportune position in the era of the Anthropocene: Landscape architects have a long legacy of crafting restorative environmental systems and creating livable spaces within human-dominated mosaics across scales; from the scale of the garden, to the city, and to urban-rural regions[3]. While landscape architects are system thinkers and trained in observing complex environments through different thematic layers, they also have developed the skills to represent and simulate spatial processes and relationships in diverse contexts across territories. Combining this multi-dimensional sensitivity to critically observe and analyze different geographies with the ability to propose and visualize design solutions for an anticipated future makes them powerful agents in the planning and development of territorial landscape systems. Therefore, landscape architects are uniquely situated to guide alternative modes of development that reconcile human impact with ecological sustainability.[4]-[6] However, Landscape Architecture is often overshadowed by other disciplines and excluded from the process of leading large-scale efforts towards climate resilience and territorial conservation.

The environmental and societal issues the world is facing today demand a critical examination of processes of extraction, production, and consumption, and a grounding of these systems

设计师通过将"景观"视作一种合作媒介和一种着眼于空间的过程，来吸引并引领不同的利益相关者和学科参与到多尺度的人类干预措施中，从而发挥或开拓他们的作用。

就这一点而言，需要指出的是，支持向跨学科、多尺度景观方法转变的基础早已根植于北美景观设计学的起源之中——景观行业最先确立于北美地区——而城市和区域规划专业的发展轨迹也与其大致相同[7]。1900年，哈佛大学在科学学院中设立了第一个景观设计学专业项目。后来，景观设计师在哈佛大学的城市规划课程中发挥了关键作用，并最终在1923年开设了第一个城市规划专业项目——景观设计学硕士（城市规划方向）。[8]这一事件似乎影响了此后的景观设计学与城市规划的尺度划分，景观设计学更关注于场地尺度的设计，而城市尺度的规划（城市规划）则正式发展为了独立的专业领域[8]。

正如安妮·惠斯顿·斯本所说，景观设计师不仅仅关注场地尺度的问题，也致力于解决大都市区的城市增长，以及卫生、排水和废水

to the ecological challenges and opportunities that are specific to the respective region. To ensure this connection to the place, designers, planners, and landscape architects have to acquire the agency to influence environmental policy, land management regimes, engineered systems, and socio-ecological processes that impact much larger scales than design and planning professionals have been accustomed to. The book *From the South: Global Perspectives on Landscape and Territory* therefore promotes an approach which allows landscape architects to establish — or rather reclaim — their agency by positioning the landscape as a collaborative medium and a spatially grounded process that can engage diverse stakeholders and disciplines to guide human interventions at multiple scales.

In this regard, it is helpful to point out that the foundation to support this shift to an interdisciplinary and multi-scalar landscape approach is already embedded in the origins of the discipline of Landscape Architecture in North America, where it was first formalized as a profession, sharing a common path with City and Regional Planning[7]. Harvard University established the first professional Landscape Architecture program in 1900 within the Scientific School. Landscape architects later played a key role in shaping the city planning curriculum at Harvard and the first city planning professional program was eventually established in 1923 — the Master in Landscape Architecture with Special Reference to City Planning.[8] This event seems to

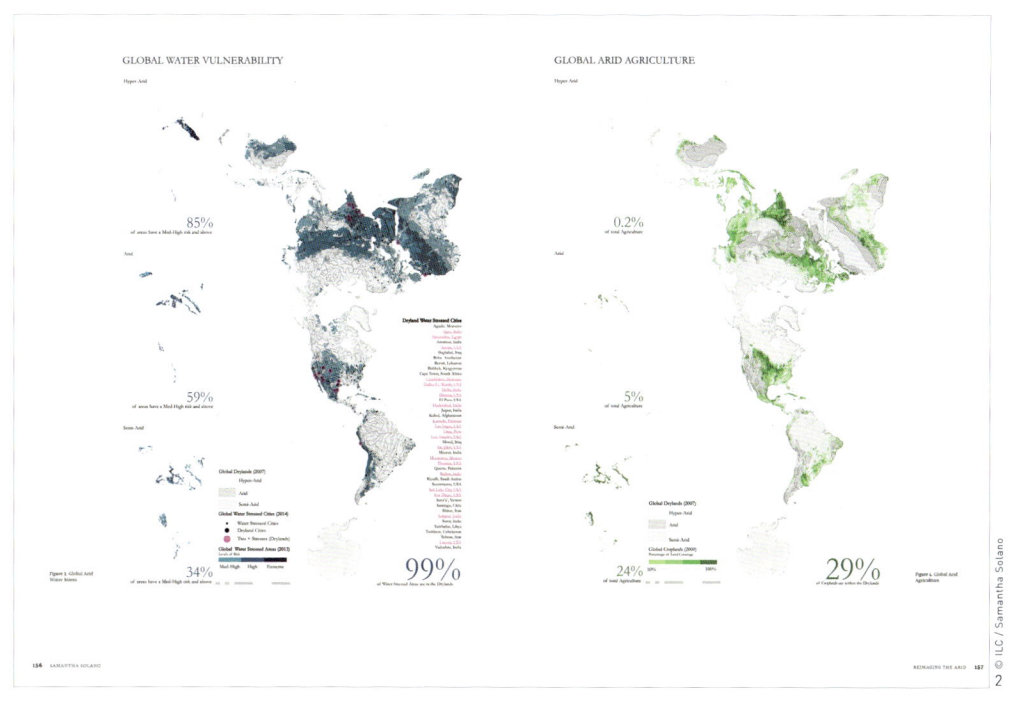

2. 全球范围的水资源短缺和旱地农业空间分析。图片来源于萨曼莎·索拉诺的《重塑干旱》一文。

2. Spatial analysis of water stress and arid agriculture in a planetary scale. From "Reimaging the Arid" by Samantha Solano.

3. 利用现有景观特征为多伦多大都市区打造一个潜在的新框架。图片来源于索尼娅·万杰利的《将城市景观重新视作关键性基础设施：多伦多潜在的景观框架》一文。

3. A potential new framework for the Toronto metropolitan area taking advantage of existing landscape features. From "Rethinking Urban Landscapes as Vital Infrastructure: Toronto's Potential Landscape Framework" by Sonja Vangjeli.

处理管理等问题[9]——例如早期弗雷德里克·劳·奥姆斯特德、查尔斯·艾略特、约翰·诺伦等人在区域规划方面所做的工作。加之20世纪下半叶在地域规划方面的一些创新之举——如伊恩·麦克哈格的适宜性分析方法的提出或GIS的使用——均证实了景观设计学不仅学科根基强大，还发展出了一些方法工具，以便在地域尺度上战略性地处理环境和发展问题。大量适用于专业实践、政策框架和行政机构的学术成果不断涌现，以保证规划设计方案的实施[10]。全球多地的环境冲击与压力的持续增加，以及新的合作渠道的出现，已经为景观设计师创造了施展专业技能的契机。

景观设计师和城市规划师可以通过与生态学家、经济学家、工程师、地理学家、自然资源管理者和社会学家等相关人士以及当地社区协作来解决一些最为紧迫的"棘手问题"[11]。而这需要设计师和规划师基于分析提出有力的跨尺度的设计驱动型方法，且这些方法能够促进基于景观的模型的研发，来协调建成环境和自然系统[12]。为了更具针对性地应对不同地区的环境条件和政治背景，在解决与土地规划和韧性提升相关的重重问题时，需要引入跨学科思维。以环境科学和人文科学为指导的系统研究和设计方法[13][14]可以提供一种审视"人类与自然系统耦合关系"[15]的细致入微的视角，并且可以使景观从业者有足够的能力在科学性和经济性（这二者常常会影响自然资源管理和发展的方式）之间进行权衡。景观因此成为了多方利益相关者以及不同学科之间的媒介，发挥着协调自然和人工化系统之间关系的作用，以确保随着时间和尺度的变化，整个系统在生态、社会和经济层面仍然具备可持续性[16]。这一进程——连同景观这一媒介的广义概念——有助于理解

have laid the foundations for a scalar divide where site design became the cornerstone of Landscape Architecture while the planning of urban systems (Urban Planning) moved into its own professional trajectory[8].

At the onset of this specialization, as Anne Whiston Spirn pointed out, landscape architects were not only interested in phenomenological concerns at the site scale, but also addressed metropolitan urban growth and issues such as sanitation, drainage, and waste-water management[9]. Early examples of this are the works of regional planning advocates such as Frederick Law Olmsted, Charles Eliot, or John Nolen. Considering this context but also innovations in territorial planning in the second half of the 20th century, such as the suitability analysis method developed by Ian McHarg or the use of Geographic Information Systems (GIS), it seems evident that the discipline builds on a strong tradition and developed the methodological tools to strategically work on environmental and development issues at a territorial scale. It created a bulk of academic work that was adapted into professional applications, policy frameworks, and administrative bodies to sustain the plans that were envisioned[10]. The increasing occurrence of environmental shocks and stresses in multiple geographies across the globe along with the emergence of new avenues for collaboration have created an opportunity for landscape architects to reclaim this legacy.

Landscape architects and urban planners can tackle some of the most pressing "wicked problems"[11] together with allied professionals such as ecologists, economists, engineers, geographers, natural resource managers, and sociologists alongside local communities. This effort requires design-planning professions to develop robust, analytical, and design-driven methods that can operate at multiple scales and promote landscape-based models to mediate built environments and natural systems[12]. Multi-sectoral issues of land planning and resilience require interdisciplinary thinking to respond to the environmental constraints and political challenges of the place. Systematic research and design methodologies, informed by environmental science and humanities[13][14], allow for nuanced reading of "coupled human and natural systems"[15] and equip landscape advocates with the skills and the credibility to negotiate between scientific and economic models which often guide normative approaches to natural resource management and development. Landscape then becomes the medium over which multiple stakeholders and disciplines negotiate the relationship of natural and designed systems to ensure ecological, social, and economic sustainability over time and scale[16]. This process, together with the inclusive notion of the

各利益相关方的需求与意图，并以一种全面而可持续的方式协调他们不同的诉求与利益，以制定未来具体的景观设计方案和发展战略。

2 国际景观合作组织

ILC成立于2017年，成员包括景观设计师、城市设计师和规划师。ILC以景观为媒介，建设性地探讨与当代自然及建成环境相关的议题，同时希冀能够在更多其他学科和地理环境中发挥更大的影响力。ILC创始成员们已经对基于景观的设计和规划方法进行了较为前沿的探索，并都在此框架之上继续在世界各地拓展各自的研究领域。

在批判性地研读特定环境及场地具体条件时，观察者会自然而然地依赖以往的经验，因而其社会、文化和学术背景尤为重要。通过聚集不同地理和文化背景的专家，ILC积极促进核心小组的交流对话，使拥有不同学术和专业背景的人士能够分享他们的研究和实践经验。ILC希望能够发展成为一个独立的智库，为景观设计、城市和区域规划，以及其他相关学科的研究人员和从业者提供一个平台。通过促进来自世界各地的专家间相互交流，ILC旨在加深人们对于景观，以及与景观相伴相生的地域文化的理解。此外，尤其是在规划的基础设施系统尚未纳入法规或尚未成形的情况下，ILC试图将景观途径作为社会和政治改革的工具。虽然这些新兴的地区尚未进入传统学科视野，但它们所

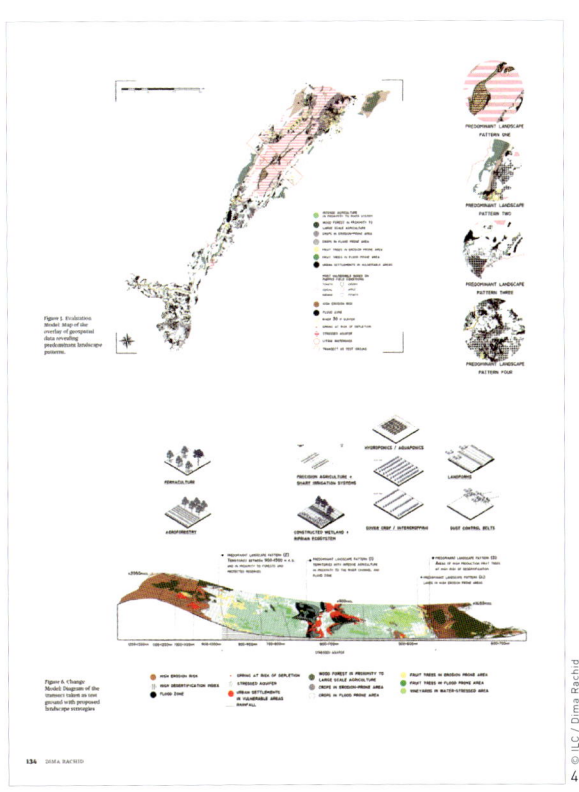

medium of landscape, helps understand the different needs and intentions of all the stakeholders that are involved. It allows to coordinate their different interests and benefits in a comprehensive and sustainable fashion for the respective landscape's future design and development strategy.

2 International Landscape Collaborative

The ILC was founded in 2017 by an interdisciplinary group of landscape architects, urban designers, and planners. Its members, who all share a common interest in using the medium of landscape to productively interrogate contemporary issues of natural and built environments, but also the ambition to broaden the scope of Landscape Architecture and engage with other disciplines as well as different geographical contexts. With a sensitivity towards landscape-based approaches in design and planning, the initial core group continued to develop this framework through individual career trajectories in different parts of the world.

The critical observer who studies a certain environment and its specific conditions naturally relies on past experiences. The observer's social, cultural, and academic background is thus critical. As an international collaborative with members from different geographies and cultural contexts, the ILC serves as a common forum to share experiences from research and practice within different academic and professional environments. The ILC aspires to grow as an independent think-tank that offers a platform for researchers and practitioners from landscape architecture, city and regional planning, and an expanded set of allied disciplines. By connecting experts from around the world, the ILC intends to deepen the understanding of landscapes and the cultures that co-produce and depend on them. Moreover, the ILC seeks to position the landscape approach as a tool for social and political transformation, particularly in contexts where planned infrastructural systems are not yet codified or consolidated. Such emerging regions generally lie outside the traditional disciplinary discourse, yet they contain a challenging field of research and practice. They offer productive opportunities to rethink urban form and question dominant spatial or political organizations.

In January 2018, the ILC organized an inaugural conference in Santiago, Chile. As one of the southernmost territories in the world, Chile provided a symbolic platform to showcase a diversity of interesting work and research that is happening outside the traditional centers of landscape discourse in North America and the Global North. With

4. 为饱受争议的黎巴嫩利塔尼河流域制定的景观策略。图片来源于迪马·哈西德的《后军事化景观的生态规划：以黎巴嫩利塔尼河流域排雷区为例》一文。

4. Proposed landscape strategies for the contested Litany River Watershed in Lebanon. From "Ecological Planning in Post-Militarized Landscapes: The Case of the Demined Territories in the Litany River Watershed-Lebanon" by Dima Rachid.

涉及的研究和实践领域极具挑战性，为重新思考城市形态并向占主导地位的空间或政治形态发出质疑提供了机会。

2018年1月，ILC首次学术研讨会在智利圣地亚哥举行。将智利作为会议举办地的意义在于，这个地处全球较南端的国家极具代表性，这里有发生在北美等北半球传统景观语境中心之外的各种有趣的实践与研究。借由智利的案例，ILC旨在通过细致研究当前存在于景观设计学理论和实践层面的北半球向南半球席卷之势，来展现南半球较之于北半球截然不同的景观途径。《南半球的观察》一书的封面也意在回应这种趋势，即将常见的、工业化程度较高的北半球在上的世界地图进行了颠倒。

那些常被归为"南半球"的部分地区需要在规划过程中加强对景观和地域环境的考虑，其中许多区域出于城市化、交通发展、工业生产或资源开采等目的，正在经历人口激增和大规模基础设施快速建设等过程。因此，当前迫切需要跨越多种文化和经济背景，以跨尺度、跨地域的方式来解决这些地区的地域冲突问题。ILC在《南半球的观察》一书中既强调了在界定紧迫的地域问题时重新重视景观设计学作用的必要性，也展示了景观设计学在全球范围内处理此类问题的能力。

3 《南半球的观察》内容概述

《南半球的观察》一书包括18篇文章，作者来自五大洲的9个不同国家，并通过5个章节来说明景观途径与特定系统和尺度的相关性。第一章"大都市公园系统规划"包括4篇文章，讨论了波士顿、多伦多和圣地亚哥这几座城市在区域规划方面的工作。文章基于每座城市的现有环境条件和生态原则，追溯了它们各自的城市发展史，描述了城市如何与其周边景观结构和生态系统协同发展，以及空间概念和规划框架如何指导并调控这些发展。经过几十年的发展，这三座城市都已成为大都市区，因而这些文章也就如何在区域尺度上协调未来发展提出了策略，可依据这些地区的自然环境特征来制定具体的规划框架，从而为提升城市区域的宜居性、韧性、生态连续性及绩效，以及建立公私合营伙伴关系、城市投资和发展等提供机遇。

the case of Chile, the ILC aims to reframe the north-south dichotomy by adding nuance to a predominantly north-to-south vector of transferring theory and practice in Landscape Architecture. This suggested paradigm shift is also visualized on the cover of the book where the traditional conventions of the world map, with the industrial countries of the northern hemisphere at the top, are turned upside down.

The need for a stronger consideration of the landscape and territory in planning processes has become critical in parts of the world which are often referred to as being part of the Global South. Many of these regions are rapidly transforming through population growth and large-scale infrastructure projects, such as for urbanization, transportation, industrial production, or resource extraction. Thus, there is a strong sense of urgency in addressing territorial conflicts in these regions that demand multi-scalar and cross-boundary integration across various cultures and economies. With the book, the ILC advances the landscape approach in two ways: it highlights the need to reclaim Landscape Architecture's agency in defining pressing territorial issues and it demonstrates the discipline's capacity to address such issues across the globe.

3 Book Content

The book contains 18 essays that are written by authors from nine different countries and five continents. It is structured in five chapters along themes that highlight the relevance of the landscape approach to specific systems and scales. The first chapter, "Planning Metropolitan Park Systems," presents four essays that discuss the cities of Boston, Toronto, and Santiago in terms of regional planning. For each of the cities, the authors trace back the history of urban development under the scope of the existing environmental conditions and ecological considerations. They describe how the cities grew in relation to their surrounding landscape structures and ecosystems, and how the development was steered and regulated by spatial concepts and planning frameworks. Over the past decades, all three cities have grown to large metropolitan areas. The essays therefore provide strategies of how future development can be coordinated and synchronized in a regional scale. Place-specific characteristics of the natural environment offer a set of opportunities and serve as planning frameworks that help improve the city region in terms of its livability, resiliency, and ecological connectivity and performance, but also in terms of public-private partnerships, urban investment, and development.

第二章"生态基础设施建设"讨论了来自印度(孟买、加尔各答)和智利(兰奇胡亚)的三个案例,展示了景观系统作为高绩效城市基础设施的潜力。其中,孟买的案例聚焦于沿城市海岸线分布的红树林湿地,它们因城市扩张和基础设施建设而遭大面积破坏,但这些湿地可以消减风暴潮和保护城市免受洪水侵袭,是一种成本效益合理、生态价值较高的基础设施。在另一个令人瞩目的景观基础设施案例中,东加尔各答湿地已经逐渐发展为一个社会生态系统,能够净化城市用水、维持社区生计并提供重要的生态系统服务。兰奇胡亚的案例讲述了这座智利南部城市的绿色基础设施系统规划,以及区域公园和开放空间在城市中发挥的重要功能,包括雨洪管理、生物多样性和连通性提升、城市美学品质优化和休闲空间营造。

第三章"解读社会政治景观"包括4篇文章,论述了政策、社会政治关系和等级制度作为城市化的驱动因子,如何影响地域景观的塑造。文章指出,为了与利益相关方合作并对争议性的环境采取干预措施,了解不同行动者的土地利益和政治力量是至关重要的。在中国台湾,当今大型景观基础设施的制度化管理方式被视为权力下放和民主化进程的结果。中国大陆地区快速而多维度的城市转型则被解读为一种在政府高度层级化的背景下,在土地所有权斗争中处于高度动态变化且本质上去中心化的过程。黎巴嫩的利塔尼河流域既是一处遭到严重污染的后军事化景观,也是重要的生态和社会经济资源,文章为重

"Building Ecological Infrastructure" discusses three cases in India (Mumbai and Kolkata) and Chile (Llanquihue) to demonstrate the potential of landscape systems which serve as performative urban infrastructures. The case of Mumbai discusses how the city's mangrove wetland habitats along the coastline, which have been largely destructed by urban expansion and infrastructure development, but bear the potential to mitigate storm surges and protect the city from flooding as a cost-effective, ecologically valuable infrastructure. The East Kolkata Wetlands provide a compelling example of a landscape infrastructure that has grown over time as a socio-ecological system that cleans water for the city, sustains communities' livelihoods, and provides important ecosystem services. The case of Llanquihue in Southern Chile describes the city's systematic green infrastructure plan and how regional parks and open spaces provide critical functions for the city such as managing rain water or fostering the biological biodiversity and connectivity in addition to aesthetic qualities and the supply of recreational spaces.

"Reading the Sociopolitical Landscape" contains four essays that describe how policies, socio-political relationships, and hierarchies act as drivers of urbanization which shape the territorial landscape. It is crucial to understand different actors, their territorial interests and political forces in order

5. 智利南部兰奇胡亚市的城市绿色基础设施规划细节。图片来源于奥斯瓦尔多·莫雷诺的《城市绿色基础设施:以智利兰奇胡亚市为例探讨提升区域性城市韧性和社会生态适应性的景观规划和设计策略》一文。
6. 东加尔各答湿地与城市土地利用相关的高产景观基础设施分析。图片来源于索爱弗·库玛·比斯瓦斯的《为东加尔各答湿地制定景观规划》一文。

5. Details from the Green Urban Infrastructure Plan for the city of Llanquihue in southern Chile. From "Green Urban Infrastructure, Landscape Planning and Design Strategies for the Resilience and Socioecological Adaptability of Regional Cities in Chile — The Case of Llanquihue" by Osvaldo Moreno.
6. Mapping the highly productive landscape infrastructure of the East Kolkata Wetlands in relation to urban land uses. From "Mapping a Landscape Planning Agenda for the East Kolkata Wetlands" by Sourav Kumar Biswas.

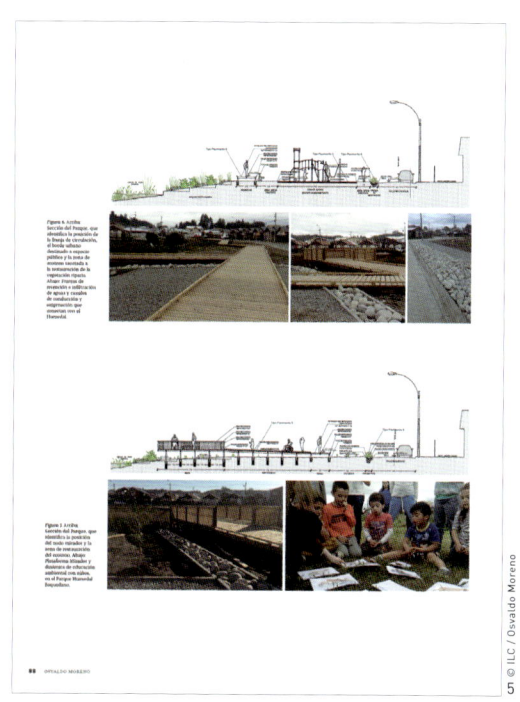

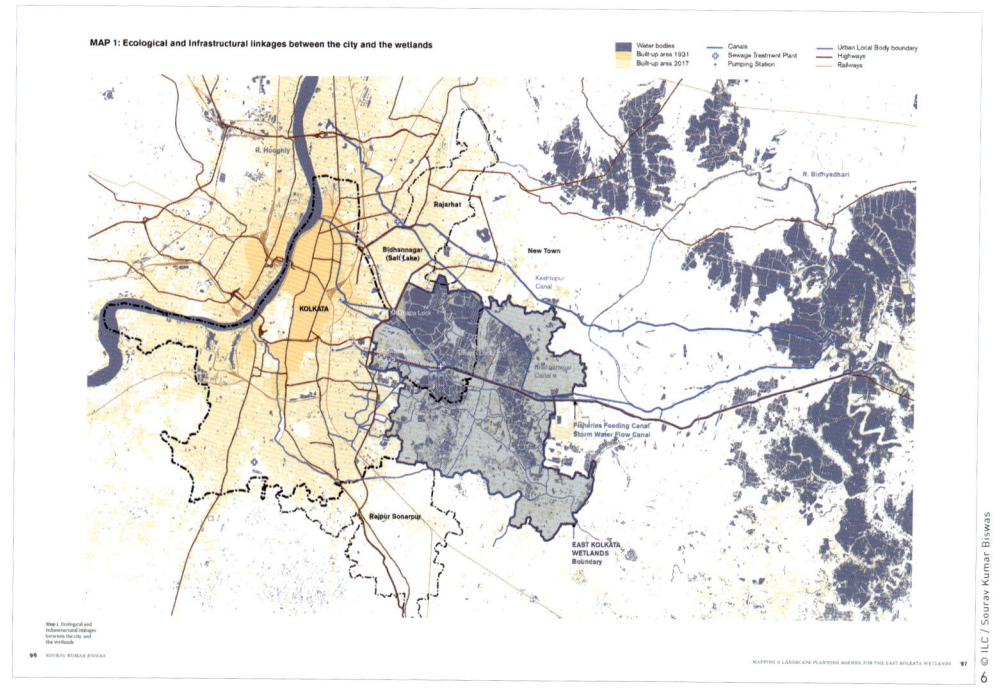

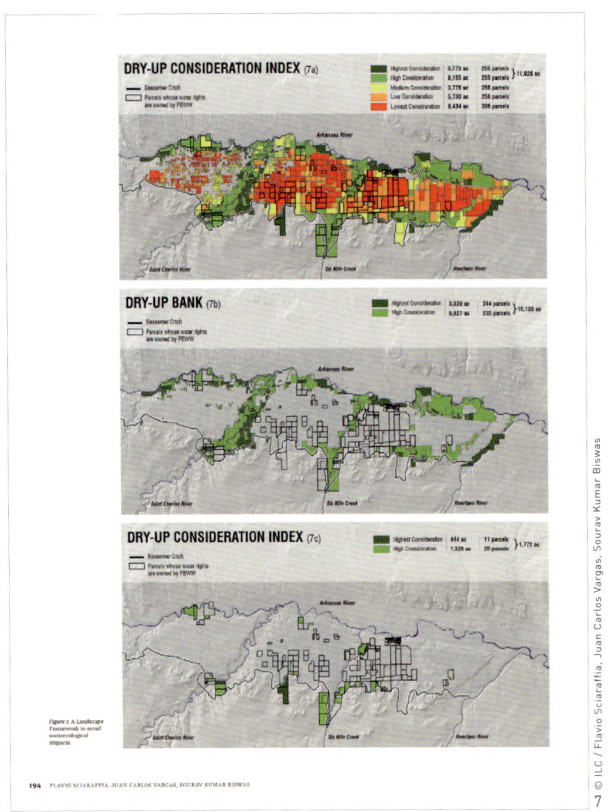

7. 阿肯色河流域干旱农业用地的可持续水系统空间概念。图片来源于弗拉维奥·萨瑞弗、胡安·卡洛斯·瓦格斯和索爱弗·库玛·比斯瓦斯的《解决农业和城市之间的水冲突：为避免科罗拉多州水权转让造成的社会生态影响而设计景观框架》一文。

7. Spatial concept toward a sustainable water regime in the dry agricultural lands of the Arkansas River Basin. From "Addressing Water Conflicts between Agriculture and Cities: Designing a Landscape Framework to Avoid the Socioecological Impacts of Water Rights Transfers in Colorado" by Flavio Sciaraffia, Juan Carlos Vargas, and Sourav Kumar Biswas.

新利用这片备受争议的土地提出了生态规划措施。在葡萄牙塞图巴尔科伊纳河上进行的跨学科性环境教育项目则积极鼓励当地社区的直接参与，并讨论生态系统能够为人类和环境提供哪些服务。

第四章"地域系统规划"聚焦于极端气候条件下的全球水资源与粮食供给问题以及气候变化的长期影响。第一篇文章关注全球背景下的干旱地区，这些在景观语境中往往较少涉及的地区却居住着超过三分之一的全球人口和一些发展最为迅猛的城市。第二篇文章讲述了不同地区的政府如何启动大型水利工程项目来应对水资源短缺问题，以跨流域远距离调运淡水资源的方式来维持城市的增长与繁荣。就此，文章作者建议采取分散式建设模式并加强局地水循环模式转换。另外两篇文章则讨论了与水供给密切相关的可持续粮食生产方式：一篇探讨了智利首都圣地亚哥所进行的城市及城郊农业地区规划，另一篇关注于美国科罗拉多州的阿肯色河流域。在阿肯色河流域案例中，作者建议建立一个更具可持续性的水资源分配景观框架，并防止因短视的水权转让而造成的不利影响。

最后一章"新型实践模式"探讨了景观和地域环境对城市空间的规划与管理，以及相关学科课程体系的影响。在加拿大蒙特利尔的案例中，作者介绍了将景观管理的实践经验纳入跨学科发展计划的初期阶段，可为城市环境带来多层面上的长远效益。作者还介绍了恰当地选择和维护单株树木以在更大的城市环境尺度上发挥巨大影响的具体

to cooperate with allied stakeholders and intervene in contested environments. In Taiwan, China today's institutional management of large-scale landscape infrastructures is described as the result of decentralization and democratization processes. Mainland China's rapid and multi-dimensional urban transformation is explained as a highly dynamic and essentially decentralized process of battles for the possession of land within a strong governmental hierarchy. The Litany River Watershed in Lebanon is a post-militarized and heavily contaminated landscape, yet it serves as a vital ecological as well as socioeconomic resource. An ecological planning methodology is proposed to repurpose these highly contested grounds. A transdisciplinary environmental education project on the Coina River in Setubal, Portugal, serves as a catalyst to engage directly with local communities and discuss the services which ecosystems are able to provide for both people and the environment.

The fourth chapter, "Planning for Territorial Systems," addresses global issues of water and food supply under extreme climatic conditions and the long-term effects of climate change. The first essay discusses arid regions in a global context. These regions are often neglected in the landscape discourse, yet they host more than one third of the global population and some of the fastest growing cities. The second essay describes how water scarcity led governments of different geographies to initiate massive hydro-engineering projects to transport fresh water over vast distances and across watersheds in order to sustain urban growth and prosperity. Alternatively, it suggests a shift to decentralized models and the local circulation of water. Sustainable modes of food production, which are closely linked to the availability of water, are addressed in two essays: First, in the context of metropolitan Santiago through plans of urban and peri-urban agriculture; and second, in a territorial scale in the Arkansas River Basin in Colorado, USA. In the latter case, a landscape framework is suggested for more sustainable practices of water allocation and to prevent deleterious impacts of shortsighted sales of water rights.

The last chapter "New Models of Practice" discusses how landscape and territory influence the planning and management of urban spaces as well as academic curricula. In the case of Montreal, Canada, experiences from practice are shared of how the inclusion of landscape management in an early stage of interdisciplinary development plans benefits the urban environment on different levels in the long run. It describes how specific methods for the proper selection and maintenance of individual trees can have tremendous impacts on the larger urban context. In Pretoria, South Africa, an urban design project is presented which is driven by the revitalization

方法。南非比勒陀利亚的案例介绍了通过前瞻性地确定潜在景观改造场地来复兴一个被忽视的景观基础设施，从而改善城市环境的项目。第三篇文章展示了随着时间推移及在不同的学术语境下，在智利圣地亚哥发展大学的建筑课程中，景观议题和地域环境如何影响相关学科的课程体系。

《南半球的观察》中探讨的所有话题既具有普遍性，又具有地域性。为了向更多的拉丁美洲读者推广，该书以英语和西班牙语出版。作者们通过审视景观——这一人类与特定地区的自然环境长期系统互动的结果——从政治、社会、经济和环境各个方面对不同地区进行了多维度探讨。因此，该书通过详实的、多层次的叙述向不同学科背景的读者和潜在合作伙伴进行了介绍。

为了表现某一地区中的各类空间关系，地图成为了重要的研究和交流工具，用于展现作者的研究成果和理念。由于地图绘制所需的数据建立在特定的地理和空间环境之上，所以将错综复杂的关系，以及历史数据或量化数据进行图形空间化的本质也是一种设计思维。借助地图和空间示意图，作者得以重新绘制分析图并研究场地。为避免因循守旧，在书中的许多其他项目中，作者以未来视角来展现他们的想法与研究成果，并基于不同预景提出了具体建议或设计策略。这些面向未来的项目并不仅仅是一个个分散的个例，更是从地域尺度出发——这一点至关重要，因为这一尺度最终会影响未来的空间建设。书中收录了135幅原创地图、平面图、示意图、表格和照片，旨在生动地呈现景观途径案例，并为新的合作模式提供思路。

4 结论

景观途径是解决当今世界上一些最为紧迫问题的有力方法。为了全面恢复和改善生态系统，有必要将一个个单独的场地置于其所处地域乃至整个地球背景中来解读并因地制宜地进行设计。通过构建跨越地理、文化和学科边界的国际网络来共享和共同探讨此类研究和设计

of a neglected landscape infrastructure. It illustrates how the potential to improve urban environments can be unlocked by a practice of proactively identifying possible sites for landscape transformation. The third essay of this chapter presents how, over time and through different academic courses, the themes of landscape and territory have restructured the curriculum and started to play an important role in the architecture program at the Universidad del Desarrollo in Santiago.

All the topics addressed in the book are universal in nature but they are grounded in specific geographic locations. To make the content accessible to a Latin American audience, the volume is published in bilingual form with Spanish translations. By putting the landscape — the result of systematic human interaction with the natural environment in a specific region over time — as a focal point, the authors discuss the different geographies through multiple dimensions, including political, social, economic, and environmental aspects. The diverse geographies are therefore presented with a thick, multi-layered narrative that addresses readers and potential collaborators from different disciplinary backgrounds.

Mapping, the spatial representation of various interrelations across a territory, is an important tool of research and communication and helped the authors to convey their findings and concepts. The graphic spatialization of different relationships as well as of historic data or quantitative figures is essentially an act of design thinking as the data needs to be grounded in a specific geography and its physical conditions. Through maps and spatial diagrams, authors are redrawing and thus rethinking the sites that are discussed. Many project their ideas and findings into the future and propose specific recommendations or design solutions for alternative scenarios instead of, as in many other cases, deep-rooted and deadlocked paradigms. Imagining and visualizing the future, not only through individual, site-specific projects but also in a territorial scale, is critical, as it allows to eventually have a hand in shaping it. With 135 original maps, plans, diagrams, tables, and photographs, this book aims to make a compelling case for the landscape approach and provide avenues for new forms of collaboration.

4 Conclusion

The landscape approach is a powerful method to tackle some of the most pressing challenges the world is facing today. Connecting individual sites to their territorial and, in some cases, planetary context — intellectually as well as physically through design interventions — is necessary in order to holistically

8. 系统分析洛杉矶地区干旱区域的水循环过程和基础设施。图片来源于托马斯·尼德瑞斯特的《当我们仅有的只剩灰水：将景观视为应对水资源短缺的框架和媒介》一文。

8. Systematic analysis of water cycles and infrastructures in the context of the arid Los Angeles region. From "When the Only Water Left Is Gray: The Understanding of Landscape as a Framework and Medium to Approach Water Scarcity" by Thomas Nideroest.

理念，是ILC的一项宏大且颇具建设性的使命。未来，ILC计划定期在世界各地举办学术研讨会，与来自当地及世界其他地区的专家进行交流，并将知识成果以出版物的形式加以记录、凝结。除了全球视野及跨学科合作，ILC还前瞻性地将这些理念付诸实践，以减轻对环境和社会经济的负面影响，并同时开拓韧性、公平且更具针对性的发展与保护模式。**LAF**

注释

本文是对《南半球的观察》一书的介绍与延伸。该书由4位作者合作撰写，分别是费拉维奥·赛瑞夫、苏拉夫·库玛尔·比斯瓦斯、托马斯·尼德瑞特和哈尼兹·詹德，他们均已获得景观设计学硕士学位。作为一本非营利性学术出版物，该书由智利国家文化艺术委员会、智利发展大学出版社和智利非盈利基金会Cosmos于2018年提供资金支持。全书可在ILC官网上免费下载。

restore and improve ecosystems. Sharing and discussing such inquiries and design concepts through an international network across geographic, cultural, and disciplinary boundaries is an ambitious, yet constructive mission. In future, the ILC intends to periodically organize conferences in different parts of the world to engage with local experts and diverse geographic contexts and in order to allow knowledge to be distilled and recorded in future publications. In pursuing this global and interdisciplinary model, the ILC looks ahead to implement these concepts to mitigate negative environmental and socio-economic impacts while fostering resilient, equitable, and place-specific models of development and conservation. **LAF**

NOTE

This text is an extended version of the introductory essay in the book *From the South*, written by four co-editors, Flavio Sciaraffia, Sourav Kumar Biswas, Thomas Nideroest, and Hannes Zander, who all hold Master in Landscape Architecture degrees. The publication was supported by Fondart Nacional, Convocatoria 2018 (Chilean National Council of Culture and Arts), the publisher Universidad del Desarrollo, and the Chilean non-profit Fundación Cosmos. As a non-commercial publication, it is intended for institutional distribution. However, the full content of the book is available in digital format on the ILC website for free download.

REFERENCES

[1] Crutzen, P. J. (2002). Geology of Mankind. Nature, 415(6867), 23.
[2] Ellis, E. C., & Ramankutty, N. (2008). Putting People in the Map: Anthropogenic Biomes of the World. Frontiers in Ecology and the Environment, 6(8), 439-447. https://doi.org/10.1890/070062
[3] Spirn, A. W. (1984). The Granite Garden: Urban Nature and Human Design. New York: Basic Books.
[4] Liu, J., & Taylor, W. W. (2002). Coupling Landscape Ecology with Natural Resource Management: Paradigm shifts and New Approaches. In J. Liu & W. W. Taylor (Eds.), Integrating Landscape Ecology into Natural Resource Management (pp. 3-19). Cambridge: Cambridge University Press.
[5] Nassauer, J. I., & Opdam, P. (2008). Design in Science: Extending the Landscape Ecology Paradigm. Landscape Ecology, 23(6), 633-644. https://xs.scihub.ltd/https://doi.org/10.1007/s10980-008-9226-7
[6] Forman, R. T. T. (2001). Foreword. In V. H. Dale & R. A. Haeuber (Eds.), Applying Ecological Principles to Land Management. New York: Springer.
[7] Spirn, A. W. (2000). Ian McHarg, Landscape Architecture and Environmentalism: Ideas and Methods. In M. Conan (Ed.), Context, Environmentalism in Landscape Architecture (pp. 97-114). Washington, D.C.: Dumbarton Oaks.
[8] Simo, M. L. (2000). Coalescing of Different Forces and Ideas: A History of Landscape Architecture at Harvard 1900-1999 (pp. 4-10). Cambridge: The Harvard University Graduate School of Design.
[9] Spirn, A. W. (2000). Ian McHarg, Landscape Architecture and Environmentalism: Ideas and Methods. In M. Conan (Ed.), Context, Environmentalism in Landscape Architecture (pp. 97-114). Washington, D.C.: Dumbarton Oaks.
[10] Tishler, W. H. (1989). American Landscape Architecture: Designers and Places. Washington, D.C.: The Preservation Press, National Trust for Historic Preservation.
[11] Rittel, H. W. J., & Webber, M. M. (1973). Dilemmas in a General Theory of Planning. Policy Sciences, 4(2), 155-69. https://xs.scihub.ltd/https://doi.org/10.1007/BF01405730
[12] Botequilha-Leitão, A., & Ahern, J. (2002). Applying Ecological Concepts and Metrics in Sustainable Landscape Planning. Landscape and Urban Planning, 59(2), 65-93. https://doi.org/10.1016/S0169-2046(02)00005-1
[13] Castree, N., Adams, W. M., Barry, J., Brockington, D., Büscher, B., Corbera, E., ... Wynne, B. (2014). Changing the intellectual climate. Nature Climate Change, 4(9), 763-768. https://xs.scihub.ltd/https://doi.org/10.1038/nclimate2339
[14] Collard, R.-C., Dempsey, J., & Sundberg, J. (2015). A Manifesto for Abundant Futures. Annals of the Association of American Geographers, 105(2), 322-330. https://doi.org/10.1080/00045608.2014.973007
[15] Liu, J., Dietz, T., Carpenter, S. R., Folke, C., Alberti, M., Redman, C. L., ... Provencher, W. (2007). Coupled Human and Natural Systems. AMBIO: A Journal of the Human Environment, 36(8), 639-649. https://doi.org/10.1579/0044-7447(2007)36[639:CHANS]2.0.CO;2
[16] Whatmore, S. J., & Landström, C. (2011). Flood Apprentices: An Exercise in Making Things Public. Economy and Society, 40(4), 582-610. https://doi.org/10.1080/03085147.2011.602540

本文引用格式 / PLEASE CITE THIS ARTICLE AS

Shi, H., Lin, Z., & Chen, J.(2019). Observations beyond the Site: Unfolding of Landscape Process in the Design of Duke Garden in Kunshan. Landscape Architecture Frontiers, 7(5), 108-119. https://doi.org/10.15302/J-LAF-1-040006

超越场地的多维度观察：
昆山杜克花园的情境生成

OBSERVATIONS BEYOND THE SITE: UNFOLDING OF LANDSCAPE PROCESS IN THE DESIGN OF DUKE GARDEN IN KUNSHAN

https://doi.org/10.15302/J-LAF-1-040006　收稿时间 RECEIVED DATE / 2019-09-17　中图分类号 / TU986　文献标识码 / B

时惠来
美国注册景观设计师，Futurepolis未来都市规划建筑设计事务所设计总监

林中杰
宾夕法尼亚大学斯图尔特－韦茨曼设计学院城市设计副教授，Futurepolis未来都市规划建筑设计事务所设计总监

陈嘉诚
宾夕法尼亚大学斯图尔特－韦茨曼设计学院景观设计学在读硕士

SHI Huilai
PLA; Principal of Futurepolis

LIN Zhongjie*
Associate Professor of Urban Design, University of Pennsylvania Stuart Weitzman School of Design; Principal of Futurepolis

CHEN Jiacheng
Master Student in Landscape Architecture, University of Pennsylvania Stuart Weitzman School of Design

*Corresponding Author
Address: University of Pennsylvania Stuart Weitzman School of Design, G5 Meyerson Hall, 210 S. 34th St, Philadelphia, PA 19104, USA
Email: zlin@design.upenn.edu

摘要

观察是阅读场地与启发设计的开始。当设计场地缺乏明显特征时，设计者不仅需要细致观察，同时也要跳出场地现状限制，通过研究拓展观察范围。这个过程包括对场地内在因素的思考，以及针对设计对象的核心内涵进行场景参照与延伸，形成情境的模拟、选择与表达。江苏省昆山市杜克花园的场地现状属于典型中国城郊景观，缺乏明显的地理特征，这迫使设计师进行场所精神的深度挖掘。这样依托于情境生成的另类观察过程从三个角度入手：一是对同一脉络下异地先例的审视比较；二是对超越场地范围的区域生态开展地文学研究；三是从时间维度考察前期项目的效果及其与后期项目的关联性。这三个方面的观察使杜克花园的设计得以探索"花园"一词的当代精神内涵，最终表达为具体的设计形式。

关键词

杜克花园；花园精神；异地性；地文学；延时性；情境；观察与表达

ABSTRACT

Observation is the beginning of reading site and inspiring design. When the site lacks obvious features, designers not only need to observe in detail but also step out of the site's physical boundaries and expand the scope of observation. This process involves reflection on the intrinsic factors of the site, seeking landscape reference in the broader context according to the subject's core connotations, through which design concepts can emerge from the simulation, selection, and expression of scenarios. The new Duke Garden, located in the city of Kunshan in Jiangsu Province, is situated in a typical Chinese suburban area, which bears little distinction in geographical features. The ordinary site condition forced designers to search for deeper characteristics of the place through alternative methods which allow designers to examine the site from three perspectives: 1) through the study and comparison of precedents which share a spiritual lineage; 2) through the physiographical investigation on regional ecosystem to which the site belongs; and 3) through a revisit of the preceding phases of the project and a probe into the temporal connection between adjacent sites. Observations from these three perspectives have enabled the design of Duke Garden to explore contemporary spiritual connotations of the landscape typology of "garden" and intepret it through this project.

KEYWORDS

Duke Garden; Garden Spirit; Off-Site; Physiographical; Time-Lapse; Scenario; Observation and Representation

1 项目背景

杜克大学昆山校区坐落于江苏省昆山市西北部的高教园区内，是由昆山市支持，杜克大学与武汉大学联合创办的学校。校园总面积约77.5hm²，其中杜克花园位于校园东部与东北部，占地约28.9hm²（图1）。目前，一期校园已经建成，二、三期校园和杜克花园正在同步建设中。

杜克花园场地现状为典型的城郊景观（图2），以农田为主，包含部分苗圃，一条市政道路从场地中部穿过。场地北部人工挖掘形成的白窑湖约9.5hm²，东侧为宽约25m的渠化河道。由于长期的土方挖掘，湖岸和水渠岸线呈规则几何形。水体最深处达11m，穿透两层地下水层，但水质只达到IV~V类。场地中植物品种与栖息地类型单一，仅在北侧岸际有部分成熟乔木，中部有小片苗圃植被。如何通过设计修复遭到破坏的场地特性，还原生态活力，提升水质，增加生物多样性；以及如何在缺乏设计依据的情况下赋予杜克花园新的、鲜明的场所精神，成为杜克花园设计面临的两大挑战。

2 场地观察与设计过程

在西方造园理论中，设计师通过造园过程将自然与人造物进行融合式演绎，形成了所谓的"第三自然"。这一概念最早由文艺复兴时期的史学家雅各布·彭法迪奥和巴尔托罗莫·迪亚吉奥几乎同时提

基金项目
国家自然科学基金面上项目"健康城市视角下的紧凑城市形态量化指标体系研究：以苏南城市为例"（编号：51878428）

RESEARCH FUND
Research of a Compact City Indicator System from the Healthy City Perspective: Studies of the South-Jiangsu Region, General Program of National Natural Science Foundation of China (No. 51878428)

编辑　冉玲于　汪默英　翻译　尹奕涵　陈嘉诚
EDITED BY　RAN Lingyu　WANG Moying　TRANSLATED BY　YIN Yihan　CHEN Jiacheng

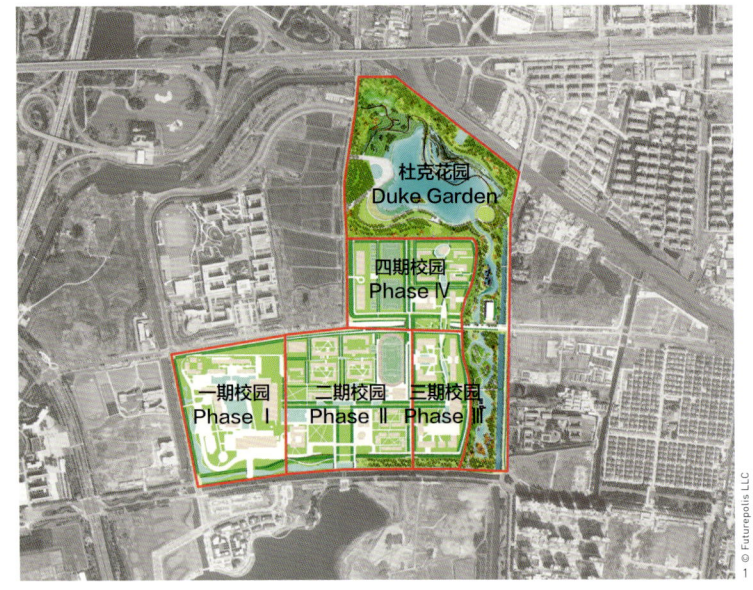

出；当代艺术史学家克劳迪娅·拉扎罗将其解释为自然与艺术交织而成的难以分辨的整体。自然成为了艺术的创作者并具备了艺术本质，二者结合后创造了一种区别于自身的全新存在——"第三自然"[1]。

美国杜克大学本部的杜克花园即是基于"第三自然"理念设计的经典案例。花园场地位于北卡罗莱纳州的山麓地带，这片曾经鲜有人迹的原始景观构成了"第一自然"，以宗教、科教、园艺为代表的一系列人工元素通过造园过程融入了当地的自然生境，从而营造出兼具人工与自然特征的"第三自然"。

昆山所属的中国江南则代表了另一种与之相通又相异的造园传统。江南私家园林在建造之初往往没有太多特殊地形和显著自然特征，大多只是由围墙从城市或郊区中切割出来的平地，区别在于地块大小和围合度。造园者基于对场地的观察和对南方山水的理解，将选择与合成的情境投射到场地上，所形成的"第三自然"呈现出高低错落、山水相间、楼台掩映的景象。尽管景观元素大同小异，每个园林却都独具特色。

昆山杜克花园延续了中国江南园林的情境塑造方法：它没有简单地复制杜克大学本部花园的形式或元素，而是在精神传承的基础上，通过广泛了解场地文脉，深入挖掘场地潜力，从而形成根植于本地的景观解决方案。人与自然的关系是随着历史与文化变迁的，"花园"的内涵也随之拓展。杜克大学本部花园的历史发展为昆山的设计设定了坐标，而新的情境塑造过程则立足于江南水乡的区域背景。设计师既需要回应当代生态语境下的校园文化，也需要以回应生态环境问题为切入点寻找当代花园精神。在这一思路下，基于三个不同视角的深度观察逐步帮助设计师形成设计概念，分别是异地性考察、地文学考察和延时性考察。这三个过程不仅包括通常的地形地貌与植被的视觉感知与记录，还切入了深层的分析与思考——从"观察"（observation）的范畴深入到了"考察"（investigation）的范畴。

2.1 异地性考察

异地性考察，即通过洞悉"别处"相似的文化景观与文化传统，达到精神境界的迁移。在昆山杜克花园项目中，设计团队通过对杜克大学本部花园的景观情境考察，思考如何将一部分相似的花园文化精神植入昆山杜克花园。

杜克大学本部围绕著名的杜克教堂而建，它刚柔并济的布局与东西交融的设计体现了杜克大学"博学笃信"的校训，即知识与信仰的融合。在美国杜克花园的克伯森亚洲树木园中，符号化的日式红桥是美国造园师对东方异国情调的援引（图3），反映当时西方社会对东方

① 拉扎罗在《意大利文艺复兴花园》一书中的原句是"自然和艺术是不可分割的整体，自然既是艺术的创造者也具有艺术的精髓。它们共同缔造了一个既非自然也非艺术，而是由两者共同创造出来的存在"。

1. 分阶段建成的校园及杜克花园区位图
2. 场地现状航拍照片（向西）。一期校园已经建成，二、三期校园和杜克花园正在同步建设中。

1. Location of the phases of campus construction and Duke Garden
2. Bird's-eye view from east. Phase I of the campus has been built up while Phase II and III as well as the Duke Garden are still under construction.

3. 杜克大学本部花园日式红桥。在克伯森亚洲树木园内，这座木桥横跨在园内的小河上，掩映于竹林中，反映了美国景观设计师对东方文化的想象。
4. 水袖桥渲染图。平行于水上森林的人行栈道，灵感来源于昆曲中的水袖。
5. 鱼鳞铺装渲染图。滨水步道的铺砖灵感源自"太湖三白"中的白鱼形象。
6. 区域土壤分析。昆山区域内主要由夯实土、高活性强酸土和强淋溶土组成。场地位于大面积的夯实土区与高活性强酸土区的交界处。

3. The red bridge in Japanese style in the original Duke Garden. Located in the Culberson Asiatic Arboretum, the wooden bridge hides itself behind the bamboo, reflecting the curiosity in and reception of the oriental culture in the West world at the time of its building.
4. Rendering of the water sleeve bridge. The bridge runs parallelly to the promenade in the wetland forest like a long dance sleeves of Kunqu Opera costume.
5. Rendering of the fish-scale-liked pavement. The pattern comes from the scales of whitefish, which is known as one of the three famous "white" symbols of Taihu Lake in Jiangsu Province.
6. Analysis of soil at regional scale. The soil of Kunshan is mainly composed of compacted soil, highly active acid soil, and highly leached soil. The site is located at the transition belt of compacted soil and highly active acid soil.

文明的好奇与接纳。在当代的语境下，以杜克大学为代表的美国高等教育被引入中国，杜克大学本部花园成为即将建成的昆山杜克花园的"别处"。因此昆山杜克花园在设计上回应了杜克大学本部花园对东方文化的想象，二者在精神上一脉相承，但在表现上需要加以区分。设计团队相信这个项目需要基于明确的地域性，而地域文化应以当代的尺度和与西方对话的方式来传达。具体落实在对江南园林的理解上，江南文化以无胜有，大面积的白墙黛瓦犹如中国山水画的留白；江南园林中的短桥往往是最简单的石板，连栏杆都没有。在昆山杜克花园中，江南园林的这些特质以含蓄的方式表达在了一些被抽象化了的景观元素中（图4、5）。

但在功能与绩效层面，杜克大学本部花园对昆山的设计具有很强的借鉴意义。1935年夏，北卡罗莱纳州暴雨造成的洪涝摧毁了刚刚兴建一年的杜克花园。重建时，设计师艾伦·彼尔德·希普曼刻意抬高了地势，并更换了植栽。1980年，设计师琳达·朱厄尔又开挖了蓄水湖，使花园能够更加韧性地应对洪水[2]。

相应地，设计团队保留并将白窑湖水体转化为中央水景，遵循填挖方平衡原则改造周边水深与岸线形态，恢复了有益于重塑湿地栖息地的水体特征；设定调蓄容量，使中央水体成为周边区域的大"海绵"；针对不同水源设计不同的净化路径，逐步提升水质，并通过东侧水道，为周边地块和待建校区输送净化水源。这一系列设计既垂范了杜克大学本部花园的设计，也反哺了昆山本地的生态环境。

2.2 地文学考察

地文学考察来源于伊恩·麦克哈格开创的生态分析与设计的方法体系。它是对大尺度区域环境的多维度X光透视式检查，通过分类法和

② 贝里兹拜迪亚在《阿姆斯特丹森林》一文中的原句是"景观的价值（或是个体的或是社会的）通过一个开放设计的体系来表达，这个体系通过诸如风和水的冲蚀和植物的轮替建立一个生物进程，并通过对场地产生的作用来塑造它的景观"。

③ 对一期校园水处理策略的具体介绍详见曾颖发表于《时代建筑》2017年第4期的《水生态在空间与时间维度上的塑造：昆山杜克大学校园作为微型海绵城市设计的解析》一文，以及时惠来和林中杰发表于《建筑学报》2018年第3期的《"上善若水"：昆山杜克大学生态景观设计》一文。

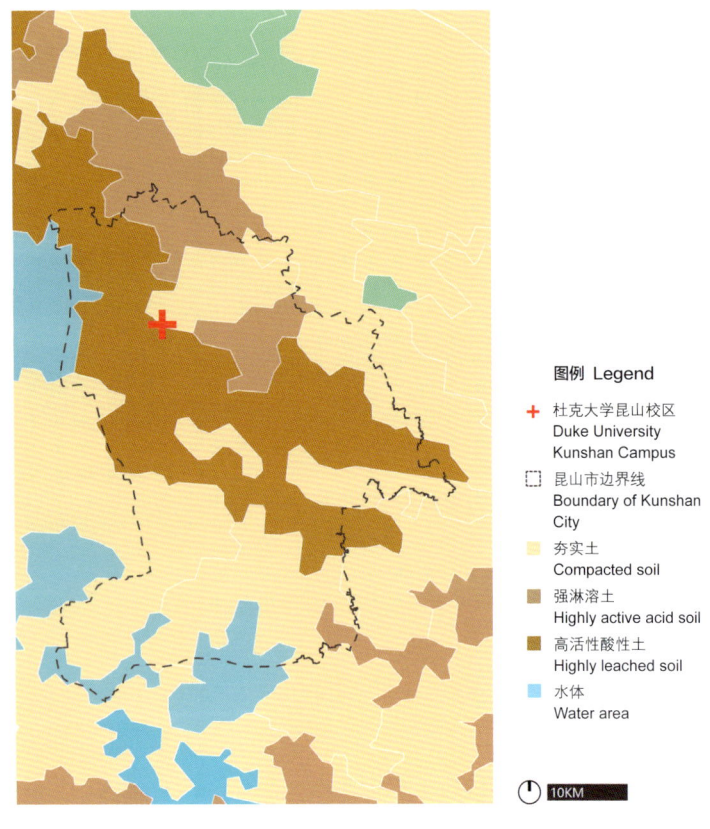

图例 Legend
+ 杜克大学昆山校区 Duke University Kunshan Campus
⋯ 昆山市边界线 Boundary of Kunshan City
夯实土 Compacted soil
强淋溶土 Highly active acid soil
高活性酸性土 Highly leached soil
水体 Water area

10KM

© Futurepolis LLC

队结合气候与植被等其他元素的地文分析最终得出了能够反映区域原始景观多样性的组合类型：森林、草甸与淡水湖泊的组合。设计借此围绕湿地森林、湿地草甸与水岸混合带创造出新的栖息地，强化生态结构，提升生态连通性，并恢复温带草地景观，用更可持续的景观类型替代高作业强度的农地景观（图7）。

在勾画平面草稿时，设计团队从水滴滴落在纸面的印迹与动态中获得灵感，并在具化过程中参考各个栖息地所需的最小面积做出相应调整，使水面轮廓与栖息地功能形态基本吻合（图8~10）。同时，设计团队尽量让以上几种栖息地以其自身最朴实的状态呈现在使用者眼前，并依托开敞的湖面，让光线、水、倒影提升游览体验，这种趋于自然的表达方式力图将人带回到一个不事雕琢的情境中（图11）。

2.3 延时性考察

延时性是景观都市主义具有代表性的概念，即景观不是创造出来的静态场景或画面，而是在很长的一个时间段中逐步成长、演化、成熟乃至最终衰退的过程。景观设计需要考虑社会与自然因素的不断介入，更有效地设定与引导城市景观生态的演变[4]。正如景观理论家安妮塔·贝里兹拜迪亚的观点，后现代的设计在结果预期上是开放式的，它通过设置"生物性的过程"让所设计的景观在时间轴上演变，在逐步呈现的过程中景观得以构建②[5]。

昆山杜克大学作为一个系列项目，提供了很好的延时性考察的机会。在一期校园设计中，设计团队即构建了对整个场地生态功能与空间营造的初步设想。该设想在一期到二期再到杜克花园的递进式设计过程中得到不断检验和修正。在一期校园设计中，设计团队即从生态系统的视角出发考虑如何模糊人工与自然界限，使其相互渗透。由此带来的动态平衡和冗余，为校园空间创造了更多韧性，从而能够有效应对极端气候事件。如一期校园的中央景观湖具有系统管理雨洪的中枢功能，湖心平台亦可适应水位变化而呈现出不同的空间状态（图12~14）。场地周边看似自然的水生池塘实际上也暗含着一套完整的雨水处理系统，并很好地运行了生物净化的一系列程序③[6][7]。这在一定程度上引导了杜克花园的设计方向——杜克花园中心水体的设计采取了类似的水位调控方法，使水生态处理和景观空间的塑造合二为一（图15）。

在表达手法上，如果说一期校园是江南私家园林的当代阐释与海绵城市的微缩模型，那么杜克花园则是以花园之名融合江南地区的地理特征，是江南景观系统在当代语境的呈现。一期校园中以土木工程方法为主，景观配合建筑去塑造室外空间，强调设施的系统作用；而在杜克花园的设计中，景观成为主体，开阔的空间促生了一种更加简练和独具意境的创作。但是从整体来看，一期、二期与花园是密不可分的，它们不但带来空间上的系列收放和流线变化，而且在水量和水质方面互相调蓄。杜克花园与主校区共同形成了一个"海绵"，使校园整体上具备更高的生态韧性（图16，17）。

剖面法的结合，对不同地文特征进行立体剖解，得到适宜性结论[3]。这种对地理要素的深入考察可帮助设计者发现不同地理人文信息在各层面的联系，从而推导出地文特征背后的因果关系，使设计因地制宜。

针对基地缺乏景观特色的现状，设计团队将场地放置于更为宏观的生态尺度下进行考察，从而更好地确定场地在区域中的定位。首先，昆山地区湿地密布，是候鸟迁徙路线上的重要驿站，而杜克花园则位于城市近年着力打造的高教区绿网系统内，使其成为连接周边绿地、湿地及生态廊道的有机组成部分。这些条件为解答场地绿化密度低和生态条件不佳等现状问题提供了线索。同时，设计团队从水文、土壤和植被等方面对昆山所处的苏南冲积平原栖息地进行深入调查，采用地文学分析方法，获取更为精确的生态信息，帮助设计团队构筑新的景观情境。

在水文层面，昆山地区所在的苏南冲积平原是以水为基底的自然冲积地带，地形平整、地质柔软有弹性且渗水性较强。杜克花园的设计通过大面积的"软质元素"还原与原始地貌相近的空间形态布局，有意模糊水地分界，凸显出江南景观中的柔性感官特征。在土壤和植被方面，历史上苏州地区长期的水稻种植已基本改变了区域内原本的土壤结构，一般认为主要由人为夯实土组成。但分析发现，昆山地区的土壤构成中还有高活性强酸土和强淋溶土（图6）。其中，强淋溶土的存在使设计团队有理由推断这里曾存在大面积的森林景观。设计团

在使用中，一期校园的空间营造和美学理念得到了师生的普遍认

可（图18）。与此同时，校园的湿地景观也成为了生态课程的教学场所，学生在科学教育中更加认同校园的文化定位（图19）。可以说，对一期校园建成效果的观察和使用的反馈鼓励了设计团队在杜克花园中更坚定地摈弃流于表面的形态设计，转而将设计融于生态功能和多样化的空间体验中，通过空间序列和节点而不是符号化元素来突显地域文化，将注意力全面聚焦于有长期效应的生态重建上。

3 讨论与评述

"观察"一词的涵义是多解的。在昆山杜克花园的设计过程中，观察不仅包括在场行为，还引入了研究，将"观察"拓展到"考察"的范畴。这个拓展的过程包含了异地性考察、地文学考察和延时性考察三个方面。这三种考察过程帮助设计师逐步厘清思路、反思"观察"的内涵、发掘场地潜力。这种工作方法也将设计考察的范围从在地扩展到区域乃至全球，同时把时间维度纳入空间设计的考察范畴，搭建起景观情境的演化框架。

杜克花园项目也让我们有机会重新审视"花园"这一古老的景观类型。麦克哈格在《自然不止于花园》一文中曾说，与其他设计类型相比，花园是在做一种简化的工作，在其创造过程中排除了很多自然现象[8]。而昆山杜克花园的设计则试图将多种景观生态浓缩于花园之中，这证明二者未必互斥。设计团队不仅借助延时性考察给出了一个跳出追求静止与永恒之美的传统花园的局限而去拥抱"时间与变化"的设计方案，同时也在异地性考察中思考了"花园的当代意义"。这些思考促使设计师尝试对花园精神作出基于场地特征的诠释，并在地文学考察的辅助下，实现了生态景观的系统化布局。

需要强调的是，设计团队在项目中所采用的"考察先于设计，分析贯通设计"的方法虽然已是欧美设计实践中的主流思维，但在中国仍待普及。随着中国更多的城市发展计划付诸实践，郊区景观的设计需求也会持续增长。在面对缺乏场所精神的场地时，设计师同样可以跳出直观景象的限制，开展一些溯源性的、区域性的、延时性的考察工作，并以此为出发点展开设计，摈弃过度表达，追求以"空"为"多"、用"境"生"景"的设计目标。**LAF**

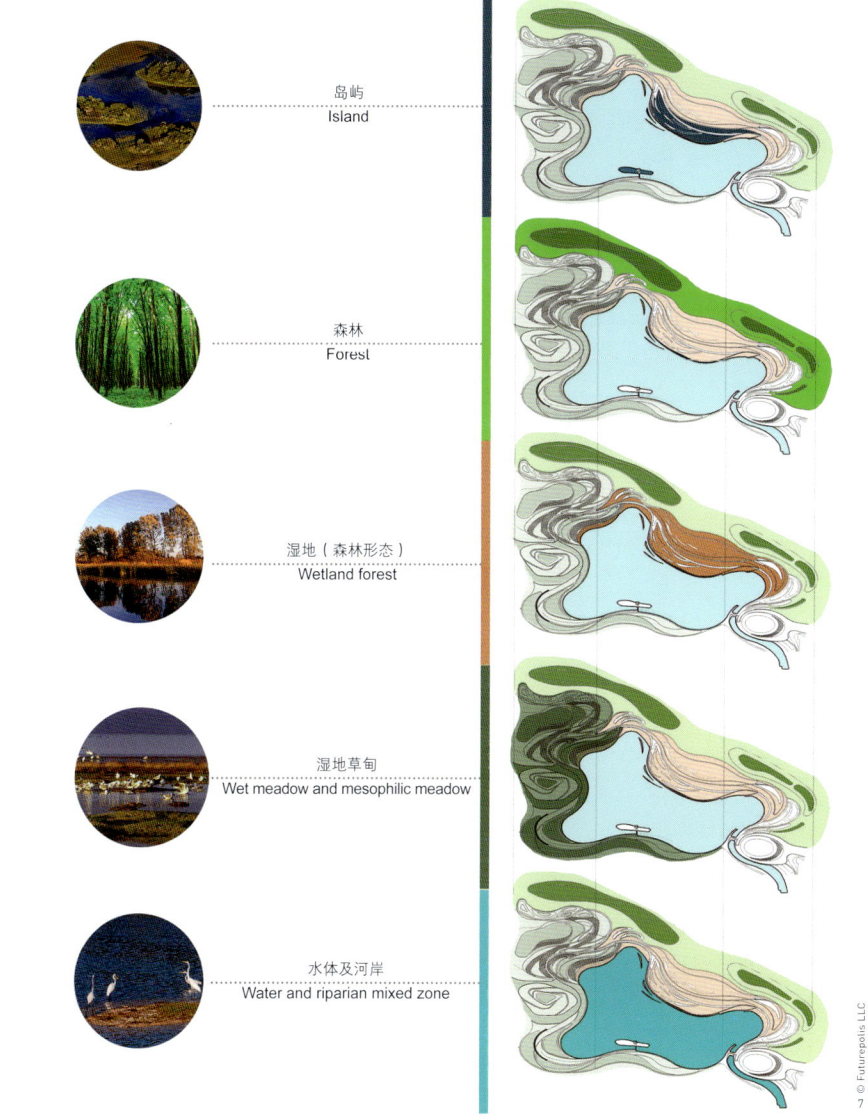

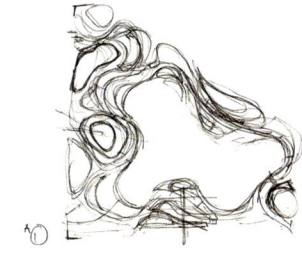  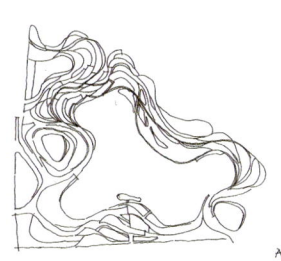

7. 杜克花园中不同种类的栖息地。将新造的栖息地具体化为景观形态，由水体向周边扩展，彼此相连形成一个微生态系统。
8. 杜克花园平面设计草图

7. Different habitats in Duke Garden. The proposed habitats are represented into specific landscape patterns according to the outline of the water body, together forming a micro-ecosystem.
8. Sketches of the site plan of Duke Garden

项目信息

项目地址：中国江苏省昆山市高教园区
项目面积：28.9hm²
项目委托：昆山创业控股集团有限公司
景观设计：Futurepolis未来都市规划建筑设计事务所
首席设计师：时惠来
设计团队：林中杰、高伟、庞会涛、郑立
合作团队：法国Biotope生态工程咨询公司
设计时间：2018年9月~2019年10月
施工时间：2019年9月至今

致谢

感谢中国美术学院曾颖副教授、Futurepolis未来都市规划建筑设计事务所高伟、宾夕法尼亚大学郑盛远和尹奕涵对本文的协助与建议。

1 Project Background

Duke University Kunshan Campus is located in the Higher Education District in the northwest of Kunshan, Jiangsu Province, China. It is a new research university jointly created by Duke University in the USA and Wuhan University in China and funded by the government of Kunshan. The total area of the campus is around 77.5 hm^2. Duke Garden is located in the east and northeast of the campus with an area of about 28.9 hm^2 (Fig. 1). Phase I of the campus has been built up while Phase II and III as well as Duke Garden are still under construction.

Kunshan Duke Garden is situated in a typical suburban landscape (Fig. 2). It is occupied by farmland and several plant nurseries, with a municipal road passing through. The excavated Lake Baiyao in the north of the site is around 9.5 hm^2. In the east, there is a canal of around 25 meters in width. Due to the long-time practice of excavation, the edges of the lake and the canal are shaped in regular geometry. The deepest depth of the water body is around 11 m, penetrating two layers of groundwater. However, the water quality are found in Class IV and V. The site is monotonous in terms of plant species and ecological habitats; there are only some matured trees to the north of the lake and small clusters of plant nurseries in the middle of the site. Therefore, the two primary challenges of the design of Duke Garden include: 1) how to restore the natural character of the site that has been damaged during excavation and farming, while enhancing ecological vitality, water quality, and biodiversity; and 2) how to provide Duke Garden with a fresh spirit of the place under the limit of the absence of distinctive site identity.

2 Site Observation and Process of Design

In Western garden theories, designers merge nature and artifact through garden making to form the so-called Third Nature. This concept was initially proposed by Renaissance historians Jacob Bonfadio and Bartolomeo Taegio. Contemporary art historian Claudia Lazzaro revisited the interpretation of this concept as the interweaving of nature and art into an indistinguishable whole. The nature becomes the creator of art and gains the essence of art. The combination of the two creates a completely new being, which is neither one nor the other, but a "Third Nature." ①[1]

The original Duke Garden of Duke University in the USA is a beautiful manifestation of this theory. The garden is located in the Piedmont region of North Carolina, characterized by its wild landscape with little intervention by humans, which constitutes the First Nature. A series of artificial elements, represented by

① Lazzaro's original statement in *The Italian Renaissance Garden* is "nature and art are united into an indistinguishable whole, in which nature becomes the creator of art and shares the essence of art. Together they produce something that is neither one nor the other, and is created equally by each."

9. Site plan of Duke Garden. The north part functions as an ecological purification and a gathering area while the south part provide more private spaces to stay in quiet.

religion, science, education, and gardening, were integrated into local habitats when the garden was built, thereby creating a Third Nature that claims both artificial and natural characteristics.

The Jiangnan Region (South-eastern area of lower Yangtze River Delta), where Kunshan is located, represents a similar yet different garden-making tradition. The potential sites for private gardens in Jiangnan urban areas usually lack distinguished topographies or natural features. Most of them were simply parcels of flat lands framed by walls separating them from the busy city, although these plots vary in size and peripheral circumference. Based on the observation of the site and understanding of the Jiangnan landscape, literatis projected a selected and synthesized scenario onto the site, forming a Third Nature through the interaction between nature and buildings, and between water and terrains. Although the landscape elements are similar, specific employment of such a method, however, makes each garden unique.

The design of Kunshan Duke Garden further develops the scenario-making method of the gardening practice in Jiangnan. It does not simply replicate the form or elements from the original Duke Garden; instead, it is based on spiritual inheritance to invent a landscape design solution that is rooted locally through investigation of the city's cultural context and exploration of the potential of the site. The relationship between human and nature is related to the vicissitude of history and culture, and the connotation of "garden" has also been extended. The evolution of Duke Garden in the USA gives a reference to its counterpart in Kunshan, which combines with new contemporary interpretation of the local water-town landscape tradition in Jiangnan. The designers need to respond to the university culture with the contemporary ecological context, and look for the contemporary garden spirit with an environmental consciousness as the point of departure for the design. Based on this idea, deep observations in three perspectives gradually assist the designer team to come up with design concepts, which consists of off-site observation, physiographical investigation, and time-lapse observation. Besides the commonly-used perception and recording of topography and vegetation, these three processes also have involved analytical thinking at a deeper level, which go beyond the realm of "observation" towards the territory of "investigation."

2.1 Off-Site Observation

Off-site observation describes the migration of the spiritual state through insights into similar cultural landscapes and traditions located elsewhere. In Kunshan Duke Garden project, the design team considered how to embed a portion of similar garden cultural spirit into the design by studying the landscape of the original Duke Garden.

Duke University in North Carolina was built around the renowned Duke Chapel. Its forceful yet harmonious layout and integrated aesthetics of the East and the West reflects Duke University's motto, "Eruditio et Religio," i.e., the merge of knowledge and faith. In Culberson Asiatic Arboretum which is part of Duke Garden, the symbolic red bridge in Japanese style represents the American garden designer's imagination of oriental exoticism, which reflects the curiosity in and reception of the

10. 花园中心水体鸟瞰图
11. 水上森林效果图

10. Rendering of the central pond of Duke Garden from bird's-eye view
11. Rendering of forest wetland

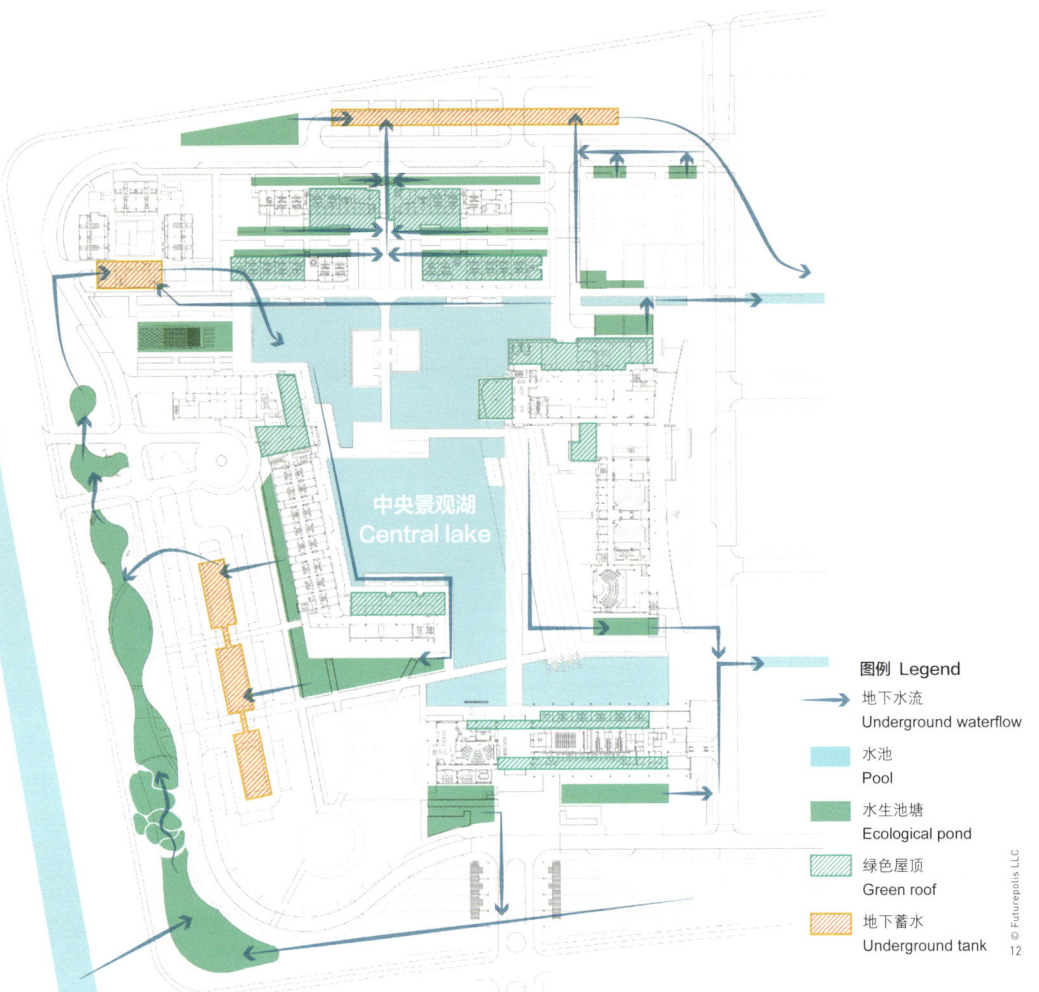

洪水期
Flood period

常水期
Ordinary condition

枯水期
Drought period

12. 一期水处理。一期南侧的地表污水先进入一连串的水生池塘，再存储在地下蓄水池中。溢出部分汇入中央景观湖。中央景观湖向西可以进入二、三期校园的排水渠，最终汇入杜克花园的中心水体中。
13. 一期校园湖心平台水位变化模拟图。在不同的水位条件下，平台不同的状态增加了场地的趣味性。
14. 一期校园的湖心平台

12. Water treatment of Phase I. The surface wastewater from the south of Phase I is stored in the underground tanks after purified with a series of ecological ponds. The overflow running into the central lake is discharged into the drainage ditches in Phase II and III, and finally conveyed into the central pond of Duke Garden.
13. Platform on the central lake of Phase I under different water levels. The varied scenarios raise interesting experience to the site.
14. Platform on the central lake of Phase I

oriental culture in the West world at the time of its building (Fig. 3). Today, American higher education represented by Duke University is introduced to China, and the Duke Garden in the USA becomes the "elsewhere" of the upcoming Duke Garden in Kunshan. Therefore, the new garden design needs to respond to the cultural imagination of the orient in old Duke Garden. The vision embedded in both gardens are consistent, yet their representations should be distinguished. The design team believes that this project needs to build on the recognition of regional characters, and the regional cultures should be conveyed at a contemporary scale as a dialogue with the West. As one of the outstanding features of Jiangnan gardens, the culture prefers simplicity to complexity. Large areas of white walls and black

tiles resemble the emptiness in Chinese landscape paintings. The short bridges in Jiangnan gardens are often built in the simplest form with stone slates but without railings. In Kunshan Duke Garden, these qualities of Jiangnan gardens are represented in abstract forms of contemporary culture (Fig. 4, 5).

However, in terms of function and performance, the Duke Garden in the USA serves as a valuable reference to the design in Kunshan. In the summer of 1935, a flood caused by heavy storms hit the city of Durham in North Carolina and almost completely destroyed the Duke Garden, which had only been built for a year. During its reconstruction, landscape architect Ellen Bilddle Shipman intentionally elevated the terrain and changed plant species to better adapt to extreme climate events. In 1980, Linda Jewell, who renovated the garden, dug a pond for water storage, enhancing the resilience of Duke Garden against flooding[2].

Accordingly, the design team of Kunshan Duke Garden retained and transformed Lake Baiyao into a central waterscape, remoulded the bathymetry and edge form through on-site cut-and-fill, and restored the water features beneficial in reshaping wetland habitats. The design team also modified the water level for the central pond to act as a big sponge for surrounding areas. Different purification paths were designed for different water sources, in order to gradually improve the water quality. Purified water is transported to surrounding areas and other campus areas through the east waterway. This series of design strategies not only inherit the idea of resilence in the Duke Garden in the USA but also respond to the local natural environment in Kunshan.

2.2 Physiographical Investigation

Physiographical investigation originated from the methodology of ecological analysis and design pioneered by Ian McHarg. It represents an in-depth multi-dimensional investigation of large-scale regional environments. Through a combined work of classifying and sectioning, an appropriate conclusion is obtained through three-dimensional dissection of different physiographical features[3]. This in-depth study of geographical features can help designers discover the connections of various information in geography and humanity at different levels. Thus it derives the logics behind these physiographical features, allowing design to adapt to the local conditions.

Given the lack of in-situ landscape characteristics, the design team examined the site by placing it at a macroscopic ecological scale to better understand its physiographical conditions. First of all, the location of Kunshan is a node on the migratory route of birds, and the city is characterized by a high density of wetlands. The new Duke Garden is situated in the green space network system of the Higher Education District that the city has been developing in recent years, with an attempt of making it an integral part in connecting the surrounding green space, wetland, and ecological corridors. These conditions provided clues for solving some of the current problems on site, such as low green coverage and poor ecological conditions. Meanwhile, the design team conducted in-depth investigations of the habitats of alluvial plains in southern Jiangsu in the aspects of hydrology, soil, and vegetation. Analytical methods of Physiography were employed for more precise ecological information, which helped construct new landscape scenarios.

On the hydrological level, the alluvial plains in southern Jiangsu is a natural alluvial zone under-layered with water. The terrain is flat, and the geology is soft and elastic with a high water permeability. The design of Duke Garden uses large areas of "soft elements" to restore the spatial layout similar to its original topography, intentionally blurring the water boundaries to highlight the sensorial characteristics in Jiangnan landscape. In terms of soil and vegetation, the long-term rice farming in Suzhou has changed the regional soil structure. It is generally believed that the soil type is mainly composed of artificially compacted soil. However, analysis revealed that, in Kunshan

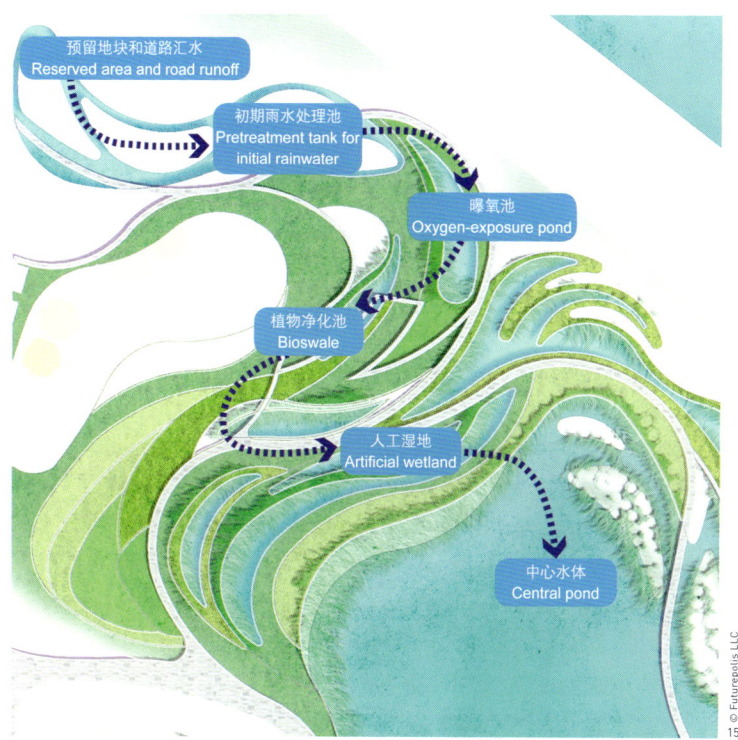

15. 杜克花园水处理分析图。相嵌的月牙形湿地景观与净水功能相结合，将场地外的地面汇水以低成本的生态方法处理排入中心水体，并加以重复利用。
16. 校园海绵功能分析图。杜克花园与主校园的水量和水质方面互相调蓄，不仅缓解了极端气候的危害，也节约了水资源。

15. Water treatment of Duke Garden. The crescent wetlands serving as an aesthetic landscape and purification system collect surface runoff from the surrounding areas, purify it in a low-cost ecological method, and then discharge it into the central pond for a reuse.
16. Campus sponge. Duke Garden and the main campus can adjust water of quantity and quality with each, relieving the challenge of extreme climate events while saving water source.

② The original sentence of Berrizbeitia described in "The Amsterdam Bos" is "In landscape, these values (individual over collective) are expressed through a system of open-ended design that is also largely based on setting up a biological process, such as erosion by wind or water, or plant succession, and letting the process through time, shows its effect on the site, constructing its landscape."

③ The detailed water treatment strategies can be learned in "Shaping the Spatial and Temporal Dimensions of Hydro-Ecological Landscape: The Design of the Duke University Kunshan Campus as a Micro Sponge City" by Zeng Ying published in the 4th issue of *Time Architecture* in 2017 and "'The Supreme Virtue Is Like Water': Ecological Landscape Design of Kunshan Duke University" by Shi Huilai and Lin Zhongjie published in the 3rd issue of *Architectural Journal* in 2018.

图例 Legend
- - ▶ 湖体泄洪方向 Flood discharge
- ▶ 雨水收集方向 Rainwater collection
- ▶ 景观供水方向 Supply to waterscape
- I~III 类水 Water quality of Class I and III
- IV~V 类水 Water quality of Class IV and V

area, there are still highly active acid soil and highly leached soil in the soil composition (Fig. 6). Among them, the presence of strongly leached soil provides the design team with clues to infer that there used to be a large area of forest landscape. The design team combined the geological analysis of other elements such as climate and vegetation to reveal indigenous Kunshan landscape in terms of landscape typologies: a combination of forest, meadow, and freshwater lakes. The design thus created three new complementary habitat types of wetland forest, wetland meadow, and riparian mixed zones, in order to strengthen the ecosystem structure, enhance ecological connectivity, and restore temperate meadow landscapes. By so doing, the labor-intensive agricultural landscape would be replaced with more sustainable ones (Fig. 7).

The design concept was also inspired by the dynamics of water on paper surface, as often seen in Chinese painting or calligraphy. Articulating details of the garden, the design team adjusted the layout based on the minimum area needed for each habitat and matched water contour with the habitat functions and forms (Fig. 8 ~ 10). Meanwhile, we also tried to expose the aforementioned habitats in their most authentic states to visitors, relying on the open lake surface to let light, water, and reflection enhance the recreational experience. This natural means of expression that favors austerity of nature aims to bring visitors back to a place that is not prevalent with sculpted artifice (Fig. 11).

2.3 Time-Lapse Observation

Time-lapse is a representative concept in the theory of Landscape Urbanism, in which landscape is not a static scene or picture, but a long-term process of gradual growth, evolution, maturity, and decline. Landscape design is required to consider the continuous intervention of social and natural factors, and more effectively set and guide such a transformation of urban landscape ecology[4]. As the landscape theorist Anita Berrizbeitia notes, postmodern design is open-ended in anticipating for a result; it allows the designed landscape to evolve over time by setting up a "biological process," which is capable of building landscape as it gradually proceeds②[5].

As a series of projects, the whole campus of Kunshan Duke University provides a great opportunity for time-lapse observation. In the Phase I of the campus design, the design team built a preliminary framework for the ecological system and the space-making layout of the entire site. The idea was continuously inspected and corrected during the progressive design process from Phase I to II then to the Duke Garden. In Duke University Campus Phase I, the design team approached the issue from the perspective of ecosystem and considered how to blur the boundary between the artificial and the natural, enabling both to permeate each other. The resulted equilibrium and redundancy enhance the resilience of the campus against extreme weather events. For example, the central lake in Phase I has the pivotal function of systematic stormwater management, and the platforms on and around the lake respond to the fluctuation of water level to present different spatial characteristics (Fig. 12 ~ 14). The seemingly natural aquatic ponds on the outskirt of the central campus are equipped with a hidden stormwater treatment system and can effectively carry out a series of biological purification procedures. This precedent experiences, to a certain extent, informed the design of Duke Garden③[6][7]. The design team has used similar methods to control the water level of the central pond in the garden, so that the ecological treatment of water and shaping of the landscape are combined into one (Fig. 15).

In terms of design expression, if Phase I of the campus is a contemporary interpretation of the classical Jiangnan gardens as well as a miniature model of the Sponge City, the new Duke Garden would be an amalgam of geographical characters in Jiangnan area reflecting the changing culture of garden and a

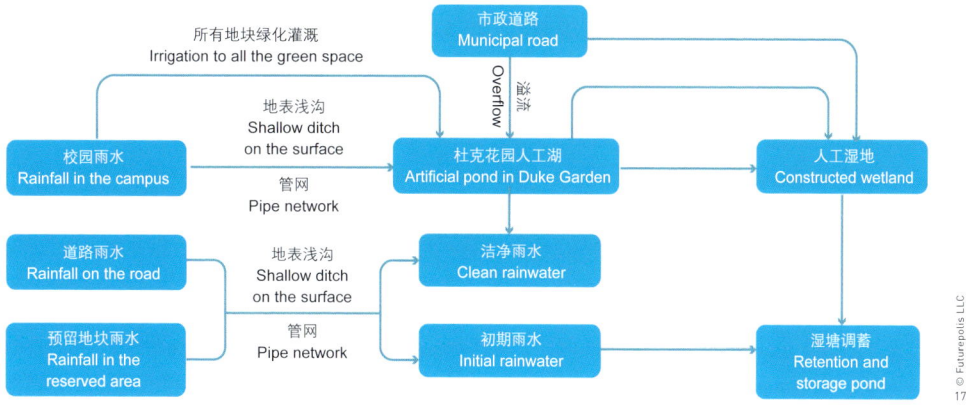

17. 校园径流分析示意图
18. 一期校园围绕水生态形成具有教育功能的海绵校园
19. 一期校园中的外圈湿地渗滤系统

17. Runoff analysis of the campus
18. Phase I acts as an ecological sponge in the campus with educational programs
19. Infiltration wetland system set along the border of Phase I

representation of Jiangnan landscape system in a contemporary cultural context. An engineering approach dominated the design of Phase I, where landscape cooperates with buildings to shape the outdoor spaces and prioritize the systematic function of the facility. In contrast, in the design of Duke Garden, landscape becomes the focus as the open spaces prevail to shape its unique atmosphere. As a whole, however, Phase I and II are inseparable from the garden. Not only do they bring a sequence of compression-decompression spatial variance with changes in circulation, but also adjust water of quantity and quality with each other. Together the garden and the campus form a large "sponge," enabling the local environment to achieve a higher level of resilience (Fig. 16, 17).

Since it is put in use, the landscape of Phase I with its space-making and aesthetic concepts (Fig. 18) has been widely recognized by teachers and students of the university. Meanwhile, the wetland landscape of the campus has become a teaching venue for ecological classes. Students are more aware of the cultural orientation of the university through science education (Fig. 19). It can be said that the observation of the performance of the earlier phases and users' feedback have encouraged the design team to abandon superficial designs that are concerned only about forms. Instead, the design is expressed in ecological efficiency and diverse spatial experiences, which reflect the regional culture in sequence and with nodes spatially rather than symbolically, by focusing on ecological reconstruction that has long-term effects.

3 Discussion and Review

The meaning of "observation" can be interpreted in multiple ways. During the design of Kunshan Duke Garden, observation is no longer confined as in-situ behavior, but introduces research that expands "observation" to the realm of "investigation." This act of expansion includes three aspects: off-site observation, physiographical investigation, and time-lapse observation. These processes help designers gradually clarify ideas, reflect on the meaning of "observation," and explore the potential of the site. This method also expands the scope of design observation from a site scale to a regional and even global scales. It simultaneously incorporates temporality into the design work, so that an evolutionary framework of landscape scenarios is built.

Kunshan Duke Garden also gives us an opportunity to revisit the ancient landscape typology of "garden." Ian McHarg once discussed in his essay "Nature is More Than a Garden" that gardens are works of simplification in comparison with other design categories, during which many natural phenomena are excluded[8]. The design of the Kunshan Duke Garden, however, tries to condense a plethora of landscape ecologies into the garden, proving that there might not be such a schism between "garden" and "nature." The design team used the time-lapse method to make a plan that embraces time and change, which is different from a limiting pursuit for stability and eternal beauty in traditional garden-making. Furthermore, they also paid attention to the contemporary significance of "garden" during the process of off-site observation. These contemplations prompted designers to interpret "garden spirit" based on specific local characters, with the assistance of physiographical investigation, to achieve a systemized layout of ecological landscapes.

It is worthwhile to note that, although the aforementioned design methods (investigate before design and design with analysis) have already been the mainstream thinking in European and American design practice, it is yet to be popularized in China. As more urban growth plans in Chinese cities are put into construction, the need for suburban landscape design will continue to grow. In the face of the sites that lack notable characters, designers have the choice to step out of site limitations and carry on alternative observations. Then, design is set off in such direction that abandons over-expression to achieve design goals which favor "less" as "more" and pursue "scenario" over "scenery." **LAF**

PROJECT INFORMATION

LOCATION: Higher Education Park, Kunshan, Jiangsu Province, China
AREA (SIZE): 28.9 hm^2
CLIENT: Kunshan Chuangye Holding Group Co., Ltd.
LANDSCAPE ARCHITECTURE: Futurepolis
CHIEF DESIGNER: Shi Huilai
PROJECT TEAM: Lin Zhongjie, Gao Wei, Pang Huitao, Zheng Li
COLLABORATOR: Biotope
DESIGN PERIOD: September, 2018 – Octorber, 2019
CONSTRUCTION PERIOD: September, 2019 to present

ACKNOWLEDGEMENTS

Thanks for the assistances and suggestions provided by Associate Professor Zeng Ying of China Academy of Art, Gao Wei from Futurepolis, and Zheng Shengyuan and Yin Yihan from University of Pennsylvania.

REFERENCES

[1] Lazzaro, C. (1990). The Italian Renaissance Garden. New Haven: Yale University Press.
[2] Sennett, S. (2017). Ellen Biddle Shipman's Design Intent for the Sarah P. Duke Gardens: Tracing This through Virtual and Physical Augmentation. Studies in the History of Gardens & Designed Landscapes, 37(3), 261–272. https://doi.org/10.1080/14601176.2017.1281036.
[3] McHarg, I. L. (1969). Design with Nature. Garden City, New York: Natural Historical Press.
[4] Waldheim, C. (2016). Landscape as Urbanism: A General Theory. Princeton: Princeton University Press.
[5] Berrizbeitia, A. (1999). The Amsterdam Bos: The Modern Public Park and the Construction of Collective Experience. In J. Corner (Ed.), Recovering Landscape:Essays in Contemporary Landscape Architecture (pp. 186-203). Princeton: Princeton Architectural Press.
[6] Zeng, Y. (2017). Shaping the Spatial and Temporal Dimensions of Hydro-Ecological Landscape: The Design of the Duke University Kunshan Campus as a Micro Sponge City. Time+Architecture, (4), 52-57.
[7] Shi, H, & Lin, Z. (2018). "The Supreme Virtue is Like Water": Ecological Landscape Design of Kunshan Duke University. Architectural Journal, (3), 94-100.
[8] McHarg, I. L., & Steiner, F. R. (1998). To Heal the Earth: Selected Writings of Ian L. McHarg. Washington, D.C.: Island Press.

本文引用格式 / PLEASE CITE THIS ARTICLE AS

Wu, Z. (2019). Jinhua Memorial Park in Suining. Landscape Architecture Frontiers, 7(5), 120-133. https://doi.org/10.15302/J-LAF-1-040007

遂宁锦华记忆公园
JINHUA MEMORIAL PARK IN SUINING

https://doi.org/10.15302/J-LAF-1-040007　收稿时间 RECEIVED DATE / 2019-08-26　中图分类号 / TU986　文献标识码 / B

吴兆杰*
美国注册景观设计师，SWA设计董事、合伙人

*通讯作者
地址：上海市徐汇区嘉善路508号尚街时尚园区1号楼7楼718室
邮编：200031
邮箱：jwu@swagroup.com

WU Zhaojie
PLA; Principle of SWA Group

摘要

观察与表达是景观设计中最基本也是最核心的过程与方法。本文通过将遂宁市锦华棉纺厂遗址改造成具有现代休闲功能的城市文化公园，来展示在后工业改造类景观设计项目中设计师如何进行观察与表达。设计师通过对场地的初始感知、反复探索、系统分析等循序渐进的观察方式不断深入对场地的了解；研究发掘工业生产流程并以相关产品作为设计灵感的来源、空间排序的依据和形态转化的原型；以场地干道为空间骨架和主要流线来串联记忆公园的各个功能和空间节点；以原位保留、换位保留、材料保留、外观保留、精神保留五大设计策略重新梳理和组织场地的工业遗迹；以或直观、或含蓄的景观设计手法桥接了场地的过去、现在和未来，同时满足了各类使用人群的需求。

关键词

工业遗址改造；城市更新；观察；设计表达；城市公园

ABSTRACT

Observation and representation are the fundamental and core processes and methods in landscape design. By transforming a historical industrial site into an urban cultural park for citizens' recreational needs, the Jinhua Memorial Park in the Suining City demonstrates how landscape designers observe and represent in post-industrial renewal practice. Designers continuously deepen their understanding of the site through a process from site observation and perception, research and exploration to systematic analyses. During this process, designers were inspired by the industrial production process and textile products, and then applied such concepts in spatial arrangement and prototype for physical renovation. As the skeleton of spatial arrangement, the main road of the campus connects various functional spaces and landscape nodes of the park. Five design strategies, including in-situ preservation, transposition retention, material reuse, appearance protection, and spiritual revitalization, are applied to protect and reorganize the industrial heritages to recall the past prosperous scenes. Landscape design approaches, intuitive or implicit, are adopted to tie up the past, present, and future of the site while making a park that meets the needs of all kinds of users.

KEYWORDS

Post-Industrial Renovation; Urban Renewal; Observation; Design Representation; Urban Park

编辑 田乐　**翻译** 田乐　张健
EDITED BY Tina TIAN　**TRANSLATED BY** Tina TIAN　Angus ZHANG

1 项目背景

四川省遂宁市锦华棉纺厂位于船山老城区的核心位置，紧邻渠河，包裹于西山与涪江之间。在遂宁，没有一片区域像锦华棉纺厂一样承载了几代人的光辉与梦想，镌刻了几代人的青春和岁月。时光重回20世纪50年代，锦华棉纺厂担负起中国轻工业发展的重任，遂宁辉煌的工业时代也就此拉开序幕。从年产3万锭、5万锭到8万锭，锦华棉纺厂的生产规模不断扩大，巅峰时期达到20万锭之多[1]。这些数字既体现了无数遂宁纺织人的热血奋斗史，也是这座城市工业发展历史的辉煌见证。锦华棉纺厂就像一个独立的文化王国，拥有自己的电影院、篮球场、幼儿园、活动中心、医院，甚至职工住房——当时有种骄傲，叫"我是厂里的"。但随着改革开放后遂宁的产业结构调整，及中国城镇化进程的加剧，锦华棉纺厂的繁华悄然褪色，先后经历了多轮改制和重组，仍然无法避免最终关停的命运。

为了留存和延续遂宁人对这片土地的深厚记忆与情感，同时融合当地工业文脉与现代生活需求，遂宁市政府与绿地集团计划在锦华

1. 项目场地区位图（地图来源：Google地图）
1. Site location (Source: Google Maps)

纺厂旧址上联合打造一个城市地标级的文创产业园区，SWA则受邀设计一座纺织遗址记忆公园，面积约2.2hm^2，需要包含纺织博物馆、文化创客基地、青少年趣乐中心等设施。

2 场地观察

2.1 场地初识与感知

设计团队初次场地踏勘时，发现在这片现如今几近荒废的厂区中，看似凌乱的遗迹碎片仍然透露着昔日的辉煌，令人追忆曾经高效的生产场景及活泼的生活场面。根据上位规划的要求，拥有锯齿天窗与大跨度圈梁立柱的主厂房、结构稳健的大小锅炉房、外观保存良好的红砖烟囱，以及隐蔽在树林中、锈迹斑驳的水塔等主体构筑物将被加以保留并改造成各具特色的文化建筑场所或设施。

在林木现状方面，环绕主厂房的成排的高大水杉（*Metasequoia glyptostroboides*）形成了一道辨识度极高的绿环，原厂区入口处有两棵巨大的黄葛树（*Ficus virens*），香樟树（*Cinnamomum camphora*）线性排植于主干道一侧，与周边混植的乔木林形成了鲜明对比。设计团队决定对这些历经变迁的骨干乔木加以保护，它们将和那些主体构筑物共同构建起锦华记忆公园的景观框架。

锈迹斑斑的热水管道横跨主干道路，已成断壁残垣的红砖墙依稀围合出曾经的生产庭院，散落的混凝土碎块间生长着顽强的肾蕨（*Nephrolepis auriculata*），尺寸划一却又棱角凹陷的深色条石铺陈在挡墙一侧，纺织器械零件被杂草掩盖，场地一侧的涂鸦墙展现出工业生产中的文艺情节。设计师通过对场地空间的体验和氛围的感受，对留存工业物件的观察和材料的触摸，形成了许多将过去的生产记忆与现代的文化生活相连的改造利用的想法。

2.2 场地探索分析与深入了解

通过与委托方的反复沟通和大量的现场工作坊，设计团队对场地和项目本身有了更为深入的理解：从前期部门了解到遂宁政府明确要求项目展现锦华的光荣历史和奋斗精神，并建议以文字、照片等直观的方式向访客讲述这段记忆；与设计部门就景观设计和构筑物改造的风格与方向进行了沟通，达成了结合建筑改造设计形成室内外空间转换与延续的共识；从营销部门获知项目需引入的各类文创产业的业态及位置，公园也需设计与之匹配的户外功能空间；最后，基于成本部门提出的具体的造价预算，设计需尽可能地回收利用现场留存的元素与材料，并通过设计途径使场地景观焕然一新。

另外，设计团队与委托方相关部门人员还对其他城市的类似项目进行了细致考察，通过系统分析和横向比较来进一步明确场地的工业文化特征。对历史元素的保留和挖掘，对特色工业的提炼，对文创产品的包装和推广都是当前后工业改造项目的常用手法，而且往往都是以建筑为主要载体来展现工业遗迹，唯有锦华纪忆公园项目拥有由成片乔木林构成的绿色柔性空间，她既是承载城市记忆与市民情感的文化地标，又能满足周边居民的日常休闲需求。

与此同时，设计团队还对曾经长期工作、生活在此的居民进行了走访。他们从精神传承到场景细节等多个角度进行了历史还原，同时也以未来潜在使用者的身份对公园的功能活动提出了建议和憧憬：除了散步、遛狗、棋牌空间外，还表达了希望引入儿童游乐空间、趣味互动体验设施、棉纺知识科普展廊的需求。尤其是，在此工作生活了50多年的李大爷还叮嘱设计团队务必将锦华棉纺厂30周年纪念币运用到设计中，因为那是他最值得骄傲的回忆之一。

3 设计表达

3.1 设计概念

经过对场地的全方位观察和系统分析，以及依托场地L型的地块特征，设计团队确定了公园的设计概念——"重走似'锦'繁'华'之路"：以场地干道为空间骨架和主要流线来串联记忆公园的各个功能和空间节点，以满足各种使用者的需求；运用原位保留、换位保留、材料保留、外观保留、精神保留五大设计策略重新梳理和组织场地的工业遗迹，重现过往的"繁华"景象。

场地设计围绕生产记忆与文化生活两大线索展开。作为由北侧主入口入园后的主要游览线路，空间设计以"棉花原料进厂—纱线形成—纱锭、棉布和锦缎成品产生"的生产流程为故事线，依次划分出五大生产主题景观片区[2]。其中，"植棉为田区"借助遗址庭院中的装置设施和梭织广场上的迷雾效果呼应棉花主题；"纺棉成线区"通过活力草坪上的时代标语纤维艺术装置和五彩丝织装置来突出棉线主题；旧石步道、静水之塔、乐享之园、纱锭乐园等空间的设计都源自"绕线为锭区"中的纱锭原型，并以同心圆的形式和不同的体量来表现；"织锭成布区"则从传统布料织法纹样中提炼出空间排布的方式；"染布为锦区"以不同颜色肌理的组合来烘托商业街区的热闹氛围。针对周边居民的需求，项目依托园区内构筑物改造后的不同功用——文创书店、纺织博物馆、趣乐中心，设计了多样的全龄户外活动场所。园中设立了清晰的标识解说系统，即使访客从东、南两侧入口进入公园，也能便捷地游览各个功能场所——有时逆向游览生产故事线，也能获得独特的游览体验。

3.2 主要景观节点与元素

3.2.1 遗址庭院

作为从北侧主入口进入公园后的第一组景观节点，设计通过材料保留及重组的方式来表现厂区废弃后的景象，既突显了场地的工业精神，又营造了全新的空间体验。设计团队利用遗留的条石与红砖组合建造了新的挡墙，围合形成纺织博物馆（经保留改造的大锅炉房）前方的遗址庭院。庭院内利用原厂区最常用的混凝土材料，从规整的矩形混凝土板渐渐过渡至散置的混凝土碎块，通过保留并补植场地已有的肾蕨，形成强烈的工业遗址氛围。庭院内有序布置着大锅炉房中保存下来的设备零件，并结合解说系统，让访客深入了解棉纺生产的步骤及相关设备的功能。

3.2.2 梭织广场

设计将梭子形状抽象为石材铺装单元来强调棉纺概念。梭织广场中央设置的水雾装置，以迷雾效果呼应棉花印象。林荫草阶鼓励访客们驻足享受活力草坪的开阔视野，在台阶踢面设置了以五彩丝织为主题的艺术装置。为了既保证安全照明，又不产生明显眩光，设计在每个台阶末端都运用通长的透明玻璃砖来弱化光源。考虑到尽量减少使用者活动对新移植乔木的树球的压迫，设计利用耐候钢围合出梭形的树池外框，也与棉纺主题相得益彰。

红砖烟囱原位完整保留并加固了基底，其独有的高度使之成为了项目的标志。平日的夜晚里，红砖烟囱会通过灯光投影设备讲述棉纺厂的发展历史，节假日则可结合特殊事件上演艺术灯光秀。设计将4组充满年代感的标语以耐久纤维丝线编织的方式重现于活力草坪北侧的红砖景墙上。活力草坪既可满足周边居民日常的休闲活

| 大锅炉房 | 红砖烟囱 | 仓库 | 主厂房 | 水塔 | 小锅炉房 |
| Large boiler house | Red brick chimney | Warehouse | Main plant | Water tower | Small boiler house |

| 水杉林 | 香樟树列 | 黄角兰 | 黄葛树与混植林 | 成熟混植林 |
| *Metasequoia glyptostroboides* | *Cinnamomum camphora* | *Michelia alba* | *Ficus virens* and mixed grove | Mixed mature grove |

| 热水管 Hot water pipes | 条石红砖组合墙 Wall made with ashlar and red brick | 混凝土碎块与旧红砖挡墙 Concrete pieces and the existing red brick retaining wall | 条石挡墙 Ashlar retaining wall | 条石 Ashlars | 混凝土碎块 Concrete pieces |

| 锅炉房设备 Boiler | 锅炉房设备 Boiler | 混凝土碎块 Concrete pieces | 路灯 Lamp | 设备零件 Machine parts | 涂鸦墙 Graffiti wall |

2. 设计要求对场地中的主体构筑物加以保留并进行改造。
3. 场地中得以保留的乔木
4. 场地中得以保留的小型构件与其他工业遗迹

2. The main structures on the site to be preserved and restricted.
3. Preserved trees on the site
4. Small structures and other industrial elements remained on the site

动需求，又可举行各类聚会活动或户外艺术展览。现状红砂岩条石基座与旧红砖墙在颜色与质感上相互呼应，设计决定对此外观进行保留。结合周边空间分割和氛围营造的需求，设计对挡墙整体高度做出调整，条石和红砖的高度比例也因四周墙体高度不一而几经优化。最终，综合考虑时代标语的布置和面积要求，设计团队决定将外侧处理为竖直面而内侧使用砖叠出斜面，由此形成独特的纹理效果。

3.2.3 大道小径

丝缕大道是场地中的一个重要节点，其保留了厂区原有混凝土道路充满年代感的外观特征，仅对路面宽度进行了适当缩窄。纺织工艺流程图标及科普文字以耐候钢板的形式被蚀刻于大道上，借此加深来访者对纺织工业的了解和记忆。而在文化创客基地（经保留改造的主厂房）外侧林荫大道上方则设置纱线主题的艺术装置，以多组彩色纤维模仿机织纱线，同时在地面上形成微妙投影，与高大乔木一同勾画出灵动的空间氛围。

在场地踏勘阶段，设计团队发现厂区内数条现状道路因年久失修而碎裂坑洼，杂草丛生。为了突出这一细节特征，设计进行了换位保留：文化创客基地入口步道以大块混凝土碎拼混合混凝土细砾来还原厂区内具有历史感的斑驳地面肌理。同时，环绕成片原位保留的葱郁水杉林设置蜿蜒的衫林小径，丰富游人的空间体验。

3.2.4 水塔石道

坐落在项目西南角的现状水塔是公园次入口的标志物，设计保留了其体量外观并进行了艺术化处理。设计团队希望邀请遂宁本地涂鸦艺术家们在水塔上进行棉纺主题的喷绘艺术创作，以此形成独特的涂鸦墙景观，为公园注入年轻时尚气息的同时为遂宁打造一处"打卡胜地"。

设计原位保留了两株巨型黄葛树和老旧红砂岩条石，并通过回收重组这些材料，建造了一条静谧的旧石步道，结合林荫营造出冥想空间，悠悠绿意使访客心旷神怡，与园中其他活跃的场所氛围形成了反差。

3.2.5 全龄乐园

乐享之园设计以纱锭为灵感，以同心圆的形态围绕黄葛树营造出适宜中老年人活动及休憩的花园。其中，靓丽的黄色烤漆不锈钢座椅并未采用常规尺寸，使用者可以跨坐其上，同时结合凸起的桌面进行棋牌活动。场地原有的仓库屋瓦被回收利用为铺装材料，进一步强化了纱锭的同心圆语汇。

由小锅炉房改造而来的青少年趣乐中心同样以同心圆为原型，组织串联了零件花园与纱锭乐园。现场遗留的纺织设备零件材料被保留并成组地摆放于花园步道的两侧，与金叶女贞（*Ligustrum × vicaryi*）、金边黄杨（*Buxus megistophylla*）、黄金菊（*Euryops pectinatus*）和金桂（*Osmanthus fragrans*）等植物一起营造了一处金

1	大锅炉房	Large boiler house
2	遗址庭院	Ruins Courtyard
3	北入口（主入口）	North entrance (main entrance)
4	红砖烟囱	Red brick chimney
5	时代标语	Old-time slogan banners
6	活力草坪	Lawn of Vitality
7	梭织广场	Shuttle Square
8	林荫草阶	Shaded grass terraces
9	丝缕大道	Yarns Avenue
10	入口步道	Passage
11	衫林小径	Grove Pathway
12	主厂房（改造为文化创客基地）	Main plant (Cultural Innovation Center after a renewal)
13	旧石步道	Old Stone Walkway
14	黄葛树	*Ficus virens*
15	小锅炉房（改造为青少年趣乐中心）	Small boiler house (Joyful Youth Center after a renewal)
16	零件花园	Garden of Machine Parts
17	南入口	South entrance
18	静水之塔	Tower of Water
19	涂鸦墙	Graffiti Wall
20	纱锭乐园	Spindle Garden
21	运动休闲庭院	Courtyard for sports and recreational activities
22	光影步道	Walkway of Light and Shadow
23	荣光之林	Woods of Glory
24	乐享之园	Garden of Enjoyment
25	东入口	East entrance

黄色的芳香花园，丰富了游人的感官体验；抽象保留纱锭形式的主题攀爬塔通过步道与静水之塔相连，同时借助蜿蜒而下的滑梯，为使用者提供了亲子活动空间；垂挂纤维丝线的互动艺术装置则为孩子们提供了与众不同的穿梭游乐空间。

3.2.6 荣光之林

设计从传统织法纹样中获得灵感，在公园的东侧打造了一处"荣光之林"，并邀请对锦华纺织厂乃至遂宁纺织业发展做出过卓越贡献的劳动者认植树木。树木的分布以斜线交织的肌理象征织法纹理，而相对规则的格局则象征机械高效的工业生产[3]。通向运动休闲庭园的"光影布道"两侧分别设计了支架，以黄色半透明塑胶材料模拟织布悬挂于生产支架上的效果，突出布匹主题的同时也界定了穿行与活动空间，营造出妙趣横生的场所体验。运动休闲庭园的地面利用金属蚀刻的方式抽象还原了锦华厂30周年的纪念币，作为对锦华历史的礼赞。

4 讨论与评述

观察与表达是景观设计中最基本也是最核心的过程与方法。观察是景观设计师感知场地、吸收信息的首要渠道，而表达则是景观设计师消化信息、融入思考、输出想法的途径，两者相辅相成、紧密结

5. 场地设计平面图
5. Master plan

合才能生成专业而全面的解决方案。遂宁锦华记忆公园项目场地具有悠久的工业背景和深刻的时代演变内涵，通过以不同的视角、层面和方式对场地进行观察和研究，景观设计师对场地的理解完成了由感性到理性、由具象到抽象的演变，并考虑了场地现在及未来的功能需求——设计永远是为使用者服务的，而不是一味展现设计师的喜好与品味。

项目设计过程收集到的数据是设计团队对未来同类型项目进行的一种"提前观察"[4]。设计团队计划在公园建成开放后进行定期回访，了解公园的维护情况，并与使用者沟通交流，收集来自不同维度的使用后评价和意见，为项目设计优化和调整提供依据——这也是对项目"再观察"的开始。

后工业改造项目一直广受设计师青睐，不仅因为改造设计本身更具挑战，需要考虑更多的限制条件和现存元素的利用，同时，新与旧的共存共生更能突显设计师的设计才能和审美价值。委托方在宏观愿景及项目基调方面可以为设计师提出明确的框架建议或要求，而在创意集成、空间转换和材料搭配上可以更倚重设计师的专业素养。通过建成更多前瞻性的、符合时代价值和需求的项目，景观设计师可以发挥专业力量，来逐渐提高人民群众的普遍审美水平和环境保护意识。**LAF**

项目信息

项目地址：中国四川省遂宁市
项目面积：2.2hm²
项目委托：绿地集团西南事业部
景观设计：SWA集团
首席设计师：吴兆杰
设计团队：林荟、石钰、王冠仪
合作团队：成都基准方中建筑设计有限公司、扩道建筑设计事务所
设计时间：2019年4~9月
施工时间：2019年8月至今

致谢

作者感谢遂宁经济技术开发区政府的刘帆，绿地西南事业部的王瑞、沈策、谢君恺、王小均、谢英鉴、李小兵、谢佳，以及绿地集团技发部的胡宇鹏对本项目的贡献。

6. 项目分区及节点区位示意图
   Zoning plan and landscape nodes

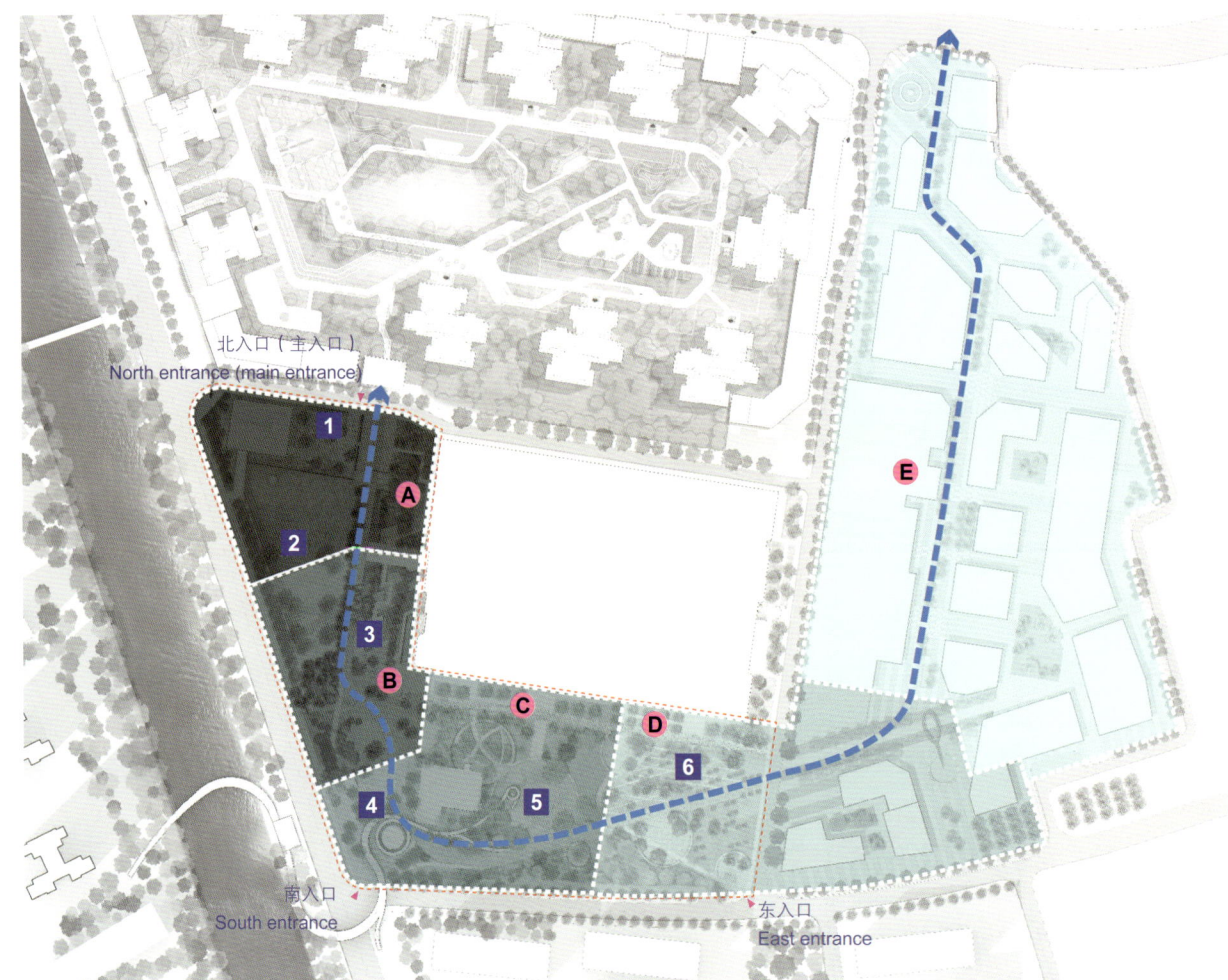

A 植棉为田区 Zone of Cotton Farms
B 纺棉成线区 Zone of Yarns Spinning
C 绕线为锭区 Zone of Spindles Spinning
D 织锭成布区 Zone of Cloth Weaving
E 染布为锦区 Zone of Brocade Dyeing

1 遗址庭院 Ruins Courtyard
2 梭织广场 Shuttle Square
3 大道小径 Avenues and pathways
4 水塔石道 Water tower and stone path
5 全龄乐园 Recreational area of all ages
6 荣光之林 Woods of Glory

1 Project Background

Jinhua Textile Factory in Suining City, Sichuan Province is located in the historic center of the Chuanshan District, sitting next to the Quhe River and connecting the Xishan Mountain and the Fujiang River. In Suining, there is no other areas like Jinhua Textile Factory which had carried the glories and dreams of generations. Back in the 1950s when Jinhua responded to the nation's call of an ambitious development of light industries, the city of Suining opened its industrial era. The production scale of the factory kept increasing, reaching an annual production of 200,000 spindles in its peak period[1]. These figures reflect the glory of those hard-working days, as well as the history of the city's industrial boom. Jinhua was once like an independent "kingdom" which not only had its own culture and identity, but also was well built physically, including cinema, basketball court, kindergarten, recreational center, hospital, and workers' residential building. Jinhua's workers were also very pound of the factory. However, with Suining's industrial restructuring after China's reform and opening up policy, as well as the aggressive urbanization throughout the country, the industrial and social prosperity of the factory has gone and eventually had to face the shutdown after several rounds of restructuring and reforms.

Considering Suining people' memory and deep feelings about Jinhua, the city's industrial context, and citizens' daily needs, the Suining City Government and Greenland Group jointly launched a project, a cultural industry park on the site of Jinhua Textile Factory that acts as a new city landmark. SWA Group was invited to design a textile heritage memorial park, which covers an area of approximately 2.2 hm^2 and will accommodate a textile museum, a cultural innovation center, and a joyful youth center.

2 Site Observation

2.1 First-Sight Perception of the Site

When the design team first visited the site, they were impressed by the derelict factory structures that still tell the flourishing days of the past, reminding people that the site was once one of the busiest industrial campuses in the city. According to the current land use planning, the main plant with oblique-angled windows and long-span ring-beams and columns, the well-structured boiler houses, the red brick chimney with a good appearance, and the rusty water tower hidden in the woods are planned to be preserved and transformed into different cultural buildings or facilities.

The existing tress on the site are also well preserved. The rows of tall trees of *Metasequoia glyptostroboides* form a distinctive green ring surrounding the main plant. Two huge *Ficus virens* stand at the entrance of the campus. *Cinnamomum camphora* alley are planted on one side of the main road, contrasting with the mixed grove nearby. The design team decided to protect these trees that have witnessed the changes in decades and leverage them together with those main factory structures on the site as the skeleton of the park.

The rusty hot water pipes span across the main road, the

7. Ruins Courtyard: first-sight perception of the site and a rendering.

ruins of a red brick wall roughly define the previous production courtyard, *Nephrolepis auriculata* robustly grow between the scattered concrete pieces, the dilapidated dark-color stones in a uniform size are laid down at the bottom of the retaining wall, the parts of textile machines are covered by weeds, and a graffiti wall adds an artistic atmosphere to the industrial campus. Wandering through the site, designers' sensitivity of the space, the perception of the site, and the observation of the remaining features, all together inspired them with ideas to bridge the past and nowadays and to combine people's industrial memories with citizens' modern cultural life.

2.2 A Deeper Understanding of the Site through Investigation and Analyses

Through a long-time communication with the client and a large number of on-site workshops, the design team deepened their understanding of the site and the project. The client conveyed a clear desire of making the park a place to narrate the unique history and spirit of Jinhua with interpretations, photos, or other intelligible ways. Based on the discussion with the client's design department on the style and focuses of landscape design and structure transformation, a decision was made that the landscape design continues the tune of architectural design to create a harmonious spatial experience between the indoors and outdoors. From the marketing department, the design team learned all the types and locations of varied cultural and creative programs that need to be introduced into the site, which requires the spatial design to match with. Finally, according to the specific cost budgets informed by the finance department, the design team were expected to recycle the remained elements and materials on the site and to revitalize the site through design approaches.

The design team, together with the client, also conducted a cross comparison with similar projects in other cities through site visits, in order to further extract the industrial cultural characteristics of the Jinhua project. Methods including preserving and reusing historical heritages, extracting and refining industrial features, and commercializing cultural creative products are commonly used in current post-industrial renewal projects that often focus on architectural / structural construction. What makes the Jinhua Memorial Park project special is the flourishing green patches on the site, offering a great opportunity to create a cultural landmark which not only recalls the industrial bond of the city and the citizens, but also meets the daily recreational needs of surrounding residents.

The design team also interviewed the residents who have worked and lived in the community long since. They provided valuable information about the Jinhua spirit and the production scenes and expressed their desires about the new park as future potential users: In addition to create spaces for strolling, dog-walking, and chess and card playing, children's playfield, recreational interactive facilities, and educational gallery of textile knowledge are mostly mentioned among the survey feedback as well. Impressively, a gentlemen who had lived and worked here for over 50 years hoped that the 30th anniversary commemorative coins of Jinhua Textile Factory can be reflected in the design, because he sees it as a symbol of those glorious years working in the factory.

3 Design Representation

3.1 Design Concepts

Base on a comprehensive observation and understanding of the site, the design team conceived a path of "retracing the prosperity of Jinhua" that leverages the site's L-shaped topography. As the skeleton of spatial arrangement, the main road of the campus connects various functional spaces and landscape nodes of the park. Five design strategies, including in-situ preservation, transposition retention, material reuse, appearance protection, and spiritual revitalization, are applied to protect and reorganize the industrial heritages to recall the past prosperous scenes.

The design and programs are curated with two major clues: production memory and cultural life of the textile factory. The path starts from the main entrance in the north and follows the production process of "cotton stocking — yarns spinning — spindles, cotton cloth, and brocade production." Five themed landscape zones are planned in order along the path[2]. The zone of Cotton Farms highlights its theme with an installation in the Ruins Courtyard and the foggy landscape effect on the Shuttle Square; the zone of Yarns Spinning highlights the theme of yarns production with an artist installation of old-time slogan banners and the design of colorful yarns of the Lawn of Vitality; the design of the Old Stone Walkway, the Tower of Water, the Garden of Enjoyment, and the Spindle Garden in the zone of Spindles Spinning are all conceived from the prototype of spindles and represented in a form of concentric circles in different sizes; the zone of Cloth Weaving refers its spatial design from the traditional textile patterns; the zone of Brocade Dyeing creates a lively landscape of busy retail blocks with a combination of various textures in different colors. In addition, in response to the needs of the surrounding residents, the project combines a variety of outdoor programs with the renovated structures, including

8. Rendering of the Shuttle Square
9. Rendering of the shaded Grass Terrace
10. The design uses the shape of shuttles into stone paving units to reflect the site's textile history.

the Cultural Creative Bookstore, Textile Museum, and Joyful Youth Center. An interpretation signage system is also set up in the park, so for visitors who enter the park from other entrances, it will be easy to find their ways to various spaces — sometimes more fun and surprise arises through a reverse tour along the path.

3.2 Major Landscape Nodes and Features
3.2.1 Ruins Courtyard

As the first group of landscape nodes of the path, the design represents a post-industrial atmosphere of the site through material reuse and recombination, which suggests the industrial history of the campus, create a new spatial experience. A new retaining wall is formed by recycling the remained stones and red bricks, defining a courtyard in front of the Textile Museum (the larger boiler house after a renewal). In the courtyard, concrete, the most commonly found materials in the existing campus, is used to create an experience transition from regular rectangular concrete slabs to crushed pieces, together with the preservation and introduction of *Nephrolepis auriculata*, which manifest a strong industrial sense. Machine parts found in the large boiler house are orderly arranged in the courtyard combined with an interpretation system, from which visitors can learn the knowledge about textile production.

3.2.2 Shuttle Square

The design uses the shape of shuttles into stone paving unit to reflect the site's textile history. A water mist installation in the center of the square creates a foggy effect to represent an image of cotton. The shaded grass terraces invite visitors to sit and enjoy the open view of the Lawn of Vitality, and colorful yarns are set up on the risers of those steps. In order to ensure night safety and avoid glare, the lights are installed at the end of each tread and long transparent glass bricks are used to soften the lighting effect. Minimizing visitors' impact on the roots of the newly planted trees, corten steels are used to form a shuttle-shaped border of the tree wells, which also complements the theme of the square.

11. 时代标语：场地初识与感知，以及设计效果图与局部建成实景。

11. Old-time slogan banners: first-sight perception and a rendering, and a photo of the built-up red brick retaining wall.

12. Yarns Avenue: first-sight perception and a rendering.
13. Grove Pathway: first-sight perception and a rendering.

As the hallmark of the project, the red brick chimney was preserved in situ and its base was reinforced. The chimney acts as a canvas for lighting projections visualizing the history of the factory on weekdays and for lighting shows at festivals and for specific events. Old-time slogan banners found in the plant are reappeared on the northern wall of the Lawn of Vitality with interwoven durable fiber materials. The lawn itself is a place that not only meets users' daily activity needs but also can accommodate various gatherings and outdoor exhibitions. The design preserves the look of the existing wall made with red bricks with a red sandstone base since they appear a harmony in color tune. Considering spatial layout and visit experience, the height and size of the retaining walls were accordingly adjusted to the surrounding heritages. Taking into account the layout and size of the slogan banners, design team eventually decided to make the outer side of the retaining walls straight up and the inner side tapered, forming a unique pattern and texture.

3.2.3 Avenues and Pathways

The Yarns Avenue is a focal node of the site. It imitates the historical appearance of the concrete road in the campus only with a reduction in width for a more pleasant pedestrian experience. The textile production line and knowledge is etched on the corten steel panels inlaid along the avenue regularly. A yarn-themed art installation is placed above the boulevard nearby the Cultural Innovation Center (the main plant after a renewal

and reprogramming), which is made with colorful fibers to mimic a woven fabric and casts subtle shadows on the ground. Together with the tall trees, a unique, refreshing space is created.

During the site investigation, several existing roads were found in a state of disrepair with weeds overgrown. The design preserves and highlights this detail through transposition retention. At the passage to the Cultural Innovation Center, large concrete blocks were mixed with small crushed concrete pieces to restore the historic pavement texture. At the same time, a winding pathway round the lush *Metasequoia* grove preserved in situ helps enrich visitors' spatial experience.

3.2.4 Water Tower and Stone Path

The existing water tower, located in the southwest corner of the site, is a landmark of the park's secondary entrance. The design preserves its appearance with an artistic improvement.

14. 静水之塔：场地初识与感知，以及设计效果图。
15. 旧石步道：场地初识与感知，以及设计效果图。

14. Tower of Water: first-sight perception and a rendering.
15. Old Stone Walkway: first-sight perception and a rendering.

Inspired by the graffiti wall on site, the design team plans to strengthen this feature by inviting local graffiti artists to create textile-related art pieces on the water tower, in a hope of bringing a vibrant and fashion sense to the park and creating a selfie destination for the city.

The Old Stone Walkway is formed by recycling and spatially reorganizing the old red sandstones with preservation of the two giant *Ficus virens* in their original places. Contrasting with the active recreational areas of the park, the design realizes a tranquil and intimate place surrounded by lush greenery.

3.2.5 Recreational Area of All Ages

Inspired by spindles, the Garden of Enjoyment creates a place for the seniors where a bright yellow seating amenity in a concentric form was designed around the existing *Ficus virens*. Made of stainless steels, the seats adopt an unusual size and are partly elevated, allowing users to straddle on and play chess or cards comfortably. The roof tiles reclaimed from the previous warehouse are recycled as materials for a concentric-pattern pavement.

The Joyful Youth Center, which was transformed from the small boiler house, echoes with the concentric pattern in its spatial layout, connecting and integrating the Garden of Machine Parts and the Spindle Garden. The reused textile machine parts are carefully placed in clusters on both sides of the garden path; both gardens are vegetated with mixed plants such as *Ligustrum × vicaryi*, *Buxus megistophylla*, *Euryops pectinatus*, and *Osmanthus fragrans* to create a golden-colored fragrant landscape, offering visitors with a visual and olfactory pleasure. A climbing tower, which reflects the spindle theme in an abstract way, is featured with a twisting slide, not only connecting the Tower of Water through a pathway, but also providing a space for parent-child activities. The interactive art installation with hanging fiber threads invites children running through and around joyfully.

3.2.6 Woods of Glory

The design draws inspiration from traditional weaving patterns and creates a Woods of Glory on the east side of the park. Meanwhile, the design team invites workers who have made outstanding contributions to the factory or the development of city's textile industry to adopt and foster the trees. Tree rows are diagonally arranged to symbolize a weaving texture, contrasting with the foursquare path network that

16. Garden of Enjoyment: first-sight perception and a rendering.
17. Rendering of the Garden of Machine Parts
18. Rendering of the Spindle Garden
19. Rendering of the Walkway of Light and Shadow
20. Rendering of and the Woods of Glory

symbolizes the efficient industrial production[3]. On both sides of the Walkway of Light and Shadow which leads to a courtyard for sports and recreational activities, semi-transparent yellow plastic materials are suspended with brackets to mimic dyeing clothes, defining spaces for different activities and sparkling the site in an exceptional way. On the ground of the courtyard, metal etching was again used to abstractly reproduce an image of Jinhua's anniversary coins, as a paean to its golden history.

4 Discussion and Review

Observation and representation are the fundamental and core processes and methods in landscape design. Observation is the primary means that landscape architects use to perceive and learn from the sites. Representation, on the other hand, is the way to process information, integrate thoughts and knowledge, and convey ideas. The two complement each other and both matter the design outcomes. The site of Jinhua Memorial Park project has a rich industrial heritage and a profound cultural significance of time changes. Through observation and research from different perspectives, levels, and ways, designers' understanding of the site evolves from sensible to rationale, from physical to abstract. Besides, designers always need to consider users' present and future needs, rather than showing off designers' personal preferences.

Data collection during a design process is also a kind of "pre-observation" of future projects in the same type[4]. The design team plans to regularly visit the site after its completion, in order to collect post-occupancy feedbacks from park managers, citizens, and visitors, which can inform the adjustment and improvement plans for the park — this is also the beginning of a "re-observation" of the project.

Post-industrial transformation projects are always favored by designers, not only because the cases themselves are more challenging — more limits or constraints, as well as the possibilities of reuse of existing elements — but also because between the old and the new, designers can give a full play of their talent and aesthetic capability. Client could direct the project by providing macroscale visions or images, while creative integration, space revitalization, and material combination shall be more relied on designers' professionalism. By building more forward-looking projects that reflect the values and needs of the times, landscape designers play an important role in improving the public's aesthetics and the awareness of environmental protection. **LAF**

PROJECT INFORMATION

LOCATION: Suining City, Sichuan Province, China
AREA (SIZE): 2.2 hm²
CLIENT: Greenland Group
LANDSCAPE ARCHITECTURE: SWA Group
CHIEF DESIGNER: Wu Zhaojie
PROJECT TEAM: Lin Hui, Shi Yu, Wang Guanyi
COLLABORATORS: Chengdu Ji Zhun Fang Zhong Architecture Design Co., Ltd., Quad Studio
DESIGN PERIOD: April - September, 2019
CONSTRUCTION PERIOD: August, 2019 to present

ACKNOWLEDGEMENTS

The author would like to thank Mr. Liu Fan, from the Suining Economy and Technology Development Zone, Mr. Wang Rui, Mr. Shen Ce, Mr. Xie Junkai, Mr. Wang Xiaojun, Mr. Xie Yingjian, Mr. Li Xiaobing, Ms. Xie Jia from the Southwest Division of Greenland Group, and Mr. Hu Yupeng from the Headquarter Technology Development Department of Greenland Group, for their contribution to the project.

REFERENCES

[1] Hu, Q., & Sun, G. (2018, May 20). 5.20 Love Suining: Recall the Gone Fanghua of Suining. Suining Daily. Retrieved from http://m.sohu.com/a/315324064_119895
[2] Love, H. (2017). Textile Production Procedure. Retrieved from https://wenku.baidu.com/view/d4a99a230a1c59eef8c75fbfc77da26925c59694.html
[3] Kennel, K., & Kirkwood, N. (2015). Phyto: Principles and resources for site remediation and landscape design. London: Routledge. https://doi.org/10.4324/9781315746661
[4] Schlickman, E., & Domlesky, A. (2019). Field Guide to Life in Urban Plazas: A Study in New York City. Retrieved from https://www.dexigner.com/news/32354

本文引用格式 / PLEASE CITE THIS ARTICLE AS

Sun, C. (2019). Observation and Reflection of the Country Park — Nanchang Red Earth Heritage Park. Landscape Architecture Frontiers, 7(5), 134-145. https://doi.org/10.15302/J-LAF-1-040008

城市郊野公园的观察与思考
——南昌红土遗址公园设计实践

OBSERVATION AND REFLECTION OF THE COUNTRY PARK — NANCHANG RED EARTH HERITAGE PARK

https://doi.org/10.15302/J-LAF-1-040008　　收稿时间 RECEIVED DATE / 2019-10-08　　中图分类号 / TU986.2　　文献标识码 / B

孙翀*
水石设计项目总监

SUN Chong
Project Director of SHUISHI

*通讯作者
地址：上海市徐汇区古宜路188号
邮编：200235
邮箱：evaasun@163.com

1 背景概况

随着城市化进程的加快，日趋紧凑的生活节奏和不断增大的工作压力使得城市居民亲近自然、回归乡野的诉求日益强烈。城市郊野公园在为居民提供近郊休闲空间的同时，也可发挥保护乡村自然风景资源、保护生态环境、开展环境教育等作用[1]。

本次设计的场地即位于江西省南昌市郊县安义县，距离南昌市中心36km，占地面积约16hm²（图1）。场地东望梅岭国家森林公园，周边为安义古村群等旅游景点。随着当地乡村振兴和文旅开发的推进，这块方圆50km内仅存的网纹红土地貌得以被发现并有望打造为一处城市郊野公园。

网纹红土是长江中下游地区的一种地质地层，是第四纪冰川期的冰碛物在湿热气候条件下经淋溶和风化的产物，其断面特征为不同年代的红色土层中夹杂着蠕状白斑。因土质黏重板结，降水不易下渗，

摘要

南昌红土遗址公园位于江西省南昌市近郊，定位为城市郊野公园。场地以成片的网纹红土和马尾松林为主。根据对场地的资料研读和实地踏勘，设计团队发现场地水土流失情况日渐严重，动植物群落单一，且受人工影响严重。考虑到场地本身已具备"红土"这一标志性符号，且造价受限，此次设计旨在打造一处低介入、低维护的城市郊野公园。通过地质科普、自然教育的方式使人们参与其中，并创造不同的互动体验。在此过程中，团队尝试从不同维度审视场地，不断梳理思路、完善设计。从站在宏观视角、跨越时间维度观察场地历年来的变化更迭，到通过微观层面的实地踏勘发现场地特质，建立与场地的对话与连接，最终呈现这处与自然和谐共处的城市郊野公园。

关键词

城市郊野公园；网纹红土；观察；生态修复；低介入；自然体验

ABSTRACT

Located in the suburb of Nanchang City in Jiangxi Province, the Nanchang Red Earth Heritage Park is positioned as a country park that features vast vermicular red earth and *Pinus massoniana* forest. The off-site review and on-site exploration suggested that the site was confronting with problems of severer soil erosion, biodiversity loss, and intensive human intervention. Both to preserve the symbolic red earth in the site and to reduce cost due to limited budget, a country park requiring low intervention and maintenance was proposed. The park would also engage citizens with geological and scientific education programs and create diverse interactive experience.
The design strategies were optimized through continuous site observation and reflection, both with historical and existing data in a broader sense and individual feeling by on-site exploration. This way of dialogue and connection to the site finally gives birth to a natural country park that stays in harmony with nature.

KEYWORDS

Country Park; Vermicular Red Earth; Observation; Ecological Restoration; Low Intervention; Natural Experience

编辑　汪默英　　翻译　王颖　肖杰
EDITED BY WANG Moying　**TRANSLATED BY** WANG Ying　XIAO Jie

1. 项目位于南昌市近郊，可东望梅岭国家森林公园。
2. "红色荒漠"与网纹红土细节

1. The site is located in the suburb of Nanchang City, neighboring the Meiling Mountain National Forest Park to its east.
2. The landscape of "red desert" and the vermicular red earth

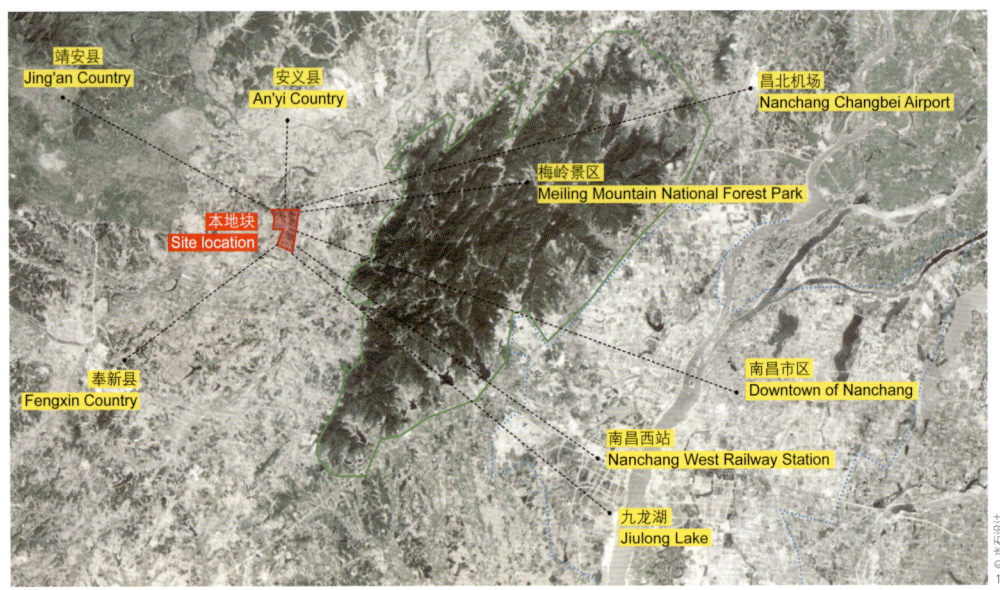

地表径流引起坡面冲刷致使水土流失，常年累月形成了植被稀疏、沟壑纵横的"红色荒漠"景观（图2）。在长期的淋溶作用下，网纹红土几乎丧失了各种营养元素（有机质、氮和钾的占比分别仅为0.2%、0.007%和30ppm）。且因其酸性特性，能在网纹红土上生长的植物品种十分有限。[2]

2 场地初探与实地踏勘

现状场地中既有大片壮阔的红色荒漠地貌，也有呈斑块状镶嵌于其间的大片马尾松林（*Pinus massoniana*）。为了研究场地变化趋势，设计团队首先研究了近几年的卫星地图（图3），发现2013~2018年间，场地内裸露的红土在逐渐减少。一方面是由于植被覆盖率（主要为低矮灌木）在慢慢增加，大自然在进行缓慢的植被演替。另一方面，则是由于极端天气、开荒修路等致使场地外围的红土遭到破坏和蚕食。

随后，设计团队利用GIS数据对场地的高程、坡度、水文径流等信息进行了系统研究。发现场地地势西高东低，高差为15m左右。在场地西侧，因降水引起的坡面冲刷加剧了红土的流失，雨水径流逐渐汇集至地势低洼的东侧区域，在适宜的自然条件的催化作用下，目前场地东侧生长着马尾松林和草甸。

在完成前期研究后，设计团队进行了实地踏勘，期望通过使用者观赏和体验场地的视角，利用五感获取一些更有温度、可共情的感受。在抵达场地之后，设计团队即被眼前壮阔的红土景观所震撼，认

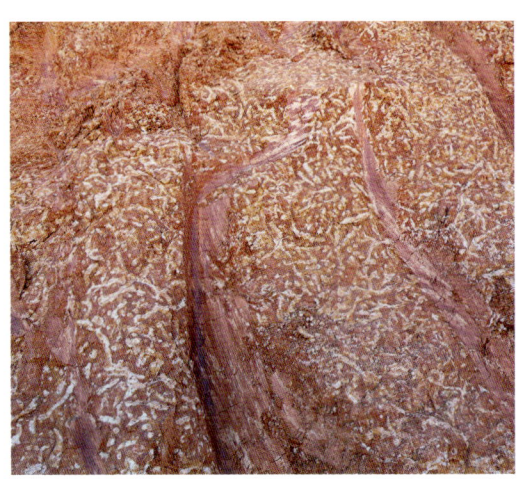

2013年1月
In January, 2013

2016年12月
In December, 2016

2018年2月
In February, 2018

为不应过多地干预场地,以免喧宾夺主。行走在场地之中,可以直观感受到马尾松对视线开合的影响,并据此初步拟定不同地块的介入程度——保留原状、弱干预或适度设计。

通过对场地进行跨越时间维度的研读和细致的实地考察,设计团队发现,场地水土流失情况日渐严峻,动植物群落单一,且受人工影响严重,亟需利用合理的设计策略来对这一独特场地加以保护和修复。为了发挥场地"城市郊野公园"的特性,亦需思考如何将人带入场地进行互动。

3 设计思路和策略

考虑到场地本身已具有足够吸引人的标志性符号,以及低至50元/m²的造价限制,此次设计旨在打造一处低介入、低维护的城市郊野公园。通过地质科普、自然教育的方式使人们参与其中,去了解这种仿若"大地之殇"的自然景观。并基于场地实地踏勘时的感受与发现,创造不同的互动体验。最终的设计策略(图4,5)兼顾生态修复、社会科普、自然体验、成本效益等多个维度,提出三个设计目标:首先,修复场地群落生态环境,为提升场地动植物多样性创造良好基础;其次,在减少对原生动植物和雨水径流影响的前提下,创造连续的低介入慢行栈道系统,提升使用者参与感;最后,营造多样化的空间节点,丰富在地体验、推广自然科普教育。

3.1 塑造基础:修复场地生态环境

生态问题是场地面临的首要问题,塑造良好的生态基底是整个公园发展的根基。设计期望依靠生态系统的自我恢复能力,通过实施适度的人工辅助措施,使受损的生态系统逐步恢复,并不断朝着良性循环的方向发展[1]。最终,设计团队提出了林相更替(图6)和水源涵养相结合的应对策略(图7)。

南昌本地气候特征为亚热带湿润性季风气候,当地的稳定植物群落结构为亚热带常绿阔叶林。而目前场地内是以马尾松为代表的常绿针叶林,且乔木品种过于单一,与稳定的群落结构相差甚远。因此,通过林相更替策略,在对现有植被进行保护的基础上,新增多种乡土树种,可以使物种更加丰富,逐步实现常绿针叶林—常绿针叶阔叶混交林—常绿阔叶林的自然过渡,最终停留在稳定的群落状态。

已有研究发现,植被重建是实现侵蚀退化红壤生态修复的根本措施之一[3]。因此,设计团队首先引入刺槐(*Robinia pseudoacacia*)、马尾松等先锋物种进行斑块化混合种植和土壤改良(图8)。在不同演替阶段,植被对土壤质量的恢复改良均有促进作用[3],因此经过一段时间的生长和竞争后,树种根系和落叶绿肥可以逐步改良红壤的营养与酸碱度,最终改善至更适合多数物种生长的条件。在土壤逐渐改良后,可适当引种一些乡土阔叶类树种,逐步向亚热带常绿阔叶林群落演替——这一过程通常需要数十年的时间。从已有研究可知,亚热带常

3. 2013~2018年间场地卫星地图变化
4. 采用低介入、低影响的设计策略,进行区域生态修复,实现带状栈道串联和点状空间营造。

3. Satellite maps indicating changes of the site from 2013 to 2018
4. Strategies with low intervention and low impact were proposed to realize regional ecological restoration and to link dotted nodes by the linear boardwalk.

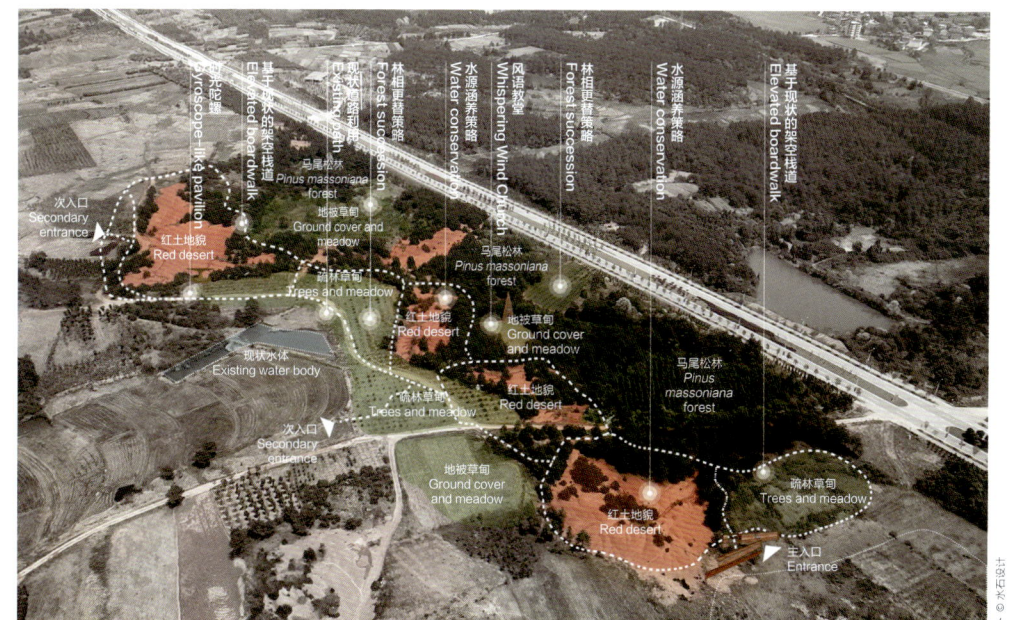

绿阔叶林群落乔木层的建群种是壳斗科、樟科和山茶科植物，下层为杜鹃花科、山茶科和冬青科植物[4]，因此设计团队也建议从这些科中选取适宜植物进行配植。

此外，在现有场地地势和坡向现状下，雨季时的水文径流会冲刷红土，造成水土流失，因此水源涵养也是生态修复的重要部分。设计团队在径流冲沟中种植了喜湿的旱生植物，如芦苇（*Phragmites communis*）、千屈菜（*Lythrum salicaria*）、蒲苇（*Cortaderia selloana*）等，用以降低土壤粘度，提高土壤渗透性，截留径流并使其下渗，恢复植被并形成水源涵养区，从而减缓雨季径流对红土沟壑地表的直接冲刷，达到固结土壤、保持水土的目的[5]。同时在周边已被村民开垦的经济林和农田区域，重新种植乡土优势宿根类和观赏草类植物，如芒草（*Miscanthus sinensis*）、蒲苇等，以涵养水源，改良土质（图9）。

生态修复带来的生态及美学价值毋庸置疑，但由于自然的演化过程较为漫长，这些价值往往需要假以时日才能逐渐显现。对于一个即将投入使用的城市郊野公园而言，立竿见影的休闲游憩价值也不容忽视。因此，在生态基底修复后，迎来了下一个问题：人们要如何与场地互动？设计根据不同的场地条件和功能区位，给出了多元的答案。

3.2 加强参与：建立交通廊道体系

针对红土裸露面积较大的区域，设计团队在充分尊重现状地貌和植被的基础上，以最小介入方式引入了交通廊道体系，并明确了三条道路系统布置原则：一是避免穿过裸露的网纹红土区域；二是尽量避让现状大乔木点位；三是尽量利用场地西侧原有的土路基础，减少不必要的土方开挖。

团队在此原则基础上进行了多次实地踏勘，利用GPS定位工具和CAD平面定位反复核验，确认廊道的最终走向，并用彩色旗帜在场地中进行定位放线标注，指导最终的施工（图10）。为了减少对现状地貌和植被的破坏，同时避免阻隔场地内的雨水径流，设计最终采用了浅基础形式的架空栈道（图11）。由于场地条件复杂、空间狭小，为了避免施工过程中对场地的破坏，施工期间基础开挖和材料运送均依靠人力而非机械设备完成，最大程度地保护了场地原貌（图12~14）。

在交通廊道系统内部，设计团队还选取了空间相对开阔和视野较好的位置，设置不同朝向和尺度的观景平台——或可观赏壮阔的红土地貌，或可远眺梅岭山峦。基于场地踏勘时寻得的一处最佳视野，设计团队建造了名为"时光陀螺"的观景亭（图15、16）。当人们身处其中，望向眼前壮阔的红土景观，感受沉静的周边环境，会觉得时光仿佛静止了一般（图17）。

3.3 丰富体验：创造多样活动空间

在场地外围和已经形成了茂密草甸的区域，设计则希望引入多样化的活动空间，加强使用者与场地的互动——既包括身体层面对场地的使用，也包括精神层面对场地的感知。空间节点的设计均充分借助客观的场地条件和主观的实地踏勘体验，希望将设计师们敏锐的观察

图例 Legend
1 公园入口 Entrance
2 松果草甸 Meadow
3 红色荒漠 Red desert
4 自然荒野 Natural area
5 赤脚乐园 Playground
6 风语教堂 Whispering Wind Church
7 迷雾森林 Fog Forest
8 植被复育 Forest restoration
9 时光陀螺 Gyroscope-like pavilion
10 呐喊峡谷 Shout Canyon
11 次级入口 Secondary entrance
12 松林栈道 Broadwalk

5. 这处占地16hm²的城市郊野公园集生态修复、自然体验和科普认知为一体。
5. This 16-hectare country park realizes a balance between ecological restoration, natural experience, and public education.

林相更替策略　Forest succession

3年　　　　　　　　1~2层群落（引入先锋树种）
3 years　　　　　　One to two layers (pioneer species introduced)

10年　　　　　　　2~3层群落（常绿针叶阔叶混交林）
10 years　　　　　Two to three layers (the evergreen coniferous and broad-leaved forest)

30年　　　　　　　4层群落（常绿阔叶林）
30 years　　　　　Four layers (the evergreen broad-leaved forest)

乔木层：马尾松、刺槐
草本层：芒萁、壳斗科、山茶科阴生幼树
Arbor layer: *Pinus massoniana*, *Robinia pseudoacacia*
Herb layer: *Dicranopteris dichotoma*, Fagaceae, Theaceae (shade sapling)

乔木层：壳斗科、樟科
亚乔木层：山茶科、木兰科
草本层：莎草科
Arbor layer: Fagaceae, Lauraceae
Sub-arbor layer: Theaceae, Magnoliaceae
Herb layer: Cyperaceae

乔木层：壳斗科、樟科
亚乔木层：山茶科、木兰科、冬青科
地被层：杜鹃花科
草本层：莎草科、禾本科
Arbor layer: Fagaceae, Lauraceae
Sub-arbor layer: Theaceae, Magnoliaceae, Aquifoliaceae
Ground cover layer: Ericaceae
Herb layer: Cyperaceae, Gramineae

水源涵养策略　Water conservation

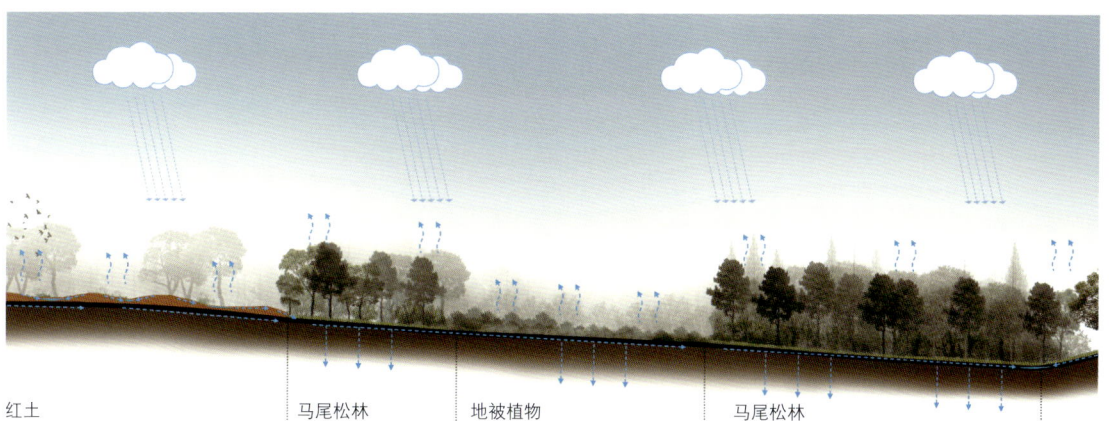 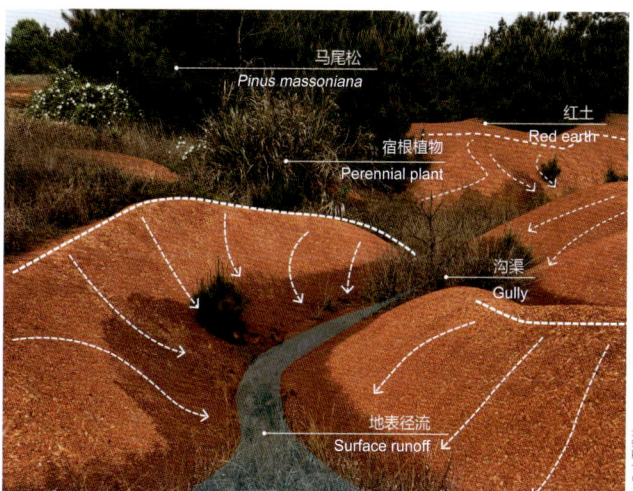

红土　Red earth
低洼冲沟处选择喜湿的旱生植物，用以固结土壤、涵养水源，降低水土冲刷影响。
Hygrophilous xerophilous plants were chosen to plant in the low-lying gullies to consolidate soils, conserve water, and reduce soil erosion.

马尾松林　*Pinus massoniana* forest
通过植物呼吸作用将有机物氧化成水和 CO_2，植物根系可蓄水固土、改善土壤持水能力。
The plants' respiration could oxidize organic matters into water and carbon dioxide, while the roots can retain water and consolidate soils.

地被植物　Ground cover
选用依靠自然降水就能生长的籽播宿根类植物，可降低土壤粘度、提高土壤渗透性。
Seed-sowed perennial plants that could grow with rainfall were used to reduce soil viscosity and improve soil permeability.

马尾松林　*Pinus massoniana* forest
保留原有植被，引入先锋类物种进行演替，逐步改良红土的营养与酸碱度，使群落结构逐步更替至稳定状态。
After introducing pioneer species into the preserved forest, a stable community will be realized by forest succession when the nutrition and pH of the red earth reach a more favorable condition.

结果呈现给公园使用者，带领他们观察和感受场地，创造一种与场地的连接。

例如，在公园入口处，场地内外有4m的高差，这一高差断崖恰好将网纹红土不同年代的断面层次呈现了出来（图18）。受到这一地质断面的启发，设计确定了直接在现场取土筛土再逐层夯实的方法塑造入口处的夯土景墙，以回归传统、回归匠作的方式，传递出一种拙朴之美。人们一到入口处，即可感受到红土遗址公园的主题和气质，通过这一前奏融入场地的氛围之中（图19~21）。

此外，除视觉外其他感官的调动也非常重要。在现场踏勘时，当设计团队到达一处被大片高大的马尾松林包围的呈矩形的天然草甸时，耳畔响起了风吹过松林的沙沙声，一种强烈的仪式感油然而生。在这一场所中，耳畔的声响（听觉）、风拂过皮肤的凉爽之感（触觉），超越了场地大部分区域因红土热烈的颜色而占主导的视觉感知。面对这一偶得的人与自然对话的机会，设计把这种感受放大，结合乡土芒草在场地中设置了一处"风语教堂"——在高处悬挂定制风铃的三角构筑，最终形成了一处独特的与自然之声对话的空间（图22）。

6. 林相更替策略：常绿针叶林－常绿针叶阔叶混交林－常绿阔叶林群落更替过渡
7. 水源涵养策略：在径流的冲沟中种植喜湿的旱生植物，降低土壤粘度，提高土壤渗透性，对径流进行截留和下渗，缓冲雨季径流冲刷。
8. 公园局部鸟瞰图。近观红土大地，远望梅岭山峦。
9. 乡土的野草荒原

6. The forest succession strategy: From the evergreen coniferous forest to the evergreen coniferous and broad-leaved forest, and finally to the evergreen broad-leaved forest.
7. The water conservation strategy: Hygrophilous plants planted in the gullies could help reduce soil viscosity, improve soil permeability, intercept surface runoff, and facilitate runoff infiltration, to reduce runoff erosion in rainy seasons.
8. A bird's view of the park. Visitors can look close at the red earth and overlook the Meiling Mountain.
9. Rural wild meadow

4 讨论与评述

景观是一门关于大地的学科，不管是何种类型的设计项目，都应从场地入手，从观察切入。但"看见"不等于"看到"，能否"看到"场地的核心和特质取决于观察的角度，这其中的差别是微妙的。观察可以是多维度的，既包括从宏观层面跨越时间与认识视角的限制（例如借助历史/现状卫星图和GIS数据），也包括从微观层面调动感官进行细致的感受。观察、思考、策略、表达、建造是一个环环相扣的过程。在这一过程中，观察与思考通常是呈正比的——观察角度的多元决定了思考层面的多维。但表达和建造却并不一定与前二者成正比。最终的表达和建造方法可能是简单的，这是因为在多维的观察和思考后，发现适度的介入才是最合适的。作为中间环节的"策略"则扮演着媒介和纽带的角色。红土遗址公园看似"少"的设计，却也包含着"多"的思考，并尽可能地营造出了"多"的体验。既尊重了场地本身的特质，同时又拓展了场地的意义。

设计的结束绝不是观察与思考的终点，跨越时间维度的观察不仅要回顾历史，同样也要追踪未来。项目建成后的不断观察、跟踪和记录，也能为初始的设计和思考提供验证，检验场地是否真正按照设想的轨迹演替发展，为下一次的实践提供数据和佐证。因此从这一角度上讲，设计还远远没有完成。

设计团队希望从多维观察与思考入手，最终回归情感与自然。用一种对自然的敬畏之心，回应大地的雕刻时光。**LAF**

项目信息

项目地址： 中国江西省南昌市安义县
项目面积： 16hm²
项目委托： 绿地集团江西事业部
景观设计： 水石设计
首席设计师： 孙轶
设计团队： 水石设计景观事业二部；祁锋、赵晓东阳、陈佳毅、龙勇、陈宇奇、王文珍
设计时间： 2018年5~7月
施工时间： 2018年8月~2019年5月
所获奖项： 2019 IFLA亚太地区景观设计专业奖公园与开放空间类杰出奖

致谢

在本文撰写过程中，得到了赵谷风博士的悉心建议，在此表示感谢。

1 Background

Urban dwellers are eager to get closer with nature as they are pressed by faster pace of life and growing stress at work under rapid urbanization. Country parks, providing an entertaining option for citizens, could also function to protect the natural resources and ecological environment in rural areas while educating the public[1].

The site of this design is located in Anyi County, a suburb country of Nanchang in Jiangxi Province which is 36 kilometers away from the downtown (Fig. 1). Neighboring the Meiling Mountain National Forest Park to its east, the 16 km² site is also surrounded by tourist attractions such as ancient villages. Taking full advantage of the rejuvenation of rural areas and the development of local cultural and tourist resources, this site covered by rare vermicular red earth was found and expected to be built into a country park.

Unique to the middle-lower reaches of the Yangtze River in China, the vermicular red earth was made from the moraine of the Glacial Epoch in the Quaternary Period after a long-term leaching and weathering under a humid climate. Layers of red earth formed in different periods and myrmekitic white spots can be found in its section. The thick and hardened soil prevents the surface runoff from infiltration, resulting in soil erosion. After years of water erosion, the landscape of "red desert" that features scarce plants and interlaced ravines comes into being (Fig. 2). Subject to the long-term leaching effect, the vermicular red earth almost loses all the nutrition, retaining only 0.2% of organic matter, 0.007% of N, and 30 ppm of K. Worse, few plants could grow here for its being acid.[2]

2 Off-Site Review and On-Site Exploration

There were both extensive red desert and patches of *Pinus massoniana* in the site. To study the history of the site, the team reviewed satellite maps over past few years (Fig. 3) and discovered that the bare red earth within the site was diminishing from 2013 to 2018, which were attributed to the gradually increasing vegetation coverage (mainly by short shrubs) and the encroachment on the outside red earth resulted from extreme weather events, farmland reclamation, and road construction.

The following systematical analyses of the site's elevation, gradient, and runoff based on GIS data suggested that it was about 15 meters higher in the west than the east. The rainfall aggravated soil erosion in the west and ran to the east, where the *Pinus massoniana* forest and the meadow grew thanks to the favorable natural conditions.

On finishing the off-site review, the design team visited the site and examined it from the perspective of ordinary visitors to collect subjective senses. Shocked by the grandeur of the red earth upon arrival, the team decided to conserve the red earth

10. Nodes and viewing platforms with different views were arranged and connected by the pedestrian system in the park, avoiding existing vegetation and territory while making use of the original road foundation.
11. The elevated boardwalk with shallow foundation in construction.
12. The red earth and the boardwalk in the forest
13. Night scene of the boardwalk in the *Pinus massoniana* forest
14. The snow-covered boardwalk

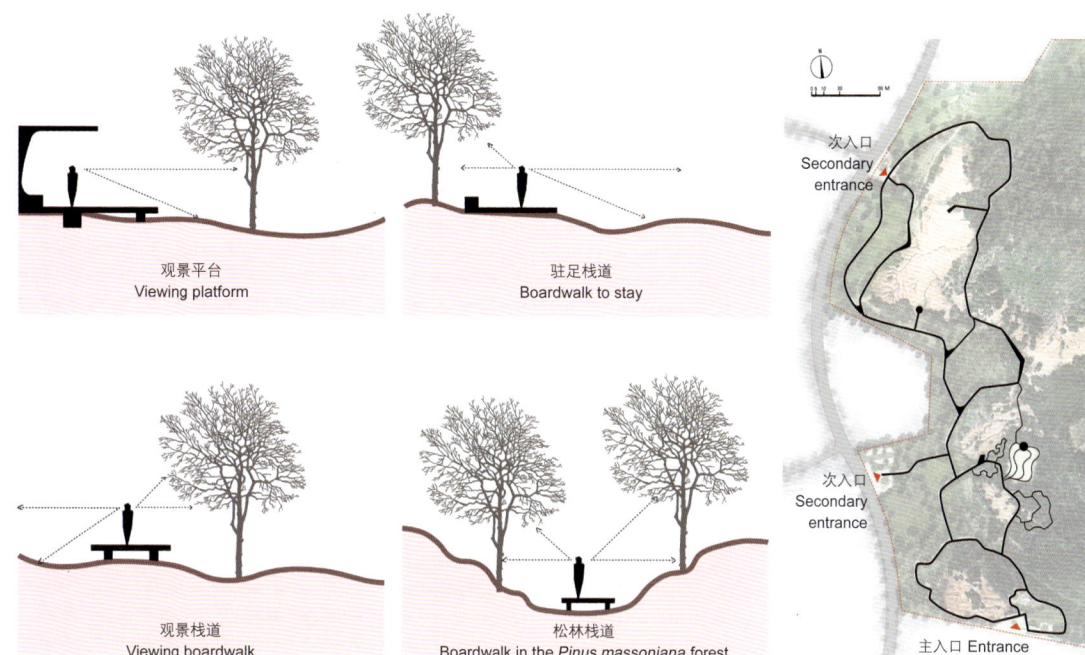

and avoid any aggressive change. The views varied from open to sheltered as the design team moved in the site, according to which different intervention strategies were proposed at different nodes, either to conserve, to intervene minimally, or to design appropriately.

Through careful off-site review across time and on-site exploration, the site was found to be suffering from severer soil erosion, biodiversity loss, and intensive human interventions. It was in urgent need to adopt proper strategies to protect and restore this unique area, while encouraging public engagement to make the site function as a country park.

3 Design Concepts and Strategies

Both to preserve the symbolic red earth in the site and to reduce cost due to limited budget, a country park requiring low intervention and maintenance was proposed. The park would also engage citizens with geological and scientific education programs and create diverse interactive experience basing on this peculiar natural landscape. The final proposal (Fig. 4, 5) was aimed first to restore ecosystems for biotic communities and enhance biodiversity; second to create low-intervened pedestrian paths to better engage the public while minimizing impacts on native flora and fauna and the runoff; and third, to create spaces serving diverse purposes, so as to realize a balance between ecological restoration, public education, natural experience, and cost efficiency.

3.1 Restoring the Ecosystem to Lay the Foundation

As one of the essential tasks, ecological restoration was given priority to lay the foundation of the park. To realize a naturally resilient ecosystem that could recover gradually with proper human intervention and function well in the future[1], the design team suggested a solution of forest succession (Fig. 6) combined with water conservation (Fig. 7).

The existing site was covered by evergreen coniferous forests — with *Pinus massoniana* as the dominant species, indicating a loss of plant diversity and discrepancy from the local stable plant community composed of evergreen broad-leaved species under the subtropical humid monsoon climate. Regarding this problem, the strategy of forest succession could help preserve existing plants while introducing more native trees in order to enrich the plant species. With a natural succession from the evergreen coniferous forest to the evergreen coniferous and broad-leaved mixed forest, a stable community of the evergreen broad-leaved forest would finally be realized.

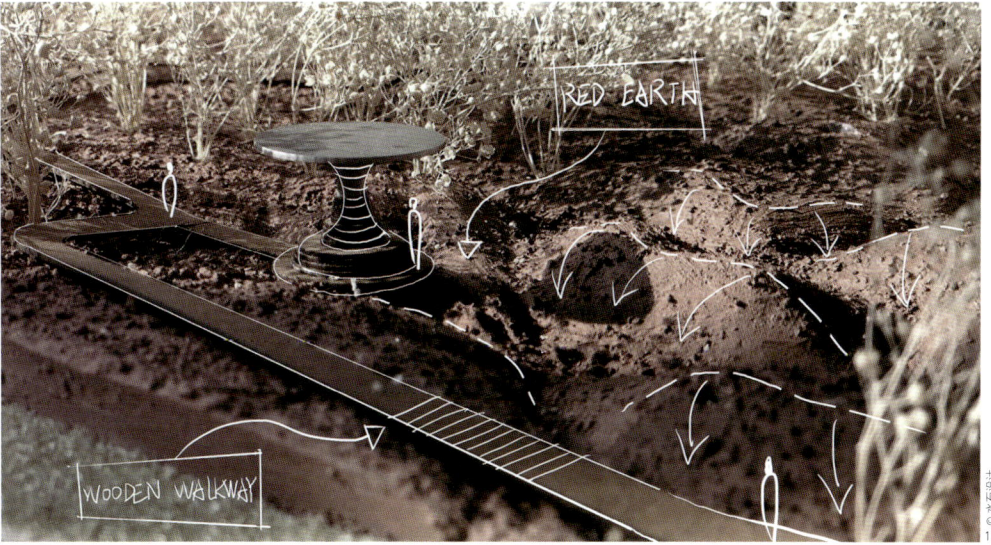

15. 用于研究节点与红土空间关系的工作模型
16. 红土大地与时光陀螺间的对话
17. 身处时光陀螺之中，时间仿佛静止一般。

15. The model to study the spatial relationship between different nodes and the red earth
16. The red earth and the gyroscope-like pavilion
17. The gyroscope-like pavilion makes visitors feel lost in the intertwining space and time.

Existing findings suggest that revegetation is core to restore the eroded red earth[3]. Thus, the design team employed pioneer species such as *Robinia pseudoacacia* and *Pinus massoniana* to mix them into patches and to improve soil conditions (Fig. 8). Vegetation can slowly recover the soil throughout the whole succession process[3], so that over a period both the tree roots and fallen leaves could nourish the red earth and balance its pH to reach a more favorable condition for most plants to grow. Soil conditions improved and some native broad-leaved trees introduced, the final community of evergreen broad-leaved forest would come into being after decades of succession. Plant arrangement of this community may also learn from findings that the constructive species of tree layer are from Fagaceae, Lauraceae, and Theaceae, while species from

Ericaceae, Theaceae, and Aquifoliaceae would be ideal choices for the lower layers[4].

Water conservation is also significant to ecological restoration. To slow down the runoff and address soil erosion of the site in rainy seasons, hygrophilous xerophytes, such as reeds (*Phragmites communis*), willow herbs (*Lythrum salicaria*), and pampas grass (*Cortaderia selloana*), which could help reduce soil viscosity, improve soil permeability, intercept surface runoff, facilitate runoff infiltration to protect vegetation and conserve water, were designed to plant in the gullies on the red earth[5]. Another strategy was to replant native dominant perennial and ornamental grasses, such as the *Miscanthus sinensis* and pampas grass, in existing economic forests and farmlands to conserve water and improve soil quality (Fig. 9).

Although the ecological and aesthetic values of ecological restoration are undeniable, they cannot be soon perceived as it is time-consuming for nature to evolve. However, for this country park about to put into use, another urgent problem is what should be done to encourage public engagement in realizing the park's significant recreational function, to which the design team responded with multiple choices considering varied site conditions and functional zonings.

3.2 Establishing Pedestrian System to Enhance Engagement

For areas with large exposed red earth, the design team introduced a pedestrian system by minimal intervention to fully preserve the existing topography and vegetation. The arrangement of this system should follow three principles of avoiding crossing the exposed red earth area, avoiding existing arbors, and making the most of existing unsurfaced roads in the west side to minimize earthwork.

Under these principles, the pedestrian system's final routes are determined based on on-site exploration and positioning schemes verified by GPS and CAD. To better guide the construction, colored flags were used as location markers (Fig. 10). Finally, an elevated boardwalk with shallow foundation was chosen as it could minimize impacts on the existing topography and vegetation and allow the runoff to flow through (Fig. 11). Instead of utilizing machinery, fundamental excavation and material transportation were conducted manually to protect the small-scale site with complicated conditions (Fig. 12 ~ 14).

Along the boardwalk, visitors could enjoy the grandeur of the red earth and overlook the Meiling Mountain through vantage points where viewing platforms in different directions and scales were set (Fig. 15, 16). In the node with a panoramic view, a gyroscope-like pavilion was designed for visitors to stay, feeling immersed in the red earth landscape and lost in the intertwining space and time (Fig. 17).

3.3 Creating Multi-Functional Spaces to Enrich Experience

In the periphery of the site and areas with dense meadow, multi-functional spaces were introduced for visitors to interact with the site both physically and mentally. The subjective on-site observation by designers integrated with the objective site condition supported the design of each node, aiming at representing the detailed findings of designers to visitors and creating a link between human and nature.

For instance, inspired by a 4-meter elevation difference at the park entrance, which exactly presented the multi-layered section of the red earth formed in different periods (Fig. 18), the design team raised an analogous landscape wall tamped layer by layer with earth excavated and sieved in the site to apply the traditional craftsmanship and to better bond with the nature. This plain but conspicuous entrance may immediately attract visitors to the park featured with red earth (Fig. 19 ~ 21).

Perceptions other than the visual one are also crucial to on-site exploration. For example, when arriving at a naturally formed rectangular meadow in the site, the design team was impressed by the rustle from the surrounding *Pinus massoniana* forest and captured the feelings about the grandeur of nature. Here, the auditory and tactile perception of breeze dominated the visual impact by the major red earth area. To represent this special way to dialogue with nature, the designers established a triangular architecture named "Whispering Wind Church" surrounded by *Miscanthus sinensis* with a customized wind chime hanging on the top (Fig. 22).

4 Discussion and Reflection

Landscape Architecture is the discipline on the earth, for which the observation of the site is principal to any project. However, the difference between "seeing" and "observing" should also be noticed, as the latter requires a deeper understanding of the site's core traits through certain perspectives. We may observe both with objective data from historical and existing satellite maps and GIS in a broader sense and individual subjective feeling through different senses by

18. 利用公园内外4m的高差，采用现场取土的夯土作为入口的挡墙，夯土的肌理呼应网纹红土的地质断面。
19. 研究入口竖向设计和比例关系的模型
20. 夯土墙与无障碍坡道
21. 公园入口建成效果

18. Making use of the 4-meter elevation difference at the park entrance, the retaining wall was tamped with earth excavated in the site, which exactly presented the multi-layered section of the red earth.
19. The model to support analyses on the vertical design and proportions between elements of the entrance
20. The rammed-earth landscape wall and the barrier-free ramp
21. The park entrance

22. In the Whispering Wind Church, visitors can dialogue with nature, feeling the rustle from the surrounding *Pinus massoniana* forest.

on-site exploration. Basing on the observation and reflection of the site, we could then come up with strategies to make them better represented and realized, during which process we may reflect more thoroughly if with diverse observing perspectives. However, the final construction might be simple as "less may be more." How to make the detailed observation and reflection into the optimum design proposal becomes the core. The Nanchang Red Earth Heritage Park is a good example of this idea — transforming "elaborate" ideas into "little" intervention to preserve the site while providing "abundant" spaces for experience. The proposal finally enhanced the value of the site with respect to its original conditions and features.

The observation and reflection of a site will never end even though the design proposal is finished. A post-occupancy investigation could also provide evidence for proposal verification to help optimize practices in the future. In this view, the design of a site will be ongoing.

Through a multi-dimensional observation and reflection, the design team hopes to celebrate nature with full respect, while responding to its voyage in time. **LAF**

PROJECT INFORMATION

LOCATION: Anyi County, Nanchang City, Jiangxi Province, China
AREA (SIZE): 16 hm^2
CLIENT: Greenland Group Jiangxi Division
LANDSCAPE ARCHITECTURE: SHUISHI
CHIEF DESIGNER: Sun Chong
PROJECT TEAM: Qi Feng, Zhao Xiaodongyang, Chen Jiayi, Long Yong, Chen Yuqi, Wang Wenzhen from Department II of Landscape, SHUISHI
DESIGN PERIOD: May ~ July, 2018
CONSTRUCTION PERIOD: August, 2018 ~ May, 2019
AWARD: Award of Excellence of Park and Open Space Category, IFLA Asia-Pac Landscape Architecture Awards

ACKNOWLEDGEMENT

The author sincerely acknowledges Dr. Zhao Gufeng for his important suggestions to this article.

REFERENCES

[1] Zhuang, W., & Duan, Y. (2019). Ecological Restoration and Reconstruction of Plant Diversity in Country Parks — A Case Study of Shanghai Binjiang Forest Park. Landscape Architecture, 26(1), 42-46. doi:10.14085/j.fjyl.2019.01.0042.05
[2] Zhu, J. (1988). Genesis and Research Significance of the Plinthitic Horizon. Geographical Research, 7(4), 42-46.
[3] Wang, X. (2004). Study on soil biological quality changes during secondary succession of vegetation on severely eroded red soil. The Tenth National Congress of Soil Science Society of China and Fifth Cross-Strait Soil and Fertilizer Academic Exchange Seminar Proceedings (Special Subject Soil Science about Agricultural and Environmental Health) (p. 2), Shenyang.
[4] Gao, Y., Yang, J., Wu, L., & Mo, Y. (2012). Application of Ecology Principle in the Plant Disposition. Heilongjiang Agricultural Science, (6), 90-92. doi:10.3969/j.issn.1002-2767.2012.06.032
[5] Zuo, C. (2007). Characteristics and Development Trend of the Soil Conservation Technology in the Red Soil Area. Subtropical Soil and Water Conservation, 19(1), 1-3, 6. doi:10.3969/j.issn.1002-2651.2007.01.001

探索与过程
作为调和过程的设计表达

专栏编辑

陆小璇

香港大学建筑学系园境建筑学部助理教授

我们很难为"景观"找到一个具体而包罗万象的定义。当代语境倾向于将景观视为基于感官感受或文化理解的认知对象。而无论是在物质还是文化层面，对于景观的认知都倚赖于某种调和过程，例如前者多借助图像或模型，后者则在意识层面借助某些信息分类或描述。长久以来，视觉表达一直是景观设计领域中的一种主要调和过程，而人们对环境认知的不断发展也同时激发出各种全新的表达方法，这些方法又反过来推动了景观干预策略的不断创新。

在很长一段时间内，平面图和鸟瞰图曾是景观设计传达的主要途径，这类将人为秩序强加于自然之上的视觉表达方式直到18世纪末才受到挑战。作为质疑这一表达惯例的先驱，尤维达尔·普莱斯爵士指出：无须人类干预，自然本身就能产生如画美景。而后，受这一变革性见解的启发，汉弗莱·赖普敦开创了众所周知的、用于对比改造前后景观的水平视角表现图，体现出自然过程与人为干预和谐共存的设计理念。直至今日，水平视角表现图仍是景观设计表达的重要途径之一。

20世纪亦不乏像普莱斯和赖普敦那样挑战传统的景观感知、表达和干预方式的变革者。地图叠加法（或"千层饼法"）是伊恩·麦克哈格所采用的核心方法，他倡导一种与自然和谐相处、以生态为导向的设计过程。阿德里安·高伊策和West 8城市规划与景观设计事务所应用的基本技术——拼贴法，颂扬了平凡之美并模糊了人的日常生活与自然神秘主义之间的界限。雷姆·库哈斯和大都会建筑事务所主要采用生成性图解来阐释、探索环境和吸引观察者，其中的植物元素和建筑元素都为空间机能而服务。这些多元的景观感知方式共同激发了景观设计领域关于历史、场所和生态的新语汇。

时至今日，数字技术的迅猛发展不仅改变了以观察、视觉表达、分析、转译和干预为主的传统设计过程，也促进了对环境状态、人类主观性和行动力，以及环境与人类因素之间复杂关系的批判性反思。本期的两个项目探讨了作为调和过程的设计表达如何将景观感知与景观干预联系起来，及其所带来的人类与环境之间的新的互动形式。

在《Íchni：欢乐建筑中的装置》一文中，来自伦敦大学学院巴特莱特建筑学院的王芷序分享了Íchni项目的关键构思和实施过程。Íchni作为一种"舞蹈装置"，旨在研究交互式物理–虚拟系统如何引发不可预测的复杂行为。装置由一系列简单的几何构架组成，表演者以拉、推、抓等多种方式参与其中。嵌入装置中的传感器记录了表演者的运动轨迹并将其存储为数据点，再将由这些数据点转换生成的可视化几何图像和粒子行为投射回物理环境之中，以进一步激发身体做出反应。这一系统实现了物理空间和数字空间之间的交互，是对诸多未能实现与使用者的互动，且难以给人带来愉悦或乐趣的传统景观空间的批判。

在《视域策划：朝鲜半岛金刚山风景区景观规划设计》一文中，香港大学建筑学系景观设计学硕士李玉寒讨论了将基于GIS的景观视域分析与朝鲜传统山水画共同运用在景观设计与表达中的尝试。该项目旨在提高从朝韩非军事区两侧眺望金刚山美景的视域范围。承载着丰富历史传奇、政治象征和自然美景的金刚山是该地区文化的标志。但自20世纪中叶以来，位于朝鲜境内的金刚山风景区便成为了游客难以抵达之地。李玉寒首先选定了分别位于朝鲜和韩国境内的16个制高点，建议通过对边境地区树木进行策略性移植或补植来改善从制高点观察到的视域，加强朝韩人民在边境区域的视线联系。与此同时，受朝鲜名画家谦斋郑敾（1676 - 1759）的启发，项目方案采用水平视角的表现图来呈现，一方面是为克服场地数据和现有视觉材料不足的问题，另一方面则期望人们对场地展开畅想，进而体验其所承载的文化和情感。

尽管这两个项目尺度相差巨大——前者为装置尺度，后者为国土尺度——却都意在发掘视觉表达的潜力。在这两个案例中，视觉表达不是用来传达静态的最终设计成果的工具，而是联系并调和景观感知和景观干预的关键过程，以及基于物质现实促生迭代设计的过程。在充分运用自动化和电子计算技术力量的同时，两个项目都将人的力量置入先进的技术系统中，或是回应人们对喜悦之感和身体感受的渴望，或是回应人们对乡愁、文化和身份特征的本真需求。

EXPERIMENTS & PROCESSES
REPRESENTATION AS A PROCESS OF MEDIATION

COLUMN HOST

LU Xiaoxuan
Assistant Professor of Landscape Architecture at the University of Hong Kong

The idea of *landscape* defies a specific and all-embracing definition. Contemporary discourses predominantly interpret it in cognitive terms, understood as perceived by our physical senses and in terms of cultural conventions. The communication of both kinds of understanding requires some process of mediation, either physically by means of an image or a model for example, or consciously by means of classification or description. Visual representation has long been landscape architecture's primary process of mediation within which ever-changing perceptions of the environment inspire new methods of representation. It in turn gives rise to innovative interventions on the physical landscape.

Up until the end of the 18th century, the use of plans and bird's-eye views to communicate how landscape design imposed its artificial order on nature was questioned by Sir Uvedale Price who argued that nature could well provide its own picturesque beauty without human meddling or interference. This revolutionary insight inspired Humphry Repton's celebrated eye-level "before and after" illustrations depicting an ideal harmony between natural and human elements and processes, which remains a primary means of landscape design representation to this day.

The 20th century was not without its own revolutionary redefinitions of the conventions that determine how we perceive, represent, and impose design interventions on the landscape. The map-overlay method was a key technique proposed by Ian McHarg who advocated an ecologically orientated design process in harmony with nature. Collage is a technique fundamental to the work of Adriaan Geuze and West 8 Urban Design & Landscape Architecture celebrating the beauty of the ordinary and blurring the boundary between the mundane and the mysticism of nature. Rem Koolhaas and OMA's generative diagrams, in which both vegetative and architectural elements are in the service of programs, explain, explore, and seduce the observer. Collectively, these ways of perceiving landscape stimulate new vocabularies of history, place, and ecology within landscape architecture.

More recently, the mushrooming of advances in digital technology not only is transforming the traditional design process of observation, visual representation, analysis, interpretation, and intervention, but necessitates much more sophisticated critical reflection on the state of the environment, human subjectivity and enterprise, and the inextricable entanglement of all these factors. Two projects in this issue explore the role of landscape representation as a mediation process linking perception and intervention thereby enabling new types of interaction between humanity and environment.

In Íchni: Devices for a Joyful Architecture, Isabella Ong from The Bartlett School of Architecture, University College London, shares the key ideas and processes behind the development of Íchni, "choreographic devices" that explore how complex, unpredictable movements can emerge in a playable physical-virtual system. Íchni consists of a collection of simple geometrical sculptures, where performers engage in various ways, pulling, pushing, and grabbing. Sensors embedded within the sculptures record participants' movements and capture them as data points. These are translated into geometrical visualizations and particle movements which are projected back into the environment that in turn stimulate the body to respond. The system enables interaction between physical and digital, and is a critique if not a rebuke of many traditional landscape spaces that hardly ask the user anything and give little in the way of delight and joy.

In Curated Viewshed: Landscape Planning and Design of the Mount Kumgang International Tourist Zone on the Korean Peninsula, Li Yuhan, master of Landscape Architecture of Faculty of Architecture, the University of Hong Kong, explores the use of GIS-based viewshed analysis and traditional Korean landscape painting in a landscape planning project that aims to improve the visibility of scenic views of Mount Kumgang from both sides of the Demilitarized Zone. Mount Kumgang is an icon of cultural identity of this region replete with historical legend, political symbolism, and flush natural beauty. The Mount Kumgang International Tourist Zone has remained largely inaccessible to visitors in the middle of the 19 century. Li identifies 16 overlooking points located in DPRK and ROK, and proposes the establishment of carefully curated viewsheds by means of strategic removal and replanting of tree cover within the border region in order to establish visual connections between the two countries. Eye-level perspectives are inspired by Korean artist Jeong Seon (1676–1759) partly to overcome the problem of the deficiency of data and existing visual documentation and partly to enable people to image the site and experience the culture and emotion behind it at the same time.

Despite their wildly divergent sculptural and territorial scales, both projects explore the potential of visual representation beyond just the communication of a static final design outcome. In both cases, landscape representation serves as a mediation process that arbitrates between perception of and intervention on the landscape, and draws on a physical reality that nourishes an iterative design process. While relying largely on the power of automation and computation, both projects integrate human agency within advanced technical systems, one by appealing to our desire for joy and physicality, and one to our instincts for nostalgia, culture, and identity.

本文引用格式 / PLEASE CITE THIS ARTICLE AS

Ong, I. (2019). Íchni: Devices for a Joyful Architecture. Landscape Architecture Frontiers, 7(5), 148-155. https://doi.org/10.15302/J-LAF-1-050007

ÍCHNI：欢乐建筑中的装置
ÍCHNI: DEVICES FOR A JOYFUL ARCHITECTURE

https://doi.org/10.15302/J-LAF-1-050007　　收稿时间 RECEIVED DATE / 2019-09-10　　中图分类号 / J5, J59　　文献标识码 / B

王芷序
伦敦大学学院巴特莱特建筑学院建筑师、创意工艺师

Isabella Zhixu ONG*
Architect and Creative Technologist, The Bartlett School of Architecture, University College London

*Corresponding Author
Address: Here East, 8-9 East Bay Lane, Queen Elizabeth Olympic Park, London, E15 2GW, UK
Email: isabellaong@gmail.com

摘要

建筑是否能够激发身体产生更为复杂的行为？活跃的身体往往处于愉悦状态，久坐会大幅减少我们与美好空间邂逅的机会。故而建筑应当激发人们积极参与其中的意识。

íchni是一项有趣的探索，旨在研究空间装置如何通过互动技术激发身体的行动意愿，以及如何通过物理-数字系统促使身体与周边物体形成情感反馈回路。项目设计了一个嵌入了物理传感器的互动"舞蹈装置"，通过投射在幕布上的虚拟影像来追踪舞蹈动作的物理作用力，并将捕获的数据信息进行转译，再投射至原有环境中，以此来提高人们的行为意识，影响人们在这一生成的环境中的行为方式。

关键词

空间；运动；情感反馈；物理传感器；虚拟投影；互动；技术

ABSTRACT

Can architecture prompt the body into more complex actions? An active body is a joyful body, and our sedentary behaviors are inhibiting the delightful encounters of spaces. Architecture should, in fact, inspire active and engaging experiences.

Íchni is a playful exploration into how spatial devices can increase the body's potential to act through the use of interactive technology; an investigation in generating affective feedback loops between surrounding objects and the body through a physical-digital system. Through developing "choreographic devices" — playable structures embedded with physical sensors — and a virtual projection overlay, the physical forces of movements are captured as data points, then translated and projected back into the environment, heightening the awareness of our actions to affect the manner in which we move through a generative environment.

KEYWORDS

Space; Movement; Affective Feedback; Physical Sensors; Virtual Projection; Interaction; Technology

翻译　肖杰　王颖
TRANSLATED BY　XIAO Jie　WANG Ying

1 引言

活跃的身体往往处于愉悦状态，因此令人愉悦的建筑也必定能够激发更多的肢体动作。游乐场便是此类建筑的有力证明——在这里，孩子们释放天性，尽情攀爬奔跑，欢声笑语不断。即使偶有小摩擦，所有挥洒汗水的瞬间也都是幸福的。

斯宾诺莎式哲学思想认为愉悦之感源自人的主动（或本能）探索，基于这一思想，"欢乐建筑"主张通过空间邂逅来激发身体的行动意愿[1]。例如，在荒川修作与马德琳·金斯的建筑作品及威廉·福赛斯的装置作品（图1）中，空间均能够让身体保持活跃的张力。古罗马建筑师马库斯·维特鲁威·波利奥认为，好的建筑应该具备稳定性、实用性和趣味性三大特征[2]。如果说愉悦感与趣味性是建筑的核心，而行动又是快乐的源泉，那么于建筑而言，激发行动的能力至关重要。

2 建筑的动词属性

"我身边的物体映现了我的身体对其的反作用。"

——亨利·柏格森[3]

我们早已习惯通过常规方式来欣赏建筑，与建筑相关的论述也多局限于其静态实体、形状和线条等设计语言。除非是运用了拟人化的形态，否则人们往往不会将建筑与身体联系起来。因此，我们应该构思新的建筑语汇，关注建筑中的行为与互动，而非仅仅将欣赏停留在静态层面。正如芬兰建筑师尤哈尼·帕拉斯马所认为的，建筑意象的动词属性远比名词属性丰富[4]。例如，我们可以由一扇门联想到出入行为，而非只是一块带有把手的木板；由一把椅子联想到坐下这一隐含行为，而非只是由四条腿支撑的面板。由此，建筑所代表的就不仅是其物理属性，更是其喻义行为。而空间要素则应被解读为人类

生活的背景条件或促发因子，或者如帕拉斯马所说，是对行为的"允诺和邀请"[5]。

心理学家詹姆斯·J·吉布森指出，功能可供性是指由动物所在的环境赋予其的"行动的可能性"[6]。吉布森对物体的物理属性及其隐含行为——即其名词属性与动词属性——进行了辨析。例如，物体表面的隐含行为包括人类（或动物）"爬上、跌落、进入或撞到（它）的可能"[6]。基于建筑的功能可供性定义，我们不再只通过其表面的物理轮廓来感知空间元素，而是将其理解为种种实现身体、行为与环境之间连接的暗示与诱因。

3 íchni装置

Íchni一词在希腊语中意为"痕迹"，涵盖了瞬间动作和符号标记双重含义。通过追踪转瞬即逝的物理运动，将捕获的数据信息进行转译与可视化处理，构建身体、装置和环境之间的情感反馈回路，以此改变人们的行为模式，激发非常规行为（隐含行为）。

Íchni装置旨在研究交互式物理-虚拟系统如何触发不可预测的复杂行为，重点关注人们的动作意识对自身行为及与物质环境互动方式的不同影响。研究中所采用的混合现实"舞蹈装置"由可用于舞蹈表演的金属装置和虚拟投影设备组成。从某种意义上说，这些能够激发使用者行为、鼓励使用者对其施加影响的装置其实就是舞台。每个装置中都嵌有物理传感器，用于捕捉使用者的物理运动，进而将其转译为可视化数据信息，再重新投射至原有环境中。这一过程使得运动效果与行动传播过程变得可见，也强化了使用者对于动觉的感知。

帕拉斯马指出，对建筑意象的传达不应仅停留在其名词属性上，而应更多地关注其动词属性[4]。但这种观点仍旧因语言表达的局限而限制了行为的广度。然而，在转译并可视化捕捉到的物理运动后，物体的动态行为便超出了语言表达的范畴，物质环境中承载的行为也更加丰富。由此，对物体的阐述由规定性定义转变为了描述性定义，透过虚拟投影这一视角，使用者可感知到帕拉斯马名-动词二元论之外的物理属性。

装置的设计保留了材料的原始性能，并依据其功能可供性来建造，旨在激发使用者产生开放而有趣的解读。例如，数条横向的金属棒连接起了两根平行的弧形金属条，构成了形似跷跷板的装置，能够让人联想到类似于摇摆的动作（图2）。可以发现，人们对于与装置积极互动有着特有的直觉倾向。1971年，罗伯特·莫里斯在伦敦泰特现代美术馆举办的展览（该展览于2009年再次举办），通过设计一系列"行为装置"，有意吸引参观者与装置互动，从而挑战并扩展了"装置"原本的概念。展览取得了惊人的成功：参观者与装置亲密接触的热情一路高涨，很多人甚至在互动过程中受伤。

尽管Íchni装置是作为一项调查研究提出的，团队将其作为布景工具进行了测试，邀请具备一定动作掌控力的舞蹈演员在舞台布景中表演。舞蹈演员在装置内部舞动身体，仿佛在"演奏"一项乐器，同时控制着数字投影的效果（图3、4）。在这一过程中，Íchni装置成为了表演的一部分。并且，除专业舞蹈演员外，业余舞蹈爱好者以及动作略显笨拙的老年人和儿童的参与，还将为进一步探究装置中的行为增添不少趣味。此时的Íchni既是交互式游乐场，又是戏剧表演道具，还是沉浸式艺术装置。

1. 威廉·福赛斯的编舞作品《无处又遍处》（2013）
1. *Nowhere and Everywhere* by William Forsythe (2013)

4 技术是答案……

舞台装置中嵌入的传感器包括开源电子原型平台Arduino和各类经济型传感器——如压电式传感器及由加速度计和陀螺仪构成的惯性测量单元（IMU），它们可通过一系列数值读取基于使用者行为的模拟输入信号（图5~7）。以安装于"跷跷板"上的六轴IMU传感器为例，其可测量摆动的加速度、方向和角度（图8，9），再通过Wi-Fi将这些数据传输到计算机中Processing语言的sketch操作界面中，以传感器读数为数据点，由程序生成几何可视化图像和粒子行为，并投射至屏幕上（图10~12）。

在过去数十年中，许多艺术家和设计师已经开始将创意计算应用到设计实践中。尽管直至当前，鉴于复杂性与计算能力的限制，软件和硬件编码始终只能依靠科学家和工程师在实验室中的超级计算机上完成，但更为先进的个人计算机和日渐发展的编程语法推动了新技术的普及，也降低了非专业人士掌握技术的门槛。

当前已有艺术家专门针对视觉艺术开发了类似Processing语言的编程集成开发环境，用以服务更多的艺术家。艺术与技术的交融也催生了多种多样的全新艺术形式，如互动装置、数字艺术、程序或衍生艺术、互联网艺术、虚拟现实、增强现实、参与式艺术等。由Arduino等公司生产的即插即用微控制器也使得不具备电子学或编程背景的人员能够轻松理解物理计算。与此同时，交互设计也开始摆脱屏幕，渗透到日常的空间实体中，继而走进建筑领域。

5 ……那么问题是什么？

1966年，英国建筑师塞德里克·普莱斯曾发出诘问："如果技术是答案，那么需要用技术解决的问题是什么？"[7]随着技术门槛的降低，人们往往过度强调工具的作用，而忽略了问题本身。伊丽莎白·格罗斯曾写道：

"在某种意义上，技术虽然是由人开发、为人所用的，但也在改变着人类的行为：技术的价值不在于引发更好的行为，而在于带来更多的行为可能性。"[8]

当代空间常常不能满足身体的需求——既难以让身体与之互动，又无法让人产生愉悦之感。究其根源，在于行为的缺失。对于人机交互的参与天性激发了使用者在物质环境中积极参与的欲望，促进了身体和空间之间更为密切的互动。回顾基于Íchni装置的舞蹈表演，当表演者逐渐摸索到人体力学、装置与环境之间的关联后，这一物理—数字系统便促生了一段舞蹈设计。

回到最初有关表演与愉悦的问题上来，我们应该利用新技术来挑战对行走、就座、行动和移动等行为的固有认知，而对于技术的具体化呈现则应鼓励人们积极地与日常建筑碰撞出更多愉快的火花。这就是需要解决的那个问题。**LAF**

2. 鼓励人们进行行为交互的跷跷板、绳带和可移动金属框架等舞蹈装置及屏幕。
3. 舞者与布景结构的互动——通过动作的变换来控制数字投影。

2. Choreographic devices (seesaw, ropes, and movable frame) that invites playful actions, and the screen.
3. A performer "playing" the scenographic architecture by using their movements to manipulate the digital projections.

1 Introduction

An active body is a joyful one. Accordingly, a joyful architecture is one that encourages the body into more actions. One need not look far to find proof for this: the playground. The untamed scene of kids climbing and running about is often accompanied by the discordant din of their shouts and laughter. Amongst the sweat and despite the scraps, it is hard to find an unhappy child in a playground.

By adopting a Spinozist attitude which associates joy with active effort (or conatus), an Architecture of Joy describes spatial encounters that increase the body's potential to act[1]. The architecture of Shusaku Arakawa and Madeline Gins and William Forsythe's works (Fig. 1) are examples of such Spinozist architecture, with spaces that maintain the body in a state of active tension. Marcus Vitruvius Pollio declared that the three principles of good architecture are stability, utility, and delight[2]. If joy and delight are fundamental to architecture, and action is fundamental to joy, we can thus conclude that it is essential for architecture to facilitate actions.

2 Architecture's Verb Form

"The objects which surround my body reflect its possible action upon them."

— Henri Bergson[3]

We have grown accustomed to the formal appreciation of architecture. Architecture discourse is primarily confined to the language of static solids, shapes, and lines, often with no relation to the body other than its anthropomorphic fit. It is high time we conceive of an alternate architecture vocabulary that consists not of nominative terms that limit spatial appreciation to the formal; one in which action — and interaction — is the form. Juhani Pallasmaa observes that architectural images have less of a noun form than a verb form[4]. Rather than thinking of a door as a panel with a knob, we can think of it in its suggested act of entering and exiting; instead of thinking of a chair as a surface supported by four legs, we can think of it in its implicit action of sitting. Architecture then can be conceptualized in terms of its solicited actions instead of its physical attributes. Spatial elements thus function as a condition and facilitator for human life, or as Pallasmaa describes, "promises and invitations" for actions[5].

According to psychologist James J. Gibson, affordances define as the "action possibilities" offered to an animal by its

4. 舞者与Íchni装置进行互动
4. Dancers performing with Íchni

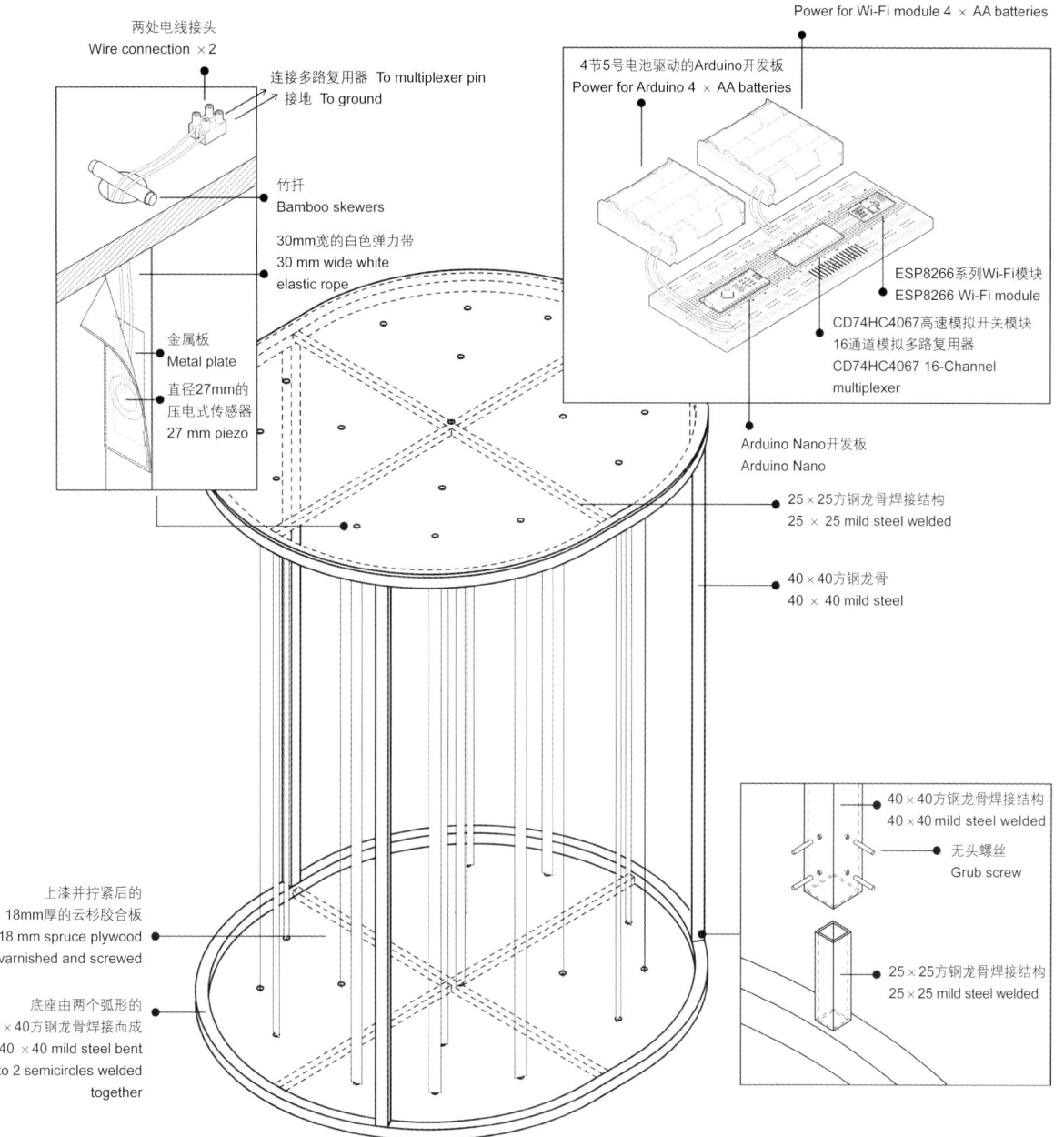

5. Technical and construction drawing of the rope set up
6. A device built using Arduino and an IMU to measure the oscillation of the seesaw.
7. A piezoelectric sensor is attached to each rope, detecting when it is activated.

environment[6]. He distinguishes between the physical properties of an object from its implicit actions — noun versus verb form. The suggested actions of material surfaces can be what we, the animal, perceive as "climb-on-able or fall-off-able or get-underneath-able or bump-into-able"[6]. By adopting an affordance-based definition of architecture, we perceive spatial elements not by the physical delineation of their surfaces but as cues and triggers, ensuring the non-disassociation between body, behavior, and environment.

3 Íchni

Íchni is the Greek word for "traces," and it encapsulates both the concepts of passing movements and notational markings. Physical movements, which are usually so fleeting, are captured into data points, translated and visualized to create an affective feedback loop between the body, devices, and the environment, altering the way we behave and cueing the body into unconventional movements.

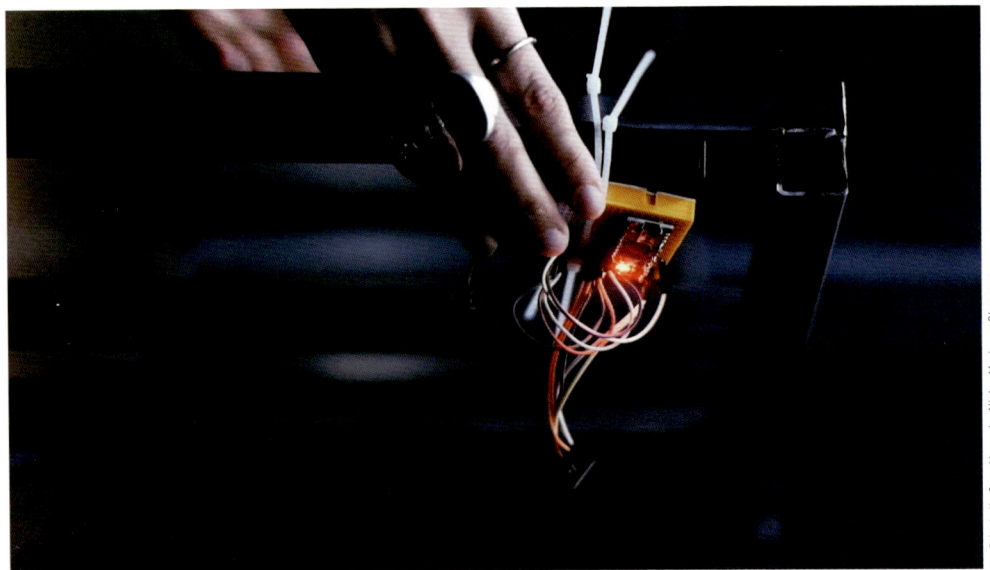

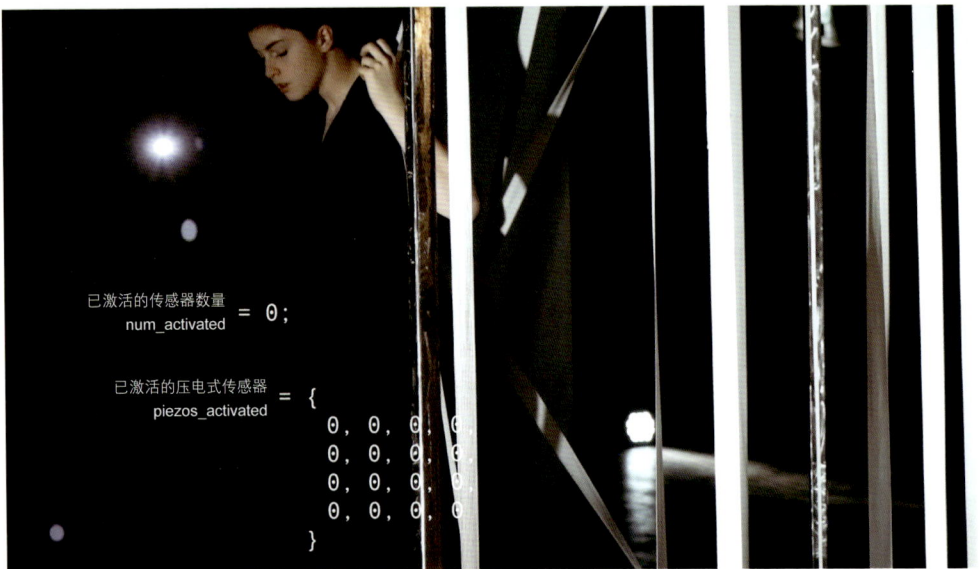

translated into digital visualizations that are then projected back into the environment. This makes visible the effects and propagations of the movements and amplifies users' kinesthetic awareness.

Pallasmaa proposed to communicate architectural images in their verb instead of their noun form[4]. This, however, still reduces the range of actions to the limits of language. By translating the captured physical forces into visualizations, it opens up the active form of the object beyond linguistic limits and accommodates the richness of movements afforded by the material environment. Objects then become descriptive rather than prescriptive, with the virtual projection operating as a viewing scope through which users can perceive the physical beyond Pallasmaa's noun-verb dichotomy.

The designs of the sculptures were kept rudimentary to evoke open, playful interpretations of their use and were constructed with their affordances as references. For example, two curved rods held parallel by horizontal bars hint at the actions of rocking, swaying, or oscillating, similar to that of a seesaw (Fig. 2). There is a particular intuitiveness for active participation in playing objects. In Robert Morris' 1971 exhibition (recreated three decades later in 2009) at the Tate Modern, he challenged and expanded the notion of what a sculpture is by designing a series of "action sculptures" to intentionally include visitors' participation in the works. This proved unexpectedly effective as visitors took the invitation to play a little too enthusiastically and went berserk, with many hurting themselves in the process.

Although developed as a research investigation, Íchni was tested as a scenographic tool where dancers — people exercising certain mastery over their movements — were invited to perform within the system. The architecture became an instrument that the performers could "play" by using their body movements to manipulate the digital projections (Fig. 3, 4). The research apparatus thus became part of the performance. It will be interesting to gather further insights by expanding the application of this installation to include a range of body types, from professional performers to the amateur, clumsy bodies, from older folks to young children. Íchni can take the form of an interactive playground, a theater prop, or an immersive art installation.

4 Technology Is the Answer...

The embedded sensors of the choreographic devices were built using Arduino and various inexpensive sensors such as piezoelectric sensors and IMUs (an accelerometer and gyrometer combined), which read the analogue inputs of users' movements

Íchni investigates how complex, unpredictable movements can emerge from an interactive physical-virtual system, with an emphasis on how conscious awareness of our movements affects our actions and causes us to negotiate with the material environment differently. The research took the form of a mixed-reality play installation, composed of playable, metal sculptures — "choreographic devices" — and virtual projections. These sculptures are choreographic in the sense that they invite actions from the users and elicit forces to be acted upon them. Each of these devices is embedded with physical sensors that measure and capture the physical movements, which are procedurally

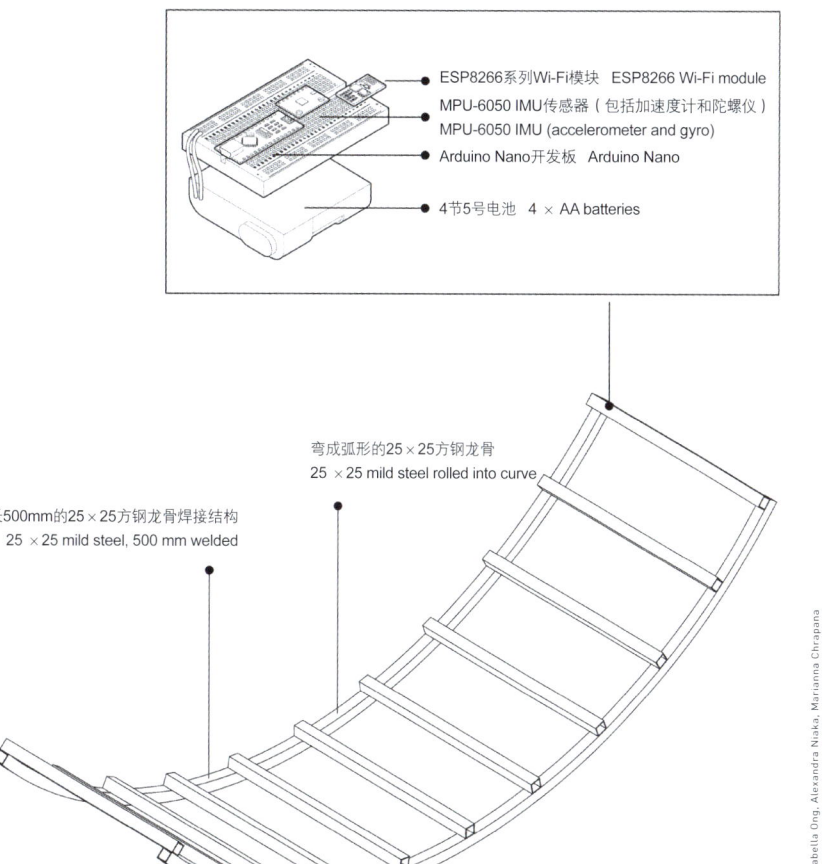

8. 跷跷板的技术图和施工图
9. 传感器感知到跷跷板角度的变化。

8. Technical and construction drawing of the seesaw
9. The sensor reading of angle change of the seesaw.

through a range of values (Fig. 5 ~ 7). In the example of the seesaw, a 6-axis IMU sensor was attached to measure the acceleration, direction, and angle of the oscillation (Fig. 8, 9). These values are transmitted via Wi-Fi to a Processing sketch on a computer, which uses the readings as data points to procedurally generate geometrical visualizations and particle behaviors that are projected on a screen (Fig. 10 ~ 12).

In the last few decades, many artists and designers have started to incorporate creative computing as part of their design praxis. Hitherto software and hardware coding have always been confined in the labs of scientists and engineers with their supercomputers due to the complexity and computational power required. But personal computers becoming more powerful and programming syntaxes less esoteric engender the democratization of new technologies, lowering the barrier of entry for non-experts to adopt them.

Programming IDEs (Integrated Development Environments) like Processing are created by artists, for artists, and are specifically produced within the context of visual arts. The intersections between art and technology have spawned a diverse range of art categories: interactive installations, digital art, procedural / generative art, Internet art, virtual and augmented realities, participatory art, etc. Physical computing is also rendered more accessible for people with no background in Electronics or programming with companies like Arduino making plug-and-play microcontrollers. As such, interaction design starts to break out of the screen and seep into the hardware of our everyday spaces, into the domain of architecture.

5 ... But What Was the Question?

In 1966, Cedric Price posed the rhetorical question, "technology is the answer, but what was the question?"[7] With technology becoming more accessible, there is the temptation of overemphasizing the tool while ignoring the problem. Elizabeth Grosz writes,

"Although technology is in a sense made by us and for our purposes, it also performs a transformation on us: it increasingly facilitates not so much better action but wider possibilities of acting, more action."[8]

Contemporary spaces often fall short in serving the body: they require little from the body and do not aspire towards delight and joy. Underlying all, these is the absence of action. The participatory nature of human-computer interaction, when embedded into our material environment, presents the opportunity to demand a greater involvement of the users,

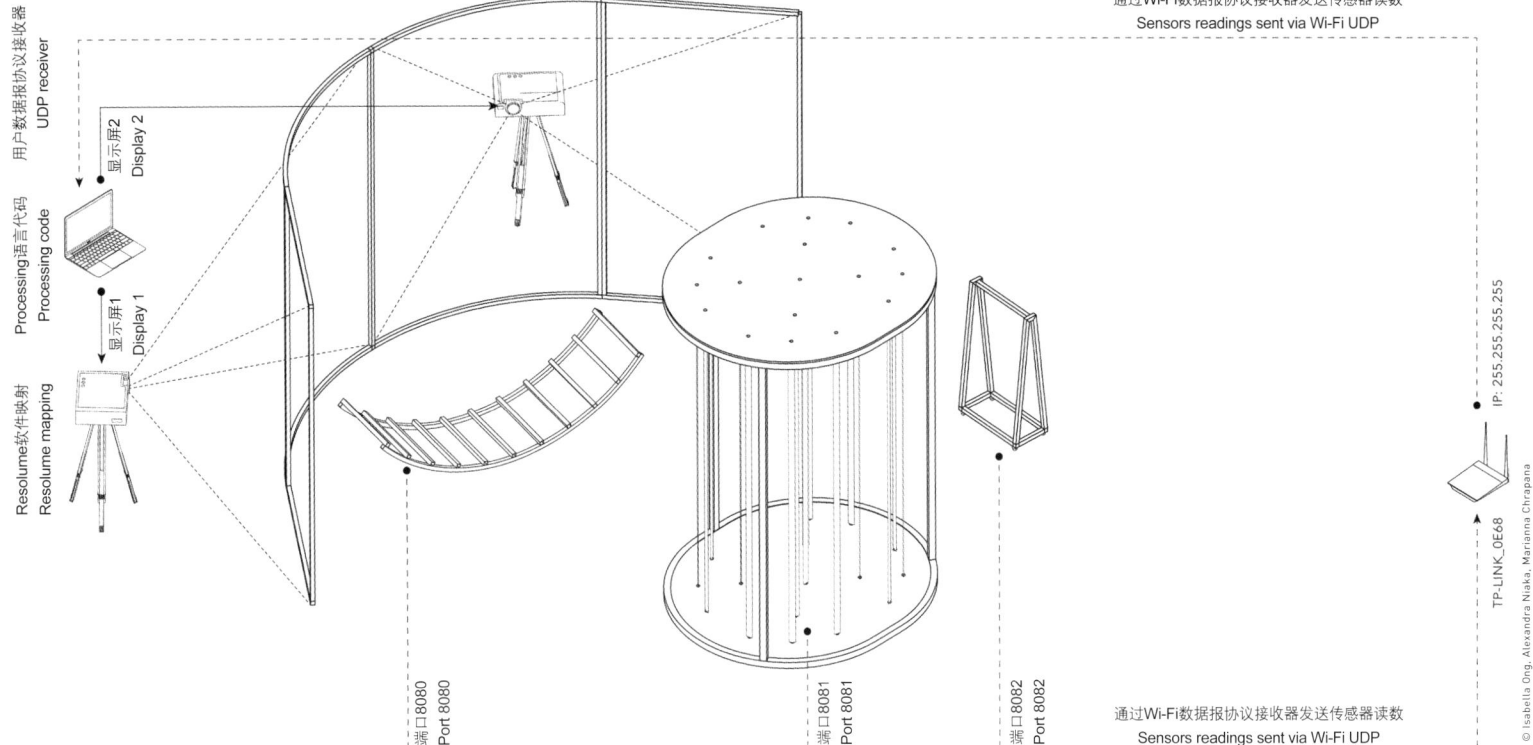

10. 在将影像投影至弧形屏幕之前,通过Wi-Fi由Arduino开发板向Processing语言的sketch操作界面中传输模拟数据。
11. 通过利用Processing语言的编程集成开发环境将动作的模拟信号转化为程序化的视觉影像。
12. 将运动行为映射为可视几何元素的初步研究。

10. Analogue inputs are sent via Wi-Fi from the Arduinos to the Processing sketch, before being projected on the curved screen.
11. Procedural visuals are generated from the analogue signals of the movements, using the Processing IDE.
12. Initial studies on the behavioral mapping of the movement to the geometrical visual elements.

facilitating a more intimate interplay between body and space. During the dance performances of Íchni, a generative choreography emerged from the physical-digital system as the performers progressively find complicities between the mechanics of their own bodies, the sculptural devices, and the environment.

Going back to fundamentals, such as play and joy, we should utilize new technology to challenge the basics: how we walk, sit, act, and move. Our embodiment of technology should inspire active and delightful encounters in our everyday architecture. The question is simply that. **LAF**

REFERENCES

[1] Lambert, L. (2013). The Funambulist Pamphlets 1: Spinoza. New York: Punctum Books.
[2] Vitruvius. (1960). Vitruvius: Ten Books on Architecture (M. H. Morgan, Trans.). Mineola: Dover Publications.
[3] Bergson, H. (1990). Matter and Memory (N. M. Paul & W. S. Palmer, Trans.) (p. 21). New York: Zone Books.
[4] Pallasmaa, J. (2005). The Eyes of the Skin: Architecture and the Senses. West Sussex: Wiley Academy.
[5] Pallasmaa, J. (2011). The Embodied Image: Imagination and Imagery in Architecture (p. 123). Chichester: John Wiley and Sons.
[6] Gibson, J. J. (1979). The Ecological Approach to Visual Perception. Boston: Houghton Mifflin.
[7] Price, C. (1966). Technology is the answer — But what was the question?. Retrieved from https://monoskop.org/images/archive/0/09/20181205204255%21Price_Cedric_Technology_Is_the_Answer_but_What_Was_the_Question.pdf
[8] Grosz, E. (2001). Architecture from the Outside: Essays on Virtual and Real Space (p. 177). Cambridge: MIT Press.

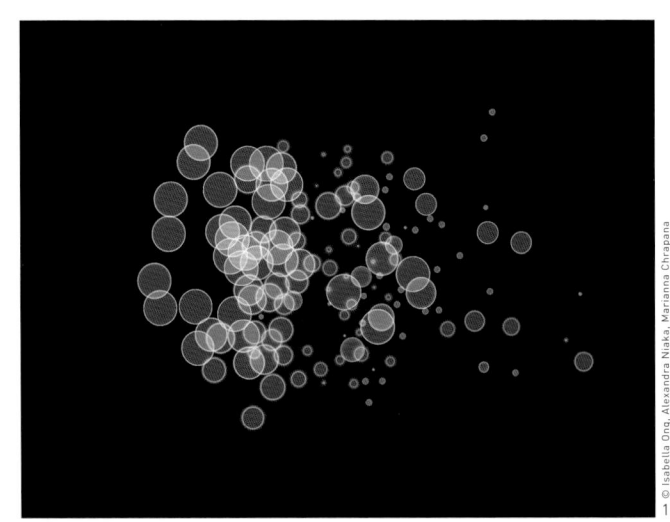

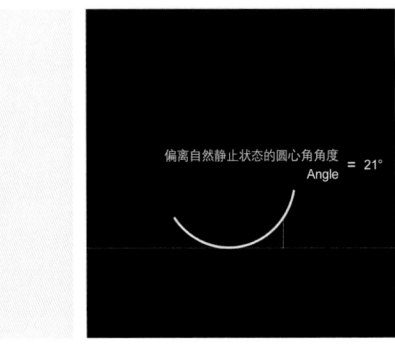

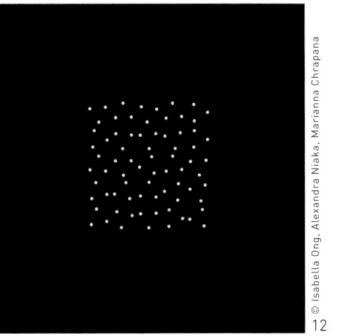

本文引用格式 / PLEASE CITE THIS ARTICLE AS

Li, Y. (2019). Curated Viewsheds — Landscape Planning and Design of the Mount Kumgang International Tourist Zone on the Korean Peninsula. Landscape Architecture Frontiers, 7(5), 156-165. https://doi.org/10.15302/J-LAF-1-050008

视域策划
——朝鲜半岛金刚山风景区景观规划设计

CURATED VIEWSHEDS — LANDSCAPE PLANNING AND DESIGN OF THE MOUNT KUMGANG INTERNATIONAL TOURIST ZONE ON THE KOREAN PENINSULA

https://doi.org/10.15302/J-LAF-1-050008　收稿时间 RECEIVED DATE / 2019-07-02　中图分类号 / TU982, K312　文献标识码 / B

李玉寒*

土人设计景观设计师，香港大学建筑学系景观设计学硕士

*通讯作者
通讯地址：北京市海淀区中关村北大街127-1号
邮　编：100080
邮　箱：betty_li091@foxmail.com

LI Yuhan

Landscape Architect of Turenscape; Master of Landscape Architecture of Faculty of Architecture, the University of Hong Kong

摘要

金刚山位于朝鲜半岛中东部临海区域，横跨朝韩边境，从古朝鲜时期起就是该地区的文化象征。由于朝鲜坐拥金刚山总面积的三分之二以及大部分自然风光和文化遗迹，因此整个金刚山风景区都位于朝鲜境内。为了调动金刚山丰富的地理及人文资源，回应朝韩人民渴望彼此了解的情感，笔者尝试利用视觉网络构建景区规划系统，为当地政府合理进行土地开发建设提供参考，为双边居民塑造欣赏金刚山风景的绝佳视野。面对文献不足、资料缺失、难以涉足场地进行实地调研等问题，笔者通过解读该片区的文化内涵，借鉴古代山水画《金刚全图》和"金刚山全景地图"（1939）中青绿山水和白描的描绘手法，结合电脑制图进行图面表现。同时引入了两种实体模型，以增强场地的可读性。最终，通过针对性的设计策略和深思熟虑的表现方式，为金刚山地区后续的开发建设提供建议。

关键词

视域分析；景观规划；风景区；图像表达；文化景观

ABSTRACT

Mount Kumgang, located in the middle of the eastern coastal area of the Korean Peninsula, has been a cultural symbol of this region historically. It stretches across two countries, the Democratic People's Republic of Korea (DPRK) and the Republic of Korea (ROK). The former enjoys two thirds of the total area and rich natural landscape and cultural relics, which is now known as the Mount Kumgang International Tourist Zone. The design responds to the bond of both DPRK and ROK people through design approaches while celebrating the rich natural and cultural resources of Mount Kumgang. By building a tourist zone planning system based on a visual network, the design would improve the sight-seeing system for the both sides of Mount Kumgang and provide references for the local government on the future development of the area. However, when faced with challenges such as the inadequacy of literature, missing data, and difficulties in field survey, the author explored into the Korean culture and studied the blue-and-green-color landscape painting and line drawing techniques from the famous Korean painting *Geumgang Jeondo* and the "Panorama Map of Diamond Mountain" (1939), combining with computer-generated graphics in the design drawing. Meanwhile, to help audience better read the site and design concepts and strategies, two types of material models were also introduced. Finally, the suitable design strategies and deliberated representation together provide thoughts for the development and construction to Mount Kumgang in the future.

KEYWORDS

Viewshed Analysis; Landscape Planning; Tourist Zone; Graphic Representation; Cultural Landscape

编辑　汪默英　　翻译　李慧彦
EDITED BY　WANG Moying　　TRANSLATED BY　LI Huiyan

1 金刚山丰富的地理及人文资源

金刚山位于朝鲜半岛中东部临海区域，横跨朝韩边境，从古朝鲜时期起就是该地区的文化象征。整个山脉三分之二的面积以及大部分自然风光和文化遗迹都位于朝鲜境内。

1910年，在日本殖民期间，朝鲜境内的金刚山区域首次作为景区被开发。1953年停战协定签订后，金刚山一直拒绝接待韩国访客。直到

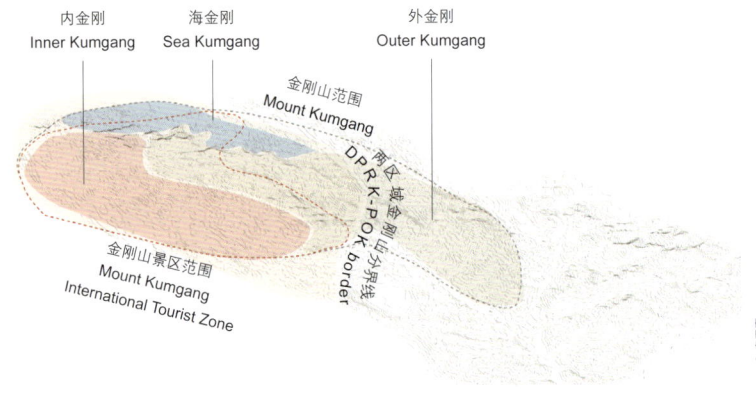

1. 金刚山景区区位
2. 山地非军事区战前及战后游客类型

1. Location of the Mount Kumgang International Tourist Zone
2. The nationalities of visitors to the demilitarized zone in mountainous areas before and after wars

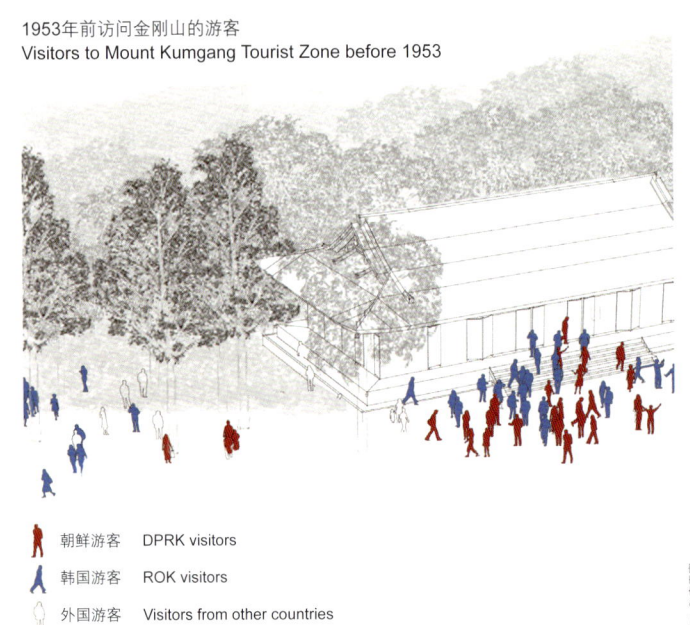

1953年前访问金刚山的游客
Visitors to Mount Kumgang Tourist Zone before 1953

朝鲜游客　DPRK visitors
韩国游客　ROK visitors
外国游客　Visitors from other countries

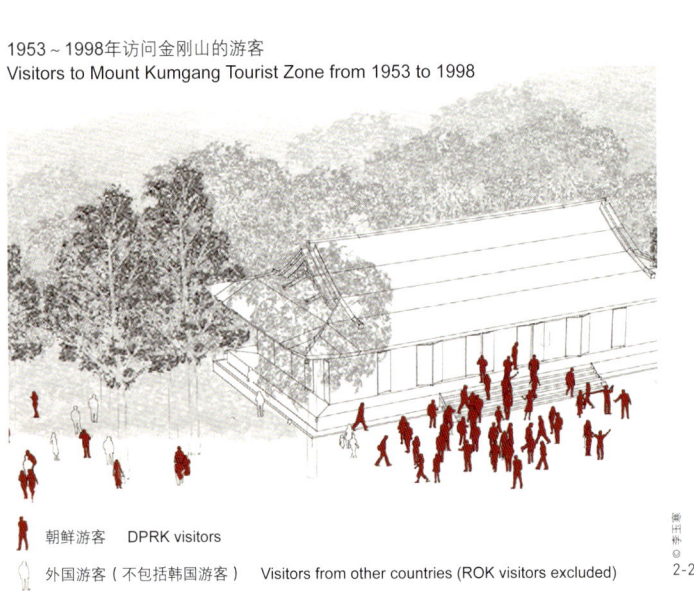

1953~1998年访问金刚山的游客
Visitors to Mount Kumgang Tourist Zone from 1953 to 1998

朝鲜游客　DPRK visitors
外国游客（不包括韩国游客）　Visitors from other countries (ROK visitors excluded)

1998年，韩国现代峨山公司与朝鲜亚太和平委员会达成协议，启动金刚山旅游合作项目。该项目是在之前景区的区划范围内进行的再开发，即整个景区仍位于朝鲜境内，但是打破了对韩国访客的禁令。据资料记载，很多韩国人（尤其是老人）在踏上金刚山时，都喜极而泣。然而，由于2008年的一次韩朝冲突，金刚山再次对韩国访客关上了大门。[1]

即使韩朝边界冲突不断，但分治两国的局面毕竟是第二次世界大战后才形成，细数起来不过70余年，很多老一辈人民仍深陷在隔界相望的乡愁之中。在经历过历史变迁的朝韩人民眼中，横跨边界的金刚山也成为了两国和平关系的寄托。

整个金刚山被分为海金刚、外金刚和内金刚三个部分：海金刚东侧与日本海相邻，西侧为延锦江，南部靠近边境线，其最早因优美的山地与海洋风光而闻名，而现在主要充斥着军事景观。剩余区域被分为东西两部分，东部为外金刚，西部为内金刚。外金刚地势相对平坦，曾经有大量基础设施集中兴建于此，如今却只留下废弃的金刚山电气铁路大桥、车站及民居[2]。由于大部分边境区域都与外金刚相切，因此该区域现阶段还设立有部分边境机构及军事设施。内金刚的环境相对闭塞，仅南端略与边境线相连，是寺庙等古建筑的聚集地，眼下正有越来越多的森林被转变为农田，以获取更多经济效益。而一般意义上的金刚山景区则包括全部内金刚及部分海金刚和外金刚。[3]

2 以视线连接两侧

笔者希望通过设计，在充分调动金刚山丰富的地理及人文资源的同时，回应朝韩人民渴望彼此了解的情感。考虑到政治因素的限制，视域连接是相对有效、且可行性较高的方式。因此，笔者尝试利用视觉网络构建公园规划系统，为当地政府合理进行土地开发建设提供参考，为双边居民塑造赏金刚山风景的绝佳视野。需要说明的是，规划设计范围主要集中在金刚山风景区，但考虑到韩国人民对于眺望金刚山景区的需求，因此也将边境线东南侧韩国境内的山脊线纳入了考量。

笔者首先利用地理信息数据对地形、用地类型、文化标志物等信息[4]进行分析，沿边境线朝鲜一侧和韩国一侧的山脊线分别选定了8处制高点，计算出可视区域。分析结果显示，俯瞰海金刚区域的视野相对开阔，而俯瞰外金刚和内金刚的可见区域则相对较少。作者随后根据地块基底条件叠加出不同地块的潜在用地类型，进行针对性开发，让人们可以在不同制高点上俯瞰到各种不同的景观。[5]

经过分析，方案叠加得到了16个制高点的可视范围，并以此为基础结合植被种植设计来引导人们的视线。笔者将重要的历史遗迹、自然风光等落位于可视范围内，并在视线廊道内重新种植低矮的植被；而对于军事设施、政府基建等需要隐藏的目标来说，一方面可设置在不可视区域之中，另一方面也可以在其前方种植高大植物——如当地常见的红松（*Pinus koraiensis*）、油松（*Pinus tabuliformis*）等——进行

海金刚
Sea Kumgang

资料中的海金刚景象描述
Historical images and narratives about the Sea Kumgang

在早期的邮票和照片中可以看到因优美的自然风光而闻名的海金刚。
Old stamps and pictures showing the beautiful scenery in Sea Kumgang.

海金刚景象现状意向图
Drawing about the existing landscape of Sea Kumgang

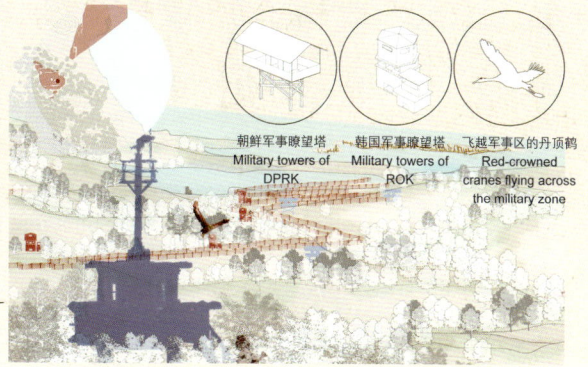

朝鲜军事瞭望塔 / 韩国军事瞭望塔 / 飞越军事区的丹顶鹤
Military towers of DPRK / Military towers of ROK / Red-crowned cranes flying across the military zone

外金刚
Outer Kumgang

资料中的外金刚景象描述
Historical images and narratives about the Outer Kumgang

因为相对平坦的地势，外金刚在日本殖民时期修建了金刚山电气铁路大桥及接驳车站，用以运输煤矿和游客。
Many infrastructures such as Mount Kumgang Electric Railway Bridge and major stations for transporting coals and visitors were built by the Japanese in the Outer Kumgang due to its relatively flat landform.

外金刚景象现状意向图
Drawing about the existing landscape of Outer Kumgang

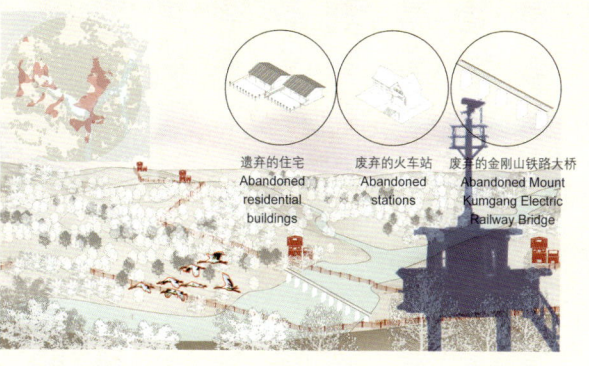

遗弃的住宅 / 废弃的火车站 / 废弃的金刚山铁路大桥
Abandoned residential buildings / Abandoned stations / Abandoned Mount Kumgang Electric Railway Bridge

内金刚
Inner Kumgang

资料中的内金刚景象描述
Historical images and narratives about the Inner Kumgang

内金刚环境相对闭塞，拥有诸如佛寺、石刻等历史文化遗迹，是金刚山景区文化的代表。
The relatively remote Inner Kumgang with many ancient temples and carved stones is the cultural hub of the Mount Kumgang International Tourist Zone.

内金刚景象现状意向图
Drawing about the existing landscape of Inner Kumgang

农田 / 飞越军事区的丹顶鹤
Farmland / Red-crowned cranes flying across the military zone

3. 古代（左）及战后（右）金刚山景象
4. 朝韩双边视点可视范围及高程

3. The ancient Mount Kumgang (on the left) and that after the war (on the right)
4. Viewsheds and elevations of the 16 overlooking points

遮挡。由于大部分边境区域都与外金刚相切，因此上述策略主要应用于外金刚景区。其中，金刚山电气铁路大桥作为金刚山区域最重要的地标之一，需尽可能保证在最多视点可见。[5]

除上述主要措施外，笔者还针对海金刚和内金刚的使用现状进一步制定了生态系统保护策略。在海金刚中分布着很多丹顶鹤栖息地，由于丹顶鹤对栖息地环境的要求很高，因此种植在这里的水稻也被认为是无污染的，可以以较高的价格售卖[6]。但是丹顶鹤也会以水稻为食，会影响水稻产量。为了保证粮食的经济收益，笔者利用地理信息数据识别出了丹顶鹤栖息地，在部分栖息地周围建立沙洲屏障，在满足丹顶鹤粮食需求的基础上，防止它们过度侵袭稻田。内金刚区域已有部分土地被开垦为不同种类的粮食作物（诸如土豆、玉米等）及人参种植区，但这些种植区的分布随意且分散。因此，笔者试图通过分析地块坡度、土壤条件等信息，找出适宜这些物种生长的区域，以避免在不适宜种植区进行不必要的森林开垦，从而在保障农业经济效益的同时保护该地区的生态系统。

在对制高点视域范围进行分析的过程中，发现部分视域包含部分韩国范围内尚未开发的山区，虽然这些地块不在金刚山风景区范围内，但笔者亦希望通过此次规划设计为这些区域的未来开发提供参考。

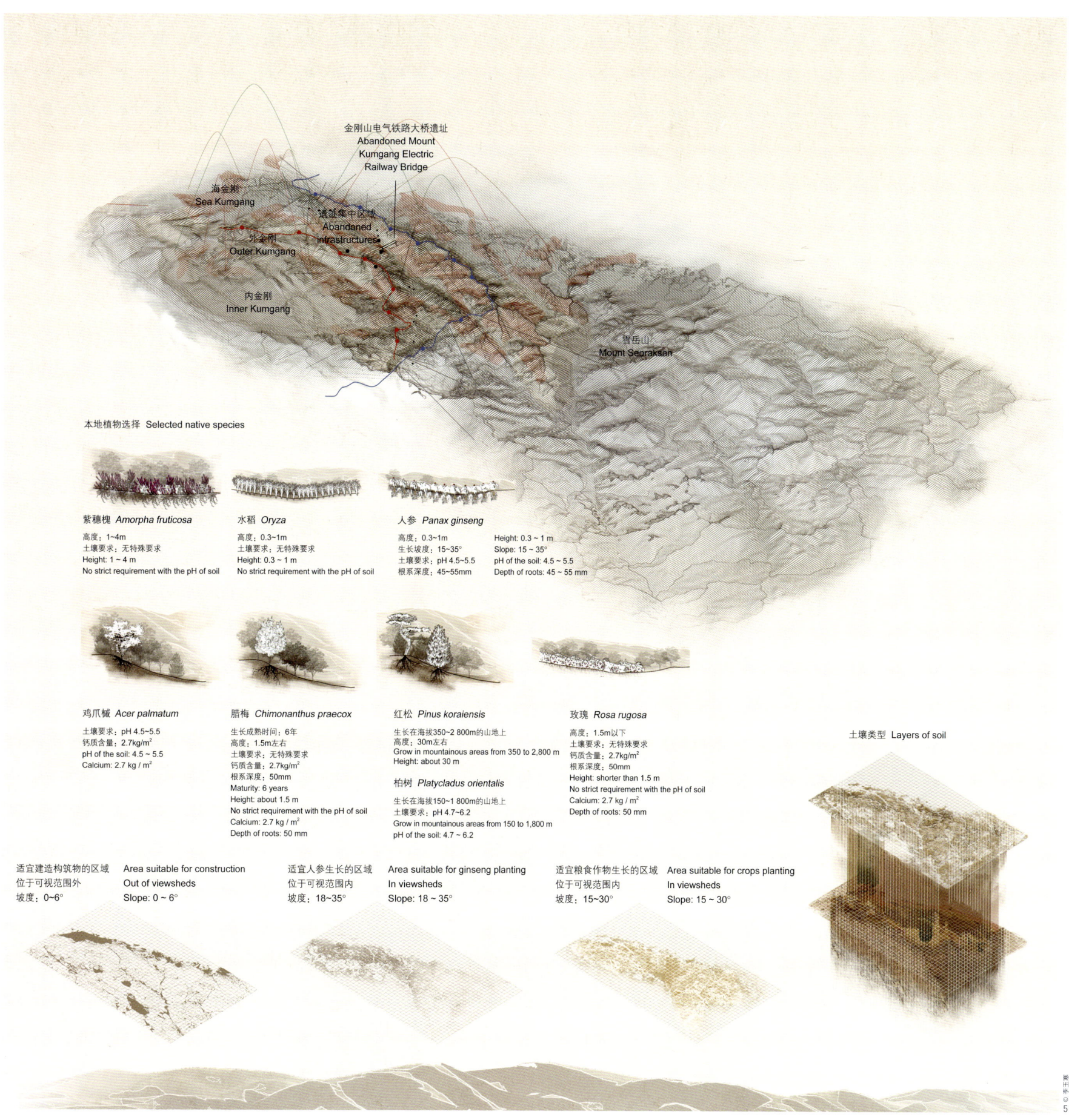

海金刚可视范围
Viewsheds in Sea Kumgang

打开更多的视野，满足观赏风景的需求
Increase viewsheds to open the scenery horizon
种植低矮的水稻，回应场地现有对于水稻种植的需求
Plant more rice which will not block the sight-lines while ensure agricultural needs

外金刚可视范围
Viewsheds in Outer Kumgang

通过视线叠加分析，甄别可以看到电气铁路大桥遗迹的视点
Identify the overlooking points which cover the abandoned Mount Kumgang Electric Railway Bridge based on viewshed analysis

内金刚可视范围
Viewsheds in Inner Kumgang

通过视线范围的叠加分析，甄别可以被用于农业种植的土地，指导朝鲜进行合理的土地利用
Identify the land for agricultural cultivation based on viewshed analysis to provide a reference to the DPRK government for future development programs

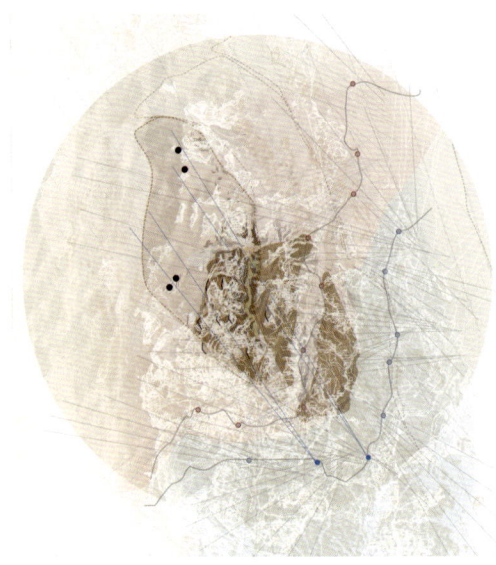
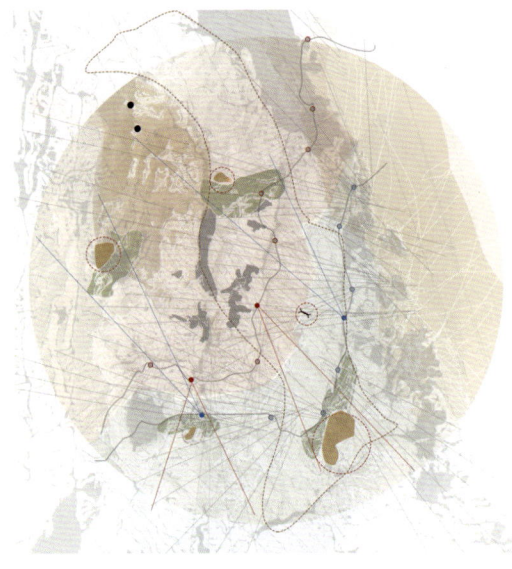

视线范围打开前 Before
由于遮挡，美丽海景无法被欣赏
Beautiful scenery of the sea was blocked

视线范围打开后 After
在得以欣赏海景的同时，满足水稻种植需求
Meet both the needs of sight view and rice cultivation

视线范围打开前 Before
由于遮挡，无法看到标志性的铁路大桥
The Railway Bridge was blocked

视线范围打开后 After
标志性的铁路大桥可以在尽可能多的视点被看到
The Railway Bridge can be seen at the most overlooking points

视线范围无遮挡 No block
朝鲜土地开发利用情况可以被看到
Land occupancies in DPRK expose to visitors

视线范围有遮挡 Blocked
种植高大乔灌木，达到对视线范围的遮挡
Block the sight lines with tall trees and shrubs

营造浅滩水岸，创造更多丹顶鹤的栖息环境
Restore shoals to create more habitats for red-crowned cranes

种植植被，保障韩国境内的山地开发利用状况被遮挡
Plant vegetation to conceal the land occupancies in ROK

对适宜开发地块进行进一步处理，以满足人参等作物的生长需求
Meet the needs for planting ginseng and other crops

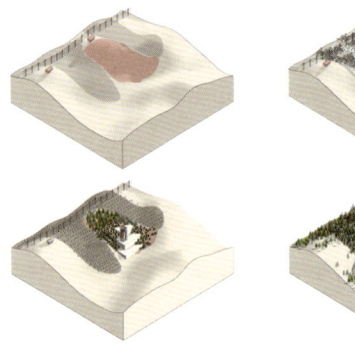

5. 视线连接及叠加策略分析
6. 针对不同区域的设计策略

5. Analysis of the connection of the sight-lines by overlaying different elements
6. Design strategies for different zones

3 表现手法的选择

由于场地位置的特殊性，在资料收集的过程中出现了文献不足、资料缺失、难以涉足场地进行实地调研等问题。在此情况下，后期的景观设计表现手法就显得至关重要。为了更好地呈现设计方案，笔者通过解读该片区的文化内涵，借鉴朝鲜名画家谦斋郑敾的山水画作品《金刚全图》和"金刚山全景地图"（1939）中青绿山水和白描的描绘手法，结合电脑制图进行图面表现。笔者还以代表朝鲜的红色与代表韩国的蓝色贯穿整个制图过程的始终，来表现两方的隔离与联系。最终奠定了整个项目的图面的色彩基调——以棕黄、灰白、青绿色系为底，红蓝两色为点缀。

其中大部分图纸都是基于地理信息数据模拟场地条件进行计算机建模，再通过后期技术增加多种元素，来展现场地的景观特征。在具体设计策略部分，笔者通过多组轴测图来直观表现改造前后的效果。效果图则采用了照片、图面资料、手绘相拼贴的方式进行表现。

与此同时，为了引导观者更好地阅读场地、理解项目设计理念及策略，笔者还引入了实体模型这一重要表现方式。此次设计中主要包括了两种实体模型。其一为高程断面模型，笔者将部分地区的高程起伏直观地体现在模型之中，之后将打印好可视区域的透明纸板叠加于其上，通过探讨地形与可视区域之间的关系，综合选择目标策略。其二，通过在建模软件中研究金刚山区域的山脊线和相对高度来提炼其方向和走势，笔者以折纸的方式抽象出山脊与山谷。随后通过地理数据分析，在实体模型中将某一观测点在朝鲜境内和韩国境内的可视范围分别涂成红色和蓝色，加以区分。在场地信息缺失的情况下，对于整个片区的全局性分析往往难以进行，上述两种实体模型则起到了很好的辅助说明作用。

4 讨论与评述

通过确定视域范围，针对不同场地提出合理的规划方案，笔者试图重申金刚山对于朝鲜半岛人民的特殊意义——边境不是一条线，或是一个军事区域，而是承载着文化象征意义的连接空间，也是两国人民的情感寄托。

虽然目前大多数设计作品都习惯于应用电脑后期制图来展现场地的设计愿景，但笔者更希望每个设计都可以有其自身独特的阐述方式，做到"图能达意"。因此，笔者尝试在电脑制图的基础上借鉴青绿山水和白描的描绘手法，以更好地传达地域景观特征。此外，图片表现还突破了鸟瞰图、效果图等多种惯常的透视展现方式，让人们可以对项目设计地点进行无限畅想，体会场地背后的人文感情。景观图像的表达不仅要思考如何绘制精美的图像，给人以赏心悦目之感，更重要的是通过图像的绘制表达一种有序的设计过程，并引导观者阅读和思考，以产生共鸣。最终，通过针对性的设计策略和深思熟虑的表现方式，为金刚山地区后续的开发建设提供建议。 LAF

7. 作物种植效果图
8. 人参种植效果图

7. Rendering of crop cultivation
8. Rendering of ginseng cultivation

1 Geographical and Cultural Resources of Mount Kumgang

Mount Kumgang, located in the middle of the eastern coastal area of the Korean Peninsula, has been a cultural symbol of this region historically. It stretches across the Democratic People's Republic of Korea (DPRK) and the Republic of Korea (ROK). The former enjoys two thirds of the total area and rich natural landscape and cultural relics, which is now known as the Mount Kumgang International Tourist Zone.

Mount Kumgang was first planned and developed as a tourist zone in 1910 under the Japanese colonization. For a long period of time since 1953 when the Korean War Armistice Agreement was announced, ROK visitors were not allowed to enter the tourist zone. The isolation did not change until 1998 when Hyundai Asan Cooperation of ROK and the Korea Asia-Pacific Peace Committee launched the Mount Kumgang Tourism Cooperation Project that was a redevelopment of the former tourist zone in DPRK and open to tourists from ROK. It was said that many ROK visitors (especially senior ones) wept for joy when they reached the mount. However, due to a conflict between the two countries, Mount Kumgang shut its door to ROK visitors again in 2008.[1]

It has been about 70 years since the Korean Peninsula split into two countries at the end of the Second World War. Many senior Koreans, who had witnessed such changes in history, have been dreaming about seeing their families and friends in the other side. Therefore, Mount Kumgang is a place full of good wishes of a peaceful relationship between the two countries.

Mount Kumgang consists of three parts, namely Sea Kumgang, Outer Kumgang, and Inner Kumgang. Sea Kumgang, to the west of the Sea of Japan, east of the Yeongeum River, and north of the border area, was renowned for its beautiful scenery of mountains and sea but now is filled with military construction. For the rest of the mountain, Outer Kumgang sits in the east and Inner Kumgang in the west. Infrastructures were concentrated in Outer Kumgang due to its relatively flat landform, while only the abandoned Mount Kumgang Electric Railway Bridge, stations, and residential buildings left now[2]. The adjacency to the border area also made it accommodate some governmental agencies and military facilities. The relatively remote Inner Kumgang only slightly connected with the border on its southern tip, with many ancient temples and other buildings dotted in the flourishing forests. However, today more and more forestlands are being converted into farmland for greater economic benefits. Basically, the Mount Kumgang Internaional Tourist Zone now includes the entire area of Inner Kumgang and some parts of the other two.[3]

2 Establishing Sight-Line Connection of the Two Sides

The design is expected to respond to the bond of both DPRK and ROK people through design approaches while celebrating the rich natural and cultural resources of Mount Kumgang. Considering the political restrictions, the author finds out that establishing sight-line connection between the two sides seems to be a relatively effective and feasible way. By building a park planning system based on a visual network, the design would improve the sight-seeing system for the both sides of Mount Kumgang and provide references for the local government on the future development of the area. Considering the needs of ROK visitors to see Mount Kumgang International Tourist Zone in the distance, the design also takes the ridges on the southeast of the border area in ROK into consideration.

Through an analysis of the geographic data in terrain, land use, and cultural sites[4], eight overlooking points on each ridge lines in DPRK and ROK were identified, which further informed the calculation of the viewsheds. It is found that the visibility to destinations in Sea Kumgang is relatively clear while that in Outer Kumgang and Inner Kumgang is somewhat blocked. Then, an suitable development planning was conducted by overlapping multiple layers of land use requirements to determine the potential land use types of the sites while creating varied overlooking landscapes at different points.[5]

Based on the identified viewsheds of the 16 overlooking points, the author attempts to strengthen these sight-lines through planting design. To the viewsheds that cover important historical sites and sound natural landscapes, short vegetation is (re)introduced; to the viewsheds that cover military facilities, civil infrastructures, and other sight objects which need to be concealed are not included in any viewsheds as much as possible, or covered with tall native vegetation, such as *Pinus koraiensis* and *Pinus tabuliformis*. These strategies are mainly applied in the Outer Kumgang because of its adjacency to the border area. Besides, the Mount Kumgang Electric Railway Bridge as one of the most remarkable landmarks in the area should be ensured visually connected with as many overlooking points as possible.[5]

The design further offers strategies to Sea Kumgang and Inner Kumgang in ecosystem protection. Sea Kumgang sees a number of red-crowned cranes habitats. This bird species has a very high environmental requirement of habitats, therefore the local rice production enjoys a good quality and a great economic return[6]. However, red-crowned cranes are rice-eating birds which impacts the yield of rice. As a response, the design examined the local geographic possibilities and identified some of the bird habitats that can be surrounded with sandbanks to keep the birds away

9. Conceptual models of the relationship between the viewsheds and topologies
10. Material models of viewsheds
11. Design scenarios

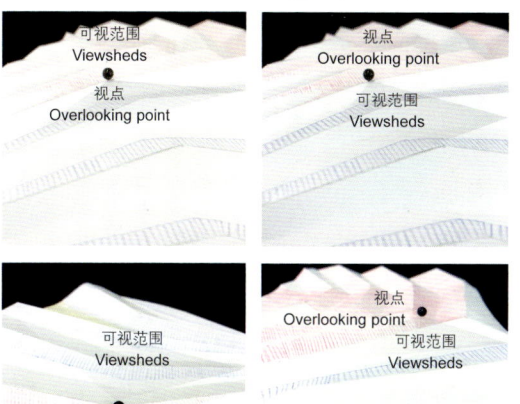
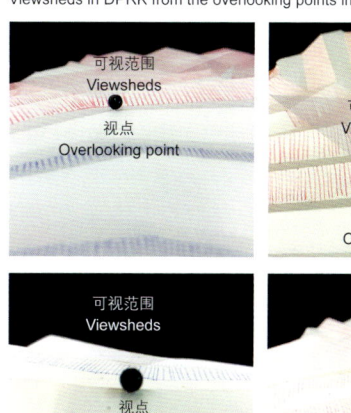
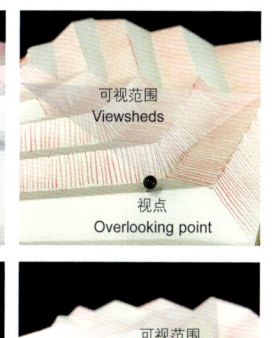
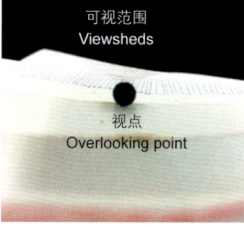
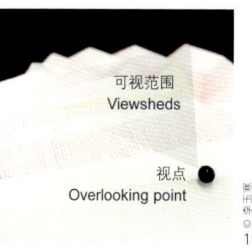

from most rice fields while reserve a few paddies as the food source for the cranes. In Inner Kumgang, lands have been partly transformed from forestlands to farmlands and planted with crops such as potato, corn, and ginseng. However, the existing farming is fragmented and in poor management. To avoid unnecessary reclaimation in forests, the design studied the existing slope and soil conditions to identify the plots suitable for growing such species, protecting the forest ecosystem and ensuring economic benefits of local agriculture.

The viewshed analyses also reveal that part of the undeveloped area of Mount Kumgang in the ROK side can be reached. Though it is not a part of the tourist zone, the design proposes several ideas for its future development.

3 The Ways of Representation

Due to the uniqueness of the site, the design encountered problems such as the inadequacy of literature, missing data, and difficulties in field survey, making it tricky for the representation of design ideas. The author explored into the Korean culture and studied the blue-and-green-color landscape painting and line drawing techniques from the famous painting *Geumgang Jeondo* by Jeong Seon, an ancient Korean artist and the "Panorama Map of Diamond Mountain" (1939). Computer-generated graphics were then used in the design drawing. Especially, color red and blue, representing DPRK and ROK respectively, is emphasized in all the drawings to narrate the separation and connection between the two countries, while the hue of the whole set of drawings are defined by brown-yellow, gray-white, and blue-green.

Most of the drawings were generated by computer modeling that simulates the site conditions based on geographic data, to which multiple elements were then overlapped to render the landscape characteristics of design proposals. In the representation of specific design strategies, several groups of axonometric drawings are adopted for a clear and strong comparison before and after the design. The renderings are represented through an assemblage of photos, drawing materials, and hand paintings.

Meanwhile, to help audience better read the site and design concepts and strategies, material model, an important tool of representation, was also introduced. In the design, two kinds of material models were made. One is to simulate the elevation changes of the terrain, in a form of a series of cross-sections, onto which transparent paperboards with printed viewsheds are overlaid, to disclose the relationship between terrain and viewshed to inform the selection of targeted strategies. The second is paper folding model. The topography of the ridges and valleys of Mount Kumgang are extracted with modeling software and further abstracted by means of paper folding. Then, through geographic analyses, the viewsheds in DPRK and ROK at a certain overlooking point are painted in red and blue, respectively. The data missing about the site made it hard to conduct a comprehensive analysis of the whole area, and these two kinds of models help audience understand the design concepts in a direct way.

4 Discussions and Review

Through viewshed planning of the site, the design highlights the cultural significance of Mount Kumgang to people in the Korean Peninsula — the border here does not mean a separation line or a military zone, but a sanctuary of unison to both countries.

Although a majority of designers are accustomed to visualize their design ideas with computer-generated graphics, the author hopes that each design can show its uniqueness of graphic representation that narrates design concepts. When faced with the challenge of the absence of image data, the author tried to combine the traditional blue-and-green-color landscape painting and line drawing techniques with computer-generated graphics to better show the characteristics of the site. Moreover, in addition to conventional aerial views and renderings, the drawings of the design offer audience with a new perspective to imagine the site and reflect the national culture and bond behind the representation. In landscape design, representation is not only about generating delicate pictures to offer aesthetic pleasure, but also to reveal the logic of thinking and lead viewers to read the design and understand the reasons. Finally, the suitable design strategies and deliberated representation together provide thoughts for the development and construction to Mount Kumgang in the future. **LAF**

从韩国境内远眺
View from ROK

从朝鲜境内远眺
View from DPRK

REFERENCES

[1] Kim, S. (2011). Staging the "Cartography of Paradox": The DMZ Special Exhibition at the Korean War Memorial, Seoul. Theatre Journal, 63(3), 381-402.

[2] Xu, Z. (2016). Protection and damage: Ecological environment of the peaceful Demilitarized Zone. Koreana, 24(3), 5-14.

[3] Atkins, P. J. (1993). The dialectics of environment and culture: Kimilsungism and the north Korean landscape. In A. Mukherjee & V. K. Agnihotri (Eds.), Environment and Development: Views from the East and the West New (pp. 309-332). Delhi: Concept.

[4] Kim, J. (2008). An Integrative Area Selection Method for Biodiversity Conservation in the DMZ and the CCZ of South Korea (Doctoral dissertation, The University of Texas at Austin, Texas, USA). Retrieved from https://repositories.lib.utexas.edu/bitstream/handle/2152/17876/kimj.pdf?sequence=2&isAllowed=y

[5] Kim, K. (2013). The Demilitarized Zone (DMZ) of Korea: Protection, Conservation and Restoration of a Unique Ecosystem. Retrieved from http://lees.geo.msu.edu/dmz.pdf

[6] Lee, S. D., Jabłoński, P. G., & Higuchi, H. (2007). Winter foraging of threatened cranes in the Demilitarized Zone of Korea: Behavioral evidence for the conservation importance of unplowed rice fields. Biological Conservation, 138(1-2), 286–289.

（图片：深圳福田记忆公园实景）

广州土人景观
GUANGZHOU TURENSCAPE

TEL: 020-34500022 FAX: 020-84594786
EMAIL: gzturen@vip.163.com

更多沟通请关注:新浪微博 @ 广州土人景观, @ 庞伟_景观观点

广州土人欢迎更多对景观设计行业有愿望的高手加入。并长期提供实习机会。

广州土人景观于2000年创立,已成为中国本土最具创作影响力的景观综合公司之一。十多年来,我们完成了中山岐江公园、深圳东部华侨城湿地公园、深圳福田记忆公园、南昌市利玛窦广场、美的总部大楼景观、深圳观澜大水田村版画原创产业基地、广州天河软件园(天河智慧城核心区)、东莞万科建研基地等一系列获得社会广泛赞誉和行业尊重的项目,为中国景观的本土创作做出了重要的实践和努力。

广州土人重视城市化过程中土地与人良好关系的营造,重视设计的创造力并尊重不同课题和项目的差异。致力于创造对城市有贡献的景观、时光铭记的景观、有文化含义的景观。重视景观作为城市文化本身的表达,广泛融和政治、经济、生态、社会学和艺术的共生力量,为基于城市和国土健康之上的"美丽中国"而工作。

长沙·卓越中寰

奥雅设计——创造更美好的人居环境
L&A Design — To Create a Better Environment

www.aoya-hk.com

灵活运用场地高差，营造场景记忆点，长沙·卓越中寰让自然与城市共融，现代简约，线条明朗，在城市空间里共生、漫游。通过形态及空间的表达，形成都市"峡谷"，室内借由建筑空间内的柱网表达"林"的意象，结合溪流穿梭在室内向室外延展的设计，提出"林地空间漫游"的想法。

奥雅设计于2001年在改革开放前沿深圳蛇口创立，公司前身为1999年在香港成立的奥雅园境师事务所。经过近二十年的引领发展，奥雅设计以景观规划设计为基础，逐渐发展成为致力于新型城镇化土地开发及综合文旅开发的大型文创机构。目前以深圳为总部，在全国各地设有15家分子公司，拥有由1200余位行业精英组成的国际化专业团队。

深圳南山蛇口兴华路南海意库5号楼3层 / 4层404　T 0755 26826690　F 0755 26826694　E sz@aoya-hk.com

城乡规划 Urban-Rural Planning	城市设计 Urban Design	景观设计 Landscape Architecture	建筑设计 Architecture	生态规划 Ecological Planning
开发策划 Development Strategy	文创旅游 Cultural Tourism	招商运营 Investment and Operation	公共艺术 Public Art	品牌运营 Branding & Media

LAURENT

FRESH-
IMPETUS

CONTACT US

联系电话 | 021-65977085
邮箱 | lr@laurent-creative.com
地址 | 上海市杨浦区杨树浦路2866号
国际时尚中心13号楼3层

保利·天悦，哈尔滨

电话： 020-37039822 / 37039090　　**商务专线：** 020-37039313 / 18565090221(侯先生)
合作热线： 020-37039822-8027　　**招聘热线：** 020-37039822-8022
商务邮箱： spi@gz-spi.com　　**招聘邮箱：** gz-spi-hr@gz-spi.com

山水比德广州总部： 海珠区新港东路1166号环汇商业广场南塔2-4F

广州 | 北京 | 上海 | 深圳 | 青岛 | 昆明 | 长沙 | 武汉 | 重庆 | 成都 | 珠海 | 南京

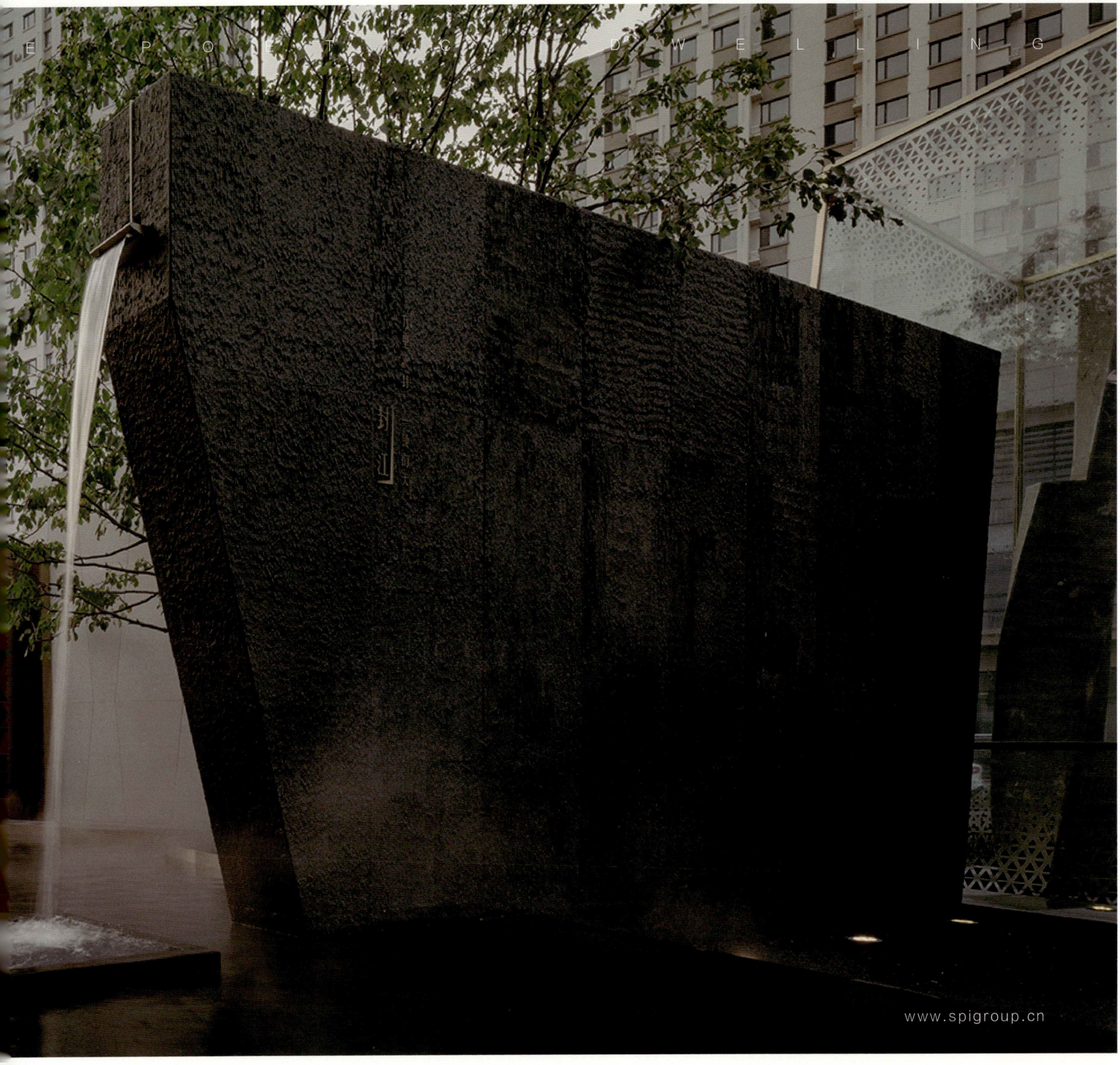

www.spigroup.cn

广州山水比德设计股份有限公司成立于2007年，目前已于广州、北京、上海、深圳、青岛、昆明、长沙、武汉、重庆、成都、珠海、南京十二地成立公司。已形成"山水地产"和"山水文旅"两大板块，在全国100+城市落地2000+精品项目，与中国TOP20地产集团形成了深度合作关系，为全国各级政府提供优质的城市环境解决方案。拥有"国家风景园林工程设计专项甲级"资质，获得"中国建筑规划设计最佳创意品牌机构""全国十佳园林设计企业"等荣誉称号。连续2年蝉联金盘奖第一，荣获IFLA国际大奖、园冶杯、勘察设计奖、地产设计大奖等多项国内外设计大奖，多次荣获行业新媒体影响力全国第一。

作为系统化景观服务专家，山水比德致力于"创新·引领诗意栖居"的企业使命，以新山水设计方法论在社区环境、商业综合体、文化旅游、特色小镇、城市设计、区域规划等领域定制系统化、一体化的专业解决方案。未来，山水比德千人设计团队将为共同的栖居理想持续奋斗，深深地根植于跨学科合作、工艺、社会和环境责任感，以非凡的设计、全程化服务与运营理念营造每一个诗意空间，不断追求设计创新的极致美学，矢志成为世界一流的景观机构。

阿普贝思作品 · 成都万科建筑装配式产业园建研中心景观设计

UP+S | 可持续景观理念践行者

阿普贝思（北京）建筑景观设计咨询有限公司

联系电话　　010-82423101
公司邮箱　　upshare@126.com
官方网站　　ups2006.com

大目湾新城

重庆龙湖两江长滩原麓示范区入口

中国
FRP 复合材料
景观制品
著名品牌

秦皇岛耀华新材料有限公司

绿色环保 \ 轻质高强 \ 耐候耐腐 \ 造型新颖 \ 色彩丰富 \ 军工品质

FRP 复合材料是于二十世纪中期研发的一种新型材料，它是由两种以上的物理和化学性质不同的物质复合而成的多相固体材料，其主要特点包括：可塑性强、材料与结构统一、轻质高强不变形、耐候耐腐抗老化、防水绝缘阻燃隔热、保色自洁透光。

联系人 / 商务 张涛 13930393940，技术 孙刚 13363359031
地址 / 秦皇岛市北部工业区耀华高新技术产业园昊月街9号　**邮编** / 066000
网址 / www.yhfrp.com　**传真** / 0335-7955600　**E-mail** / yhfrp@yhfrp.com

◀ "时空的扭转"景观盒

景观盒位于北京市大兴区
内部空间约 30m²
整体采用轻质高强的 FRP 复合材料
与内部钢结构一体成型
外部呈三角曲面形
利用未来概念造型体现时空的扭转
代表大兴永兴河生态恢复的华丽转身

设计单位：土人设计

北京"千荷泻露"大桥 ▶

北京"千荷泻露"大桥位于通州中心商务区
全长 210m
主体为钢拱结构
外部自由曲面封护造型采用复合材料夹心芯板
面积约 9000 ㎡
景观步道如同四条白色飘带穿在八片荷瓣中间
呈现"千荷泻露"的唯美造型

设计单位：北京市政设计院

◀ 重庆龙湖两江长滩原麓示范区入口

重庆龙湖两江长滩原麓示范区
位于重庆两江新区龙兴镇
入口处的弧形曲面大门长 37m
由复合材料组装而成
形态优美
气势磅礴

设计单位：重庆纬图景观

秦皇岛红飘带公园 ▶

秦皇岛红飘带公园位于河北省秦皇岛市
2006 年竣工
园中座椅全长约 600m
首创集观赏、照明、科普和休憩功能于一体的
复合材料景观制品
2007 年荣获美国景观设计师协会景观设计大奖
2008 年荣获国际建筑奖

设计单位：土人设计

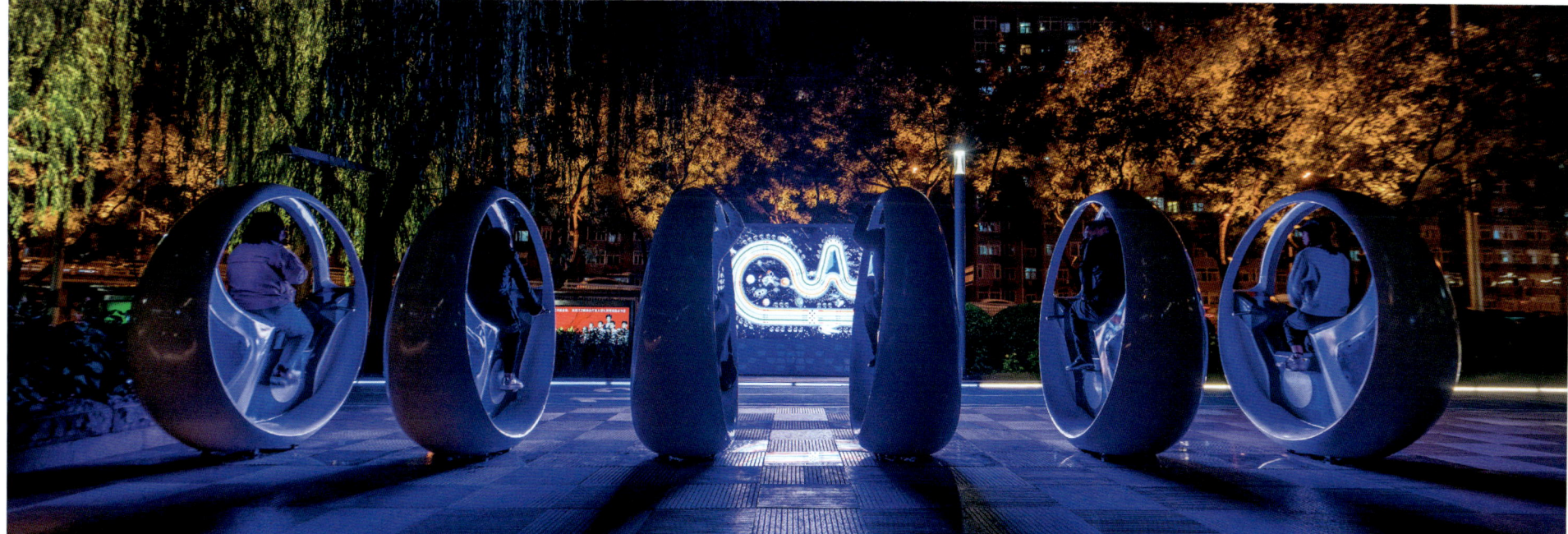

智慧景观所带来的并非人与机器的交互，而是增进人与人之间的互动。它让我们看到公共空间更多的可能性 —— O&M SMILE 城市微笑™ *

SMART LANDSCAPE: CONNECTING PEOPLE, MAKING POSSIBILITIES. (O&M SMILE PROJECT)

北京市西城区·街头公园智慧升级

偶木景观
O&M International Design

致力于以国际化的团队及可持续的创新能力服务城市，
坚持弹性生态的设计理念，以最低的环境承载塑造最丰富的生活空间，
融生态基底、智慧途径为环境空间注入更新活力。

城镇更新 | 医疗康养 | 儿童教育 | 公共空间 等领域首选设计服务商

O&M偶木景观·北京总部
电话：+86-010-59111184
邮箱：om@omdesign.email
地址：北京市朝阳区望京东园四区5号楼昆泰嘉瑞4006室 | 100102

O&M偶木景观·巴黎工作室
电话：+33-679539984
邮箱：wangzhao41@hotmail.com
地址：56 Avenue des Tulipes, 78990 ELANCOURT, FRANCE

O&M偶木景观·西安工作室
电话：+86-18681870778
邮箱：961070707@qq.com
地址：陕西省西安市雁塔区锦业路12号迈科商业中心3003室 | 710077

* 城市微笑™ 为偶木景观智慧城市解决方案，更多信息敬请关注偶木景观咨询

| 景观建筑 Landscape Architecture | 都市生态 Ecology Urbanism | 海绵城市 Water Management | 河湖修复 Waterbody Restoration |

复式潜流湿地运行案例
为流域提供生态服务的绿色基础设施代表

瓦地® 湿地设计运营
Ecology + Imagination
www.wadistudio.com

瓦地湿地板块专注于尾水和环境水水处理人工湿地的专业设计和运营维护。云南省九溪人工湿地公园，总占地面积约1000亩，为国内最大规模人工湿地工程之一，水处理量共约20万吨/天，主要承接上游被污染的星云湖水和九溪大河河水。湿地日常出水能够满足地表水III类水质标准并供给下游城市使用，极大地修复了区域生态，洪水期间能够提供10万立方米的洪水蓄洪利用空间。作为为流域提供生态服务的绿色基础设施的典型代表，大型人工湿地具备将解决城市水污染问题和生态空间建设结合起来的潜力，"人工湿地+公园"的新模式已经呼之欲出，九溪人工湿地公园即为此方面的典型中国代表项目。

北京 Beijing
杭州 Hangzhou
荷兰 Wageningen

WADI（瓦地）设计
北京办公地址：北京市朝阳区东三环中路 39 号建外 SOHO 一号楼 504 室
合作联系方式：info@wadistudio.com 18101051037

RAMBØLL
STUDIODREISEITL

福州东二环泰禾广场东区景观设计
THAIHOT PLAZA LANDSCAPE DESIGN IN THE EAST 2ND RING ROAD OF FUZHOU

SHAPING LIVABLE CITIES
建宜居城市,绘生态未来

北京办公室地址：北京市·朝阳区化工路焦奥中心1号楼B座1705室
Address: Rm 1705, Block B, Tower 1, Jiao'ao Center, NO.59 Huagong Road, Chaoyang District, Beijing
邮箱（E-mail）：beijing@dreiseitl.com
电话（Tel）：+86-87523599
网址（Web）：http://www.dreiseitl.com

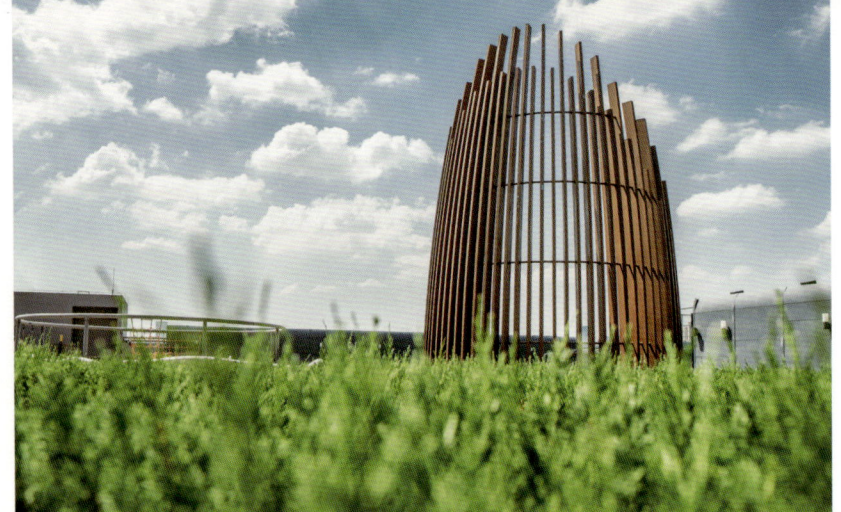

安博戴水道

RAMBOLL STUDIO DREISEITL

安博戴水道（Ramboll Studio Dreiseitl）隶属于丹麦安博集团（Ramboll Group），是集团水务部门在中国的分支机构。40多年来，安博戴水道在景观设计领域完成了众多高质量的城市景观设计和城市水文环境项目。我们致力于将人的需求、可达性强的公共生活空间、干净的水环境、宜人的景观等融合到从设计到实施的整个过程中。我们以国际设计质量为标准，应用适应性生态基础设施应对全球气候变化，以实现全球宜居城市梦想！

Ramboll Studio Dreiseitl, a branch of the Ramboll Group in Denmark, is a multi-cultural landscape architecture company specializing in water in China. For more than 40 years, Ramboll Studio Dreiseitl have delivered high quality projects in urban landscape architecture and urban hydrological environment. At Ramboll, we are committed to integrating human scale, available public life, healthy water environment, pleasant landscape into the entire process from design to implementation. Based on international design standard, we utilize a methodology of climate-adaptive ecological infrastructures to respond to local conditions. Ramboll Studio Dreiseitl is committed to realizing the dream of a globally livable, climate-adaptive, and ecological sustainable living city!

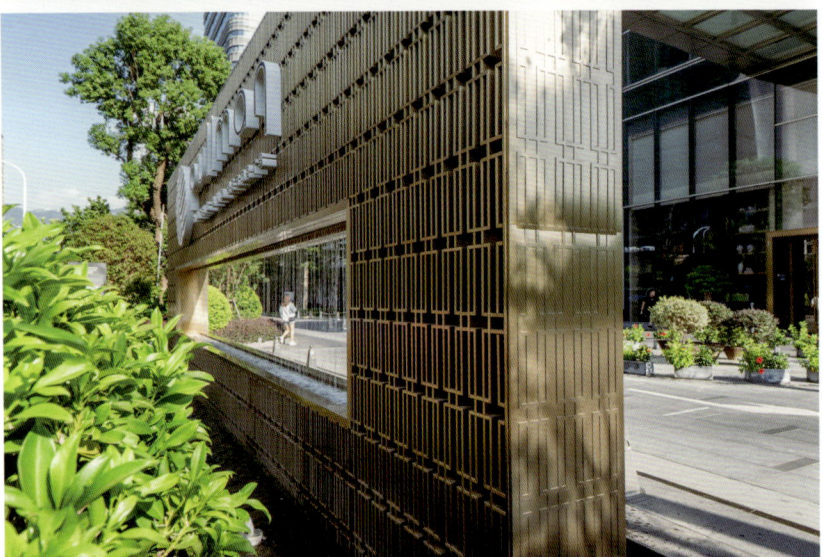

服务范围
OUR SERVICES

生态环境规划设计
Master Planning

生态园区环境设计
Ecocity District

生态河流修复设计
River Restoration

商业开发景观设计
Commercial Development

城市空间和公园设计
Urban Space and Parks

建筑 城市 土地

土人设计
TURENSCAPE
北京·上海·广州

北京土人城市规划设计股份有限公司（以下简称土人设计）由美国艺术与科学院院士、哈佛大学设计学博士、罗马大学荣誉博士、国家千人计划专家、北京大学景观设计学研究院院长俞孔坚于1998年1月领衔创立，拥有500多名职业设计师，其中包括80多位海外归国设计师，配备有城市规划设计、建筑设计、生态水利、市政设计、景观设计、环境设计、风景园林、结构及项目策划等专业人员；具有土地规划、城市规划、旅游规划、园林设计等多项甲级设计资质，是北京市高新技术企业和ISO9001：2000质量体系认证单位，自成立至今已完成大量有影响力的优秀工程项目。

土人设计以土地的名义，倡导天地、人、神和谐的"土人理念"，以解决人地关系为宗旨，坚守品质至上的职业道德，高举民族设计大旗，立足本土面向全球。多年来，土人设计在国内外200多个城市完成了2000多个规划设计项目，包括许多国内外重要工程的规划与设计。截至2017年12月土人设计已先后获得十二次全美景观设计师协会年度大奖，五次世界建筑节最高景观奖等行业权威奖项，土人设计已经成为国际上最具影响力的品牌设计公司之一。

2017年世界建筑节最佳景观奖
2016年，2017年AZ AWARDS最佳景观奖
2016年AZ AWARDS环境领导奖
2016年美国景观设计师协会荣誉设计奖
2015年世界建筑节最佳景观奖
2015年世界人道主义粮食与水奖
2015年国际能源奖
2013年，2014年美国景观设计师协会荣誉设计奖
2012年美国景观设计师协会杰出设计奖
2012年国际建筑奖
2011年世界建筑节最佳景观奖
2011年美国建筑奖
2010年美国景观设计师协会杰出设计奖
2010年美国景观设计师协会荣誉设计奖（2项）

Turenscape was founded by Doctor and professor Kongjian Yu (Doctor of Design, GSD, Harvard University; Foreign Honorary Member of the American Academy of Arts and Sciences). It was officially recognized and certificated as a first-level design institute by the Chinese government. Having over 500 professionals, Turenscape is an integrated team that provides quality and holistic services in Architecture, Landscape Architecture, Urban Planning and Design, and Environmental Design.

Turenscape's projects have earned a great reputation for innovative and environmentally sound designs. Our projects has been internationally and nationally recognized, including:

2017 World's Best Landscape Award of the World Architecture Festival
2016, 2017 Best Landscape Architecture Awards of the AZ Awards
2016 Social Good and Environmental Leadership Awards of the AZ Awards
2016 ASLA Design Honor Award (American Society of Landscape Architects)
2015 Landscape of the Year of World Architecture Festival
2015 Humanitarian Water and Food Award
2015 Energy Globe Award
2013, 2014 ASLA Design Honor Award (American Society of Landscape Architects)
2012 ASLA Design Excellence Award (American Society of Landscape Architects)
2012 International Architecture Awards
2011 World's Best Landscape Award of the World Architecture Festival
2011 American Architecture Award
2010 ASLA Design Excellence Award (American Society of Landscape Architects)
2010 ASLA Design Honor Awards (American Society of Landscape Architects)
2010 World's Best Landscape Award of the World Architecture Festival
2009 ULI Excellence Award for the Asian Pacific Region and Global Award for Excellence
2009 World's Best Landscape Award of the World Architecture Festival
2008 Excellence on the Waterfront Top Honor Award
2008 The International Architectural Award
2008 The 1st World Architecture Festival Award (Highly Commended)
2008 The Classic Habitat Planning and Architecture Double Gold Award (MOHURD,China)
2007 The Emerging Architects Award Commended (The Architectural Review, UK)
2007 Excellence on the Waterfront Top Honor Award (Waterfront Center, USA)
2005~2007 ASLA Design Honor Award (American Society of Landscape Architects)
2005 ASLA Honor Award, Planning and Analysis (American Society of Landscape Architects)
2004 The Gold Medal of Fine Arts (The Chinese Cultural Ministry, Chinese Society of Fine Arts)
2002 ASLA Design Honor Award (American Society of Landscape Architects)

北京土人城市规划设计股份有限公司　Turenscape (Beijing Turen Design Institute)
总部地址：北京市·海淀区·中关村大街127—1号北大科技园五层505室　邮编：100080
Headquarter Office Add: Rm.505, Peking University Science Park No.127–1, Zhongguancun North Street, Haidian District, Beijing 100080, P.R.C
电话（Tel）：010–62747888
传真（Fax）：010–62745656　62745680
邮箱（E–mail）：info@turenscape.com
网址（Web）：www.turenscape.com

香港大學建築學部
園境建築學系

MLA
Master of Landscape Architecture

HKU's Master of Landscape Architecture (MLA) is an advanced two year degree in landscape architecture that is taught in English, and is accredited by the Hong Kong Institute of Landscape Architects (HKILA). The program teaches landscape architecture as a broad discourse in which the core practices of the discipline are examined alongside contemporary developments in planning, conservation, urbanism, and ecology. Our experience-rich and problem-based approach to learning and thinking prepares students to lead the discipline through careers in research, teaching, and critical practice. Candidates for admission should hold a Bachelor of Arts (Landscape Studies) degree of the University of Hong Kong, or a similar degree from a comparable institution.

園境碩士學位

香港大學的園境碩士學位（MLA）課程為期兩年，以英語為教學語言。該學位項目得到香港園境師學會（HKILA）的認證。我們的課程以課題廣泛、兼收並蓄著稱；密切關注當下規劃、保護、城市化和生態學的發展來確定學科的核心實踐內容；我們注重有豐富體驗、基於問題的學習方法和批判性思維，以培養學生在研究、教學和實踐中成為帶頭人。申請者應已獲得香港大學園境學文學士或其他學校相應學位。

PDLA
Postgraduate Diploma in Landscape Architecture

HKU's Postgraduate Diploma in Landscape Architecture (PDLA) is an intensive one-year program, taught in English, that establishes foundational skills, theories, and concepts in landscape architecture for students without previous academic training in the environmental design fields. The PDLA offers an alternate pathway for students of diverse non-traditional backgrounds and experiences to enter the landscape architectural profession and aims to generate multi-skilled graduates capable of transcending disciplinary boundaries. Candidates for admission should hold a Bachelor of Arts or Bachelor of Science degree of the University of Hong Kong, or a similar degree from a comparable institution.

園境深造文憑

香港大學的園境深造文憑（PDLA）課程為期一年，以英語為教學語言。在環境設計領域尚未有學習經驗的學生，可以通過該項目的集中強化課程，了解園境建築設計的基本技能、理論和概念。園境深造文憑課程為具有非傳統學術背景和經驗的學生開闢了進入該領域的新途徑，旨在培養一支能夠跨越傳統學科界限並由內而外擴展專業領域的多技能隊伍。申請者應已獲得香港大學文學士或理學士學位，或其他學校相應學位。

THE UNIVERSITY OF HONG KONG
DIVISION OF LANDSCAPE ARCHITECTURE

For more information please visit
更多信息可見
http://www.arch.hku.hk
http://www.aal.hku.hk/tpg/
https://sweb.hku.hk/tola/html

关注美丽乡村，共建山水田园

新美学 / 新体验 / 新生活

WANGSHAN LIFE

诗意栖居慢生活

望山者 / 心归田 / 意原野

栖·居

研·学

匠·造

行·旅

DESIGN-BUILD WORKSHOP
设计建造工坊

LANDSCAPE DESIGN
BASED ON SOCIAL PRACTICE

2019/11/26 – 12/04

基于社会实践的乡村共建工作坊

Xixinan Anhui, China
安徽西溪南

带队老师：
Annacaterina Piras
LWC创始人
知名建筑师、设计师
阿尔盖罗建筑学院PhD
国际学术研讨会协调员

报名及咨询

公众号　王老师　李老师

2019 ASLA Annual Meeting & Contemporary Landscape Study Tour in Western United States

2019 ASLA年会 & 美国西部当代景观游学

2019 11月08日~11月21日

考察城市
旧金山、洛杉矶、圣地亚哥

联系人
李俊

联系电话
010-62747820 / 18161860766

联系地址
北京市海淀区中关村北大街127-1号北大科技园303-3室

了解更多详情请扫描官方微信

景观之路官方微信

李俊

行程特色

1 参加ASLA年会及主题交流活动

2 行走中的设计思维工作坊

3 六大主题·20+经典/新锐设计案例

主题一：景观和建筑项目
尔湾光谱中心景观改造项目、盖蒂中心、巴尔博亚公园、萨尔克生物研究所、金门公园、加州科学博物馆及绿色屋顶、笛洋美术馆、旧金山环湾客运中心、通格瓦公园、旧金山现代艺术博物馆及扩建项目、达格特公园、华特·迪士尼音乐厅等

主题二：硅谷高科技企业园区
Facebook新总部园区、Google园区、苹果总部游客中心

主题三：地产景观
尔湾大公园社区、尔湾伍德伯里社区、尔湾木桥社区、尔湾山顶豪宅区样板区

主题四：商业综合体
号称"全世界最尊贵商业街"的好莱坞罗德尔商业街、南加州颇负盛名的高级购物中心葛洛夫购物中心

主题五：各具特色的海滨小镇
卡梅尔小镇、圣塔芭芭拉、拉古纳海滩

主题六：著名文化地标
一号公路、斯坦福大学、金门大桥、渔人码头、环球影城等

4 全程学术解读与思维激荡
1位全程专业导师 + 若干特邀设计师讲解
5场专题讲座
20+学员头脑风暴

5 高标准住宿餐饮

LA ROAD 景观之路